Musical Worlds

Musical Worlds

New Directions in the Philosophy of Music

Edited by
Philip Alperson

The Pennsylvania State University Press
University Park, Pennsylvania

Library of Congress Cataloging-in-Publication Data

Musical worlds : new directions in the philosophy of music / edited by
   Philip Alperson.

      p.   cm.
      Consists principally of essays originally published in a special
   issue of the Journal of aesthetics and art criticism (v. 52, no. 1
   [1994]).
      Includes bibliographical references and index.
      ISBN 0-271-01769-4 (pbk. : alk. paper)
      1. Music—Philosophy and aesthetics.   I. Alperson, Philip.
   II. Journal of aesthetics and art criticism.
   ML3800.M89   1998
   781'.1—dc21   97-33027
                                                         CIP
                                                         MN

It is the policy of The Pennsylvania State University Press to use acid-free
paper for the first printing of all clothbound books. Publications on uncoated
stock satisfy the minimum requirements of American National Standard for
Information Sciences—Permanence of Paper for Printed Library Materials,
ANSI Z39.48-1992.

Contents

Preface

This book is based upon a special issue of *The Journal of Aesthetics and Art Criticism* that was commissioned by then editor of the *JAAC,* Donald Crawford, and the Editorial Board of the *JAAC,* who had noticed an unusually strong interest in the philosophy of music at meetings of The American Society for Aesthetics and in submissions to the *Journal.* It was my pleasure to edit that special issue. The present collection includes the essays in the original *JAAC* issue (*The Journal of Aesthetics and Art Criticism* 52:1 [1994]) as well as two new and original essays, "Evaluating Music," by Jerrold Levinson, and "Rock 'n' Recording: The Ontological Complexity of Rock Music," by John Andrew Fisher.

I am indebted to Donald Crawford, the *JAAC* Editorial Board, the authors of the essays, and to the many referees who provided valuable advice to me and to the authors. I add a special note of thanks to Sally Gray, Karen Fearing, Janice Theriot, and Sandy Thatcher at The Pennsylvania State University Press who provided wise and patient counsel throughout the preparation of the manuscript.

PHILIP ALPERSON

Introduction

Musical Worlds: New Directions in the Philosophy of Music

Is it not strange that sheep's guts should hale souls out of men's bodies?
—William Shakespeare
Much Ado About Nothing

[Music] is such a great and exceedingly fine art, its effect on man's innermost nature is so powerful, and it is so completely and profoundly understood by him in his innermost being as an entirely universal language, whose distinctness surpasses even that of the world of perception itself.
—Arthur Schopenhauer
The World as Will and Representation

Music is as strange as it is familiar, and questions about the elusive character of music are as old as philosophical inquiry itself. Philosophers and other theoretically minded people have wondered at music's storied ability to stir or express the deepest recesses of the inner life of human beings. They have wondered whether and to what extent music is adequately described as an object fit primarily for a certain sort of aesthetic or contemplative experience and, if so, what the central features of that experience might be. They have wondered about the various subpractices of music, from musical composition, improvisation, and performance to music appreciation and music criticism. They have wondered about the place of music in human affairs generally and its ability to transform experience in so many domains of life. In their wonderment, philosophers and theoreticians have explored connections among music and the structure of the universe, music and religion, music and the social world, and music and the good life. They have wondered at the peculiarity of a practice that seems at once so artificial, and yet so utterly intimate, natural, and important.

Western philosophical thought in the last two hundred years or so—perhaps because of the rise of public institutions and venues for the performance of concert music—has focused on a set of interlocking problems arising from a musical practice that has centered around the creation and reception of musical works that, on the surface at least, seem designed to be contemplated and appreciated for the sake of their own specifically musical qualities. Not surprisingly, then, the philosophy of music in modern times has concerned itself centrally with the question of the meaning of music. But it is hard to put questions about the nature of the meaning of music without falling prey to a form of petitio. Just what is to count as musical meaning?

It is probably not too much of an exaggeration to say that the terms of this inquiry in modern times were set by Eduard Hanslick's polemical *On the Musically Beautiful*, published in 1854, in which Hanslick distinguishes sharply between the sort of purely tonal beauty he sees as properly ascribable to music and other properties and varieties of meaning erroneously attributed to it.[1] Hanslick is especially concerned with combating what he sees as the most flagrant and widespread heresy about music, the notion that musical meaning has essentially to do with the emotions. Hanslick takes a hard line on the matter:

According to this doctrine, music cannot entertain the intellect by means of concepts the way that literature does, any more than it can the eye, as do the visual arts. . . . However, when we allow our eyes to adjust a little, we arrive at the discovery that in the prevailing view of music the feelings play a double rôle.

Of music in the first of these two rôles, it is claimed that to arouse the delicate feelings is the defining purpose of music. In the second, the feelings are designated as the content of music, that which musical art presents in its works.

The two are similar in that both are false.[2]

Hanslick does not believe that musical experience either is typically or should be devoid of feeling. In the foreword to the eighth edition of his book, he says explicitly, "I share completely the view that the ultimate worth of the beautiful is always based on the immediate manifestness of feeling."[3] But Hanslick resolutely denies the view that the purpose of music could be either the arousal of emotion in the listener or the expression of emotion in the music itself.

Beauty, Hanslick argues, is a formal property, existing independently of whatever emotions might be aroused by it. It is true, Hanslick allows, that music is an art of sensation insofar as sensation is a prerequisite to music (as it is to feeling). But this is a far cry from saying that the musically beautiful should address itself to feeling. The musically beautiful properly directs itself to the imagination in an activity of contemplative and active understanding of the tonal forms of music. "Thus we say nothing at all concerning the crucial aesthetic principal of music," Hanslick argues, "if we merely characterize music in general according to its effect upon feeling, just as little, perhaps, as we would get to know the real nature of wine by getting drunk."[4] There is not, Hanslick claims, even a stable causal relationship between pieces of music and the feelings they may awaken in us. As individuals, we are differently affected according to changes in our moods, in our musical experiences and impressions, and even in such general emotive characterizations as are advanced by entire generations are vitiated by the pronouncements of subsequent ages.

Hanslick is as unforgiving on the claim for the emotional content of music as he is on the claim for its effects. If we consider the paradigm case of musical expressiveness—the predication of definite, namable emotions such as love, longing, melancholy, or hope, of passages or pieces of instrumental music—we find that the expression of such qualities by music is impossible. The emotional states identified by these names take their character, not from mere fluctuations of inner physiological activity, but from the combination of inner perturbations with "ideas, judgments, and (in brief) the whole range of intelligible and rational thought." The feeling of hope, for example, "cannot be separated from the representation of a future happy state which we compare with the present; melancholy compares past happiness with the present."[5] Instrumental music, Hanslick insists, is quite incapable of embodying such specific representations and concepts. Music may reproduce the general dynamics of emotional life, but that is only to say that any particular musical piece or passage may be thought to be formally analogous with any of an indefinitely wide range of emotions that share the same dynamic shape. That fact explains at once why music is such a protean art, able to support the suggestion of so many different specific emotions, why emotive predicates are so often apt characterizations of musical passages, and yet why the representation of definite emotions in music is impossible. Loose talk aside, musical experience cannot properly be conceived in terms of the arousal or the expression of emotion.

Many of the issues raised pointedly by Hanslick are still the focus of contemporary debate as we near the end of the twentieth century. Few today, however, would be as inclined as Hanslick to exclude musical expressiveness from the realm of musical meaning. Nor would contemporary writers be so quick to circumscribe the range of meaning of music generally in a way that Hanslick would have approved. There is, instead, a marked effort by philosophers and theoreticians writing on music today to place music and musical practice in the broader context of human experience and practices generally. The essays in this collection of recent work in the philosophy of music exemplify that movement.

We can see this emphasis clearly in the essay that leads off the collection, Jenefer Robinson's "The Expression and Arousal of Emotion in

Music." Robinson supposes both that music arouses emotions in us and that it expresses specific emotional qualities such as sadness, nobility, aggressiveness, tenderness, serenity, and so on. Further, Robinson argues, it is often if not usually the case that feelings aroused by music are intimately related to our understanding of the music and its expressiveness.

Robinson builds her case by first examining several leading contemporary views on the relation between the expression and arousal of emotion in music. Some philosophers—Susanne Langer and Peter Kivy in particular—seek to explain musical expressiveness without recourse to the evocation of emotions in the listener, finding the locus of expression instead in forms or contours that music shares with the felt quality of emotional life (Langer) or with expressive behavior, directly or through the intermediary of a musical convention (Kivy). These approaches, Robinson argues, provide insight into some instances of musical expressiveness, but leave some important features of musical expression unexplained, even when, as in the case of Kivy, the emotion of "being moved" by the music is allowed into the picture. Robinson is somewhat more sympathetic to the view of Kendall Walton, which does allow a role for musical evocation. On Walton's view, what music arouses are imaginary feelings. Expressive music induces the listener to imagine himself or herself experiencing particular emotions: stabs of pain, feelings of ecstasy, sensations of well-being, and the like. Robinson has reservations about the view, however. There is no indication why we should be inclined to imagine our awareness of musical sounds to be an awareness of our feelings, or an account of what grounds there might be for imagining emotions in their full particularity. Robinson is also critical of Jerrold Levinson's view that musical expression involves both an incipient feeling and an imaginative but cognitively etiolated version of the emotion being expressed. Levinson is right to acknowledge a relationship between imagination and the arousal of emotion by music, but he does not adequately explain how the cognitive content of a complex feeling (such as unrequited passion) could be recognized or induced by music.

In offering her own analysis, Robinson re-turns to a possibility that Hanslick and others seemed to have authoritatively discredited, the direct arousal of feelings by music. Robinson points out first that there are cases when music simply evokes relatively primitive emotions—physiological changes and inner feelings ranging from the relatively simple startle reflex to feelings of relaxation or excitement—that are unaccompanied by complex cognitive content (rather than having, say, an "etiolated" cognitive content). These feelings are often an important part of our experience of the music, as in the case of the sense of relaxation that comes after four hours of relentless modulation and resolution in Wagner's "Tristan." These less cognitively complicated emotions are not only important for our appreciation of formal structures—a point to which Leonard Meyer had famously attested—they can contribute to our understanding of the emotional expressiveness of the music, helping to alert us to and perhaps even further characterize complex emotions expressed in the music. This is especially evident in large-scale musical structures, such as the movements of the classical sonata form, whose expressiveness characteristically relies upon the arousal of emotions of surprise, relaxation, uncertainty, satisfaction, and so on. If Robinson is right, reports of the death of the arousal theory of expression have been greatly exaggerated.

Francis Sparshott pushes the question of the varieties of musical expressiveness further in his essay, "Music and Feeling," by posing an even more fundamental question: What would the criteria of acceptability of a satisfactory theory of the relation between music and the emotions be? Sparshott's surprising answer is that though much of value can be said on the general theme of emotion and music, no useful theory of the relation will be forthcoming. "We do not know what such a theory should be," Sparshott says, and we have "no reason to seek such knowledge." The reason for this, he argues, is that, when we turn our attention from what is often studied in the classroom to the way in which music actually figures in people's lives, we find that musical practice is not something easily described in terms of an abstract formal system with musical works being defined as artificial constructions defined within the system. What we find instead is that "actual musical practices are integral to social practices," and that there is "no reason a priori to suppose that only one relationship [between music and feeling] should hold between musically formal structures and the active and affective lives they relate to, or that they should relate distinctively to any specific range of such phenomena, or that such relationships as obtain should be reducible to any system. Perhaps we need rather to consider a lot of diverse phenomena, only loosely connected."

This is precisely what Sparshott does, drawing our attention to many of the complex, subtle, and distinctive sorts of affectiveness that belong to music. Sparshott distinguishes four kinds of phenomena that lie behind the words "emotion" and "feeling": having moods (being manic, depressed, cheerful, and so forth), having reactive feelings toward events, things, and people ("love," "rage," "hope," "desire," and so forth), ascribing named types of reactive feelings to things, events, and people ("annoying," "adorable," and so forth), and experiencing a world or field of interest as affectful (as sinister, gloomy, peaceful, or as affectful in some way that resists verbal identification). Sparshott also identifies seven independent ways in which music and feelings might be generally related to one another, ranging from the possibility that a musical work can have affective qualities that can be perceived directly on the basis of musical relationships, to the possibility that a piece of music has an affective quality as a part of its meaning. But human beings are animals that respond to their environments with discriminating sensitivity. Whatever relationships between music and emotion might be identified, "We would expect music, if it existed, to be saturated with affect, to be perceived as variously and immediately moving in ways that would resist reduction to anything else but relatable in indefinitely various ways to everything else."

Sparshott also places these observations in the context of an analysis of the Aristotelian notion of "voice" (*phone*). Animals (including human beings) both generate sounds in response to events in their lives and discriminate such sounds made by others. Music may thus be considered in the context of "the natural phenomenon of voice as a communicative system, with its associated cognitive functions and capacities," including language. This greatly complicates an already complicated picture, introducing various language-like features of music-making into the account of the multifarious relations between music and feeling. Sparshott goes on to discuss many of the relations between musicians and the music they make and between listeners and the music they listen to. And to all this may be added the observation that music-making also derives its affective significance from other sorts of activity in the midst of which music-making finds itself immersed. In the end, Sparshott writes, "[T]he phenomena of 'affect' or whatever we choose to call it are irreducibly complex, simply because to be alive in a world is necessarily to be endlessly responsive to everything in that world (including the most cerebral music as experienced by the most analytically minded musicologists), and because humanity, as the culture-making species, continues to develop the system of music in the context of its general resources."

Sparshott's use of Aristotle to shed light on the relation between music and emotion is paralleled by Göran Sörbom's return to the Greeks to discuss another domain of meaning in music: musical representation and its possible connection with human character. As Sörbom points out in his article, "Aristotle on Music as Representation," music is not nowadays thought to be a representational art. What, then, could the ancients have meant in saying that music is a form of imitation and that pieces of music are images of character?

Sörbom sets the discussion in the context of the classical notion of *aesthesis*, the process by which particulars are imprinted on the mind, one variety of which is the way in which images made by human beings are apprehended. Generally speaking, an image is similar in some, but not all, respects to what it represents. An image therefore has a double nature insofar as it is a real thing in its own right and it is also an illusion having a representational function: an imitation creates an image of what it represents in the mind of the spectator who is normally aware of the illusory status of the image and reacts accordingly. If music *were* a form of imitation, as the ancients had it, it might provide us with hedonistic pleasure deriving from musical qualities (on the analogy of the pleasures of tastes and odors), with pleasure deriving from beauty (conceived as the presence of certain structural and proportional properties of the music), and with pleasure deriving from learning something about what is skillfully imitated. But we must ask again: What could music possibly imitate?

The answer begins with an acknowledgment of the Greek doctrine of *ethos*, the view that music has the means to influence the character and dispositions of persons, which it can do because listening to music is an instance of *aesthesis*. As expressively made things, pieces of music present to the listener images that, through a process of acculturation, listeners come to regard as imitations of inner states. On Sörbom's reading, "Pieces of music are *images* of character because the listeners know that they are neither real and genuine signs of a character nor the character itself; they are only similar to it. The impression the listeners get results in a mental image of, for instance, anger, i.e., an experience and conception of anger, and he or she knows that it is neither anger in itself nor real genuine signs of it." On the Greek view, music, through its direct and paradigmatic imitation of character, is well placed to affect the character of those who listen to it by imprinting the images of character onto the mind.

Sörbom's investigation of classical sources raises the interesting question of the extent, if any, to which musical expression might be subsumed under the notion of representation. This possibility is pursued from a contemporary perspective by Kendall Walton in "Listening with Imagination: Is Music Representational?" Can we regard music as representational, Walton asks, while simultaneously preserving the intuition that there remains a significant difference between the paradigmatically representational arts of painting and literature and the art of pure, absolute music?

In the case of literary and pictorial representation, Walton argues, we encounter fictional worlds replete with fictional characters and events, which is to say that literary and visual works prescribe certain sorts of imaginings. Clearly, music may prescribe imaginings of fictional musical "characters" and events in connection with musical expectations we bring to our listening, but the fictional worlds of music may also be populated with characters that are not themselves wholly features of a musical world, as when a cantabile instrumental passage

is imagined to be sung by a fictional person, or when we imagine "something" being late in a deceptive cadence. These are bona fide cases of representation, Walton argues. "The music is [not] merely indicating or expressing the *property* of lateness; it portrays a particular (fictitious) instance of something's being late, even if nothing much can be said about what it is that is late."

If there are such things as musical fictional worlds, however, they must be significantly different from pictorial or literary fictional worlds. Unlike the latter cases, the unity of a musical work does not seem dependent on the coherence of its fictional elements, in large part because musical worlds are indeterminate with respect to the identity and individuation of the agents that populate them. In addition, musical space, lacking perspective, seems less related to the listener's space than, say, pictorial space. More fundamentally, while we might have the experience of imagining seeing while perceiving a picture, we do not, in the case of music, imagine hearing. Music, in general, seems to involve less imagining *de se* than does painting and literature.

This last point would seem to run counter to the intuition that we are intimately connected with the musical world we perceive. A peculiarity of music, however, and what accounts for our sense of intimacy with it, is that, in listening to music, we can imagine introspecting or simply experiencing feelings, and this in a musical way: "Anguished or agitated or exuberant music not only induces one to imagine feeling anguished or agitated or exuberant, it also induces one to imagine of one's auditory experiences that *it* is an experience of anguish or agitation or exuberance. . . . One imagines experiencing the emotion, and one imagines one's experience of the sounds to be one's experience of it." These vivid imaginings, in addition to the fact that music can induce actual tension, relaxation, exuberance, and so forth, help to explain the proclivity of music to induce behavioral responses such as foot-tapping, singing, swaying, and so on: "the beginnings of behavioral expressions of feelings" that the listener can imagine to express the actual feeling in question. Music is an especially apt site for such imaginings, Walton argues, because sounds and feelings are conceived in analogous ways. But, in the end, music is not fully representational: it does not show the circumstances that produce experiences but only gets us to imagine the experiences. In music, Walton argues, "there are game worlds but no work worlds. . . . It is the auditory experiences, not the music itself, that generate fictional truths."

The issue of musical representation is at least as complex in the case of music wedded to text or drama, as Peter Kivy shows in "Speech, Song, and the Transparency of Medium: A Note on Operatic Metaphysics." Kivy examines the case of the representation of speech and song in opera. His starting point is Edward T. Cone's distinction between the "realistic song" of a play, sung by a character and distinguishable from the play's normal medium of speech, and "operatic song," the conventional or expressive song that takes the place, as it were, of ordinary speech in opera. Cone argues that though there can be instances of realistic song in opera, the distinction between realistic and operatic song tends to break down, primarily because the typical mode of expression in opera is singing rather than speaking. Operatic characters are usually perceived as composers of the songs they sing, whether realistic or operatic, realistic and operatic motifs are frequently interwoven, and operatic characters are often thought to be Orphaic composer-singers. The result is that, typically, one cannot say whether speech or song is being represented in opera and this, according to Cone, is "the fundamental operatic ambiguity."

Kivy argues that Cone is right, but for the wrong reasons. Kivy objects to Cone's obliteration of the distinction between realistic and operatic song and to the gap between the real world and the world of opera implied in Cone's view. Kivy instead takes his cue from Collingwood's maxim that every utterance and every gesture each of us makes is a work of art. If Collingwood is right that there is something expressive and inventive about ordinary language, then the gap between normal and operatic discourse narrows. We may therefore embrace the Orphaic view of operatic characters, not because of a distinction between speech and song, but rather because speech and song are both modes of expression: operatic characters are the "composers" of their conversations just as we are the "authors" of ours. However, this insight must be understood in both the ontological and

the aesthetic context of opera. Operatic speech is represented in the relatively opaque representational medium of singing, one that provides an apt object for aesthetic appreciation in which the "representational attitude" is intermingled with the "concert attitude." Phenomenologically speaking, what we hear in opera, says Kivy, "is characters expressing themselves not in speech represented by the medium of music but expressing themselves in the medium, the *music* itself."

In "Musical Understanding and Musical Kinds," Stephen Davies asks in what musical understanding might consist in the case of another important type of music—instrumental music in the classical tradition—but his concern here is not with musical expression or musical representation per se. Let us assume a listener who lacks proficiency as a performer and who is without technical training in music theory or analysis. Minimally, Davies argues, such a person should have an ability to recognize the overall structure or pattern of musical events of a piece, even if one lacked the customary technical terms to describe that structure. Failing that degree of understanding, a listener would be unable to distinguish one work from another.

We cannot let the matter rest there, however, Davies argues. One must understand, not merely the structure of the piece, but its function—not merely how a work is put together in the way that it is, but why it is put together in precisely that way. And that, Davies argues, presupposes a certain contextualist understanding that situates the piece among musical kinds: historical and artistic categories addressing particular sorts of problems in characteristic ways. Davies supports his view with analyses of several symphonies and concerti composed by Mozart after 1778, explaining the greater number of themes in the concerti roughly in terms of the aim of providing the soloist with new material, as against the symphonic goals of economy and precision in developing particular musical materials. Another analysis highlights respective functions of the symphonic first movement form and the opera overture. The greater the appreciation of such matters, Davies argues, the deeper the understanding of the works in question. Musical understanding is further enhanced by an awareness of the works of one composer in relation to the problems addressed by others within a given style, and an understanding of the relations of the given style to antecedent and subsequent styles and conventions—all of which is taken to embrace dramatic, social, and political, as well as more purely musical, elements.

But what about the compositional traditions and conventions themselves? Music history and music theory textbooks are replete with descriptions, proscriptions, and prescriptions for compositional practices for musical forms (the fugue, the sonata-allegro form, and so forth) taken to be standard in the literature. What is the status of these suggestions and formulae? Are there actually "rules" of composition, and, if there are, in what sense, if any, are they imperative upon composers? In "On Composing 'By the Rules,' " James Manns looks into these questions by asking first what a compositional rule might be. Some theorists (Graham George and Adele Katz, for example, following Schenker), acknowledge that the formulae given in music textbooks are as often violated as observed, but they nevertheless hold to the view that there are principles formulable at a suitable level of generality such that they do in fact encompass even the most recalcitrant examples in particular eras. On such a view, a rule of composition is construed as something universally adhered to by composers of a particular era. Manns rejects the view, however, on the grounds that the theorists in question typically appeal to (very general) principles of tonality as applying to a musical era in which nonadherence to tonal principles was not even conceivable. This runs counter to the notion of a "rule" of composition since "where there is no such possibility, there is no need to crystallize practice into principle, and no grounds for ascribing anything as strong as 'obedience' to a composer faithful to the practice." Manns is also less than enthusiastic about Donald Tovey's appeal to the authority of "artistic form," which is taken to be exemplified in great works that must be judged on their own merits, whether or not they follow the precepts of textbook formulae. Few would gainsay the profundity of Tovey's analyses of particular works, but, if the point was to preserve the notion of musical greatness through variations in compositional practice, the principle backfires: "To the extent that Beethoven's Ninth contains elements which internally dictate the nature of its formation, so too does

Neil Sedaka's 'Calendar Girl.' " Furthermore, the notion of "law" underlying the view turns out to be a vacuity. In Manns's words, "no reasonable conception of 'law' allows for individuals to be laws unto themselves."

Manns does not think, however, that we should dismiss the notion of compositional rules as misleading or meaningless. What motivated the previous views was an inappropriate notion of explanation modeled on a certain view of explanation in the natural sciences that brooks no theoretical gaps or holes, and according to which works are to be accounted for in terms of their strict obedience to rules. But one can be mindful of a rule without being obedient to it. Manns writes, "[T]hose composers can be said to be mindful of a practice who allow it to contribute to the shaping of their musical ideas, *even if* their ideas do not take on precisely the shape prescribed by that practice. . . . [T]he proper goal of musicological analysis with respect to rules of composition is not to seek out rules which encompass all cases, but rather, to determine when and why obedience to them is effective, and when and why deviance from them is desirable." The notion of compositional rule at issue must also be understood historically, in terms of its future and its past: rules of composition are accepted as regulatory within a practice after a certain measure of obedience has been established. Textbook rules, then, identify the procedures that have, for a time, served composers well, both in their observance and in their violation, and in that sense they provide a link between procedures and values.

Manns's essay leads naturally to the question of musical value itself or, as Jerrold Levinson points out in "Evaluating Music," at least two basic questions that can be asked at the outset about musical value: What is the value of music generally? and What makes particular pieces, genres, or styles valuable? Levinson concentrates on the latter question. He argues against the position of Malcolm Budd, among others, who argues that the distinctive value of a musical work of art "is determined by or is a function of the intrinsic value of the experience the work offers" when correctly understood. Such a view, Levinson argues, supposes a too sharp distinction between an experience and its effects, a too restrictive view of artistic value as intrinsic (as opposed to instrumental) value, and a too narrow construal of artistic value as constitutable only in and through the experience it offers. Regarding the last point, Levinson argues that a musical work may have what he calls "influence value"—an actual or potential positive impact that the work might have on the future course of music-making and musical thinking—as well as other non-appreciative-experience-based values, including those pertaining to problem-solving, originality, and performance.

To acknowledge the existence of the range of values of musical works is not thereby to dismiss or diminish the importance of intrinsic, experientially based musical value. Levinson himself distinguishes three possible levels of value that have figured into discussions of such value: the abstract, high-level criterion of the intrinsic rewardingness of the experience of listening; the low-level merits of particular musical features (attractive melody, significant harmonic invention, rhythmic interest, pleasing timbres, emotional expressiveness, and so forth); and midlevel principles (Beardsley's unity, intensity, and complexity, for example) that might be thought to mediate between these two. Levinson's own approach to the matter is rather different, proposing two models of the main object of musical appreciation. On the first, more basic level, one listens for "content-infused form" (or "formally embedded content"), a fusion of purposive and expressive features; that is, of "how it goes" with "what it conveys." Levinson calls this the "significant form / immanent content" of the music. At a more complex level, one listens for the fusion of expressive purposiveness ("expressive form") and purposive expressiveness ("dramatic content"), the blend of which Levinson calls the "(global) significant form / immanent content" of the music. In addition, one listens for the relationships among these various forms and contents. Levinson explores the subtleties and nuances of these aspects of music, the "value relevant dimensions of the experience of music," as he calls them, by way of a discussion of Schubert's Piano Sonata in A major, op. posth. D. 959.

Levinson's analysis has much to offer with respect to a central and important tradition in Western music. But the role of tradition itself in musical practice has been unusually fore-grounded by certain developments in our own century in the practice of music and in critical and philosophical discourse about that practice, especially in the domains of popular and avant-garde music. On the popular music scene, one must contend with the ever-increasing prominence of rock music, a phenomenon that, as some contemporary philosophers have argued, may very well offer its own distinctive aesthetic values, challenges, and rewards. In "Rock 'n' Recording: The Ontological Complexity of Rock Music," John Andrew Fisher argues that aesthetic thought must come to grips with the distinctive ontology of rock. In the central classically based tradition in Western music, as we have seen, the focus is on musical works that are thought to be determined by, though not identical with, their scores. Performances provide instances of the musical work, which is itself usually understood as a universal or a type that presents a formal sound structure that, as Levinson points out, can fruitfully be understood to feature a variety of purposive and expressive components. Recordings, in this context, are regarded, more or less, as documentations of particular performances of works.

One might try to adapt the standard view to rock, arguing that the musical work in the case of rock is the song. But Fisher argues that the rock musical work is better understood as a recording. The rock recording is not the physical object (a tape, record, or CD) but rather what he calls an "extended sound event," which is in turn identifiable as a "norm-kind," to use a notion developed by Nicholas Wolterstorff, a normative ideal within a kind that allows for the possibility of defective instances. More specifically still, the norm-kind of the rock recording is "the extended sound event (the sequence of sounds) produced by a studio quality playback (circa the time of creation) of a master tape." The ontological status of the rock recording is in that sense not far removed from the final cut of a film.

Fisher also distinguishes between "veridic" and "constructive" recordings, the former regarded as recordings more or less true to performances in accordance with certain conventions about how live performances should sound, the latter not carrying the implication that they represent live performances. Most rock recordings are constructive, Fisher argues. That is, most of the sounds on rock recordings define the work, but the sounds are not adequately understood merely as a performance of a song but rather as causal constructions. In fact, Fisher contends, rock music is more ontologically complex than pure autographic or allographic art forms, generating several entities simultaneously: primarily the recording, but also the song, and the arrangement. In consequence of this distinctive ontology, the appreciation of rock music differs significantly from music created and performed on the classical model. Rock music must be understood first of all as a collaborative affair (again, though with some qualification, in the way that one understands the ontology of movies). Further, rock music typically brings to our attention qualities predicable of recordings as such, especially timbral, rhythmic, and sonic effects, many of which, such as feedback, reverberation, electronic mixes, and so on, are achieved in the engineering of the recording, rather than focusing on the sorts of tonal structures favored by the classical music tradition.

On the avant-garde scene, probably no one has had a greater impact on the contemporary understanding of musical practice and tradition than the composer, musician, and theoretician, John Cage, whose music and views are the subject of Noël Carroll's article, "Cage and Philosophy." As Carroll makes clear, Cage sought to radicalize musical practice. Cage strove to replace traditional practices of listening-for-meaning with a new sort of attention: attending to the activities of sounds as such. This he did, in part, by replacing the traditional object of musical attention—musical sounds—with the entire gamut of sound, including what, under normal circumstances would be regarded as mere random, ambient noise. One hesitates even to call Cage's sound-events musical "works" insofar as they seem to lack even that minimal artistic quality that has been said to differentiate artworks from real things, what Arthur Danto has dubbed their "aboutness."

Or have we granted too much to Cage in saying that his compositions (if they are that) lack semantic content? Consider Cage's notorious *4'33"*. On Carroll's view, the presentational context of *4'33"* frames ambient noises as samples or, in Nelson Goodman's terminology, as exemplifications of everyday noises, that serve to illustrate "the latent potentials of noise." This is a content that has to be understood, Carroll argues, in the context of entrenched views about the nature of meaning and interpretation of music, especially with respect to the question of the role of expressiveness in music. Cage's compositions have a degree of aboutness after all, "in part by way of exemplification, and in part by contextual (art-historical–conversational) implicature in conjunction with exemplification." And as Carroll remarks, "Those offended know precisely what is at stake theoretically." Cage may not have succeeded in completely severing the link between his compositions and intentionality, but he has, Carroll argues, introduced us to "a positive aesthetic predicate, *ordinariness*, which focuses attention on a newly discovered realm of value." A musical phenomenon of the 1950s and 1960s, Cage's music and his pronouncements draw attention to a topic much discussed in the 1980s and 1990s, namely, the extent to which sayings and doings are culturally charged.

But if we want to take a philosophical view of music against the backdrop of its larger social order, where shall we begin? Lydia Goehr places the cultural embeddedness of music in a more specifically political context in "Political Music and the Politics of Music." Goehr tells the story of Hanns Eisler's exchange with the House Un-American Activities Committee in 1947, during which Eisler was required to defend himself against the charge that his music had aided the alleged Communist infiltration of the motion-picture industry. Many aspects of Eisler's musical practice might have been regarded as revolutionary, but Goehr uses Eisler's case to focus on the hardest question: In what sense, if any, could Eisler's instrumental music be thought to be political?

Goehr puts the matter the following way: "In determining the meaning and nature of musical works, to what extent, or according to what principles of selection, should we take extra-musical factors into account?" Goehr identifies two main lines of thinking about the question. Traditionally, musical "purists" or "formalists" have sought to identify the musically significant with the purely musical. In recent times, theorists, especially those influenced by certain postmodernist writings and contemporary emphases on difference and pluralism, have insisted that musical meaning can only be understood in the institutional and societal context in which musical works are created, presented, and enjoyed. Both of these positions may be articulated in extreme forms, either by insisting on the absolute purity of music with a quasi-religious zeal or by reducing music to politics, as in some of the more notorious proclamations of Marxist aesthetic theory.

At the root of this dispute, Goehr argues, is an unsatisfactory notion of musical autonomy, one that posits that a musical work must be either autonomous or political, but cannot be both. A fundamental distinction, inherited from romantic aesthetic theory, is drawn between the transcendent and the ordinary world. The purists insist upon music's placement in the former, the levelers in the latter. Goehr's own solution is to look for a philosophically acceptable middle ground according to which, "though aesthetics is separable from politics, the ideals regulating each should be neither reduced one to the other, nor formed in isolation from one another. The separation recognizes functional and categorial differences but avoids mutual isolation or exclusion." Citing a philosophical tradition that runs from Kant through Sartre characterizing beauty as a symbol or analog of the morally good, Goehr argues that the political significance of music may be found, not in the external and contingent relations between musical works and concrete political messages, but rather in the "internal, essential, and abstract relation that holds between the musical and the political." Music has a "relative" autonomy, by turn manifesting and resisting the forms imposed upon it by the social conditions of the status quo. In this way music exhibits a condition of "freedom within." Goehr allows that, ultimately, the connection between autonomous musical form and the political function of music cannot be adequately described, but, following a Wittgensteinian line of thought, she suggests that the limitation may reside as much in the inherent limitations of language as in the theory she propounds.

Claire Detels also makes an explicit effort to link our understanding of music to a social context. In "Autonomist/Formalist Aesthetics, Music Theory, and the Feminist Paradigm of Soft Boundaries," Detels attacks a particular autonomist/formalist view that defines art and artworks in isolation from other cultural practices and assesses the value of artworks in terms of purportedly universal formal and/or structural values. Musical representatives of the view Detels has in mind are the musical aesthetics of Eduard Hanslick and the music-theoretical writings and analyses of Allen Forte and Milton Babbitt. Originally a product of the rising "museum culture" in the latter part of the eighteenth century, the autonomist/formalist position generally had the effect of devaluing what Detels calls the "vital aspects of artistic experience"— the physical, emotional, historical, and cultural resonances of art—as well as disenfranchising entire artistic communities (women in particular) by relegating their work to the status of "low" art. Certain recent feminist insights, such as the importance of recognizing gendered perspectives (and the "male gaze," in particular), have provided the means to challenge the exclusionary tendency of formalist/autonomist theories in the visual arts. Can an analogous perspective be brought to bear on the aesthetics of music?

Notwithstanding the largely nonrepresentational character of music, Detels suggests the deployment of what she calls the "soft-boundaries paradigm," which she sees as applicable to such basic music-theoretical concepts as the musical work, section, period, phrase, chord progression, motive, interval, and pitch. In accordance with a particular postmodern version of feminist theory, Detels characterizes her approach as "feminist" insofar as it seeks to replace logocentric, patriarchal thinking that emphasizes totalizing, universal truths and unitary judgments, with a "careful and continuing attention to all aspects of experience, appreciation for detail . . . and allowance for pluralism, i.e., the possibility of a multiplicity of valid concepts and judgments." The approach has much in common with other culturally embedded analyses of music that have been advanced under the banners of ethnomusicology, Marxist aesthetics, hermeneutics, and poststructuralist theory. On Detels's view, standard music-theoretical analyses would be enriched and perhaps even supplanted by "experience-based" categories relating music to "the ways in which the music under consideration was composed, performed, heard, taught, danced, moved, worked, or prayed to," as well as to particular codings according to which music might be thought to bear deep cultural meanings, as Susan McClary has sought to do with respect to more specifically feminist concerns.

Some of the complexities of contextualizing the philosophy of music are also evidenced in Joel Rudinow's provocatively entitled essay, "Race, Ethnicity, Expressive Authenticity: Can White People Sing the Blues?" The interrogative in Rudinow's title raises important questions about the musical/extramusical distinction as well as about our understanding of creation and performance in music and what is to count as relevant to these aspects of musical experience. Rudinow rejects one facile but oft-heard response to the question. This is the positive reply, supported by a mere listing of white musicians whose recordings are filed in the "blues" sections of record stores. This answer only defers the question, since it will inevitably be asked, Are these people *really* playing the blues? Clearly, more sophistication is needed.

Rudinow begins by pointing out that a negative answer to the question need not proceed from racist presuppositions. That *would* be the case, Rudinow argues, if it were maintained that white people are incapable of singing the blues simply by virtue of their being white. That view, held by some, seems completely untenable. The more interesting question goes to the issue of what is to count as *authentic* performance, since what is normally being asked is a fundamentally cultural question: Is the "blues" produced by white singers "acceptably derived" from original sources within the originating culture? Rudinow also points out that, given the blues' "compositional minimalism" and its complementary emphasis on expressive elements, the question of authenticity here differs somewhat from questions typically raised in musical aesthetics concerning the relation of a performance to the work or composition. The negative answer to the question at hand is most cogently put this way: "White musicians cannot play the blues in an authentic way because they do not have the requisite relation or proximity to the original sources of the blues."

Rudinow distinguishes two general kinds of argument that have been used to support the negative position. The "proprietary argument" proceeds on the assumption that the blues is essentially a form of intellectual and cultural property. The blues, on this argument, is considered as a musical genre and style originating in African-American culture and belonging to bona fide members of the community. The proprietary argument maintains, further, that white blues musicians have misappropriated a cultural heritage of the African-American community in what Amiri Baraka has called the "Great Music Robbery" and have profited from the mainstream distribution of the music without giving credit to the music's creators, a pattern whites have followed with other aspects of African-American culture. Rudinow argues, however, that, while the argument has some force, the claim that the blues belongs to the African-American culture cannot be maintained, in part because the actual conditions of production, presentation, and enjoyment of the blues are at odds with the notion of a cultural commodity required by the argument.

The "experiential access argument" seems more promising because it more adequately addresses the cultural ontology, as it were, of the blues. The argument is now that whites lack a necessary condition for authentic expression in the blues, the felt emotion that can be had only by having the experience of living as a black person living in America, hence Baraka's claim that "[t]he idea of a white blues singer seems an even more violent contradiction in terms than the idea of a middle-class blues singer." But the variants of this argument are suspect on several counts, especially the implicit appeal to a "myth of ethnic memory" and the claim that nonblacks are incapable of having a deep understanding of basic human experiences or of their encodings in blues lyrics. In the end, Rudinow rejects both arguments: "The essence of the blues is a *stance* embodied in sound and poetry, and what distinguishes authentic from inauthentic blues is essentially what distinguishes that stance from its superficial imitations—from *posturing.*"

The last word in this developing conversation about music and its context is given by ethnomusicologist, Bruno Nettl. In " 'Musical Thinking' and 'Thinking About Music' in Ethnomusicology: An Essay of Personal Interpretation," Nettl reflects on the interaction between musical thinking (the thought processes of musicians as evidenced in the music they produce) and thinking about music (what is said about music by musicians and others in a given society).

Nettl reports his findings about several cultures in which he has lived and worked as an ethnomusicologist. In each case Nettl emphasizes the close relation between musical thinking and thinking about music. One can analyze the formal characteristics of a typical Blackfoot song, for example; some of what Blackfoot singers say about their music refers to such formal features as motif and length. However, Nettl argues, understanding what Blackfoot people say about their music cannot be complete without reference to a central cosmological myth concerning the beaver medicine bundle, a story that not only identifies and authenticates, as it were, the formal patterns of the music, but also helps to provide an account of certain compositional and performance practices in Blackfoot culture and the origins and role of music generally in the society. In the case of the Persian radif, certain structural patterns and improvisatory performance practices can be seen to mirror deeply held ideas about thinking and acting in Persian society, especially with respect to relations between the individual to society, the value of individualism, and the tension between freedom and authority.

On the basis of his many years as ethnomusicologist, Nettl inclines toward the view that all societies possess musical thinking and engage in thinking about music. This raises the interesting question whether all societies have anything like a "theory text," that is, an articulable, if sometimes informally held, music theory. Nettl finds that he can assemble various Blackfoot statements about music under various heads (The Concept of Music, Origins and History, Uses and Functions of Music, Musicianship).

Perhaps one reads through the list with bemusement, smiling at the seemingly ad hoc assortment of statements relating music to Blackfoot society. But, Nettl shows, we have our own informal theory text, our own collection of apothegms and dicta about Mozart and Beethoven that inform our understanding of our own musical practice and values and that seem not so very far removed from the sorts of things the Blackfoot say. We are left, then, with an important set of suggestions about the relation of music to the larger cultural order from which it emerges. Perhaps, as Nettl says, "the way in which musicians think musically, the ways in which they, as it were, 'think' their music, depends in large measure on ways in which they think of their world at large. And within that context, the ways in which a society thinks about the concept of music, about music in culture, about musicians, may determine much about the way in which the musicians of that society think their music." The working out of these questions will no doubt continue to receive much philosophical attention by present and future scholars.

1. Eduard Hanslick, *On the Musically Beautiful: A Contribution Towards the Revision of the Aesthetics of Music*, 8th ed. (1891), trans. Geoffrey Payzant (Indianapolis: Hackett, 1986).

2. Ibid., p. 3.

3. Ibid., p. xxii.

4. Ibid., p. 6.

5. Ibid., p. 9.

JENEFER ROBINSON

The Expression and Arousal of Emotion in Music

I

This essay is about the relation between the expression and the arousal of emotion by music. I am assuming that music frequently *expresses* emotional qualities and qualities of human personality such as sadness, nobility, aggressiveness, tenderness, and serenity. I am also assuming that music frequently *affects* us emotionally: it evokes or arouses emotions in us. My question is whether there is any connection between these two facts, whether, in particular, music ever expresses emotion *by virtue of* arousing emotion. Of course, what it means to say that music expresses emotion is a contentious issue and I shall not be directly addressing it here, although what I say will have implications for any theory of musical expression. Nor will I be examining all the possible contexts in which music can be said to arouse emotion. My focus in this essay will be narrower. The question I shall try to answer is this: Are the grounds on which we attribute the expression of emotion to music ever to be identified with the arousal of that same emotion in listeners?

II

According to some theories of musical expression, the grounds on which we attribute expressive qualities to music have nothing to do with the arousal of emotion in the audience. According to Peter Kivy's account in *The Corded Shell*, a musical element such as a melody, a rhythm, or a chord expresses a feeling not because it arouses that feeling in anyone but for two quite different reasons. (1) It has the same "contour" as expressive human behavior of some kind and thus is "heard as expressive of something or other because heard as appropriate to the expression of something or other" (for example,

the "weeping" figure of grief in Arianna's lament from Monteverdi's *Arianna*) or it contributes in a particular context to the forming of such an expressive contour (as the diminished triad in a suitable context can contribute to a *restless* quality in the music, although all by itself it does not express anything). (2) The musical element is expressive by virtue of some custom or convention, which originated in connection with some expressive contour. The minor triad, for example, is "sad" by convention, although it may have started life as part of some expressive contour.[1]

There are many examples of musical expression for which Kivy's argument is convincing. Thus it does seem to be true that Arianna's lament mirrors the passionate speaking voice expressing grief, that Schubert's "Gretchen am Spinnrad" mirrors Gretchen's monotonous, leaden gestures at the spinning wheel and her correspondingly dejected, leaden heart, and that the "Pleni sunt coeli" from Bach's B Minor Mass maps "bodily motion and gesture ... of tremendous expansiveness, vigor, violent motion," thus mirroring the exuberance of " 'leaping' joy."[2] At the same time, as Renée Cox, among others, has pointed out,[3] virtually all the musical examples in Kivy's book are examples of music with a text, and it is relatively uncontroversial that a text can specify a particular feeling or object which is characterized by the music. Moreover, when we look closely at Kivy's examples of particular emotions said to be expressed by music we find mainly varieties of joy, sorrow, and restlessness. The vast majority of musical examples in *The Corded Shell* can be characterized as expressions of either positive or negative emotion (joy or sorrow) of various sorts.[4] Thus although what Kivy says seems to be true as far as it goes, it does not go very far, and leaves a great deal of expressiveness in music unexplained.

Kivy holds that music can express particular emotional states such as sorrow and joy, restlessness and serenity. Susanne Langer, while agreeing that emotional qualities are to be found in the *music,* rather than in the *listener,* follows Hanslick in arguing that since only the dynamic qualities of anything (including emotional states) can be expressed by music, no particular emotions can be expressed by music, but only the felt quality of our emotional life and its dynamic development:

[There] are certain aspects of the so-called "inner life"—physical or mental—which have formal properties similar to those of music—patterns of motion and rest, of tension and release, of agreement and disagreement, preparation, fulfillment, excitation, sudden change, etc.[5]

[Music] reveals the rationale of feelings, the rhythm and pattern of their rise and decline and intertwining, to our minds... . [6]

In contrast to Kivy's view that the words of a text supply the "fine shadings" to otherwise only grossly expressive musical meanings, Langer holds that musical meanings are inherently rich and significant yet cannot be linked to any particular words. Langer's theory emphasizes the development of structures of feeling throughout a lengthy piece of music, which Kivy ignores, but she in turn ignores the expression of particular emotional qualities which Kivy emphasizes. Both theorists have insightful things to say about musical expression but neither tells the whole story.

III

A very different view of musical expression has recently been presented by Kendall Walton in a paper called "What is Abstract About the Art of Music?" Walton proposes that one important way in which music is expressive is by virtue of the fact that in listening to music we imagine ourselves introspecting, being aware of, our own feelings. As he puts it, we imagine "of our actual introspective awareness of auditory sensations" that "it is an experience of being aware of our states of mind."[7] Thus the expressiveness of music has to do with its power to *evoke* certain imaginative emotional experiences. Moreover, Walton says that if this is right, then:

music probably can be said to "portray particulars" in the sense that figurative paintings do, rather than simply properties or concepts. Presumably the listener imagines experiencing and identifying *particular* stabs of pain, *particular* feelings of ecstasy, *particular* sensations of well-being, etc., as in viewing a painting one imagines seeing particular things.[8]

However, whereas one perceives the psychological states of other people, as in figurative paintings, one "introspects one's *own* psychological states."[9]

There are at least two problems I see with Walton's account. (1) First, suppose someone denies that this is what she does when listening to expressive music; we should be able to *explain* to her why this is what she should be doing. What reason is there why we should imagine our awareness of auditory sensations—experienced sequences of musical tones—to be an experience of our feelings and other inner states? True, there are similarities between the two: the experience of auditory sensations is an introspectible state, and so is awareness of our feelings. True, part of what we are aware of in these auditory sensations is, as Langer points out, their ebb and flow, and our feelings too have ebb and flow. But beyond these points of resemblance there seems to be little explanation *why* we should be inclined to imagine our awareness of musical sounds to be an awareness of our feelings. Imagination requires some guidance if it is not to be merely free association: I can imagine the tree at the end of the garden to be a witch because it has a witch-like appearance, but it is unclear what it would mean for me to imagine the snowdrop at my feet to be a witch if there is nothing about the snowdrop to set off my imagination. Similarly, in order for me to imagine my awareness of musical sounds to be awareness of my feelings, something in the musical sounds must guide my imagination. However, if the only points of resemblance between feelings and sounds is introspectibility and ebb and flow, then I would suggest that this is insufficient to ground an imaginative identification between the two. There are, moreover, striking *differences* between the two which would seem to preclude any such imaginative identification. In particular, whereas our feelings clearly rise up inside us (as we say), musical sounds as clearly rise up at a distance from us: even when listening to music over good earphones—when the music is experienced with peculiar immediacy—we still experience the auditory sensations as coming from an external source, such as trombones and the like. That is why although we can perhaps imagine these sounds as feelings welling up inside the *composer,* or perhaps in some *character* described by the music, it is not obvious to me that we can imagine them as feelings welling up inside ourselves.

(2) There is a second problem related to this one. I am willing to grant that there are indeed movements in music which it is appropriate to call "stabbing" or "surging." According to Walton, however, the music induces me to imagine myself feeling a particular ecstatic surge or stab of pain. He says that the music *portrays* these particulars (it picks them out or refers to them). A number of questions need to be distinguished here. (1) Can the stab be identified as a stab of feeling rather than the stab of a dagger or some other kind of stab? (2) If the stab is a stab of feeling, can it be identified as a stab of pain rather than some other feeling such as excitement or jealousy? (3) If the stab is indeed a stab of pain, can it be identified as a stab of pain which I imagine myself experiencing rather than a stab of pain attributed to someone else, such as Othello or the composer? If the music *portrays* my imagined stab of pain, as Walton suggests, then the music must be able to distinguish my imagined stab of pain from all these other possible alternatives. Can music do this? Can music portray this particular stab of pain and no other?

If the music were accompanied by an appropriate verbal text, then perhaps it could. As we listen to the music we hear in it particular tones, rhythms, harmonic modulations, phrases, melodies, counterpoint sections, etc., etc. We might also hear particular movements that we characterize as "stabbing" or "surging." Given a particular accompanying text, we might then be able to identify the stabbing as the stabbing of Mercutio rather than a stab of pain. With a different text, we might be able to identify the

stabbing as Othello's stabbing pains of jealousy rather than his stabbing pains of remorse. And so on. However, in the absence of a text, Walton suggests no good reasons for identifying the stabbing in the music (1) with a stab of feeling (rather than some other kind of stab), (2) with a stab of pain (rather than some other kind of feeling), or (3) with my imagined stab of pain (rather than yours or Othello's real or imagined pain). Walton claims earlier in his paper that musical characterization is inherently *general.* It would seem to follow that without the specification of a particular context we cannot specify that the stab is even a stab of emotion, let alone the stab of a particular emotion, let alone an *imagined* stab of *my* particular emotion. However, Walton gives us no guidance as to how a particular context could be specified. In short, although we can hear a stabbing movement in a piece of music, Walton does not show us how to tell from the music alone—without any accompanying text—what, if any, particular stabbing is occurring.

IV

Although Walton's theory does not identify musical expression with the straightforward arousal of feelings, he does try to explain expression in terms of the arousal of *imaginary* feelings. I am not actually feeling a stab of pain as I listen to the stabbing music; I am *imagining* experiencing a stab of pain, so it would seem that the pain is an imaginary feeling. In his paper "Music and Negative Emotions," Jerrold Levinson makes a similar point. Levinson's paper deals with the problem of why people enjoy music when it evokes negative emotions such as sadness in them. While the paper does not develop a theory of musical expression, it does make certain assumptions about what often happens when people listen to music which we would characterize as sad. In particular, he assumes that it is a normal response for people to have a sadness-reaction to music.

When a person has a "deep emotional response" to music, this is "generally in virtue of the *recognition* of emotions expressed in music," but recognition then leads to a kind of empathic identification: we "end up feeling as, in imagination, the music does."[10] Such empathic emotional responses to music consist in "something very like experience of the emotion expressed in the music"[11] but not *exactly* like it. In both cases the physiological and affective components of emotion are present and in both cases there is cognitive content, but the "empathic" response lacks *determinate* cognitive content:

When one hears sad music, begins to feel sad, and imagines that one is actually sad, one must, according to the logic of the concept, be imagining that there is an object for one's sadness and that one maintains certain evaluative beliefs (or attitudes) regarding it. The point, though, is that this latter imagining generally remains indeterminate.[12]

I feel sad but my sadness has no determinate object; it is directed only to "some featureless object posited vaguely by my imagination."[13] Levinson illustrates his view with various kinds of negative emotion: "intense grief, unrequited passion, sobbing melancholy, tragic resolve, and angry despair."[14] Suppose, for example, that the music evokes in me an empathic response of unrequited passion. On Levinson's view, this means that I recognize unrequited passion in the music, I imagine that I am experiencing unrequited passion, and I actually experience the physiological and affective components of unrequited passion. My imagined unrequited passion has a cognitive content which is "etiolated by comparison to that of real-life emotion";[15] however, since I am not really suffering the pangs of unrequited passion, and in particular there is no special person for whom I am languishing.

I am sympathetic to some of Levinson's assumptions: I think he is right to stress that the detection of emotional qualities in music has something to do with the arousal of emotion by music, and I think he is right also to stress the role of the imagination in the appreciation of emotional qualities in music. However, the theory as it stands will not do. First of all, it is far from clear that every emotional state has identifiable physiological and affective components. For example, real-life unrequited passion might on different occasions be accompanied by a great variety of inner feelings (love, grief, longing, jealousy, wretchedness, despair, self-contempt, etc., etc.). For another thing, the particular feelings I experience on a given occasion of unrequited passion may be just the same as I have

felt on occasions of angry despair or intense grief. The truth of the matter is that there may be very little difference between the affective and physiological components of very different emotions: I may feel the same mixture of grief and rage when I am jealous or when I am grieving (without jealousy); I may have very similar feelings whether angrily despairing, tragically resolving, or suffering from the pangs of unrequited passion. The difference between these emotions lies not so much in their affective and physiological components as in their cognitive content. The chief difference between unrequited passion, tragic resolve, and angry despair is how I view or conceive of the situation.

But now we come to a second set of difficulties. Levinson argues that I can recognize unrequited passion (say) in the "emotion-laden gestures embodied in musical movement"[16] and by virtue of this recognition respond empathically with feelings of unrequited passion of my own, since I identify with the music or perhaps "with the person whom we imagine owns the emotions or emotional gestures we hear in the music."[17] However, he fails to tell us how we detect or empathically feel the unrequited passion in the music. Although we all have some idea of what *sad* music is like, I suggest that it is much less clear what a piece of music is like in which we can recognize, and hence empathize with, unrequited passion (always assuming, of course, that there is no accompanying verbal text to help us out). If I am right and there are no distinctive affective or physiological components of unrequited passion, then the obvious way to clarify the nature of music in which we can detect unrequited passion would be to specify its cognitive content. Now, Levinson claims that the cognitive content of an emotional response to music is normally "etiolated." This could mean simply that my imagined feelings of unrequited passion are not directed to any particular individual. While it is a little odd to say that one can feel unrequited passion for someone I know not whom, we can perhaps make sense of this suggestion since on Levinson's view the unrequited passion I feel empathically belongs to the music itself or to someone whom we imagine feels unrequited passion, so that we merely empathize with this imagined person's unrequited passion.

Even if we grant, however, that there need be

no specific object for the unrequited passion I detect in the music and empathize with, it would seem that there must be some identifiable cognitive content, however etiolated, which is detectable in the music in order to justify the attribution of this particular emotion. I would suggest that if my response is to count as a response of unrequited passion rather than some other emotion, then I must imagine that there is someone whom I care about deeply, that this person does not care deeply about me, and that I care deeply that this person does not care deeply about me (or something of this sort). It is a serious problem for Levinson's account that he does not tell us how such conceptions can be embodied in music and hence how we can either recognize or empathize with the corresponding emotion. We find the same problem with tragic resolve and angry despair: we cannot clearly distinguish these emotional responses by their affective and physiological components alone, but only by their cognitive content. However, Levinson gives us no clue as to how their cognitive content can be recognized in or induced by music.

In a later paper, "Hope in *The Hebrides,*" Levinson claims that perhaps it is possible for music to express "higher" emotional states, and that in addition to the affective and physiological components of an emotion, music might even be able to convey part, at least, of its cognitive content. He points out that emotions are normally intentional but that music can convey a general "sense of intentionality (aboutness)."[18] He also notes that just as ordinary extra-musical emotions are often individuated by their context of occurrence, it might perhaps be the case that *musical* context can play a similar role for emotions in music. When he illustrates his thesis by reference to the emotional state of hope, which he claims to be able to distinguish in Mendelssohn's *Hebrides* overture, he remarks that "perhaps some of the pure conceptual content of hope—its favorable assessment of future in relation to present"[19]—can be suggested by the position of the hopeful passage in its musical context. Levinson does not develop this idea very far, however, and what he does say along these lines is very tentative. Certainly he gives us no clue as to how the three marks of unrequited passion that I distinguished above could be adequately conveyed by music.[20]

V

Recently Levinson's view has been criticized by Peter Kivy on the grounds that the expression of emotion in music is entirely independent of the arousal of that emotion. Kivy argues that to have one's emotions aroused by a piece of music—in particular, to be moved by a piece of music—is quite distinct from perceiving a particular emotional quality in that piece. Music that is sad or expresses sadness is music with a sad expressive contour or music that is sad by convention, not music that arouses or evokes sadness. Levinson argues that a "deep emotional response" to sad music consists in the arousal of a kind of imaginative but cognitively truncated sadness. Kivy rightly attacks this claim, arguing on the one hand that sad music may or may not make me feel anything, depending on how great the music is (the "yards and yards of mournful music" written by Telemann[21] may fail to make me feel anything much at all), and on the other hand that there are important emotions aroused by music which are full-blown, ordinary, real-life emotions, not "truncated" or "imaginary" in any sense. He illustrates his point by reference to a performance of Josquin's "Ave verum virginitas" which, he says *moves* him deeply.

When listening to the "Ave verum virginitas" I may simply be moved by "the sheer beauty of the sound as it unfolds in its ebb and flow."[22] If my sophistication increases, however, I may also be moved by "the incomparable beauty and craftsmanship of Josquin's counterpoint"[23] and by the fact that despite its seeming effortlessness, the music is written in a particularly difficult canonic form, "a canon at the fifth, with the voices only one beat apart."[24] This, then, is the cognitive component of the emotion aroused by the music, my being moved by the music. It is not a truncated emotion in any way. It is a genuine emotional experience, arising out of my perception of the music and its qualities. Furthermore, this emotion might be directed at emotional, expressive qualities in the music, such as sadness, but it does not follow that the emotion *aroused by* the music is the emotion *detected in* the music. Part of what I may be moved by in a piece of music may be its sadness, but I can be moved by joyful, by energetic, and by serene music just as well, as well as by music which does not have any marked emotional character. The expressive qualities, if any, which I detect in the music are entirely independent of the emotions I feel as I listen to the music.

Now, Kivy is certainly right to claim that when I am moved by a piece of music, my emotion may be independent of the emotional qualities, if any, that the music happens to have. When I appreciate a piece of music I may indeed be moved in the way Kivy describes. On the other hand, Kivy has not succeeded in showing that the expression of emotion by a piece of music is always and entirely unconnected to the arousal of emotion. Kivy makes this claim based on an analysis of just one emotion, "being moved," and it may well be true that we can be equally moved by music with different emotional qualities, as well as by music which has no marked emotional qualities. However, I believe that music arouses other feelings as well and that some of these may indeed be connected to the expressive qualities that music has. Furthermore, I think Kivy is wrong to insist that *all* the feelings aroused by music have to have a complex cognitive component as in his example from Josquin. It may be true that being moved by music involves complex evaluative judgments, but being moved is not the only emotional or feeling response which music can arouse.

Let me summarize the results of my discussion so far. Walton argues that expressive music evokes the imaginative experience of the emotion expressed: more precisely, music expressive of sadness, say, induces the listener to imagine herself experiencing sad feelings. Levinson similarly claims that sad music has the power to evoke a kind of truncated sadness-response: the listener feels certain symptoms of sadness, has an "indeterminate" idea that there is something or other to be sad about and imagines that she in fact feels sad. Both writers find a connection between the presence of an emotional quality in music and the arousal of that emotion in the listener's imagination. I have urged, however, that neither Walton nor Levinson has shown *how* complex feelings such as unrequited passion, stabs of pain, or even sadness can be aroused by music whether in fact or in imagination. Furthermore, Kivy is clearly right to hold that to have a deep emotional

response to music is not necessarily to mirror the feelings that the music expresses.

At the same time, however, I believe that Walton and Levinson are right to stress the connection between the expression and the arousal of emotion in music, and that Kivy is quite wrong to think that his analysis of the one emotion "being moved" demonstrates that no such connection exists. In what remains of this paper I will try to sketch a more adequate account of what this connection really is.

VI

None of the writers I have discussed in this essay has focused on the way in which music can *directly* affect our feelings. For both Walton and Levinson the arousal of feeling is imaginative and it relies on a good deal of cognitive activity on the part of the listener. For Kivy the emotion of being moved is a real emotion, not an imagined one, but it too relies on cognitive activity, such as recognizing the clever part-writing, etc. However, some music has the power to affect our feelings without much, if any cognitive mediation. In particular, music can induce physiological changes and a certain quality of inner feeling (what Levinson calls respectively the "phenomenological" and "sensational" aspects of the "affective" component in emotion).[25] Music can make me feel tense or relaxed; it can disturb, unsettle, and startle me; it can calm me down or excite me; it can get me tapping my foot, singing along, or dancing; it can maybe lift my spirits and mellow me out.

Emotions vary in degree—and perhaps in kind—of cognitive content. At one end of the scale there is the startle response, which is an innate response, found in human neonates as well as throughout the phylogenetic scale. At the other end of the scale there is unrequited passion which, by contrast, is found only in humans with their highly developed cultural norms. What I want to suggest is that in addition to the sophisticated emotions of appreciation, which Kivy identifies as "being moved" by certain perceived aspects of the music, there are more primitive emotions aroused by music, perhaps requiring less developed cognitive mediation. There are, after all, moments in music which make us jump or startle us. Similarly, the perception of certain rhythms may be enough—without any further cognitive mediation—to evoke tension or relaxation, excitement or calm. If the melodic and harmonic elements in a piece of music affect our emotions, this would seem to require familiarity with the stylistic norms of the piece, but no further cognitions need be required in order for us to feel soothed, unsettled, surprised, or excited by developments in the music. Certainly we need not notice that we are listening to a canon at the fifth in order for that canon to soothe us.

We have seen that to feel unrequited passion necessarily involves a certain fairly complicated conception of one's situation. By contrast, to feel disturbed or calm does not require having a conception of one's situation in this way. Music can make me feel disturbed or calm just by perceiving it (listening to it). The feeling is a result of a perception and to this extent it has "cognitive content," but it is not the full-blown cognitive content required for tragic resolve, angry despair or unrequited passion. The sense of relaxation we feel at the end of "Tristan und Isolde," for example, is the result of the long-awaited resolution, after over four hours of constant modulation without resolution. The feeling is the result of a perception, but we may not even be aware why we feel as we do: the effect of the constantly shifting harmonic pattern affects us "directly" without conscious cognitive mediation (except, of course, what is required by our understanding of Wagner's style). There is some psychological evidence (from Berlyne and others) that people seek high levels of arousal in order to have them drop afterwards: "excitement and complex, conflicting information are sought because of the 'arousal jag.'"[26] The effect of the final Tristan chord may be partly accounted for in these terms.

Now, the feelings evoked "directly" by music explain some of the cases of musical expressiveness that the contour theory finds hard to deal with. Music that disturbs and unsettles us is disturbing, unsettling music. Modulations that surprise us are surprising. Melodies that soothe us are soothing. Furthermore, unexpected harmonic shifts excite us and are exciting; protracted stay in a harmonic area distant from the home key makes us uneasy and produces uneasy music; the return to the home key after a protracted stay in a distant harmonic area relaxes the tension in us and produces

relaxing music. And so on. In short, as against Kivy's position, it seems to me that the expression of a feeling by music can sometimes be explained straightforwardly in terms of the arousal of that feeling. However, the feelings aroused "directly" by music are not stabs of pain or feelings of unrequited passion, but more "primitive" feelings of tension, relaxation, surprise, and so on. These feelings do, therefore, in a sense have an "etiolated" cognitive content, in the way that Levinson specifies in "Music and Negative Emotions," but it is not an etiolated, imaginary version of an emotion which normally has a complex cognitive content (such as unrequited passion), but rather a feeling such as surprise, which by its nature just has—or can have—a relatively simple cognitive content.

VII

Even more interesting, however, is the way in which the simple feelings "directly" aroused by music can contribute to the imaginative expression of more complex emotions such as those discussed by Levinson. When we listen to a piece of music in a relatively familiar style, a succession of feelings is aroused in us: in a pattern typical of Classical sonata form, we may first be made to feel relaxed, then jolted into uncertainty, then made to feel uneasy for a prolonged period before experiencing relief and final release of tension. Now, something that most philosophical theorists of musical expression have either ignored or underemphasized is the fact that the musical expression of complex emotions is not a function of a few isolated measures here and there, as in Kivy's examples in *The Corded Shell;* rather it is very often a function of the large-scale formal structures of the piece as a whole.[27] We cannot understand the expression of complex emotions in music apart from the continuous development of the music itself. None of the philosophical writers I have discussed has fully appreciated this point. Langer has indeed stressed the importance of large-scale movements of ebbing and flowing, tension and relaxation in musical expression, but she denies that any particular emotions can thereby be expressed. Levinson suggests at times that we need to look at the total musical context before we can say what particular emotions are being expressed, but he does not explore this idea very far. In order to explain how particular cognitively complex emotions can be expressed musically, we need to look at the overall structure of a piece and at the feelings aroused by the piece as it develops in time.

In his celebrated book, *Emotion and Meaning in Music,* Leonard Meyer showed how the formal structure of works in the Classical and Romantic styles could be analyzed in terms of the emotional *responses* of the practiced listener: his was a kind of "Reader-Response" or rather "Listener-Response" theory of musical structure.[28] In order to understand a piece of music, on this view, the listener has to have her feelings aroused in a certain way. If we are experienced in the style of the piece, then we have certain expectations about the way the music will develop; in a meaningful piece of music these expectations will be either frustrated or satisfied in unexpected ways. As we listen new expectations are constantly being aroused and we are just as constantly being *surprised* by novel developments, *relieved* by delayed resolutions, made *tense* by the delays, etc., etc. In short, understanding musical structure, according to Meyer, is not just a matter of detached analysis; rather, it is impossible without the arousal of feeling in the listener.

Now, just as the formal structure of a piece of music can be understood in terms of the arousal of such feelings as uncertainty, uneasiness, relaxation, tension, relief, etc., so too can we understand the expressiveness of that piece of music in terms of the arousal of those and similar feelings. After all, as Anthony Newcomb has put it: "Formal and expressive interpretations are in fact two complementary ways of understanding the same phenomena."[29] Emotional expressiveness in music frequently corresponds to or mirrors its formal structure. The "direct" arousal of cognitively "simple" emotions such as being made surprised, disturbed, satisfied, relaxed, etc. is a clue not only to the formal structure of a musical piece, as Meyer showed, but also to its structure of emotional expressiveness. If a piece of music is heard as successively disturbing and reassuring, or as meandering uncertainly before moving forward confidently, or as full of obstacles which are with difficulty overcome, this is at least in part because of the way the music makes us feel. Disturbing passages disturb us; reassuring ones reassure. Passages that meander uncertainly make us feel uneasy: it is not clear where the music is going. Passages that move forward confidently make us feel satisfied: we know what is happening and seem to be able to predict what will happen next. Passages that are full of obstacles make us feel tense and when the obstacles are overcome, we feel relieved. It is important to notice that the feeling *expressed* is not always the feeling *aroused:* an uncertain, diffident passage may make me uneasy; a confident passage may make me feel reassured or relaxed.[30]

Now, of course we are still a long way from showing how unrequited passion can be expressed by a piece of music, but we can perhaps begin to see how the development of a complex piece of music can mirror the development of a complex emotional experience, and how we can become aware of both the formal development and the corresponding emotional development by means of the relatively "simple" feelings that are *aroused* in the listener as she follows that development. As I listen to a piece which expresses serenity tinged with doubt, I myself do not have to feel serenity tinged with doubt, but the feelings I do experience, such as relaxation or reassurance, interspersed with uneasiness, alert me to the nature of the overall emotional expressiveness in the piece of music as a whole. Consider, for example, a piece of music in sonata form in which the two chief themes in their initial formulation are respectively lively and ponderous (we can suppose that the contour theory accounts for these characterizations). Now, suppose that the initially lively theme (in the major) gets gradually but relentlessly overwhelmed by the ponderous (minor) theme in such a way that the first theme is never allowed to return to its initial lively formulation but gets increasingly distorted, becomes darker and is finally heard in a truncated form in the same minor key as the ponderous theme. Such music might well make me feel increasingly nervous and tense, even disturbed, as it develops. On the view I am suggesting, the emotional experience aroused by the music is essential to the detection of the emotional expressiveness in the music itself. At the same time, the emotions aroused in me are not the emotions expressed by the music. *I* feel nervous, tense, and disturbed; the *music* expresses cheerful confidence turned to despair, or something of this sort.[31] If this account is correct, then it shows that Kivy is wrong to suppose that expressiveness in music is just a matter of contour and convention, even if some expressive passages in music can be explained in such terms.[32] In my example, it is not enough to spot the respective lively and ponderous contours of the initial statements of the two themes; the expressiveness of the piece as a whole can only be grasped if the listener's feelings are aroused in such a way that they provide a clue to both the formal and the expressive structure of the piece as it develops through time.

VIII

We can now see that Levinson and Walton are right to insist on a connection between the arousal and expression of emotion in music. However, neither of them has succeeded in showing how music can actually arouse, even in imagination, the complex emotional states that music sometimes expresses. In my example, I did not myself have to feel cheerful confidence turning to despair in order to detect that emotion in the music. The feelings I felt, which were evoked "directly" by the music, were less cognitively complicated, such as unease, tension, and disturbance. At the same time, we can see why Levinson is tempted to say that we empathize imaginatively with the feelings expressed by the music, for in order to detect these feelings in the music I am myself emotionally involved in listening to the music: I feel genuine feelings of unease, disturbance, and so on. Moreover, if I imagine that the themes are themselves characters in a kind of musical drama, then perhaps I can empathize with the fate of the lively theme, feeling sorrow and pity for it as I might for a character in a drama, and maybe I can even feel anger and frustration at the ponderous theme.[33]

Walton wants to say that I imagine of my introspective awareness of auditory sensations that they are an experience of particular states of my own psyche, such as particular stabs of pain. Again we can see why Walton is tempted by this idea, since on the one hand the music does arouse feelings in me, although not usually the ones expressed, and on the other hand I

may perhaps imagine that the feelings expressed by the music do belong to me. However, I think this view is more problematic than Levinson's. In my example, must I imagine of both themes that they are an experience of my own emotions? In this case my imagination must take both sides in the conflict as it were. Why cannot I identify entirely with the suffering lively theme, or even—gloatingly—entirely with the powerfully insistent ponderous theme? Why, more fundamentally, should I imagine these musical events as belonging to my own psyche at all? When I watch a performance of *King Lear* I do not imagine the drama to be taking place inside my own head; it seems to me that the same is just as true of the *King Lear* overture.

In this essay I have tried to confine my attention to the question of how the expression of emotion by music is related to the arousal of emotion in the listener. Obviously I have left many questions unanswered. In particular, I have given only a skeletal account of how music can express cognitively complex emotions such as the "cheerful confidence turning to despair" of my example. I have not attempted to show how cognitive content can get expressed by music nor whether particular emotions such as unrequited passion can be so expressed. What I *have* tried to do, however, is to indicate how such analyses might proceed. And the point I have urged above all is that any such analysis must begin with the emotions that are aroused by the music in the listener.[34]

1. Peter Kivy, *The Corded Shell* (Princeton: Princeton University Press, 1980), p. 83.

2. Kivy, *The Corded Shell,* p. 54.

3. Renée Cox, "Varieties of Musical Expressionism," in George Dickie, et al., eds., *Aesthetics: A Critical Anthology,* 2nd ed. (New York: St. Martin's, 1989), pp. 614–625.

4. Anthony Newcomb has made this point effectively in "Sound and Feeling," *Critical Inquiry* 10 (1984): 614–643.

5. Susanne Langer, *Philosophy in a New Key,* 3rd ed. (Cambridge, Mass.: Harvard University Press, 1957), p. 228.

6. Langer, *Philosophy in a New Key,* p. 238.

7. "What is Abstract About the Art of Music?," *The Journal of Aesthetics and Art Criticism* 46 (1988): 359.

8. Walton, p. 359.

9. Walton, p. 360.

10. Jerrold Levinson, "Music and Negative Emotions," *Pacific Philosophical Quarterly* 63 (1982): 336.

11. Levinson, "Music and Negative Emotions," p. 336.

12. Levinson, "Music and Negative Emotions," p. 337.

13. Levinson, "Music and Negative Emotions," p. 337.

14. Levinson, "Music and Negative Emotions," p. 327.

15. Levinson, "Music and Negative Emotions," p. 337.

16. Levinson, "Music and Negative Emotions," p. 336.

17. Levinson, "Music and Negative Emotions," p. 336.

18. Jerrold Levinson, "Hope in The Hebrides" in his *Music, Art, & Metaphysics* (Ithaca: Cornell University Press, 1990), p. 355.

19. Levinson, "Hope in The Hebrides," p. 373.

20. This paper receives more detailed attention in Gregory Karl and Jenefer Robinson, "Shostakovich's Tenth Symphony and the Musical Expression of Cognitively Complex Emotions," forthcoming.

21. Peter Kivy, *Music Alone* (Ithaca: Cornell University Press, 1990), p. 162. This chapter of Kivy's book, "How Music Moves," is a later version of a paper of that title first published in *What is Music?: An Introduction to the Philosophy of Music,* ed. Philip Alperson (New York: Haven Publications, 1987; Pennsylvania State University Press, forthcoming).

22. Kivy, *Music Alone,* p. 159.

23. Kivy, *Music Alone,* pp. 159–160.

24. Kivy, *Music Alone,* p. 160.

25. Levinson, "Music and Negative Emotions," p. 332.

26. Nico Frijda, *The Emotions* (Cambridge: Cambridge University Press, 1986), p. 346.

27. This point has been stressed by Newcomb, "Sound and Feeling," and by Gregory Karl, "Music as Plot: A Study in Cyclic Forms," Ph.D. dissertation, University of Cincinnati, 1993.

28. Leonard Meyer, *Emotion and Meaning in Music* (Chicago: University of Chicago Press, 1956).

29. Newcomb, "Sound and Feeling," p. 636.

30. In his comments on an earlier version of my paper at the American Society for Aesthetics Annual Meeting, New York, 1989, Kendall Walton defends his own view by claiming that when music "actually startles, or excites, or soothes us 'we' may imagine these feelings to be components of other more complex emotions."

31. In "Shostakovich's Tenth Symphony and the Musical Expression of Cognitively Complex Emotions," Gregory Karl and I attempt to show in detail how a particular passage in Shostakovich's Tenth expresses the cognitively complex emotion of hopefulness.

32. Nothing I have said, moreover, is meant as an objection to Kivy's claim that we may be moved, awed, delighted, etc., by music and that these emotions of appreciation, as I have called them, have or can have a highly sophisticated cognitive content.

33. This idea that musical expression can be explained in terms of a "drama" in which musical "characters" take part has been suggested by Fred Maus, "Music as Drama," *Music Theory Spectrum* 10 (1988), and by Marion Guck, "Cognitive Alchemy: Transmuting Theoretical Vices into Analytical Virtues," unpublished manuscript.

34. I am indebted to Gregory Karl, Jerrold Levinson, and Kendall Walton, all of whom have read and commented on some version or other of this paper, and all of whom have greatly influenced my thinking on these topics. I am also grateful to the Charles Phelps Taft Fund for financial support during the writing of this paper.

FRANCIS SPARSHOTT

Music and Feeling

I

This paper articulates a reaction to Malcolm Budd's book on *Music and the Emotions*.[1] It is not a critique of his argument, but responds to a general impression—perhaps a mistaken impression—of his strategy. This impression was that Budd's rebuttal of leading theories about the relation between music and the emotions was facile. Whatever theory was being considered, it could always be rejected on one of two grounds. Either one said that some key term was unexplained, or one pointed out that some phenomenon was not accounted for by the theory. Such a rebuttal is too easy because, in the first place, one can always find something in the use of a term that is unexplained, left to context or to the reader's experience. Otherwise nothing would ever get said. The objection is serious only if the lack of explanation results in some real and relevant ambiguity or obscurity; and this was not always shown. And, in the second place, no theory can explain "everything," not even everything within its purported scope. It is up to the reader to see how the theory functions, how one would apply and extend it to cover what is not mentioned, and where it fits in to other explanatory schemes. Problems arise only when a relevant phenomenon is such that one does not see how the theory *could* be extended or adapted to cover it. Budd's book seemed not to be using theories for the light they could shed, but to be seeking excuses for rejecting them totally. No wonder such a book ended by giving the impression that we lacked any theory of the relation between music and the emotions.

Budd's book left the impression that the task of finding a satisfactory theory of the relation between music and the emotions remained to be carried out and was worth attempting. But his reader was left wondering what the criteria of acceptability for such a theory could possibly be. The function of the present paper is to suggest that there is no such task. There is much to say on the general theme of emotion and music; much that is of great value has already been said, some of it in the theories reviewed by Budd, much of it by Budd himself in his book, more of it in a continuing stream of work by our contemporaries.[2] But none of it amounts to anything that could be usefully called a *theory* of the relation between music and the emotions. We do not know what such a theory should be and have no reason to seek such knowledge.

Budd sets the problem up somewhat as follows. First, "Music is essentially the art of uninterpreted sounds," based on the human capacity to hear sound sequences without assigning meanings to them (p. ix); second, it is possible for specifically musical phenomena to be systematically related to non-musical phenomena; third, such non-musical phenomena include emotions. The task of the desiderated theory, presumably, would be to give a satisfactory explanation of what is related to what, and how the relations in question are established and controlled: "presumably," because Budd's formulations here are less explicit than they might be. One difficulty with this way of setting up the question is that, though a musical system as such is indeed an abstract formal system, and a musical work is an artificial construction of entities and relationships formally defined, and musicologists can discuss such works, no such art as Budd describes has ever established itself as a social or cultural practice outside the classroom, and one does not see how it could and why it should. Actual musical practices are integral to social practices. It is not the case that music-making arises as a form of mathematics which has then to be somehow worked into the fabric of life; musical systems are excogitated rather as formalizations and elaborations of a music-making that already belongs to that fabric.

In our civilization, at least, the making and enjoying of music have generally been understood, by practitioners as well as by audiences, to be intimately related to what may loosely be termed the expression and evocation of feelings. As Peter Kivy has argued, this is true in a very obvious and straightforward way of the kind of music that gave rise to and maintains the institution of the musical concert as we know it.[3] But, granted the intimate relation between musical practice and the affective side of life, there seems no reason a priori to suppose that only one relationship should hold between musically formal structures and the active and affective lives they relate to, or that they should relate distinctively to any specific range of such phenomena, or that such relationships as obtain should be reducible to any system. Perhaps we need rather to consider a lot of diverse phenomena, only loosely interconnected.

II

The terms "emotion" and "feeling," together with the more scientific-looking word "affect," have no clear and distinct meaning, but point generally and vaguely to a pervasive aspect of our lives in the world of which we are aware and within which we act: namely, that things, people, and situations affect us in ways that incline us to want to respond.[4] A moment's reflection shows us that this applies to everything we are aware of and everything we do: it covers the whole transition between input (information) and output (movement). But the term "transition" itself misleads: as just stated, we are directly aware of what we are aware of as encouraging and inhibiting actions and attitudes. Terms like "emotion" can perhaps be defined in ways that make them seem precise, but the precision is fictitious; the words belong to "folk psychology" at its worst, their use shifting from occasion to occasion as practical contexts require, so that there is no definite subject matter within which precise distinctions might be introduced. The aspect of life in

question, however, pervades our conversations no less than our lives, and I shall continue to use all three words freely in the faith that the context will suffice on each occasion to make my meaning as clear as it needs to be and can be.

In considering the relation between music and emotion, we must take into account at least four familiar kinds of phenomena, quite distinct from each other.

First, people often have moods: they are manic or depressed, cheerful or miserable, whimsical or crabby, in ways that affect the whole way they feel about everything at a given time. In fact, one could argue that every waking person is always in some mood or other, though the mood may not be conspicuous and, if it is, may not have a namable character.[5]

Second, people have reactive feelings towards events, things, and people: feelings named by such words as "love," "rage," "hope," "desire," "fear." The actual feeling on each occasion is of course specific to the occasion and the object, being intimately related to the possibility of taking precisely appropriate action. Words such as "love" stand for general *kinds* of reactive feeling, associated with types of action and perhaps with glandular discharges and other physiological modifications; but the classifications and associations connected with this vocabulary are culturally determined to an unascertained extent, and (as in the case of "moods") the actual reactive feeling towards a specific object on a specific occasion need not fall easily under any such verbalized classification.

Third, people habitually identify things, events, and people, etc., as proper occasions for named types of reactive feelings: one calls them "annoying" or "adorable" without regard to whether anyone is actually adoring or being annoyed.

Fourth, the world as the field of our action, and its parts and contents, have a specific interest for us. A field of action for any animal has to be immediately affectful in this way, or it could not function as a field, and the animal would be reduced to reacting to isolated stimuli. The kind of affective interest such a field has is no doubt derived from cumulative experience and current concern but is experienced directly as a quality of what we perceive. The perceived quality is often suitably designated by a "feeling" or "quality" word—a landscape may be felt to be gloomy, sinister, peaceful—and that suitability itself may be part of the quality as perceived; but no doubt in most cases the experienced quality is neither referred nor readily referable to any such verbal identification.[6]

The four kinds of phenomena may shade into each other, and in their most distinct manifestations may be both causally and semantically related to each other (as by having each other as part of their content). Reflection from this point of view on the actual quality of one's own life as lived should call to consciousness what needs to be borne fully in mind here: what a vast and complex range of reality lies behind those words "emotion" and "feeling" that are so casually used.

III

We experience musical works as objects—in creating them, in performing them, in listening to them, in reflecting on them, we are aware of them as full realities. There are three things about the distinctive way we experience them, the distinctive kind of intensional object they are, that call for attention here. First, music is music, a system all of its own: keys, scales, intervals defined as "fifths" and so on, tones defined as "dominant" and so forth, are elements not found in nature. Since musical qualities are derived from formal properties that are generated by artificially constituted entities in constructed relationships, it is to be expected that the affective character we experience in a piece of music should be *sui generis,* not to be described in terms derived from other areas of experience and hence not to be effectively described at all. To describe it, we would have to devise a special vocabulary for the purpose, and it is not clear what purpose such a vocabulary would serve, since the music itself can be alluded to or reproduced. Music is a world that is itself a symbol system. Of course, our general-purpose repertory of feeling-words can often be applied to this or that musical work with more or less appropriateness, and this general vocabulary will be more often and more obviously applicable than any other set of words that lack specific musical reference. But

music remains music and its affectiveness is distinctive of it.[7]

Since the possibility of making music in endlessly variable ways is always present as a real possibility, musical works are experienced as belonging to a world of their own. The second thing we have to note is that this world is experienced as in itself affectful (as we noted that the real world is), not only in a distinctive way but, for many people at least, more directly and intensely than any other sort of object. Probably it is the very fact that music as such has no reference, no descriptive content, and no subjectivity, that makes it directly affectful. I think Malcolm Budd says this somewhere; whether the thought is his or not, I would endorse it. Eduard Hanslick notoriously argued that music could not express definite feelings because what makes feelings definite is their psychological and contextual anchorage to the real world. Budd retorts (pp. 24–33) that Hanslick does not specify his criteria of definiteness, but the point to be made here is rather that what Hanslick truly points out is irrelevant, because the affectivity of music is its own and has its own precisions, which are not dependent on the range of named responses to the practical world. Mendelssohn's famous observation that the emotional meaning of music is too precise to be put into words is best understood in this light.[8]

The third thing to be noted about the way music is experienced as a world of affectful objects of experience is that music as realized tonal structure is none the less heard as in a way constituting the reality within which it is experienced. That is, the music (though it may be emanating from a complex external source, the spatial articulation of which is an important aspect of the piece and its performance) is, in a characteristic way that many authors have noted, heard as a reality that, though objective, is not located or identified as itself other or elsewhere than the listener—"You are the music, while the music lasts." The music is, perhaps, a sounding structure or a structured sound, indwelling in the listening mind. I say "perhaps" because this aspect of musical experience, though familiar, is again *sui generis* and not perfectly captured by terms primarily appropriate to other areas of experience.

In addition to the phenomena relating affect

to musical structure and variation, there is another very direct relation between musical practice and feeling, which cannot be ignored though it fits uneasily into our discussion. Many people can and do get a "high," or numb themselves, by playing or hearing very loud, very repetitious, or very insistent music (or "sound structures" if the word music be objected to). It has never been clear how this sort of thing relates to musical phenomena that depend on how the musical object is articulated. There is an uneasy transition between three things that are in principle distinct: the response to the content of a structured sign or complex of signs, the psychological seduction by the overall quality of a sound, and the causal impact and physical shock of a vibration that exceeds the capacity of the receiving instrument. Phenomena related to "moods" as identified above are especially hard to place in this regard.

Nothing seems to me clearer than that music has the double aspect I have described; that composers, performers, and listeners may be equally concerned with the articulation of a piece and with its affective life; that the concerns sometimes merge, sometimes separate; and that both concerns are equally properly directed to the music as music. There is nothing problematic about this: the structural properties of music are found culturally significant and everywhere cultivated because of the complexity, subtlety, and strength of the emotional life that only music sustains, and that life is sustainable only by the refinement and extension of musical means. But some writers have supposed that if an affectful character is meaningfully ascribed to a piece of music, or genuinely cognized in it, one of three things must obtain. Either the affect in question is assigned to the subjectivity of the composer or performer, who expresses it in the work; or it is identified with a feeling causally aroused in its hearers (presumably its appropriate or normal hearers); or it is somehow assigned to a subjectivity nonsensically ascribed to the music itself, as though the music were somehow experiencing the feeling ascribed to it. The authors who pose this choice typically go on to deride each of the three alternatives as absurd. The derision is easily shown to be well-grounded, but none of the alternatives is as absurd as the pretense that the choice has to be made. The supposition simply

ignores some of the most familiar and obvious facts of experience, that the objects of experience are experienced as multifariously affectful, and music as much as any. It is hard to see what its rationale could be: it seems to derive from a sort of doctrinaire physicalism that construes the world uniquely as a mechanical system, inhabited by perceivers in whom feelings are caused. On that understanding, any talk of "feeling" that refers to anything other than an episode in a subjectivity is mistaken. But such subjectivities could not in any meaningful way be said to "inhabit" such a world. If one is to talk of the feeling aspects of music, one's account must be phenomenological; a physicalist account must reduce its content to physicalist terms.

IV

The curious strategy I have just described, which effectively denies the existence of musical objects having the sort of properties that items in a world typically have, acknowledges an important reality that my own account has neglected. It is true that musical works and their performances are experienced as objects, items in a musical world. But it is also true that music is a communication system in which makers, performers, and hearers of music are engaged. That being so, affectful character in music may *on occasion* be assigned, wholly or in part, to subjective states of composers, performers, or listeners, either inferentially or as a heard character in the music itself (we believe the painful character of the music to be the outcome of the composer's pain; or we hear the composer's pain in the music). Such relationships may be indefinitely various, corresponding to the complexities with which human beings interact; and no such phenomenon in any way cancels out or is disqualified by the affectful character discerned in the musical object itself by composers, performers, teachers, analysts, critics, and listeners in their various relations with it. This topic will engage our attention later.

V

Setting aside for the moment the possible relationships between affective qualities putatively perceived in music and feelings subjectively experienced by persons standing in specific relations to such music, we may formulate a series of seven different propositions, all more or less plausible, such that any could be true without any of its successors in the series being true. Some of them are so formulated here that their truth appears to require the truth of one or more of their predecessors, but no inquiry has been made into whether this appearance could have been avoided by a different formulation.

1. Some or all musical pieces have affective qualities, perceived directly and based on musical relationships as heard by people whose ears are attuned to the musical system being used.

2. All musical affect is *sui generis,* being strictly dependent on musical methods and materials.

3. All musical affect belongs to a class of "aesthetic" emotions, variously defined and variously related to "real-life" emotions.[9]

4. The affective quality of some music is such that if a competent hearer is asked to apply to it one of two contrasted mood words or feeling words (e.g., sad rather than gay, vengeful rather than conciliatory) the hearer will easily be able to comply and the responses of hearers tend to be significantly in agreement.[10]

5. Musical forms are such that the affective quality of a piece may be more congruent with some named emotions than with others, largely through its dynamic qualities (quick or slow, loud or soft, tensing or relaxing).[11]

6. Some musical pieces are typically and properly heard as actually having the quality of a named emotion (actually *being* mournful), in the sense that the name of the emotion in question will in suitable circumstances be not merely accepted but *volunteered* as truly descriptive of it. People who write program notes for symphony concerts in provincial cities often proceed on this assumption.

7. Some musical pieces not only possess the quality of a named emotion but "express" it, in the sense explained by Nelson Goodman—that is, the having of the quality is a part of their meaning.[12] A stylized lament may be meant to be heard as lamentation: as Goodman puts it, it refers to the label "lamentation."

These seven propositions are certainly vague, and it is not clear that their purport could be made definite enough for any serious theoretical purpose. Some of them are also problematic in other ways. The significance of the fourth proposition, for instance, is undermined by the contention that a similar agreement in response could be achieved by asking listeners which of two pieces of music was "ping" and which was "pong," the implication being that the phenomenon depends not on any special relation between music and emotion but on some more generalized sorting capacity or tendency of the human brain.[13] There is also the (related) difficulty of determining what counts as a vocabulary of feeling words, and how such a vocabulary is organized. And there is a question (in relation especially to propositions four and five) as to what part is played in such phenomena by such global attitudes toward one's world as being up or down, active or passive, which might be expected to affect musical experience as well as everything else.[14] These problems call for continued empirical and conceptual investigation, but that is not relevant to our chief present concern, because the outcomes of such probing could hardly *reduce* the multifariousness and complexity of the phenomena concerned.

We have encountered in two or three contexts the application to music of such general feeling-words as "sad." This has sometimes been thought puzzling, so that different explanations of such usage have been offered. For reasons already given, I do not find it puzzling. If it were, I do not think the puzzle would call for a single solution. There is no single sort of occasion that is uniquely appropriate for the introduction of this vocabulary, and no consistency in use is to be expected. Calling something sad indicates only that the speaker finds *some* occasion for doing so; there is no reason to expect that the explanation would be the same on all occasions. If the word were glaringly inappropriate or anomalous, and felt to be so, there would be good reason for seeking a single explanation of the anomaly; but the usage is normal and familiar, not anomalous at all, so that reason does not apply.

To resume: if we conceive the seven foregoing propositions as assigning to musical affectivity characters that are increasingly specific, verbally differentiated, and related to recognized and named kinds of "real-life" emotions, it may well be that other possibilities could be intercalated among those stated here, or added at the end; but I do not at present have any others to suggest and have no idea what they would be. Meanwhile we have these seven; there is no evident contradiction among them, unless it is claimed that one of them represents the whole truth about the affectivity of music, the only way in which a relation between music and feeling could have musical relevance; and I know of no reason for singling any one or any group of them out for special attention when we are considering the theme of "music and human feeling."

In the light of what has been said above, it seems reasonable to think of music as follows. Music functions as a special world in which the items are wholly musical objects. Those objects are designed to stand in precisely defined and conceptually elaborated relations to each other, and are engineered with no other purpose than to reward perceptive attention. Any perceptible world, as such, can be expected to be saturated with affect, because any animal that is normally active in and dependent on an environment has to respond to that environment with discriminating sensitivity; because this has to be true of any environment, this essential capacity should be capable of extension to any possible domain of experience. All this being so, we would expect music, if it existed, to be saturated with affect, to be perceived as variously and immediately moving in ways that would resist reduction to anything else but relatable in indefinitely various ways to everything else. The human animal is uniquely the animal that makes culture, that lives by being prepared constantly to reinvent itself and the conditions of its existence. For such an animal, music, like the arts in general, would be a crucial device to maintain the necessary perceptual acuity, worldmaking flexibility, and range of emotive resource.

VI

From one point of view, no more needs to be said. But we noted in Section IV that this self-contained and self-sustaining world of feeling can interact directly, in many ways, with the real-life worlds, culturally and practically grounded, in which those concerned with music sustain themselves and interact as social and economic beings. It is time to say more about that.

The basic phenomenon here is that singled out by Aristotle as "voice" (*phone*), widespread if not universal among air-breathing vertebrates (including humans).[15] Events in the lives of these creatures cause them to emit sounds ("cries") that evoke specific kinds of reaction in their hearers (the herring gull squawks when it sees food, other gulls are attracted to the scene); they are equipped with special apparatus (e.g., vocal cords) for generating and discriminating such sounds. In animals that have feelings, these events are presumably mediated by feelings. It is ludicrous to suppose that the human voice (cooing, squealing, singing, shouting) does nothing of the same sort. The musical use of the human voice in singing (as in cantilena) may sometimes be devoid of any such quality or significance; but it is preposterous to suppose that it must always be so. The question is rather how, how often, and how far it is so, as well as the significance of the occasions when it is not so.

Some things about animal "voice" are worth remarking. First, although animal cries may evince feeling, and function as signs the meaning of which is recognized by (appropriate kinds of) other animals, an animal presumably does not *infer* anything from what it hears, but responds directly to what it hears in the voice, which is what it finds meaningful insofar as it finds anything meaningful.[16] Second, sounds appropriate to the "voice" of animals attract the attention of and are discriminated by animals of their own species (and sometimes of other interested species) with an accuracy unlike that of the hearing apparatus in general: a mother bat distinguishes and responds to the voice of her own offspring among thousands of others. We humans, too, respond to the presence and modulations of voice in a way different from that in which we hear other sounds, and to human voice especially. Our perceptions here belong to a special system, just as we respond to the expressions on human faces with a finely-tuned discrimination that belongs to a different system from that with which we recognize objects and movements in general. Like the bat with its offspring, we respond to especially fine differences in this area, and (presumably) we respond differentially to the kinds of modulation that reflect a modification in the condition of the muscular and breathing source of the voice. This difference between two auditory systems, the general and the voice-oriented, is in part a difference between making gross utilitarian distinctions and responding in a fine-tuned way to very minute differences and modifications. In its application to music, this would correspond to an appreciative grasp of the formal properties of a piece as scored as contrasted with a feelingful response to the "expressive" adjustments that go to make up specific performances of what is (or might be) written in a standardly notated score. But this differentiation between analytic/macroscopic and physiognomic/microscopic aspects of appreciative musical hearing is something that needs to be explored rather than thus baldly asserted.

Music, as we have insisted, is a wholly artificial formal world. But it now seems that vocal music must partly be an extension of the natural phenomenon of voice as a communicative system, with its associated cognitive functions and capacities. And instrumental music is, to a very large extent, an extension from vocal music. What can be sung can be played, and often is. But if independent instrumental music is a continuation and extension of the basic resources of voice by other means, it is hard to deny that it has developed into an independent realm; and the task of saying how and how far this realm remains a special use of voice is a puzzling one indeed.[17] We must not forget, though, that the human use of the resources of voice operates by developing the general style of meaningfulness involved, by extending, expanding, and transforming, into quite new domains, an unheralded range of significances. That is, the uses of and elaborations on human voice become part of culture, a distinctive and elaborate domain in human life, in a way that (as Susanne Langer has argued) is a development from the typical form of biological development.[18] The musical use of the voice, then, and music in general, is largely an extension of a physiognomic type of discrimination into a new domain.

Animal voice communicates (evinces, evokes) attitudes, feelings, responses, as experienced on the immediate occasion. A human adult's use of its voice does the same sort of thing, but not in any straightforward way: that use is often modulated by linguistic schemes and subject to reflection and conscious modification, and this can be expected to affect virtually all uses of the voice, inasmuch as they form part of the same organism's way of life. The articulate use of voice that is human language exploits an elaborate cerebral apparatus to communicate (express, suggest) ideas, thoughts, and values, and may do so generally, reflectively, and in relation to times and occasions other than here and now. The ways in which this is done may be expected to be at least as affectful as other phenomena.

VII

How, in general, is language related to voice? One part of the answer is to say that the conceptual encoding of language is in some ways superimposed on "voice" as an emotively modulated carrier, and in some ways supersedes that modulation; but emotive modulation can in turn be applied to conceptually articulated utterance. Clearly, the relations are complex, and there may be some analogy between them and the ways in which the quasi-mathematical formal codifications of music are superimposed on, supervene, and are subjected to the expanded repertory of emotion-centered or emotion-like modulations. But things are not that simple.

A general difficulty, one that in fact pervades the whole topic of this paper, is that the information-processing systems in the human brain, to which all musical procedures belong, are shown by scientific research and medical experience not to correspond to anything that sound engineering practice would suggest, or to common sense, or to Aristotelian functionalism, but are a sort of subtle bricolage. Any account of the senses as perceptual systems, or of the innervation of the sense organs and the organization of the cerebral cortex and its pathology, shows that the familiar but elusive facts of our intelligent orientation in the world are not to be explained in terms of any readily explicable mechanism. What we call "the emotions" or "the affective side of life," as we said at the start, is not something with a simple explicable identity or structure; and the behavior we identify as "language" is likely to be no less resistant to simple modeling. With that caveat, let me set out a simple account (derived from

Sebeok) of the relation between speech and language and relate it to music.[19]

Sebeok argues that language is not, as is generally assumed, a specialized development from animal voice. Vocal utterance is simply a part of non-verbal semiosis, the general signal system that animals use to coordinate their behavior. Language, on the contrary, is basically model-forming and concept-forming, the internal representation of ideas, necessary to the stabilization and generalization of memory— something that must have been developed by tool-using hominids long before Homo sapiens developed speech as a means of communication. Language unites and relates concepts by syntax, a system which (as transformational grammars show) is logical rather than causal in structure. Speech, then, is the use of language (not itself communicative) in communication, merging with the resources of voice or combining with them in subtle and various ways (as this paper seeks to show).

Music as a world of musically structured objects has nothing to do with communication, with actual uttering and hearing, and in that way is language-like; the relations between the elements in such objects are quasi-syntactical in character, though the elements themselves are emptier than the concepts of language generally are. Music as uttered and heard does not require an articulated world of musically structured objects, but is the use of voice as part of our social communication. Musical utterance in song would be a merging of verbal communication (voice as conceptually loaded and articulated) with voice communication as culturally developed, and the further cultural development of that sort of generalized capacity. And abstract musical utterance would be the articulation of abstractly-modeled (mathematical) constructions with a voice/crying-type utterance, articulated abstractly as a developed kind of formal fabrication and articulated emotively as a by-product or extension of voice-type communication. And one needs to add that, insofar as music as such is primarily language and not communication, music will be primarily articulating feeling for the musicians (as Langer suggested) rather than for others. All this adds up to a really confused situation, which I do not know how to start unraveling. It is a mess because various basic kinds of impulse and ar-

ticulation are capable of being extended and transposed into domains other than those of their origins, severally and together, in ways that are meaningful because culture is itself the way in which humans develop and discover new kinds of meaning for themselves and each other.

VIII

The considerations that reflection on language has now introduced are unmanageable, certainly within the confines of a single paper. But there are other relevant aspects of language that are easier to handle. Language in its written form separates an actual utterance both from its originator(s) and from its receiver(s). The message is there to be examined; the qualities it observably has are separated from any psychic states attributable to its originators and receivers. And, as post-structuralists have emphasized, this same separability must have been already potentially present in oral communication: writability, and hence in a sense "writing" itself, is a precondition of speech.

Music, as composed by one person, performable by others, heard by others again, is language-like in at least this last respect. The activity of music-making has as its precondition the possibility of musical systems in which musical works are encoded in a way that gives them an identity separable from the psychic processes of their originators, transmitters, and receivers. A large part of what one learns in learning music and learning about music is the ways of manipulating the system whereby such codification is performed and manipulated, which includes as a large part of itself the indefinite extensibility of the system. Objects produced in the course of such manipulation will still have the same basic *sort* of affective meaning as objects that merely transcribe heartfelt appeals, though in many cases, perhaps most cases, the meaning in question will not only not be associated with any subjective episode in anyone's career but will not be such that it could intelligibly be assigned to any such episode.

IX

If we now consider music as a practice elaborated out of (not the specific resources of the generically human "voice" but) the type of sound-making and sound-response that is represented by the way animals communicate by voice, and review all the disparate factors that have been mentioned, we can see that an animal, human or other, may emit a sound, musical or other, that is related to "emotion" in a large number of ways. The possibilities are so many one does not see how to enumerate them, but here are nine examples.

1. The sound-producer ("performer") may emit a sound that causally evinces a feeling—for instance, involuntarily uttering a cry of pain.

2. The performer may emit a sound that disguises what is really felt, or simulates a feeling that is not really felt.

3. The performer may deliberately emit a sound that draws attention to a feeling that is really felt.

4. The performer may emit a sound that he or she judges or feels appropriate to what is really felt, and may do so just because of that appropriateness.

5. The performer may emit a sound that is conventionally accepted as expressing a feeling that is really felt (for instance, by keening when one is really feeling bereft, or by cheering when one is really feeling exuberant). Such conventionally affect-laden sounds may or may not historically have been developed by elaborating, by stylizing, or by exploiting some conspicuous sound qualities of, a sound that recognizably evinces the feeling in question or is regularly used to express it. Whether any of these is the case or not, the performer is using a culturally accepted form to express what is felt; such use may be spontaneous or deliberate, depending (among other factors) on the depth and quality of the performer's acculturation in the relevant regard.

6. The performer may emit a sound, or compose a piece, that articulates a certain feeling or that has a certain affective quality, without being interested whether that quality or articulation has any relation to anything anyone actually feels, has felt, or should feel. The feeling or quality in question may not have any standard name or description, just as the formal properties a musician seeks to impart to the piece may not be susceptible to any illuminating verbal description.

7. The performer may emit a sound that expresses or evinces a mood or feeling, not through the (structural) properties of the piece as composed, but through the way the sounds are made. A cheerful piece might be played in a lugubrious manner; one may express one's gloom by the way one plays a cheerful piece in a cheerful manner. Clearly, there is room for immense variation here, in the extent to which different aspects of a piece as performed are identified as having different (supporting, contrasting, conflicting) affective tones, and in the extent to which such identifications are made by different people (or describably different sorts of people) in the same way.

8. Different parts or aspects of a piece as composed may have different affective qualities: for instance, a sprightly melody may have a dragging accompaniment. The resulting totality may have a single complex affective quality, or may be experienced as having internal tension; or, again, the different parts or aspects may simply be experienced as different. As before, such effects may be experienced in the same way by all competent hearers, or differently by different (otherwise identifiable) kinds of hearers; it is an empirical question of the musical practice that actually prevails whether such effects can be controlled.

Song-writing, in a musically developed culture, involves uniting a linguistic text that has its own complete set of meanings, which can be considered and reflected on, to a musical structure that likewise has a full set of meanings. It makes no clear sense to say that the affective meaning of the musical setting is (ever) *identical* with that of the linguistic text, though the same words may be used to characterize the quality of both. But the qualities of the two may more or less conspicuously diverge. In any case, the meaningful relations between the two may be very various. For instance, the affective quality of the music as composed may as it were contradict or comment on the implications of the text in any number of ways. This is a familiar resource of vocal music. And the singing performer's variation on or departure from the affective quality that is, so to speak, composed into the music, which we referred to in Section VII above, is matched by an ability to depart from, reinforce, or variously comment on the meaning of the words being sung.

9. The following situations may all be realized, though they may well be indistinguishable in practice in the absence of specific information:

(a) someone skillfully sings a sad song, not feeling sad at all;[20]

(b) someone sings a sad song and happens to feel sad in the way the song expresses, but their singing is not affected by their sadness;

(c) same as (b), except that the sadness the singer feels is not the sort of sadness that the song expresses;

(d) a sad singer sings a sad song, intending the song to have the meaning of expressing that sadness to the hearer;

(e) a sad singer sings a sad song, using the song to express that sadness for the singer but not intending it to have that significance for the hearer;

(f) a sad singer sings a sad song, meaning it to be taken as evincing the singer's sadness (that is, its sadness is to be taken as caused by the singer's sadness), but meaning it not to be meant to be recognized as intended to express it;

(g) a singer sings a sad song, not knowing it to be sad, so skillfully that its hearers recognize its sadness.

To these possibilities may be added innumerable others of the following general sort: a singer's singing of a sad song evinces, expresses etc., some feeling other than sadness which the singer feels, wishes to express, etc. ...

x

The relations between hearers and what they hear are as various as those between musicians and the music they make. Here are some examples.

1. A musical experience may give rise in some listener to a subjective feeling or emotion. That feeling may or may not be "identical" with (that is: appropriate bearer of the same name as), or congruent with, a feeling-tone ascribed to the music. If it is not, the relation may be a simple matter of psychological causation, dependent on the listener's personal make-up and

history; but, if that is possible, it follows that even if the aroused emotion is "identical" or congruent, its arousal may (sometimes, often, always) similarly be a matter of mere psychological causality and thus have no bearing on any meaning or quality that may be assigned to the music as such.

2. Listeners may simply identify a piece of music as having an affective quality, which they may ascribe to the moment of composition, or to the moment of performance, or indiscriminately to the music-as-performed.

3. Listeners may identify a piece of music as apt to arouse a certain feeling, whether the music actually does arouse it in them or not—and whether or not they think the music arouses it in them.

4. Listeners may (correctly or incorrectly) identify a piece of music as having, or as being meant to have, a certain conventional affective significance, such as being a coronach or a serenade.

5. Listeners may (correctly or incorrectly) identify a piece of music as evincing (being caused by, being symptomatic of) a certain feeling or disposition in composer and/or performer.

6. Listeners may identify a piece of music as standing to its composer or performer in any of such relations as we enumerated above. These relationships may or may not be the same as those that would be admitted or avowed by the musicians involved, or as those that would be identified by other (well-informed and competent) observers—or as those that "actually obtain," insofar as any clear meaning can be given to that expression in this context.

XI

The foregoing are among the permanent possibilities of relationship between music and something like feeling or emotion or affect. They are possibilities, not for reasons of historical accident, but because of the way music has to be made and heard in order to be music. At different times it may be more fashionable (or actually easier in terms of current acceptances of performance practice) to exploit some possibilities rather than others, and some of the preferred possibilities could be quite complex.[21] By the same token, it may at a given place and time be easier or more fashionable to admit or impute some possibilities rather than others. In this connection, there is notoriously a question of how, and how closely, variations in what is done correlate in this or that culture with variations in what is said to be done: it is an intricate topic.

XII

I have been writing about variations in the ways feelings as recognized or experienced may be related to musical practices and procedures. But it should be recognized that the composition or performance of a piece of music may be not merely an expression of feeling but an *act* of praise, or worship, or thanksgiving, or mourning, or courtship.[22] The performance of the act may be very variously related to the qualities actually imparted or intended to be imparted to the music in question. The writing or performance of a mass has, as such, a range of affective significance that is distinct from the quality of the music written; but whatever the relationship may be in a given case, it cannot lack complex significance that the relationship is what it is, or is believed or recognized by this or that person or sort of person to be. In addition to that, the act itself may be performed by the musicians (and by any others involved) with any degree of sincerity, or detachment, or irony. In listening to or commenting on the last Masses of Haydn, for instance, questions of this sort insistently arise, and one does not see how they can be dismissed as musically irrelevant, even if they are irrelevant to a particular sort of history or analysis in which one may oneself be exclusively engaged.

In considering the relationships between the qualities of music and the significance of the (emotionally significant) acts performed through that music, we have to recognize something that is true of much of what has been written in this paper. In some (or even in all) cases it may be a matter of opinion (to be decided, if at all, by consensus) whether such a relationship obtains or not; in other cases it may be a matter of psychological or sociological fact (to be ascertained by empirical investigation, whether or not such investigation has been carried out or

ever will be). In some cases, it may be a matter of social agreement whether such relations are judged to obtain or not; and such agreements may vary from group to group. The existence of such agreements is itself not without affectful consequences.

XIII

In accordance with my remarks in Section II, I have been quite casual and cavalier in my use of such terms as "emotion," "feeling," and "affect." Historically, various writers have introduced various distinctions in this area, to make points in specific discussions. The concept of a "passion," for instance, has been used to designate a feeling that comes over one independent of one's choices, as opposed to an "attitude" that reflects and involves one's life-plans and policies. On the whole, though, we do not have a well-sorted vocabulary at our disposal. Nor should we. The gravamen of this paper has been that the phenomena of "affect" or whatever we choose to call it are irreducibly complex, simply because to be alive in a world is necessarily to be endlessly responsive to everything in that world (including the most cerebral music as experienced by the most analytically-minded musicologists), and because humanity, as the culture-making species, continues to develop the system of music in the context of its general resources.

Even more seriously, the underlying trichotomy of "emotion," "conation," and "cognition" is itself suspect. It seems to be built deeply into the self-images and research projects of everyone in our society who has been indoctrinated into the "official" system of science and prevailing culture, and has a sort of unarguable rightness about it—we *want to do* things about our situation if and only if we have some *desires or aversions* based on what we *perceive and understand*. But the consensual evidentness the trichotomy has somehow acquired may amount to no more than a superstitious habit of reiteration. It belongs to the folk psychology of traditional theory. Until we have a better way of thinking about the experiential qualities of life and awareness, any discussion of "music" and "emotion" is bound to have a provisional character. In particular, it will be hard to see what a *theory* in this area could be a theory of, or what purpose it might serve. Meanwhile, discussions conducted in awareness of all such factors and possibilities as are canvassed in this paper should be more securely based than discussions that disregard them. Theories and experiments might be better formulated and conducted within the ambit of something like a generalization of this paper, fuller, better arranged, more consistently formulated and more successfully open to its own limitations, but itself no more than a reminder of what there is to be taken into account. Budd's book itself, though apparently proposed and here treated as a critique of extant theories in the light of a possible ideal theory, may serve best as a rich and well-arranged assortment of such considerations.

1. Malcolm Budd, *Music and the Emotions: The Philosophical Theories* (London: Routledge and Kegan Paul, 1985).

2. Some of it is in my *Theory of the Arts* (Princeton: Princeton University Press, 1982), pp. 214–223, and in "Aesthetics of Music: Limits and Grounds" in Philip Alperson, ed., *What Is Music? An Introduction to the Philosophy of Music* (New York: Haven Publications, 1987; Pennsylvania State University Press, forthcoming), pp. 55–58.

3. Peter Kivy, *The Corded Shell* (Princeton: Princeton University Press, 1980). For concerts, see William Weber, *Music and the Middle Class: The Social Structure of Concert Life in London, Paris and Vienna* (London: Croom Helm, 1975).

4. "Affect" is, so far as I am aware, not a technical term but a mere transcription from the German; we use it partly because German sounds so *wissenschaftlich* and partly because it evokes the important German-language speculation called *Affektenlehre* (referred to in note 11 below).

5. The most famous treatment of moods is Jean-Paul Sartre's *The Emotions: Outline of a Theory* (New York: Philosophical Library, 1948). But Sartre confines himself to the case where a single feeling (love, ecstasy, panic) dominates the agent to the point where observation and effective response are obliterated: it is not clear how he would relate these "emotions" to pervasive "moods" that color observation and response without necessarily rendering them ineffective or distorting them.

6. The classical exposition of the affectful character of the world as experienced is the work of David Wight Prall, especially his *Aesthetic Analysis* (New York: Crowell, 1936); the most penetrating account of the way the world is experienced as an affectful field for action is R. G. Collingwood's account of "emotion" in Part II of his *Principles of*

Art (Oxford: Clarendon Press, 1938), though his work is not usually read in this way.

7. Non-representational painting is affectful under the same conditions: we respond to the purely paintable as we respond to the purely musical.

8. See Deryck Cooke, *The Language of Music* (London: Oxford University Press, 1959).

9. People who say this can say that the sadness heard in sad music is analogous to real sadness but not identical with it (no one is really being saddened), whereas it may be identical with the sadness seen in a sad picture. I am not aware of any version of this proposition that has proved useful or persuasive (it seems to me to be a confusing way of referring to what I take to be true, that empathetically perceiving something as affectful is not the same as being existentially affected by something), but I see no reason why some proposition of this sort might not be persuasively argued.

10. The competence required involves not only relevant musical accomplishment but familiarity with the vocabulary used and its associated cultural codes.

11. This was Eduard Hanslick's thesis, taken up by Susanne K. Langer. The underlying psychology was at the heart of the "Theory of Affect" of eighteenth-century theorists: each commonly-identified human emotion involved a characteristic blend of a few simple psychological factors, no doubt physiologically based; a corresponding blend could be imparted by a musician to a piece of music, which would then be "read" as embodying the relevant emotion whether or not the listener was actually moved to experience that emotion.

12. Nelson Goodman, *Languages of Art,* 2nd ed. (Indianapolis: Hackett, 1976).

13. E. H. Gombrich, *Meditations on a Hobby Horse* (London: Phaidon, 1963), p. 370. Cf. my *Theory of the Arts* (Princeton: Princeton University Press, 1982), pp. 597–598, n. 51.

14. One might compare the concept of *rasa* or affective tone in Sanskrit music and dance theory, which singles out eight (or nine) dominant passions which may thus impart a tinge to everything involved in a situation, in life or (more relevantly) in drama.

15. Aristotle's notions are crude and antiquated, but suggestive saliences are what we need here. Scientific accuracies group phenomena in ways that do not respect our practical prejudices, and we cannot tell which would be useful rather than sidetrack us into sophisticated irrelevancies. It will be time for precisions and corrections when some usable orientations are set up.

16. It is hard to say what such distinctions can amount to in the case of animals that lack anything like the human cerebrum and linguistic apparatus.

17. Once instrumental music has achieved autonomy from the inherent affectivity of voice, if it does, that autonomy is available for song as well; performers and hearers can distance themselves from their naive reactions.

18. Susanne K. Langer, *Mind: An Essay in Human Feeling,* abridged by Gary Van Den Heuvel (Baltimore: Johns Hopkins University Press, 1988). Roughly, the argument is that evolutionary novelties tend to be new applications and developments of organs and devices that originally had quite different functions. The argument can be traced most clearly in the abridgement cited, though its plausibility

depends on the detailed corroboration in the unabridged edition, 3 vols., 1967–82.

19. Thomas A. Sebeok, *A Sign Is Just a Sign* (Bloomington: Indiana University Press, 1991).

20. Here and in the following enumeration of possibilities, the word "sad" does duty for any form of words that picks out a feeling-state meaningfully applicable to human beings. I do not mean to imply that feeling-states named by familiar single words have any special privilege or relevance here.

21. These possibilities are open in principle, but it may well be that a highly organized or stylized musical culture will deny the existence, or exclude the legitimacy, of all but a few possibilities, stipulatively defined. Accounts of classical Indian music sometimes give the impression that that is the case, but it is impossible for an outsider to judge.

22. The musical act of composition and/or performance may constitute the whole of the act in question, or it may only be a more or less integral and distinctively contributory part of the act. I leave these complications out of account here; they are sufficiently obvious, and I do not see anything specially interesting in them.

GÖRAN SÖRBOM

Aristotle on Music as Representation

In his *Politics* and *Poetics* Aristotle claims that music is a form of imitation (*mimesis*) and that pieces of music are images of character.[1] It is a view Aristotle obviously shares with Plato,[2] and this outlook seems to have been accepted by many authors throughout antiquity, even if it is not the only view held during this period of the nature of music. In our times it is, on the contrary, not natural to regard pieces of music as images of something or to say that we listen to images. In this paper I will try to reconstruct parts of the conceptual framework within which the idea that music is a kind of image has been thought and formulated in antiquity, as a background for a better understanding of the ancient outlook on music as image. First some crucial quotations from Aristotle's *Politics* in which the nature of music in terms of images and imitations is discussed:

Rhythm and melody supply imitations of anger and gentleness, and also of courage and temperance, and of all the qualities contrary to these, and of the other qualities of character, which hardly fall short of the actual affections, as we know from our own experience, for in listening to such strains our souls undergo a change. ... The objects of no other sense, such as taste or touch, have any resemblance to moral qualities; in visible objects there is only a little, for there are figures which are of a moral character, but only to a slight extent, and all do not participate in the feeling about them. Again, figures and colours are not imitations, but signs, of character, indications which the body gives of states of feeling. ... On the other hand, even in mere melodies there is an imitation of character, for the musical modes differ essentially from one another, and those who hear them are differently affected by each. ... The same principles apply to rhythms; some have a character of rest,

others of motion, and of these latter again, some have a more vulgar, others a nobler movement.[3]

I. LISTENING TO MUSIC IS A FORM OF AESTHESIS

In an attempt to understand the ancient Greek way of thinking and describing what music is, it is useful to start with the theory of *aesthesis,* i.e., the Greek conception of what it is to look at and to listen to things and generally to perceive things. An initial difficulty here is that the terms "*aesthesis*" and "perception" are not synonymous. We cannot presuppose that what we understand by "perception" is what the Greeks understood by "*aesthesis.*"

Basic here is the distinction between *aesthesis* and *noesis,* which is the distinction between what we can see (and vision is often used as the most important form of *aesthesis* and thus the representative of the other senses) and what we think. In Plato's strongly dualistic view, what we can see we cannot think and what we think we cannot see.[4] *Noesis* grasps the world of universals, whereas *aesthesis* consists of the imprints on the mind of the particulars of the world in a variety of ways.

The fundamental metaphor used by both Plato and Aristotle in describing the process of *aesthesis* is that of pressure; the particulars, i.e., the things seen, heard, touched, etc., press their individual shapes and qualities into the minds of the living organisms via the sense organs (and sometimes through a medium like air). They do so without imposing the matter of the particular on the perceiver; only their shapes and qualities appear in the mind of the perceiver. There is, of course, a large variety of opinions in antiquity regarding the nature of *noesis* and *aesthesis* and their interrelations; for instance, the atomists described *aesthesis* in terms of atoms, and the neoplatonists described the appearance of particulars in the mind as an interplay between impressions from the outside and universals residing in the mind. Alternatively, some philosophers believed that the mind sends out something like rays through the sense organs in order to "feel" the shape of the particulars.[5] But either way, it is the metaphor of pressure which is fundamental.

The process in which this pressure results in an awareness in the mind of the particulars seen and heard is often described with the terms "like" and "unlike"; there is a shift in the sense organ from unlike to like, and this shift generates the mental image of the particular thing heard and looked at. For example, when a signet ring is pressed into wax, it changes the wax from a shape which is unlike the ring to a shape which is like the ring.[6]

Now, there are five senses but just one consciousness. This fact made Aristotle postulate that there is an *aesthesis koine* (common sense) which synthesizes the "reports" from the different senses into one complex but unified image of the world of particulars.

Further, the philosophers of antiquity distinguished a number of kinds of *aesthesis*. These distinctions are drawn with regard to the relation between the mental image and the things arousing it, particularly the correctness, consistency and vividness of the mental images and the awareness of this relation in the receiver. As a rule, a mental image is taken to be correct when the shape of it is the same as the actual shape of the particular thing seen or heard. Obviously this is not always the case. The classical example is introduced by Plato: if we, when rowing, look at the oars while they are partly under water, the mental image shows broken oars. But we know they are not. The "higher part of our mind" which calculates, measures, etc., tells us the truth, Plato wrote.[7]

This latter kind of *aesthesis* is often called illusion; there is a thing outside the mind arousing a mental image, but this mental image is not adequate to the thing looked at. The perceiver believes it is, however. Vividness and consistency may be the same in both cases; the oar looks broken even if we know it is not. An hallucination, on the other hand, is a mental image generated, for instance, by drugs and fever. When we are hallucinating there is no outward object that can be correctly or incorrectly related to the mental image occurring, but the spectator believes there is; maybe the hallucination also lacks in consistency compared to correct *aesthesis*, whereas strength and vividness can be both stronger or weaker than average *aesthesis*.

Thus, correct *aesthesis*, illusion and hallucination all are forms of *aesthesis*. But there are yet other forms of awareness of particulars related to *aesthesis*. Aristotle claims that correct *aesthesis*, illusion and hallucination are passive forms of *aesthesis* in the sense that mental images are created or received in the mind without the active interference of the mind. But the mind can also on its own call forth mental images of particulars without there being anything outside the mind arousing them, as in correct *aesthesis* and illusion and, in a way, also in hallucination. When we remember something a mental image is called forth, a mental image that often lacks in consistency and vividness compared to correct *aesthesis*. It is a recalling which is partly steered by our will of things once experienced in *aesthesis*, and we know that this is the fact; otherwise the mental image would be a delusion. Memories are always of particulars. We cannot remember thoughts; we can only think them. Or in Plato's vivid metaphor of *anamnesis*, thoughts are memories of the acquaintance with Platonic ideas in an earlier existence in an eternal world. Dreams belong to another form of active *aesthesis* which certainly can be as vivid as but seldom as consistent as correct *aesthesis*. At least when we are awake we know that dreams are generated by the mind itself. But we don't know this in the state of dreaming. Plato remarks: "Is not the dream state, whether the man is asleep or awake, just this: the mistaking of resemblance for identity?"[8] Finally, daydreams and fantasies are forms of *aesthesis*. When we are imagining something we know that there is no outward thing answering to the mental image created by our imagination. When we are daydreaming we are, perhaps, balancing on the edge between knowing and not knowing that there is no outward object answering to the mental image, and this act of balance gives strength and vividness to the daydream.

II. IMAGES AND (REAL) THINGS

To look at images and imitations is, of course, a kind of *aesthesis*. But this kind of *aesthesis* has a mysterious double character which troubled Plato; it is both an illusion and a correct *aesthesis* at the same time, or something in between— neither full illusion nor correct *aesthesis*.

In *The Sophist* Plato divides the world of things, that is the world of particulars, into (real)[9] things and images. Further, these two classes can, each of them, be split into (real) things and images made by human beings and such made by God or Nature. The result was the following "map" of the world of particulars with examples of each class:

	God or Nature	Human Beings
(real) things	trees, stones, animals	artifacts
images	shadows, reflections, constellations of stars	paintings and pieces of poetry and music

In an attempt to define what distinguishes images from (real) things, Plato claims that an image is something which is similar to something else but only in some respects, and that the function or nature of images is to be nothing but similar in these respects.[10] A thing, which is similar to something else in all respects, is not an image of that something but another example of its kind.[11] The respects in which the image resembles something else are tied to the medium in which the image is made, as Aristotle remarks in his classificatory discussion of different kinds of imitation in the first chapter of the *Poetics*.[12] But things can be similar to other things in some respects without being images of the things they resemble. The crucial characteristic is that this partial similarityis the only function or form of existence the image has. Suppose we look at Myron's famous sculpture of a cow. This piece of bronze is in some respects (three-dimensional form materialized in bronze) similar to cows, and the basic function of it is to be nothing but similar to cows, i.e., when we look at it, mental images of a cow are meant to occur in the minds of the spectators.

In *The Cratylus* Plato contrasts words and images with each other with respect to what they represent or what they signify. Words signify, he maintains in one part of the dialogue, universals, whereas images signify things in their particularity. Here images are regarded as signs; it is thus natural to understand the "being nothing but similar in some given respects" as an attempt to characterize the sign function of images.[13]

Fundamental to *semiosis,* or our uses of signs, is that we know that the thing we apprehend is a sign. When we read or hear the word "beauty," we must know that it is a word referring to beauty and not beauty itself or just a series of noises. And similarly, when we look at a sculpture, it is important for us to know that it is an *image* of a beautiful person and not a living beautiful person in front of us. Even if Greek painters and sculptors tried to make their paintings and sculptures as full of life as possible, they seldom intended to trick the spectators into the belief that they had a (real) thing in front of them and not an image.[14] This borderline between knowing and not knowing whether something is an image or a real thing is also Plato's concern in *The Sophist.* He wants to show that the sophists are such tricksters. They have no wisdom but put up the appearance of having it and trick innocent people into the belief that they, the sophists, are wise. In *The Republic* Plato claims something similar: the painters can trick simple people with their paintings and that is a danger.[15] But even if this can be the case sometimes, this does not mean that all images are used in such a way or that tricking people into false beliefs is the goal of image-making. On the contrary, if we look back into history for all the different kinds of usage of images, the spectators know in most cases that it is an image and not a (real) thing they are looking at and that this awareness is intended. There are no real persons standing along the funeral road in Kerameikos in Athens, or in the Agora or on the Acropolis. And it is not the real Oedipus who investigates why Thebes is plague-stricken in the performances of Sophocles's *Oedipus Rex* in the theater of Dionysus.

To look at or to "listen to" an image implies that the spectators and listeners, to some extent at least, expect different things from images than from (real) things and that they accordingly act differently in front of an image than they would do in front of real things of the kind represented in the image. Aristotle is aware of this fact: "Objects which in themselves we view with pain, we delight to contemplate when reproduced with minute fidelity: such as the forms of the most ignoble animals and of dead bodies."[16] When we know that we are "listening to" or looking at an image we act in a way which is different from the ways in which we usually act in front of the things represented in the image. "Again, when we form an opinion that something is threatening or frightening, we are immediately affected by it, and the same is true of our opinion of something that inspires courage; but in imagination we are like spectators looking at something dreadful or encouraging in a picture."[17]

In a sense, images have a double nature, and this doubleness might be mystifying: it is both a real thing in its own right and a sort of illusion. Myron's cow is a lump of bronze which we can look at and touch. The sculpture has its own set of qualities, like yellow-brown colors, a smooth touch and formal and structural features. These the sculpture has irrespective of its being a representation of a cow or not. But secondly, it has its representational function, i.e., to create an inner image of a cow in the mind of the spectator. The spectator sees a cow but knows that it is not a real cow, just as the person who imagines things knows that the things imagined are not outside of him or her, or as the person remembering something knows that the mental image is related to something that occurred back in time.

In *The Laws* Plato comments on the double character of images and imitations. The gods gave human beings, in pity for the beastly life of the human race, the ability to appreciate harmony and rhythm in song and dance. But since songs and dances also are representative, it might happen that people take delight in the rhythms and harmonies of representations of immoral content and are thus tricked into the belief that the thing represented also is good (since most people believe that the things that give pleasure are good).[18]

Aristotle seems to have a similar outlook in the fourth chapter of *The Poetics*. The reasons why human beings use images and imitations are two (Aristotle writes about poetry in general, but what he says is clearly valid also for

other kinds of images and imitations): "First, the instinct of imitation is implanted in man from childhood, one difference between him and other animals being that he is the most imitative of living creatures, and through imitation learns his earliest lessons; and no less universal is the pleasure felt in things imitated. ... Next, there is the instinct for 'harmony' and rhythm, meters being manifestly sections of rhythm."[19] The capacity to appreciate rhythm and harmony in things heard as well as the capacity to appreciate symmetry and good proportions in things seen is unique for human beings and these qualities, namely rhythm, harmony, symmetry and good proportions, belong to images and imitations as objects in themselves irrespective of what they represent. Thus Aristotle clearly saw the twofold character of images and imitations as the following quotation also shows: "For if you happen not to have seen the original, the pleasure will be due not to the imitation as such, but to the execution, the colouring, or some such other cause."[20]

Described within the conceptual frame of *aesthesis,* looking at or "listening to" images and imitations gives the spectator and listener a double imprint—both the shape of the image itself with its rhythms, harmonies, symmetries, and good proportions, and the shape of the thing represented. Crucial here is that the spectator and listener know that the representational imprint is without counterpart in the (real) world. Or, as Plato formulates it, an image is "a sort of man-made dream produced for those who are awake."[21]

Thus an image is, according to the ancient outlook, a humanly made thing with a set of qualities of its own which might be organized into a harmonious, rhythmical, and well-proportioned whole and with an ability to create an inner image of some particular thing which it is not in itself. Primarily images and imitations are meant to call forth mental images in the minds of the spectators and listeners. Then this function can be put into a large variety of situations in which this human ability is used.[22] In most cases it is important that the spectator or listener is aware of the fact that it is an image or imitation he or she is looking at or listening to. Sometimes, however, the image can be used to trick the receiver into the false belief that he or she is looking at a real thing.

III. MUSIC, IMITATION, AND THE PLEASURES OF MUSIC

If you claim that pieces of music are images or imitations, this means, within the conceptual framework sketched above, that a piece of music is a humanly made thing the sole function of which is to create a mental image of a double character in the mind of the listener: a mental image of the piece of music as a thing with particular qualities, foremost rhythms and harmonies, and a mental image of something which the piece of music is not, that is, what it represents. Further, it is implied that the listener knows that the representational impression does not originate from a real thing of the kind shown in the mental image.

Very few persons deny that listening to music can give the listener pleasure, although there is a great disagreement about the value of such pleasure and about the role it should play in human life. There is also disagreement about the origin of musical pleasure. Musical hedonism can be described as the view that pleasure from music is direct and immediate in the same way as the pleasure of good tastes and odors.

Another way of describing pleasure in connection with music; not necessarily denying the hedonistic view, is to claim that good proportions in the thing heard arouse pleasure. This type of pleasure, tied to the structural properties of the sensuous thing, is called beauty following a very long tradition from the Pythagorean school.[23] Since taste and smell have no structural features in their sensuous objects, they cannot share this kind of beauty, and touch can only do it to a certain extent. Only sight and hearing provide us with full-fledged sensuous beauty.

Since music is a form of imitation, the pleasure experienced in listening to music can also be the pleasure of learning something. "Again, since learning and wondering are pleasant, it follows that such things as acts of imitation must be pleasant—for instance, painting, sculpture, poetry—and every product of skillful imitation; this latter, even if the object imitated is not pleasant in itself."[24]

The Pseudo-Aristotelian text, *Problemata*, makes this distinction clear by posing the question, "Why does everyone enjoy rhythm and tune, and in general all consonances?" and then answering: "We enjoy different types of songs for their moral character, but we enjoy rhythm because it has a recognized and orderly numerical arrangement and carries us along in an orderly fashion; for orderly movement is naturally more akin to us than one without order, so that such rhythm is more in accordance with nature."[25]

Thus music can give us hedonic pleasure, structural pleasure (beauty), and pleasure from learning. But what can we learn from listening to music, and what can music represent?

IV. MUSIC AND ETHOS

Music also has an influence on the character or disposition (*ethos*) of persons. Such characters or dispositions of persons are in antiquity denoted by means of words like "frenzy," "soberness," "temperance," "strength," "lasciviousness." The idea that music can influence the character and dispositions of persons seems to be the very center of Plato's and Aristotle's argument on the nature of music. Aristotle refers to it several times as something we know from our own experience.[26] When we listen to a piece of music it happens that our minds shift, and what changes is our *ethos,* i.e., our disposition or character. Sextus Empiricus tells the following anecdote: "Thus Pythagoras, having noticed on one occasion that the youths who were in a state of Bacchic frenzy from drunkenness differed not at all from madmen, advised the flute-player who was with them in their revels to play them the 'spondean' tune; and when he had done as instructed, they suddenly changed and became sober just as if they had been sober from the beginning."[27]

The fact Aristotle uses as foundation for his argument is, then, that music has the power to change the mind of its listeners so their characters or dispositions change. Since listening to pieces of music is a kind of *aesthesis,* it often is described as a change from "unlike to like." Now, the change is described as a change of *ethos,* of character and disposition. The natural conclusion would be, then, that the piece of music has a character which it "imprints" on the listener or, at least, that it is similar to such a character.

The basic assumption is, of course, that music has character and means to communicate this character to the listener. In *Problemata* the following question is put: "Why is hearing the only perception which affects the moral character? For every tune, even if it has no words, has nevertheless character; but neither colour, smell nor flavour have it."[28]

In this passage Pseudo-Aristotle claims that music has character. But in another passage close to it in the same text Pseudo-Aristotle asks about music's relation to character: "Why are rhythm and tune, which are only an emission of the voice, associated with moral character, while flavours, colours and scents are not?" In both cases Pseudo-Aristotle's answer is that they have movement. "Is it because, like actions, they are movements? Now, action is a moral fact and implies a moral character, but flavours and colours do not act in the same way."

What does it mean to say that rhythms and harmonies have character or are similar to character? Aristotle claims that it is a plain fact, something everybody knows from his or her own experience and that the explanation is found in movement. For Plato, Aristotle, and many other, but not all, ancient thinkers it was natural to use the conceptual framework of *aesthesis* and *mimesis* in order to describe these processes. A piece of music is not, for instance, anger itself in abstraction nor is it an example of anger, i.e., angry behavior, but it is an image of anger, namely something that is similar to but not an instance of anger, and this "nothing but similarity in certain respects" is the basic nature of music apart from its rhythms, harmonies, and shapes as well as it is basic for all other kinds of image and imitation. A piece of music is a humanly made thing which is expressively made in order to give us inner images of anger which are individual and particular in shape and necessarily individual and particular, since to listen to music is a form of *aesthesis*. At the same time, the receiver knows that it is neither anger itself nor an example of anger but an image of anger which she or he is looking at or "listening to"; recognizing something to be an image implies that it is not understood as a "real" thing. This knowledge and the praxis tied up to it is to a large extent culturally established and acquired by the members of the culture in a process of acculturation, in which they learn which things are images and imitations and how to react in front of them and how to use them.

Knowing this, the listener reacts differently than in "ordinary" situations: if we see a sad person it is, in many situations, natural to try to comfort him or her. But we do not comfort the performing musician or the composer. On the contrary, we enjoy the shape of sadness because we learn something by listening to it, Aristotle would say; we learn about sadness. In the same way as we enjoy looking at paintings of things which we would dislike and detest in real situations, we enjoy learning about characters and dispositions which we, if we met with them in real life, would abhor. And we would try to turn away from them as quickly as possible, which is contrary to looking at them with enjoyment.

V. THE IMITATION OF UNIVERSALS

Since Plato's challenge that images and imitations cannot represent anything but individual things in the visual and audible world, i.e., that they cannot represent Platonic ideas,[29] a central question has been: what can images and imitations represent? Can they in some way transcend the limits of the visual and audible world and represent something that is invisible and inaudible, that has no body?

In the *Poetics* Aristotle claims that poetry is more important than history because poetry represents something more universal, whereas history is the representation of individual and particular occurrences, and universality (*to kathólou*) is, to Aristotle and to many with him, of greater value than particularity. Aristotle writes in *De interpretatione:* "I call universal that which is by its nature predicated of a number of things, and particular that which is not; man, for instance, is a universal, Callias a particular."[30] Thus, can images and imitations show and teach us something about human beings in general and not only about particular human beings as, for instance, the individual fate of Callias?

At least poetic imitation can, according to Aristotle, teach us universal truths, and this feature of poems is the distinctive differentia of poetic imitation. But it is likely that also other forms of imitation in addition to poetic imitation can teach us about universals. Let us first take Aristotle's own example of poetic imitation: *Oedipus Rex* by Sophocles. The universal truth about human existence, which we can learn from this tragedy, is what the chorus pronounces in its last lines: human happiness is fickle. At any time the greatest happiness can be reversed into the greatest unhappiness. In order to communicate this universal truth to his audience, Sophocles chose to tell the story of Oedipus and the plague in Thebes. The fate of Oedipus demonstrates this universal with graphic clarity. What we see in the performance of the tragedy is not, however, the universal truth in abstraction, something a philosopher could demonstrate and clarify with arguments. And it is neither a real thing, i.e., Oedipus himself in his search of the cause of the plague, nor an image of what Oedipus actually did (that is the history of Oedipus), if he ever lived and tried to find out why Thebes was plague-stricken. It is an image which offers a particular exemplification of a universal truth about human existence, and the fate of Oedipus is chosen because it is such a striking example.

Thus, the poetic image and imitation do not present chance examples or actual examples of some general truth but paradigm examples of it. "It is, moreover," Aristotle writes, "evident from what has been said, that it is not the function of the poet to relate what has happened, but what may happen—what is possible according to the law of probability or necessity."[31] Not all images and imitations, however, are meant to be, or in fact are, presentations of paradigm examples of universal truths; many images and imitations tell about particulars.[32] But the poetic images and imitations are, Aristotle maintains, not historical in that sense. They present something more general to their audiences. Furthermore, the universal truth exemplified should be of importance to the life of human beings and the presentation of it in images and imitations should, thus, be paradigmatic. According to Aristotle, the audience does not learn this universal truth through arguments, but, through the emotions pity and fear, it reaches the insight that human happiness is fickle.

Aristotle mentions only poetic images and imitations in connection with the presentation and exemplification of universals. But it is easy to see that other forms of images and imitations can also be "poetic" in the sense that they exemplify, in paradigmatic form, some universals important to human life. Thus it is natural to

ask: What sort of universals about human life can painting, sculpture, dance, and music present in paradigmatic form to their audiences?

To know about human character (*ethos*) is important to human life. Such characters or dispositions as temperance, sorrow, and greed are universals that can be shown in paintings, sculptures, and dramatic performances. But, as both Xenophon and Aristotle maintain, they cannot be exemplified directly. The only way to show sorrow or temperance, for instance, in paintings, sculptures, and dramatic performances is through the outward signs of these characters.

Music, however, can represent character itself, Aristotle writes. Music shows us directly, through its images and imitations, paradigmatic examples of character. These examples are received immediately and directly through a change of mind of the receiver to the character imitated in the sense that the character or disposition is not attached to the behavior of an individual person as it is in what we may call physiognomic imitation of character; it is a direct imitation of characters and dispositions.

Aristotle maintains that hearing and music are unique in this respect.[33] The other senses cannot provide us with such images. Smell, touch, and taste cannot represent anything at all. Sight, Aristotle writes, can give us images of character, but only to some extent, and he also points at an important restriction: painting and sculpture can only represent the indications of character. Painting and sculpture can, according to Aristotle, only represent character physiognomically.

A similar view is found in Xenophon's *Memorabilia*. Painting can only represent "the works of the soul," Xenophon maintains in a report about Socrates's discussions with the painter, Parrhasius, on the limits of painting.[34] Character is something immaterial and cannot be represented. But it is possible to see and thus represent the difference between an angry person and, for instance, a happy person.

Thus painting and sculpture can represent persons with a certain character or in a certain mood but unable to represent the character and mood itself. This is so because not only painting and sculpture but also poetry and theater represent individuals in action. Music alone presents examples of these dispositions and characters themselves, which the listener

knows are not real things but images and imitations. Pieces of music are *images* of character
because the listeners know that they are neither
real and genuine signs of a character nor the
character itself; they are only similar to it. The
impression the listeners get results in a mental
image of, for instance, anger, i.e., an experience
and conception of anger, and he or she knows
that it is neither anger in itself nor real genuine
signs of it. It is a thing made to give just angry
"impressions" without instilling the belief that
the piece itself or its maker is angry.

VI. MUSIC AND EXPRESSION

Modern languages find it easier to talk about
emotions than images with regard to the function of music. A piece of music calls forth an
emotion of anger or expresses anger; it does not
give us an image of character. But to ancient
thought it was natural to call pieces of music
images and imitations since they were not real
things, as discussed above.

So far we have discussed music as imitation
of character from the supposition that pieces of
music have character or are similar to character
and that they stamp this character into the
minds of their listeners resulting in a change of
character. But how can we explain that pieces
of music have or are similar to character?
According to some authors there is a relation
between the character of pieces of poetry and
their creators. "Sublimity is the echo of a great
mind," Pseudo-Longinus writes.[35] And much
earlier Aristophanes ridiculed this idea in *The
Thesmophoriazusae*. In the beginning of the
play Euripides and Mnesikles visit the poet,
Agathon, in order to recruit him to participate
in a religious festival of women where Euripides is threatened to be sentenced to death for
slandering women. Euripides is anxious to
make Agathon speak in favor of him. When
they knock at his door Agathon comes out
dressed in women's clothes, and Mnesikles
expresses his amazement. Agathon answers:

> Old man, old man, my ears receive the words
> Of your tongue's utterance, yet I heed them
>   not.
> I choose my dress to suit my poesy.
> A poet, sir, must need adapt his ways

> To the high thoughts which animate his soul.
> And when he sings of women, he assumes
> A woman's garb, and dons a woman's habits.

MN. *(aside to Euripides)* When you wrote Phaedra,
        did you take her habits?

AG.   But when he sings of men, his whole appearance
        Conforms to man. What nature gives us not,
        The human soul aspires to imitate.

MN. *(as before)* Zounds, if I'd seen you when you
        wrote the Satyrs!

AG.   Besides, a poet never should be rough,
        Or harsh, or rugged. Witness to my words
        Anacreon, Alcaeus, Ibycus,
        Who when they filtered and diluted song,
        Wore soft Ionian manners and attire.
        And Phrynicus, perhaps you have seen him,
           sir,
        How fair he was, and beautifully dressed;
        Therefore his plays were beautifully fair.
        For as the Worker, so the Work will be.

MN. Then that is why harsh Philocles writes
           harshly,
        And that is why vile Xenocles writes vilely,
        And cold Theognis writes such frigid plays.

AG.   Yes, that is why.[36]

Here it is stated that the character of the
maker is carried over to his products. This
resembles the theory of poetic communication
given in Plato's *Ion*. The Muse seizes the poet
who in his turn communicates what he has
received from the Muse to the rhapsodist or
actor. And they continue the chain to the listeners. Plato describes the process metaphorically: it is like the power of a magnet which
can attract rings of iron.[37] Basic, here, is that it
is the same content that is communicated from
the Muse to the listeners. Thus the pieces of
poetry and music are not signs of the character
in question but the character itself or resem-
blances of it.

It is possible to describe the making of images
and imitations as a reverse process of *aesthesis*.
In the process of *aesthesis* the (real) world
imprints its shapes and qualities without its
matter into the mind of the receiver, whereas in

making an image, the shape and character created in the imagination of the sculptor, poet or musician are forced upon some matter.[38] Bronze, for instance. Myron created in his imagination a mental image of a cow, and with the help of his skill (*techne*) he transformed this shape into matter. Similarly, the character or disposition of the mind of the musician is stamped upon the piece of music, which in its turn acts upon the listener in such a way that he or she changes to the character of the piece of music.

So, possibly, theories of imitation and theories of expression meet in Aristotle's account of the nature of music. Maybe we have to regard Aristotle's description of musical representation as an attempt to formulate a theory of expression within the conceptual framework of *aesthesis* and *mimesis*.

1. *Politics*, 1340a 18–22 and *Poetics*, ch. 1.

2. *Republic*, 401 B–403 C; *Laws* 655 D and 668 A: "We assert, do we not, that all music is representative *(eikastiken)* and imitative *(mimetiken)*?" *The Laws*, trans. R. G. Bury (London: Loeb Classical Library, 1952).

3. 1340a 18–1340b 10. *The Complete Works of Aristotle: The Revised Oxford Translation*, ed. Jonathan Barnes, trans. B. Jowett (Princeton University Press, 1984).

4. *The Republic*, 507B–C.

5. Cf. Boethius, *De institutione musica*, 179: "Whether sight occurs by images coming to the eye or by rays sent out to sensible objects is a point of disagreement among the learned, although this dispute escapes the notice of the ordinary person." Quoted in *Fundamentals of Music: Anicius Manlius Severinus Boethius*, trans. Calvin M. Bower (Yale University Press, 1989).

6. Cf. Aristotle, *De anima*, 424a 17–28.

7. *The Republic*, 602C–603A.

8. *The Republic*, 476C in *Plato: The Republic*, trans. Paul Shorey (London: Loeb Classical Library, 1946).

9. *The Sophist*, 265C–266D. An image is, of course, also a thing. But it is a thing of a particular sort, and it is the distinguishing characteristics of images that Plato is looking for; the nature of images in contradistinction to (real) things.

10. *The Sophist*, 239D–240B.

11. Cf. *Cratylus*, 432B: "[T]he image must not by any means reproduce all the qualities of that which it imitates, if it is to be an image." Quoted in *Plato with an English Translation*, Vol. VI., trans. H. N. Fowler (London: Loeb Classical Library, 1953).

12. Cf. also Plato's *Cratylus*, 434A.

13. *Cratylus*, 423C–D.

14. Norman Bryson's idea in *Vision and Painting: The Logic of the Gaze* (London: Macmillan, 1983) that the basic goal of pictorial art up until recently was to produce the Essential Copy, a sort of thing that made the spectators believe that they looked at a (real) thing and not an image, is to my mind a very superficial interpretation of thoughts about and practices in the pictorial arts in antiquity.

15. 598 C.

16. *Poetics*, 1448b 10–12, in *Aristotle's Theory of Poetry and Fine Art with a Critical Text and Translation of the Poetics*. First published 1894. Fourth ed., trans. S. H. Butcher (New York: Dover Publications, 1951).

17. Aristotle, *De anima*, 427b 22–25, trans. W. S. Hett (London: Loeb Classical Library, 1964).

18. *The Laws*, 653C–654A, 655D–656C.

19. 1448b 5–9, 20–22. Trans. cf. note 16.

20. *Poetics*, 1448b 18–19. Trans. cf. note 16.

21. *The Sophist*, 266C, in *Plato with an English Translation: Theaetetus, Sophist*, trans. H. N. Fowler (London: Loeb Classical Library, 1921).

22. In discussing the different causes why a sculpture exists and looks as it actually does, Seneca writes: "The 'fourth cause' is the purpose of the work. For if this purpose had not existed, the statue would not have been made. Now what is this purpose? It is that which attracted the artist, which he followed when he made the statue. It may have been money, if he has made it for sale; or renown, if he has worked for reputation; or religion if he has wrought is as a gift for a temple." Epistle 65 in *Seneca: Ad Lucilium Epistolae Morales*, trans. R. M. Gummere (London: Loeb Classical Library, 1967).

23. Cf. Wladislaw Tatarkiewitz's paper "The Great Theory of Beauty and Its Decline," *The Journal of Aesthetics and Art Criticism* 31 (1972): 165–180.

24. *Rhetoric*, I.11. 1371b4–7 in *The Complete Works of Aristotle: The Revised Oxford Translation*, trans. W. Rhys Roberts (Princeton: Bollingen Series 71:2, 1984).

25. XIX.38. *Aristotle: Problems*, trans. W. S. Hett (London: Loeb Classical Library, 1957).

26. In the long passage from *The Politics* quoted above (1340a 18–1340b 19).

27. Sextus Empiricus, *Against the Professors*, VI.8, in *Sextus Empiricus with an English Translation*, trans. R. G. Bury (London: Loeb Classical Library, 1961). This anecdote was apparently standard knowledge in antiquity. It is told by several authors. Cf., for instance, Quintilian's *Institutio oratoria* 1.10.32 and Boethius *De institutione musica* 1.185.

28. XIX.27. Trans. cf. note 27. Plato also believes that music without words represents character but he is troubled about how to know which character is represented in the individual cases (*Laws* 669E): "[T]he poets rudely sunder rhythm and gesture from tune, putting tuneless words into metre, or leaving tune and rhythm without words, and using the bare sound of harp or flute, wherein it is almost impossible to understand what is intended by this wordless rhythm and harmony, or what noteworthy original it represents." Trans. cf. note 2.

29. *The Republic*, 597E ff.

30. *De interpretatione*, 17a 38–40, in *The Complete Works of Aristotle: The Revised Oxford Translation*, ed. Jonathan Barnes, trans. J.L. Ackrill (Princeton: Bollingen Series 71:2, 1984).

31. *Poetics*, ch. IX, 1451a 37–39. Trans. cf. note 16.

32. Ibid. 1451b 10–11. "The particular is—for example—what Alcibiades did or suffered."

33. Possibly dance, too, is capable of this since rhythm is a constituent part of dance.

34. *Memorabilia*, III.10. 1–8.

35. *On the Sublime*, IX.2.

36. *Aristophanes with an English Translation*, trans. Benjamin Bickley Rogers (London: Loeb Classical Library, 1963).

37. *Ion*, 533D–E.

38. Cf. my paper "What is in the Mind of the Image-Maker? Some Views on Pictorial Representation in Antiquity," *Journal of Comparative Literature and Aesthetics* 1–2 (1987): 1–41.

An earlier version of this paper was read at the joint meeting of the British Society of Aesthetics and The Scandinavian Society of Aesthetics in Durham, England, April 9–12, 1992.

KENDALL WALTON

Listening with Imagination:
Is Music Representational?

Plato characterized the music of the flute and lyre as *mimetic,* assimilating it to painting and poetry.[1] This attitude contrasts with the modern tendency to distinguish music sharply from the representational arts. Eduard Hanslick and others insist that music is just sound or sound structure, that its interest lies in the notes themselves, not in stories that they tell or anything that they "mean." Peter Kivy calls music an art of "pure sonic design."[2] There is, to be sure, explicit program music. And music sometimes combines with words or images to form a representational whole, as in song, opera, film, and dance. But some will set aside the combinations as impure instances of music, mixtures of music with other things. And purists dismiss program music as of little intrinsic interest or even as only marginal examples of music. Music itself, "pure," "absolute" instrumental music such as Bach's *Brandenburg Concerti,* Brahms's symphonies, and Anton Webern's *Five Pieces for Orchestra,* appears to be quite a different animal from the standard "mimetic" or representational arts, such as (figurative) painting and literature.

Given the strength of purist intuitions, it is disconcerting to discover how quickly qualms arise. Distinguishing "absolute" music from program music is not nearly as easy as one might have expected. There is no sharp line between explicit and subtle program music, or between subtle program music and music that is as unprogrammatic as it gets, and one can be puzzled about the location even of fuzzy lines. When music—what taken by itself would seem to be "absolute" music—teams up with words or images, the music often makes definite *representational* contributions to the whole, rather than merely accompanying other representa-tional elements. Opera orchestras and music on the soundtracks of films frequently serve to "describe" the characters and the action, reinforcing or supplementing or qualifying the words or images. Mere titles often suffice to make music patently representational; indeed I cannot imagine music which an appropriate title could not render representational. Music stands ready to take on an explicit representational function at the slightest provocation.

If music can be nudged so easily into obvious representationality, can we be confident that without the nudge it is not representational at all? Most, if not all, music is *expressive* in one way or another, and its expressiveness surely has a lot to do with its susceptibility to being made explicitly representational. To be expressive is to bear a significant relation to human emotions or feelings or whatever it is that is expressed. Why doesn't this amount to possessing extramusical "meanings," and why shouldn't expressiveness count as a species of representation?[3] What is to stop us from saying that exuberant or anguished music represents exuberance or anguish, or instances thereof?

One possible answer is that music is expressive by virtue of its capacity to elicit feelings in listeners, and that possessing this capacity doesn't amount to representation. Arousal theories of expression have not been popular recently. Theorists typically prefer to locate the feelings expressed "in the music" rather than in the appreciator, and so must face the question why the feelings "in the music," those the music expresses, aren't represented. Is exuberance "in" the music in the way that a train is "in" a picture of a train? Arousal theories have obvious difficulties, but there is more to them than is usually acknowledged.

Further considerations which I will adduce shortly do more than raise qualms; they put the burden of proof squarely on those who would resist Plato's assimilation of music to poetry and painting. They may not, however, cure the inclination to resist, or rid us of the initial intuition that there is a gaping chasm of some sort between (absolute) music on the one hand and painting and literature on the other. I prefer to understand "representation" in such a way that virtually all music qualifies. But we should not be satisfied until we can accommodate and explain the contrary inclinations.

No sophisticated theory of representation will be needed to see why music might reasonably count as representational, however unattractive that conclusion may appear initially. The hard part will be recapturing a sense of music's purity, understanding how fundamentally music differs from the paradigmatically representational arts, whether or not we count it as representational.

I. IMAGINATION IN MUSICAL EXPERIENCE

Literary and pictorial representations establish *fictional worlds*. There is the world of a story and the world of a picture. Does music have fictional worlds? We might be tempted to speak of the "world of the music" when we listen to a *Brandenburg Concerto,* for instance, but this may be a world of a very different sort. Story worlds contain (fictional) ghosts and goblins, or murderers and detectives, or jealous lovers, or tragic heroes. There are people in the world of Bruegel's *The Peasant Dance* and unicorns in that of the *Unicorn Tapestries.* But if a *Brandenburg Concerto* has a "world," it may seem to be one that contains nothing but notes, harmonies, melodies, rhythmic motives, developments, etc.—the material of the music itself—not fictional characters and fictional events "represented" by the music. (This needn't mean that the world is not a fictional one.) One can always construct a world of the usual sort for a piece of music. One can, if one wants to, make up programs for the *Brandenburg Concerti,* tell stories to go with them—stories about ghosts and goblins or murderers and detectives, or whatever one allows the music to suggest. But such stories seem irrelevant at best to an understanding of the music, and they are more likely to hinder than to enhance appreciation.

So speak purist intuitions. But let's look further. Fictional worlds are imaginary worlds. Visual and literary representations establish fictional worlds by virtue of their role in our imaginative lives. The *Garden of Earthly Delights* gets us to imagine monsters and freaks. On reading Franz Kafka's story, "A Hunger Artist," one imagines a man who fasts for the delight of spectators. It is by prescribing such imaginings that these works establish their fictional worlds. The propositions we are to imagine are those that are "true in the fictional world," or *fictional*. Pictures and stories are representational by virtue of the fact that they call for such imaginings.[4] Music also induces imaginings. If we look carefully, especially if we are willing to look under the surface, we stand to find more than a little imagining in our experience of music, even of fugues and sonatas, and many of our imaginings would seem to be called for by the music. Why doesn't the content of these imaginings constitute fictional worlds, the worlds of the music? And doesn't this make the music representational, as literature and painting are?

In what ways does music engage our imaginations? A large and diverse range of cases needs to be considered, although what is to be said about many of them will depend on how broadly one construes the notion of imagining. Imagining as I understand it can be spontaneous, nondeliberate, a passive experience rather than something one *does*. Dreaming is one kind of imagining. I also favor understanding "imagining" in a way that allows for implicit or unacknowledged or nonconscious or subliminal imaginings; one may imagine something without noticing that one does. To insist that a person imagines only if the thought of what is imagined occurs to her would be far too restrictive. (This doesn't mean that it will be easy to ascertain whether a person does engage in a given imagining when the thought does not occur to her.)

Some imaginings that listeners plausibly engage in are about elements of the music itself, about tones and harmonies and melodies. Beethoven's String Quartet opus 59 #3 opens with a diminished seventh chord, giving the impression that what we hear first is not its beginning, that it started before we heard it. Perhaps we imagine that it did. On hearing the arpeggiated *Prelude* to Bach's G-Major cello suite, perhaps we imagine the intermittently sounding pedal tone to be sounding continuously. (Heinrich Schenker speaks of imagining in cases like this.[5]) We may imagine events of a piece to be causally related in various ways. We speak of one musical idea or event growing out of another, of one interrupting or interfering with another, of one preparing the way for another. In many instances we probably imagine that there is a nomological connection of some sort between events without imagining what specifically is the cause of what. This is enough to explain our "expectation" that a tonic harmony will succeed a dominant seventh, for instance, even if, having heard the piece many times before, we know that the cadence is deceptive.[6] We imagine (subliminally anyway) that causal principles are operating by virtue of which the occurrence of the dominant seventh makes it likely that a tonic will follow, and on hearing the dominant we imaginatively expect the tonic, whether or not we actually expect it.[7] If, or to the extent that, these various imaginings are prescribed, we have fictionality.

In our examples so far, the "characters" in the fictions are elements of the music. It is fictional that the initial diminished seventh chord of Beethoven's opus 59 #3 was preceded by sounds we did not hear, that the pedal tones of the Bach *Prelude* sound continuously, that certain musical events are nomologically connected in such a way that the occurrence of some makes the occurrence of certain others likely. But the world of the music is a *fictional* one, not just part of the real world, even if it is populated by immigrants from the real world; they behave, in the musical world, in ways they do not in the real one. (Fictional worlds contain plenty of real world immigrants. There are novels, stories, yarns, about Julius Caesar, Napoleon, Richard Nixon, the Civil War, etc.)

Music, in the cases I have described, is like nonfigurative paintings which present fictional worlds populated by features of the paintings themselves, as when it is fictional that one rectangular shape lies in front of another.[8] If, as I recommend, we count such nonfigurative paintings as representational, much music will qual-

ify as well. This result need not distress musical purists. They may be willing to call music representational in a sense that applies also to paintings of Piet Mondrian and Kasimir Malevich and Frank Stella, provided that they can still find a way to distinguish both sharply enough from literature and figurative painting. This may not be easy, however, especially in the case of music. It is not easy to deny that music often has fictional worlds containing characters that are not themselves features of the music, as we shall see.

There is a lot of mimicry in music. Instrumental music sometimes mimics vocal music. Keyboard instruments, percussive though they are, sometimes play cantabile.[9] Vocal music occasionally mimics instrumental music. Dance rhythms are used in pieces that are not dances. Stravinsky mimics a baroque musical style in his *Pulcinella Suite* and so does Ernst Bloch in his *Concerto Grosso*. Mere similarities do not necessarily induce imagining or constitute make-believe. But it is surely not out of the question that one is to imagine the melodic line of the Adagio Cantabile movement of Beethoven's *Pathetique* Sonata as being sung, and that it is best played in such a way as to encourage this imagining.[10] Here, as in the previous examples, the actual sounds of the music belong to its fictional world, but so does a (fictive) person. It is fictional that a person is singing them.

This is one of many cases in which one has a sense of performers' actions by which they produced the sounds or composers' thoughts as they wrote the score. We may not care what the performer or composer actually did or thought or what feelings she might actually have been expressing thereby. The impression the music gives of having been produced in a certain manner or as being the expression of certain feelings or emotions may be what we are interested in.[11] Joseph Kerman suggests several such characteristics in the *Heiliger Dankgesang* of Beethoven's String Quartet opus 132:

> The mystic aura is furthered by the unnaturally slow tempo and the scoring or, rather, by what seems to be an unnaturally slow tempo on account of the scoring. The image is orchestral: forty strings could sustain the hymn at this speed with comfort, but four can bear it only with a sense of strain, tenuousness, and a certain gaucherie. This Beethoven certainly wanted.

... Again one thinks of the Great Fugue, another work in which the instruments are made to outdo themselves, and in which their unhappy striving is incorporated into the essential aesthetic.[12]

I take the notation, "run amok," in the score of William Kraft's *Momentum* (1966) to be advice that the performer make the music sound as though he has run amok.

It is not a large step to regarding music that gives an impression of the composer's or performer's actions or feelings or thoughts to be *representing* itself as the product of a composer's or performer's acting or feeling or thinking in certain ways, to be mandating that listeners imagine this to be so.

Expressive music, some say, is music that suggests or portrays or somehow recalls expressive human behavior, behavior by means of which human beings express exuberance or anguish or gaiety or agitation or serenity or anger or timidity or boldness or aggressiveness.[13] This will include music that represents itself as resulting from such expressive behavior, but there is no reason to suppose that music cannot simply portray expressive behavior without portraying itself as the product of such behavior. In any case, there can be no doubt that some expressive music is expressive by virtue of connections with human behavior. There is little strain in thinking of some musical passages as representing, as inducing us to imagine, exuberant or agitated or bold behavior. Vocal music portrays expressive verbal behavior, including not just the utterance of certain words but the manner of their utterance, a tone of voice. The expressive quality of an utterance, the tone of voice, remains in much instrumental music even without the words. Some music has more or less obvious connections with nonverbal behavior, with physical movement. This is evident in the case of marches and dances, but listeners' tendencies to tap their feet or move in response to rhythmic features of other music as well suggests that they understand music of many kinds to have some important connection with agitated or calm or determined or lackadaisical behavior.

Where there is behavior there is a behaver. If music represents an instance of behaving calmly or nervously or with determination, it represents, at least indirectly, someone so behaving.

So the fictional world contains human beings, anonymous fictive agents, whether or not the sounds themselves are characters in it.

The prevalence and variety of imaginings in our experience of music, including many of the examples I have mentioned and others as well, is reflected in the prevalence and variety of metaphors we use to describe it. We call passages of music exuberant, agitated, serene, timid, calm, determined, nervous. We speak of rising and falling melodies, of wistful melodies and hurried rhythms, of motion and rest, of leaps, skips, and stepwise progression, of statements and answering phrases,[14] tension and release, resignation and resolve, struggle, uncertainty, and arrival. Music can be impetuous, powerful, delicate, sprightly, witty, majestic, tender, arrogant, peevish, spirited, yearning, chilly.[15] I do not think that metaphorical descriptions always indicate imaginative experiences (even subliminal ones) on the part of listeners, but in many instances they do. We imagine agitation or nervousness, conflict and resolution. Sometimes we imagine (something's) rising or descending. (Or we can easily get ourselves to imagine thus as we listen to the music; an awareness of this possibility may color our hearing even when we don't actually engage in the imagining.) The metaphors purists are least able to avoid, those of tension and release, motion and rest, seem to me to involve imagination. To appreciate music one must feel tension and release; one must allow oneself to imagine motion and rest.[16]

What we have noticed so far seems suspiciously like the beginnings of story fragments in music, the beginnings of programs. I conclude this collection of examples with one which is a little less fragmentary. Consider the opening of the "Adagio" movement of Mozart's A-Major Piano Concerto, K. 488.[17]

The last half of bar 7 is in the dominant, heading for the tonic, F# minor. But it doesn't get there for a while—not until the cadence in bars 11 and 12. Instead, the dominant goes first to a D-major triad (the submediant), in bar 8. This is a deceptive cadence, an instance of Meyer's thwarted expectation, but a very special one. The left hand does go immediately to the tonic, on the first beat of bar 8. The right hand gets there too, but not until the second beat. And by then the bass has moved down to D. That gives us—accidentally, as it were—the D-major triad instead of the tonic. The D major is understood later as the dominant of a Neapolitan 6th, which resolves eventually to the dominant and then to the tonic.

The upper voice is *late* coming to the A in bar 8. There are precedents for this tardiness earlier in the passage. The upper voice was late getting to the A (and F#) at the beginning of bar 3; in bar 4 it participates in a suspension; in bar 6 it is late getting to the C#. In the first two cases the bass waits "patiently" for the soprano to arrive. But in the second phrase, the bass can't wait. It is locked into a (near) sequence, which allows no delay. In bar 6, as in bar 8, the bass has moved on, changing the harmony, by the time the soprano arrives.

One could tell a story to go with this:

A character, call her Dalia, is going to catch a train. She has a habit of being late. And in bar 7 she dallies—she's off chasing butterflies. She dallies so long that she misses the train (the bass), which is on a fixed schedule and can't wait. But missing the train sets up a fortuitous meeting (D major), perhaps with a member of the opposite sex, which leads to unexpected new adventures (G major).

This is silly—like musical renditions of thunderstorms or locomotives or feline serenades. The *music* certainly doesn't tell this story. We aren't supposed to think of the story as we listen. And it is likely to be distracting. But the *lateness* of the upper voice, and its *dallying* quality, the *rigidity* of the bass's progression, the *fortuitousness* or *accidentalness* of the D-major triad, the *movement to something new,* are in the music. To miss these is, arguably, to fail fully to understand or appreciate the music. And talking about the train, the butterfly chase, etc., is one way of bringing out the lateness, the dallying, the fortuitousness.[18] Some of this at least is a matter of imagining. We imagine

something's being late, probably without imagining what sort of thing it is. And we imagine a fortuitous or accidental occurrence. (The imaginings needn't involve saying to oneself that something is late, fortuitous, etc.) If the music told the story, it would certainly be representational. But why shouldn't it count as representational anyway, as representing instances of lateness, fortuitousness, etc.? (It would be inadequate to think of the music as merely indicating or expressing the *property* of lateness; it portrays a particular [fictitious] instance of something's being late, even if nothing much can be said about what it is that is late. Listeners imagine something's being late on a particular occasion; they do not merely contemplate the quality of lateness.)

Some deceptive cadences consist in a clunking, unprepared-for progression from V to VI, and give the impression of the composer playing a trick on us; we can hear him saying, afterwards, "Ha, ha; I fooled you!" But in the Mozart example, my sense is rather that things just happen, in the natural course of events, to turn out as they do; the VI chord results from occurrences earlier in the passage, including the top voice's dallying and the bass's rigid schedule. I don't think I would have this sense if I weren't engaged actively, if subliminally, in imaginings like those I have described.

Does the dallying cause or explain the lateness? Try a less dallying melodic line in bar 7.

If the lateness now seems to you less expected, less inevitable, more in need of explanation, than it did in the original, this is evidence that in Mozart's version you implicitly imagined dallying, and that you imagined it to be responsible for the lateness. ("How could she have missed the train? She was right there when it arrived!")

There is room for disagreement, concerning some of the above examples, about whether normal or appropriate musical experiences involve imagining or make-believe in the ways

I have described. But it is clear that we cannot simply dismiss out of hand the idea of musical works' having fictional worlds. It looks as though they may have worlds teeming with life, just under the surface at least—like swamp water seen through a microscope. If we follow through on our purist inclinations to reject stories or images or meanings attached to music as unmusical, if not childish or silly, we must begin to wonder how much of what we love about music will be left. Yet if we accept pervasive make-believe in music, the question of how to account for the evident contrast between ("absolute") music, and literary and pictorial representations, becomes pressing. Our experiences of music seem shot through with imaginings, yet I, at least, continue to resist the idea that Bach's *Brandenberg Concerti* and Brahms's symphonies have fictional worlds, as *Crime and Punishment* and *Hamlet* do.

II. DIFFERENCES

If musical works do have worlds, and if they involve very much of the make-believe I have suggested they might, they are zoos—full of life, but discrete bits of life, each in its own separate cage—not a working ecological system. It is not easy to make sense of the fictional world of a fugue or a sonata as a coherent whole, to see what the various diverse bits of make-believe have to do with each other. It will be fictional that there are instances of upward and downward movement, statements and answers, causes and effects, singing, unperceived sounds, determined or aggressive or timid behavior; all of these fictional truths jumbled together with few coherent links among them. There will rarely be a plot line for the listener to follow, even as brief a one as I managed to find in—or impose on—the Mozart passage.

Musical worlds will be radically indeterminate with respect to the identity and individuation of agents.[19] Is it fictional that the agent who behaves aggressively in one phrase is the same one who behaves placidly in the next? Do we imagine that a single person behaves first aggressively and then placidly, or that different agents engage in the aggressive and the placid behavior? In an answering musical phrase, is the "character" giving the answer different from the one who made the "statement" or

asked the "question," or does the original fictive speaker reply to herself? Sometimes we may have some sense of how to answer such questions; often we will not.[20]

It may seem that the various bits of make-believe do not even belong to the same fictional world, that the musical work has multiple worlds. But there is no good way of deciding where one world stops and another begins.

If we think of a musical work as a prop in a game of make-believe, the picture seems to be that of a succession of momentary skit fragments, unrelated to one another. This picture contrasts starkly with the profound sense we often have of the unity and coherence of musical works, the sense that their parts belong together, that one phrase leads naturally to the next, and that any surprising sequences ultimately seem to have been justified.[21] Perhaps the unity is to be explained in "purely musical" terms, even if the elements that are unified include ones with significant representational roles.[22] Compare a wallpaper design containing depictions of objects of many different sorts—a truck here, a dinosaur there, an ice cream cone over there—with no very salient connections among them. We may be expected to notice various individual depictions, but not to think about how they are related within the fictional world, nor perhaps even to think of them as part of the same fictional world. The overall pattern may still be a highly unified one however, even if its unity does not consist in a unified fictional world. The depictions may all be in the same representational style, and the overall design may be formally coherent. Likewise, perhaps, with music. Musical coherence may consist more in coherence of sound patterns than in unity of representational content. There may still be representational content, of course, and it may be important.

If the elements of fictionality in a musical work do not cohere well and the work's unity is based on something else, some may be inclined to deny that these elements constitute a fictional *world*. If, rather than telling the Dalia story, the Mozart passage presents more or less disassociated instances of things' being late, something's being on a fixed schedule, a fortuitous incident, and a change to something new, it may seem artificial to attribute all this to a single fictional world and presumptuous to speak of multiple fictional worlds. Even if a listener does imagine certain connections among the incidents, these imaginings may strike one as optional, as not mandated especially by the music itself, and so not contributing to a fictional world of the musical work. (They may belong to the world of the listener's imagination, however.)

There is a more important reason to hesitate attributing fictional worlds to musical works, even while recognizing the rich imaginative component in listeners' experiences that I have described. Explaining it will require further stage setting.

Paintings and novels are what I call "props" in games of make-believe, having much in common with dolls and hobby horses. All of these props provoke imaginings. The child playing with a doll imagines a baby, as the spectator of a picture of a dragon imagines a dragon. The imaginings children engage in when they participate in make-believe are not just about babies and horses, however; the children imagine about themselves as well. A child imagines (himself or herself) putting a baby to bed or riding a horse. The child belongs to the world of make-believe; it is fictional, in that world, that he or she puts a baby to bed or rides a horse. Spectators of pictures and readers of stories also imagine about themselves. On viewing a picture of a dragon, I imagine (myself) seeing a dragon. On reading "A Hunger Artist" I imagine being told (by the narrator) about a professional faster, or at least I imagine knowing about such a person. The appreciator does not belong to the world of the *story* or the world of the *picture*. But the appreciator uses the picture or story in a game of make-believe which has its own world, one to which the appreciator does belong. In the world of the picture, the work world, there is only a dragon. But in the world of the viewer's game with the picture, he sees a dragon.

(Absolute) music and the paradigmatically representational arts induce in appreciators significantly different imaginings about themselves. One difference is evident in the ways in which music and painting portray space. Pictures represent spatial properties of things. So, arguably, does music—when melodies rise and fall, when there is "movement" from one key to another, arrivals and departures, dense textures,

open fifths, etc., or at least in some such instances. (It is less clear in music than in painting what sorts of things fictionally possess the spatial properties.) But musical space, unlike pictorial space, is usually presented in a perspective-less manner. It is fictional in my game with a painting that I have a spatial perspective in the fictional world, that *I* bear certain spatial relations to the objects in the painting. Fictionally I see a mountain towering above me; I imagine seeing it from below. Or fictionally I see a ship in the distance sailing toward me. The make-believe spatiality of music seems not to give rise to similar imaginings *de se*. When a rising melody makes it fictional that something rises, do I imagine something rising up toward me from below, or something above me rising away from me? At what pitch am *I*? When there is movement from one key to another, where fictionally am I in relation to it? Am I to imagine movement toward or away from me, or from my left to my right, or what? Answers are hard to come by. Listeners seem not to have spatial perspectives, even when musical worlds are spatial. The music appears to have its own separate space, one unrelated to the listener's space.

Occasional exceptions underscore this point dramatically. The middle section of Debussy's Nocturne, "Fetes," mimics a band approaching the listener—getting louder and louder. We imagine the musicians approaching *us*. We have a spatial position in the fictional world of our game relative to them, a spatial perspective. The contrast with more usual musical portrayals of space is striking. (It is curious that crescendos and diminuendos do not very often give the impression of something drawing closer to us or getting farther away, but they don't.) Looking ahead, I should mention another possibility: that *I* am what moves, that I feel as though I am rising, or imagine myself rising, when I hear a melody as rising, and that the listener has the impression of moving from one place to another when the music moves from one key to another.

The independence of musical space from us is linked to a more general respect in which fictional worlds of musical works, if there are such, appear often to be isolated from us. The experience of perceiving pictures is, at the most basic level, an experience of imagining seeing;

on looking at a picture of a tree one imagines seeing a tree—from a certain angle and distance.[23] But the experience of listening to music, even obviously representational music, does not in general involve imagining hearing (or imagining perceiving of any kind). When music represents sounds—sounds of trains, babbling brooks, bird calls—listeners imagine hearing these sounds. But much representational music does not represent sounds at all. A rising melody portraying the ascension of a saint into heaven doesn't portray the *sound* of the ascension; I have no idea what the ascent of a saint to heaven sounds like. Music probably does not portray sounds when it portrays nonvocal behavioral expressions of emotion (aggressive rhythms). Tension and release in music, resignation and resolve, motion and rest, are likely not to involve representations of sounds. When no sounds are portrayed, listeners do not imagine hearing things as they listen to the music. They do not have the kind of perceptual access to the fictional world that spectators have to the world of paintings. One imagines instances of tension and release, but one probably does not imagine perceiving them. So one does not imagine having a particular perspective on them.

Things have taken a strange turn. We seem headed toward a conception of music that I find very unattractive, one very contrary to my experience of music. I have emphasized the importance of participation in our games of make-believe with paintings and novels, the importance of imagining doing and experiencing things in connection with what is represented, e.g., imagining seeing things. What we seem headed toward is a conception of music involving much less participation, much less imagining *de se*, than there is in painting and literature. It may be fictional in our games that we *know* about instances of tension and relaxation, and perhaps about behavioral expressions of such states; we may imagine knowing about them. But we don't imagine perceiving them. This is a little like our response to descriptions, in a literary work, of characters doing various things and experiencing various feelings and emotions. But many literary works have narrators, and it is fictional that the narrator tells us about the characters. Even this is lacking in

music. The listener doesn't imagine being told about someone's being tense or relaxed or euphoric or agitated. It would seem to be indeterminate (in many instances) how fictionally we know. We imagine knowing about them without, it seems, imagining *anything* concerning how we came to know. We don't imagine having a particular perspective on the fictional world.

To say there is not much participation is to say that there is not much of a game world, a world to which we ourselves belong. We would seem then to be "distanced" from the events of the work world, the fictional struggles and agitations and tension and release being most prominently a part of a world to which we do not belong.

My experience of music is not at all like this. My impression is the opposite of being distanced from the world of the music (if we can call it a world). I feel intimate with the music, more intimate, even, than I feel with the world of a painting. The world of a painting (as opposed to the world of my game with the painting) is *out there,* something I observe from an external perspective. But it is as though I am inside the music, or it is inside me. Rather than having an objective, aperspectival relation to the musical world, I seem to relate to it in a most personal and subjective manner.

Some will say that, yes, I am intimate with the *music,* with the auditory phenomena, but not with a fictional world that it creates. I am sympathetic, but things are not this easy. My intimacy is not just with sounds; it is with tension and relaxation in the music, with exuberance and wistfulness and aggressiveness and uncertainty and resolution. I share the purists' skepticism as to whether these add up to a fictional world like that of a picture or a novel, but we have to admit that they are part of the stuff that such fictional worlds are made of. (And we should wonder how involvement with mere sounds could be gripping in anything like the way involvement with monsters and dragons, innocent damsels, evil villains, and tragic heroes—even fictional ones—can be. Why should we care what happens to a four note motive consisting of three eighth notes on a given pitch followed by a half note a third below? We do not follow the fortunes of musical motives in quite the way we follow the fortunes of Romeo and Juliet or Anna Karenina, wishing them well or ill and worrying about what might happen to them.)

I mentioned the idea that it is by portraying vocal or other behavioral expressions of feelings that music portrays the feelings. This is how feelings are, most obviously, presented in theater and painting. Schopenhauer and others have claimed that music gets at feelings more directly.[24] If music does bypass behavior and portray feelings directly, the listener will in one sense be "closer" to the portrayed feelings. She will not have to go through the portrayal of the behavior in order to ascertain what feelings are portrayed. But this does not provide for the intimacy that I think I have with the feelings portrayed in music. We don't experience this intimacy when we read descriptions in a literary work of characters' emotional states (rather than their behavior). Consider a novel that tells us straight out that a character experiences a warm sense of security.[25] The contrast between the relevant words of the novel and a musical passage expressive of a warm sense of security—in Brahms, for instance—could hardly be greater.

III. IMAGINATIVE FEELING

Let's try something different. I suggest that music sometimes gets us to imagine feeling or experiencing exuberance or tension ourselves —or relaxation or determination or confidence or anguish or wistfulness. This accords with the idea that music sometimes portrays anguish, not by portraying behavioral expressions of anguish but more directly, and also with the thought that our (fictional) access to what is portrayed is not perceptual—we imagine introspecting or simply experiencing the feelings, rather than perceiving someone's expressing them. And it goes a long way toward explaining the intimacy I said I felt with the anguish in the music. On reading that a character in a novel experiences a warm sense of security, one will imagine knowing about an instance of a warm sense of security, someone else's, but one probably will not imagine feeling this way oneself.[26]

More needs to be said. Listeners are intimate with the feelings the music expresses, with exuberance or anguish, for instance, if they imag-

ine experiencing exuberance or anguish. But this doesn't explain their intimacy with the music, with the *music's* exuberance or anguish. Musical experiences are not just experiences caused by music; they are experiences *of* music.[27] We don't merely hear the music and enjoy certain experiences as a result of hearing it. One possibility is that music stimulates imaginings which are in part imaginings about the sounds themselves. This is almost right but not quite. Listeners' imaginings are, in many instances, about their experience of hearing the sounds rather than the sounds themselves.

The point here is analogous to one concerning pictures. A picture of a dragon induces the spectator to imagine seeing a dragon. But a vivid verbal description in a story about a dragon might do this much. The picture induces the spectator also to imagine of her actual visual experience of the picture that it is her visual experience of a dragon. One's seeing of the picture is not just a stimulus but part of the content of one's imaginative experience. Anguished or agitated or exuberant music not only induces one to imagine feeling anguished or agitated or exuberant, it also induces one to imagine of one's auditory experience that *it* is an experience of anguish or agitation or exuberance.

R. K. Elliott, in a perceptive and suggestive essay, describes what he calls experiencing music "from within"—experiencing it "as if it were our own expression" and feeling the expressed emotion "non-primordially."[28] Elliott's characterization of this experience is sketchy, but it clearly has much in common with the experience I have described. He has the listener enjoying something akin to an experience of the emotion expressed, not just (somehow) observing the emotion in the music. Arousal theories, which in their crudest and least plausible form say that music expressive of exuberance or grief is simply music that makes listeners exuberant or stricken with grief, at least recognize that to appreciate expressive music is to *feel* something. Neither Elliott nor I think the appreciator, in general, simply and straightforwardly experiences the emotion the music expresses. Malcolm Budd encourages Elliott in my direction by suggesting that feeling an emotion "non-primordially" be explained in terms of make-believe.[29] (Elliott himself speaks of "imaginatively enriched perception.") But in other respects Budd develops Elliott's account in ways I do not find plausible (and at least some of which Elliott need not accept)—before finally dismissing it. "To experience music [either "from within" or "from without"] as if it were the expression of emotion it would be necessary ... to imagine someone giving voice to the sounds of the music and in doing so to express his emotion," Budd says. "If I experience [a piece of music] M from within then I make-believe that I feel [an emotion] E and that I am expressing my E in the sounds of M: these sounds are issuing from me as a consequence of my feeling E and they bear the imprint of E."[30] Budd rightly observes that we do not very often hear expressive music in *this* way. The kind of experience I have described doesn't involve imagining oneself producing the sounds of the music, or imagining the emotion to be expressed in sound-emitting behavior at all.[31] One needn't imagine expressive behavior of any kind, nor anything at all about the sounds one hears. One imagines experiencing the emotion, and one imagines one's experience of the sounds to be one's experience of it.

Music sometimes induces actual feelings and sensations in listeners, not just imaginings of such, and it sometimes affects our actual moods, if not our emotions. There are tricky questions about how best to describe the various effects music has on listeners. A lot will depend on what intentional content one takes the various psychological states to involve. It is more plausible to say that music makes listeners tense or relaxed or exuberant or agitated, in ordinary instances, than that it arouses in them genuine, as opposed to imagined, anguish or determination or confidence or pride or grief (although the experience of vividly imagining feeling anguish or determination or grief is likely itself be an emotional one). A person who is deeply depressed might only imagine being exuberant when she listens to an exuberant fugue, whereas an originally cheerful listener might be made genuinely exuberant. I don't doubt that even someone who is depressed may become genuinely less depressed as a result of imagining being exuberant in response to the music. Rather than trying to sort out merely imagined feelings from genuine ones, I will understand the notion of imagined feelings to include genu-

ine ones as well. Music that induces me actually to feel exuberant, thereby induces me to imagine feeling thus, and music might induce me merely to imagine feeling anguish when I don't really.[32]

That listeners' experiences of music include such imagined feelings (whether they are actual or not) fits nicely with the tendency of music to elicit behavioral responses like foot tapping, dancing, or swaying with the music. Some people sing along with music; some are inclined to sing along but know better. When music swells, one may swell with it. These are the beginnings of behavioral expressions of feelings—feelings of exuberance, agitation, gaiety, anguish, pride. They may manifest, if not actual feelings of these kinds, the vivid imagining of experiencing them. Compare the filmgoer who suddenly tenses, and perhaps screams involuntarily, as he imagines being attacked by a slime and being terrified. In this case also, vividly imagining experiencing certain feelings is intimately tied up with behavior expressive of the feelings; the imagining elicits the expressive behavior, and the person imagines this behavior to express actual feelings of the kind in question.

I tried earlier to explain how music might portray feelings directly, rather than via their behavioral expressions. Now we see that behavior—the listener's expression of the feelings she imagines experiencing—has come back into the picture. But this does not mean that the music portrays an instance of the feeling by portraying someone's behavioral expressions of it. It may be that some music which can be taken to portray a person behaving in certain ways and thereby expressing certain feelings, might alternatively be understood to involve the *listener's* behavior. (It might be understood in both ways, as we shall see.) But it doesn't *portray* the listener's behavior—certainly not in anything like the way a film about me portrays my behavior if it shows me expressing my feelings. Behavior is likely to come into the picture because in listening I, or any of us, may be induced to imagine not only experiencing certain feelings but also expressing these feelings behaviorally.

Wallace Stevens describes the intimate connection between hearing music and imagining feeling (or actually feeling) as follows. Notice that he doesn't indicate anything about observing, even to empathize with, a consciousness distinct from the listener, presented or represented or portrayed or suggested by the music.

Just as my fingers on these keys
Make music, so the selfsame sounds
On my spirit make a music, too.

Music is feeling, then, not sound;
And thus it is that what I feel,
Here in this room, desiring you,

Thinking of your blue-shadowed silk,
Is music. It is like the strain
Waked in the elders by Susanna.

Of a green evening, clear and warm,
She bathed in her still garden, while
The red-eyed elders watching, felt

The basses of their beings throb
In witching chords, and their thin blood
Pulse pizzicati of Hosanna.[33]

Sounds are curiously unusual in their tendency to elicit responses like foot tapping and singing along. Visual designs in motion have no comparable tendency. I have no inclination to tap my feet or dance or even sway back and forth to abstract motion pictures, even ones with a "beat," a regular persistent rhythm. It is hard to imagine jiving with a blinking traffic light, or even a battery of traffic lights operated by a jazz percussionist. People who dance at sound and light shows dance to the sound, not the light.

There may be reasons why sounds are better suited than sights to play the role I have claimed sounds often do play; reasons to expect that, if there is an "introspective" art of the kind I have described, as opposed to a perceptual one, it is more likely to be a sound art than a visual one. Aural experiences may be better suited than visual ones to count as, fictionally, experiences of feelings or emotions; experiences of sounds, as we construe them, may be more naturally imagined to be experiences of feelings or emotions than experiences of sights are. How might this be?

Here is an easy first point: Hearing is something we cannot easily turn off; we can't close our ears as we can close our eyes. The same is true of our introspective "sense." We can't simply turn off at will feelings of agitation or serenity or anguish or a sense of foreboding or of well-being—or our access to such feelings. In this and other ways also, seeing is a more active sense than hearing is. When our eyes are open we choose what to look at. Short of moving to a different location, we can't choose what sounds we hear, although we can to some extent ignore certain sounds and pay attention to others. Likewise, we don't have much direct control over what we feel, short of changing our situation or circumstances. We can concentrate on some feelings and ignore others, to an extent. But there is nothing in feeling, any more than in hearing, much like looking at one thing rather than another.

Other analogies between hearing and feeling are related to what I call the *Cavell-Calvino* observation about sounds. Stanley Cavell remarked that we think of sounds as independent entities separate from their sources, in a way we do not think of sights; we reify or objectify sounds.[34] We speak of clatters, bangings, whinnys, murmurs, echoes, creaks, clangs, rustles, grumbles, gurgles. Sounds—like smells—fill rooms and cross streets; sights don't do that. Italo Calvino puts the point well in "A King Listens":

The music comes and goes, in gusts, it oscillates, down in the rumbling groove of the streets, or it rises high with the wind that spins the vanes of the chimneys.

And when in the darkness a woman's voice is released in singing, invisible at the sill of an unlighted window—What is it? Not that song, which you must have heard all too many times, not that woman, whom you have never seen: you are attracted by that voice as a voice, as it offers itself in song.

That voice comes certainly from a person; a voice, however, is not a person, it is something suspended in the air, detached from the solidity of things.[35]

We reify or objectify feelings and sensations, as we do sounds, and we conceptualize them and our relations to them in similar ways. We think of feelings of exuberance or anguish as entities distinct from their sources, and sometimes as leaving their sources and surrounding or entering us. A feeling, like a sound, may come over me. It may permeate my consciousness. Both feelings and sounds wax and wane, independently of changes in their sources. They get more intense, or diminish and then disappear; they can be overwhelming or hard to detect. The same loss may cause grief of more or less intensity in different people, just as the same train causes louder or softer sounds at different distances. Sounds and feelings are both individuated sometimes by their sources, and sometimes by their perceivers. And we are of two minds about whether either can exist unperceived. We reify feelings and sounds complete with their intentional properties (while thinking of them as distinct from their intentional objects). The sound of a bell may waft through the house. Anguish about a particular event may eat at me for months afterwards; determination to succeed as a pianist may permeate one's life; pangs of jealousy seep into one's consciousness. (There is, I expect, a lot more to say on this score.)[36]

We do sometimes objectify sights distinct from their sources—glimmers, reflections, flashes of light, sheens, etc. But it is only in fairly special instances that we think of things like these as the objects of our vision; usually we think of ourselves as seeing physical objects—trees, houses, people, mountains. And a glimmer or a sparkle, if not identical to the thing that glimmers or sparkles, is thought of as attached to it. Glimmers and sparkles don't come to us from things that glimmer and sparkle, as sounds do from the sounding object.

Maybe it shouldn't be surprising that auditory rather than visual experiences are imagined to be experiences of feelings of exuberance or anguish or foreboding or well-being.[37]

There is no incompatibility between a work's inducing an appreciator to imagine someone else feeling exuberance or anguish, and its inducing the appreciator to imagine feeling this herself. It may do both at once. Visual depictions often do both when they elicit empathy for a character.

Empathizing with someone, I assume, involves imagining feeling the way one takes the person to feel. I see someone slice her hand with a kitchen knife. I wince and jerk my hand back.[38] I am not in pain. But I imagine (spontaneously, unreflectively, perhaps subliminally) the knife slicing through my flesh as I watch it cut her, and I imagine feeling pain. My imagin-

ing this explains my wincing and my jerking my hand back.

What stimulates my empathetic reaction in this case is what I see happening to my friend, not, or not directly, how she feels or how she responds. But other instances are different. If I am watching my friend's face when she is cut, I might respond empathetically to the pain I see on her face. I may not even see or know about the accident. One may simply observe a person's facial or behavioral expressions and find oneself behaving sympathetically, spontaneously mimicking his expressions, contorting one's face as he contorts his. This reaction is empathetic, and I take it to consist in imagining feeling what one observes him feeling. (Maybe one actually does feel as he does, in some respects; some aspects of the feeling, as well as the expression, may be contagious.) One may empathize with a dancer or an athlete, feeling one's muscles tense and relax in sympathy. (When a visual object is or represents a person, it *can* evoke responses akin to foot tapping.)

We respond similarly to fictional characters, imagining feeling as we perceive them (fictionally) to feel. When I look at a portrait I may contort my face in sympathy with the portrayed character's facial expressions, just as I contort my face in sympathy with a real person. So a picture may induce me to imagine someone else feeling anguish or elation and also, at the same time, to imagine (myself) feeling this way. I imagine her feeling anguish or elation, and I imagine feeling the same in response to her.

When music (vocal music for instance) portrays a more or less definite character, we are likely to have this kind of empathetic response. But what needs to be emphasized is that even when there is no definite character in the music, it can get us to imagine feeling in certain ways. The music swells and I swell with it. I imagine feeling anguish or ecstasy as these qualities are expressed in the music; I imagine experiencing a sense of foreboding, as the music changes suddenly from a major key to the parallel minor. In such cases I probably do not think of the music as portraying a person (distinct from me) who swells or feels anguish or foreboding. My experience, phenomenologically, does have some affinity with that of one who watches another person's facial expressions and responds empathetically. But I may not have much of a sense of empathizing *with someone* at all. No doubt this is partly because I do not imagine *perceiving* anyone when I listen, and because music is so fuzzy about the individuation of particulars. The difference between imaginatively recognizing and feeling with another person and merely imaginatively experiencing certain feelings oneself as one listens to the music can be very subtle, especially given that the imaginings are often implicit or subliminal. I am sure that sometimes there is no fact of the matter as to which is the case. But it would be a serious distortion of listeners' experiences to suppose that whenever music gets listeners imaginatively to feel, it must be doing so by eliciting imaginative empathy with a person portrayed in the music.[39]

There are other instances in which something gets us to imagine feeling a certain way without getting us to empathize with anyone. I see my friend's knife slip and strike the cutting board. I see a guillotine operate without a victim. In both cases I wince and draw back. But I don't observe someone else being hurt. I do imagine being cut or guillotined. A film of a hurtling roller coaster empty of passengers may nevertheless get us to imagine riding in it. Just looking at a comfortable rocking chair may induce one to imagine sitting in it.

Music differs from these last cases in that it often gets us to imagine having certain experiences not by showing us circumstances that would produce them, but by doing something more like showing or indicating either behavioral expressions of the experiences in question or (somehow) the experiences themselves—but still (often) without in any very definite way portraying someone (distinct from the listener) exhibiting the expressive behavior or having the experiences. It is as though the music provides the smile without the cat—a smile for the listener to wear. How music manages this trick is a good question. But the trick itself, the result, is not mysterious. Music gets us to imagine experiencing a certain feeling, and possibly expressing it or being inclined to express it in a certain manner. It often does this without getting us to imagine knowing about (let alone perceiving) someone else having that experience or expressing it in that manner.

IV. IS EXPRESSION REPRESENTATION?: GAME WORLDS WITHOUT WORK WORLDS

I have a lot of imagining going on in the appreciation of music, a lot of imagining *de se*. There is a game world full of life. But what has happened to the work world, the fictional world of the music itself? If there were a cat, it would be in the work world. But if there is only a smile and the smile is mine, the listener's, maybe there isn't even a place for a cat; maybe there is only a game world. The work world is supposed to contain fictional truths generated by the music alone. But the only fictional truths there are may be ones generated by the listener's experience with the music, ones that belong only to the game world.

In the case of a picture of a dragon, there is a fictional world, the world of the work, even when no one is looking at the picture. This is a large part of what it means to say that the picture is representational. The picture, standing alone, establishes a fictional world. But in music, when appreciation involves imagining experiencing feelings in the way I described, there are game worlds but no work worlds. This gives us an important sense in which music is not representational.

Dragons exist independently of anyone's perceiving or knowing about them, if they exist at all. If there is a dragon in my garden, it is there regardless of whether or not I see it. When it is fictional that a dragon exists, it is fictional that it exists independently of its being perceived. So it isn't surprising that we should understand something which actually does exist independently of perceivers to make it fictional that a dragon exists. A picture fills the bill. It is there whether or not anyone sees it, and it, by itself, makes it fictional that a dragon is there, whether or not it is fictional that anyone sees the dragon. Work worlds comprise fictional truths generated by the work alone. But feelings (of agitation, foreboding, ecstasy) do not exist independently of people who feel them. (Even if they can exist "unperceived" or unnoticed, they don't exist *unowned*.) So there is no pressure to regard the music itself as establishing a fictional world in which there are feelings (unless it is fictional that there is a person distinct from the listener whose feelings they are). It is the listener's auditory experiences, which, like feelings, cannot exist apart from being experienced, that make it fictional that there are feelings. When the listener imagines experiencing agitation herself, there is no reason to think of the *music* as making anything fictional. It is the listener's hearing of the music that makes it fictional that she feels agitated. The only fictional world is the world of her game, of her experience.

The absence of a work world goes a considerable way toward recovering the "abstractness" or "nonrepresentationality" of music, toward explaining the impression that music is not representational in the way painting and literature are. Insofar as music is expressive in the manner I have described, it does not have fictional worlds of the kind that (figurative) paintings and novels do.[40] The music itself is not a prop, as a painting or a novel is. What the music does is to supply us with experiences when we listen to it, and we use these experiences as props. It is the auditory experiences, not the music itself, that generate fictional truths. I can step outside of my game with a painting. When I do, I see the picture and notice that it represents a dragon, that it *calls for* the imagining of a dragon (even if I don't actually imagine this). But when I step outside my game with music and consider the music itself, all I see is music, not a fictional world to go with it. There are just the notes, and they themselves don't call for imagining anything.[41]

The absence of a work world does not, however, prevent the listener's imagination from running wild, as she participates in her game of make-believe.

1. This is a revision of the third of three Carl G. Hempel Lectures given at Princeton University in May 1991. It develops a suggestion I broached in "What Is Abstract about the Art of Music?," *The Journal of Aesthetics and Art Criticism* 46 (Spring 1988): 359–360, and mentioned in *Mimesis as Make-Believe: On the Foundations of the Representational Arts* (Cambridge: Harvard University Press, 1991), pp. 335–336. I am indebted to Karol Berger, David Hills, Marion Guck, Anthony Newcomb, and Alicyn Warren for helpful discussions and comments.

2. Kivy, "Is Music an Art?," *The Journal of Philosophy* 88 (October 1991): 553.

3. This possibility alone shows Kivy's peremptory declaration in "Is Music an Art?" that music is not representational to be seriously premature.

4. This is the central feature of the account of representation I develop in *Mimesis as Make-Believe*.

5. Heinrich Schenker, *Counterpoint* Volume II, Book II, Chapter 2, §2, trans. John Rothgeb, pp. 56–59.

6. See Leonard Meyer, *Emotion and Meaning in Music* (Chicago: University of Chicago Press, 1956).

7. See Edward Cone, "Three Ways of Reading a Detective Story—or a Brahms Intermezzo," in *Music: A View from Delft*, ed. Robert P. Morgan (Chicago: University of Chicago Press, 1989), p. 87.

8. Cf. *Mimesis as Make-Believe*, 1.8. I follow Richard Wollheim in understanding representationality in a way that covers much nonfigurative painting.

9. "The left hand begins to sing like a cello." David Lewin, "Auf dem Flusse: Image and Background in a Schubert Song," *Nineteenth Century Music*. Vol. 6, No. 1, p. 53.

10. The slow section of the third movement of Beethoven's A♭-Major Piano Sonata, opus 110, is titled "Recitativo," and obviously mimics a vocal recitative. (Alicyn Warren pointed out this example to me.)

11. The notion of composers' *personae* comes under this heading. See Edward T. Cone, "Persona, Protagonist, and Characters," in *The Composer's Voice* (Berkeley: University of California Press, 1974), pp. 25–26; Jerrold Levinson "Hope in the Hebrides," in *Music, Art, and Metaphysics* (Ithaca: Cornell University Press, 1990); Fred Maus, "Music as Drama," *Music Theory Spectrum* 10 (1988); and Bruce Vermazen, "Expression as Expression," *Pacific Philosophical Quarterly* 67 (1986). Also, my "Style and the Products and Processes of Art," in Berel Lang, editor, *The Concept of Style*, Second edition (Cornell University Press, 1987), pp. 72–103.

12. Kerman, *The Beethoven Quartets* (New York: W.W. Norton, 1966), p. 256.

13. See, e.g., Stephen Davies, "The Expression of Emotion in Music," *Mind* 89 (1980); R. K. Elliott, "Aesthetic Theory and the Experience of Art," in H. Osborne, *Aesthetics* (Oxford: Oxford University Press, 1972); Peter Kivy, *The Corded Shell: Reflections on Musical Expression* (Princeton: Princeton University Press, 1980); Levinson, "Hope in the Hebrides"; Vermazen, "Expression as Expression."

14. Lewin speaks of "the mimesis of a giant question mark." ("Auf dem Flusse," p. 54.)

15. These last examples are Hanslick's. (*On the Musically Beautiful*, trans. Geoffrey Payzant [Indianapolis: Hackett, 1986], pp. 9, 10, 32.)

16. For a discussion of the ways in which metaphors do and do not involve imagination and make-believe, see my "Metaphor and Prop-Oriented Make-Believe," *The European Journal of Philosophy* 1:1 (1993).

17. I am indebted to Marion Guck for introducing me to this passage and pointing out many of its interesting features. She discusses it in "Taking Notice: A Response to Kendall Walton," *The Journal of Musicology* 11:1 (Winter 1993): 45–51.

18. Susanne Langer calls a program for pure music a

crutch. (*Philosophy in a New Key,* 3rd. ed. [Cambridge: Harvard University Press, 1942], pp. 242–243). Crutches are sometimes helpful and sometimes get in the way. This one does no harm *as long as* the make-believe the story introduces is understood to be "prop-oriented," in the sense I explicate in "Metaphor and Prop-Oriented Make-Believe."

19. See Fred Maus, "Music as Drama."

20. Uncertainty about identity and individuation may be no accident in an aural representational art. Hearing, in real life, is typically less important than sight in the acquisition of knowledge *de se,* knowledge about particular things. On hearing the thunder of a team of galloping horses, I may have little notion which clops are made by the same horse and which by different ones. But I can do much better, when I see the horses, in identifying which seen bits of horse belong to the same horse and which do not.

21. Anthony Newcomb emphasized to me the difference between a high degree of *connectedness* among the parts of a whole, and the whole having a coherent or intelligible *shape;* some theme and variation movements possess the former and lack the latter. My remarks in this paragraph apply to both of these varieties of unity.

22. See Peter Kivy, "A New Music Criticism?," *The Monist* 63 (1990): 260–267, and "Auditor's Emotions: Contention, Concession and Compromise," *The Journal of Aesthetics and Art Criticism* 51:1 (1993): 9–11. I owe the wallpaper example to David Hills.

23. Sometimes the distance can be specified only approximately, and sometimes the angle is ambiguous, e.g., in some Cubist works.

24. Schopenhauer objects strenuously to musical imitations of "phenomena of the world of perception." *The World as Will and Representation,* Vol. I, trans. E.F.J. Payne (New York: Dover, 1969), p. 264. See also pp. 257, 259–260, 262–264.

25. Many literary works indicate characters' feelings by means of a narrator's description of their feelings. The following portrayal of a character's warm sense of security seems not to be indirect even in this way: "Chance circumstance which facilitated [Pancho's] intentions: the approach of a ferocious-looking stray dog who frightened Fanny and gave rise to an unmistakable show of courage on the part of Pancho, which awakened in Fanny a warm sense of security." (Mañuel Puig, *Heartbreak Tango,* trans. Suzanne Jill Levine [New York: Random House, 1969], p. 85.)

26. Not anyway when reading something like the above Puig passage. In other cases one might empathize with a character's feeling of warm security, imagining feeling this way oneself. I will discuss such instances shortly.

27. See Malcolm Budd, *Music and the Emotions* (New York: Routledge, 1985), p. 123.

28. R.K. Elliott, "Aesthetic Theory and the Experience of Art," p. 152.

29. Budd, *Music and the Emotions,* pp. 127–131.

30. Budd, *Music and the Emotions,* pp. 131, 135.

31. Elliott makes it clear that *expression* of an emotion is, for him, not limited to behavior ("Aesthetic Theory and the Experience of Art," p. 146).

32. "The affections of the will itself, and hence actual pain and actual pleasure, must not be excited, but only their substitutes, that which is in conformity with the *intellect* as a *picture or image* of the will's satisfaction, and that which more or less opposes it as a *picture or image* of greater or lesser pain." (Schopenhauer, *The World as Will and Representation,* Vol. II, p. 451. Italics in original.)

33. Wallace Stevens, "Peter Quince at the Clavier," stanza I.

34. Stanley Cavell, *The World Viewed,* Enlarged Edition (Cambridge: Harvard University Press, 1979), Ch. 2.

35. Italo Calvino, "The King Listens" in *Under the Jaguar Sun,* trans. William Weaver (San Diego: Harcourt Brace Jovanovich, 1988), pp. 50, 53–54.

36. Susanne Langer claims that particular feelings and particular sounds have similar "logical structures." *Philosophy in a New Key,* pp. 226, 228, 244; *Feeling and Form* (New York: Scribners, 1953), p. 27. But my point is that feelings in general and sounds in general are conceived in analogous ways. It is possible that conventions of some sort have a place in the explanation of how particular sounds get associated with particular feelings. And it is possible that the natural affinity Langer finds between certain sounds and certain feelings is a result of, rather than the source of, the tendency of the sounds to get us to imagine experiencing those feelings.

37. "As tone is itself inwardness and subjectivity, it speaks to the inner soul." Hegel, *Hegel's Philosophy of Nature,* Vol. II., trans. Michael John Perry (London: George Allen & Unwin Ltd., 1970), p. 71.

38. The example is borrowed from Richard Moran.

39. Elliott sometimes characterizes experiencing music, or a poem, "from within" as putting oneself in the shoes of another person, e.g., the poet.

40. There is a work world insofar as music portrays characters behaving expressively. And as I mentioned, most or all music has a fictional world and is representational in the way nonfigurative painting usually is, though the fictional worlds in these cases differ importantly from the worlds of figurative painting and literature.

41. It is misleading or worse to say, as Susanne Langer does, that the sounds are *symbols* for feelings, even "nondiscursive" symbols (whatever that is supposed to mean). "If music has any significance, it is semantic ... music is *about* feelings, it is their logical expression" (*Philosophy in a New Key,* p. 218). I disagree. Langer's obscure notion of *presenting* emotions for our contemplation, however, might be understood as getting us to imagine experiencing them.

Speech, Song, and the Transparency of Medium: A Note on Operatic Metaphysics

I

When Desdemona sings the "Willow Song" in Verdi's *Otello,* she sings a song in the world of that work, *her* world, just as I sing a song in the real world, *my* world, when I sing "Melancholy Baby" in the shower. But when Desdemona converses with Iago, she also sings, whereas when I converse with my plumber about why my shower won't work I do not sing: I *speak.*

To distinguish between what Desdemona does when she sings the "Willow Song" and what she does when she converses with Iago, Otello et al., Edward T. Cone has coined the phrase "realistic song" for the former, "operatic song" for the latter. And he then goes on to suggest that frequently in opera the line between realistic song and operatic song becomes blurred, or even tends to break down entirely. This is because, on Cone's view, operatic song and realistic song are frequently so intertwined, one with the other, that it is difficult or impossible to prise them apart and say, with clarity, at any given time, which is which.

What Cone has in mind here can be summed up in three points. First, even when realistic song is going on, the realistic song is usually such an intimate and spontaneous expression of the character's inner states and feelings that it stands to them much more as my own speech to my own inner states and feelings than as a song I might sing, by Schubert or Richard Rogers, could stand to them. And thus even where it is clear that realistic song is going on, it seems almost always the case, because of this intimate connection between song and singer, that, in sharp contrast to our world, realistic singers in the world of opera are best seen as composers of their own realistic songs. "In opera, however, a song, whether realistic or operatic, is so inti-mately connected with the character who sings it that he or she is usually to be accepted as its composer."[1]

Second, the musical themes of realistic song in opera frequently burst their boundaries and transmigrate, as, for example, in the place in Act I of *La traviata* where Alfredo (on Cone's reading of the scene) is serenading Violetta— so a case of realistic song—but weaves into the tune of his serenade a previously heard theme that we took in the earlier place for operatic song: "his serenade depends on a crucial trans-formation: the musical motif that we assumed originally to be not realistic but conventional [i.e., operatic] song (representing normal speech) now appears in such a way that it must be taken as 'really' sung—in some sense—the first time, else there would be no actual music for Alfredo to recall and for Violetta to hear." So: "The scene strongly suggests that the rigid distinc-tion between realistic song on the one hand and conventional or operatic song on the other can-not be sustained."[2]

Third, it is a matter of no small significance that the characters in opera are, quite fre-quently, people who tend to be *singers* in the worlds of their works, that is to say, fictionally singers, beginning, of course, with the very first operatic hero, Orpheus himself, the quintessen-tial singer of songs. Carmen is another. Their number is legion; and this "suggests that Orpheus is not the prototypical operatic hero for histori-cal reasons only: his role as composer-singer symbolizes what it means to be an operatic character."[3] But if what it means to be an oper-atic character is to be a composer-singer; and if, as is so often the case, expression is achieved by characters singing realistically, as in the case of Orpheus or Carmen, there seems little use left at all in the world of opera for the distinction between operatic and realistic song. Since, in the world of opera, unlike our own world, so much of a character's inner thoughts and feelings are expressed in realistic song, of which the character, therefore, must be thought the composer, it seems only a small next step to the conclusion that, for all intents and purposes, operatic characters just are, all of them, one way or another, composer-singers: creatures whose natural form of expression is music.

This three-faceted blurring of the distinction between realistic and operatic song Cone calls "the fundamental operatic ambiguity (Is speech or song being represented?)."[4] Further, he claims that "an adequate comprehension of opera ... rests on appreciation of this ambiguity."[5] Even when the ambiguity is not pressed to its *ultimate* conclusion, its recognition makes clear that "song is the natural medium of expression for operatic characters. ... [I]magine a world in which singing is the norm and speaking the exception: that is the world of opera."[6] But if there really is this ambiguity, if we really always can read operatic song as realistic song, then, truly, all operatic characters are composer-singers. And that, indeed, is the conclusion in which Cone seems to want to leave us, with his parting shot: "When Arnalta, the nurse, hears Poppea exulting after the death of Seneca [in Monteverdi's *L'Incoronazione di Poppea*], she remonstrates, ... 'You're forever going around singing songs about your wedding.' But that is just what characters in opera do: *they go around singing songs all the time*."[7]

II

Cone's notion that operatic characters might be all imagined in the image of Orpheus, the improvisatory composer-singer, seems to me to be an intriguing and important one, and to capture something palpable about our experience of the opera. In a previous essay I attempted to reach Cone's conclusion by a rather different route.[8] In the present one I want to try to carry that project forward. But before I do I must give a brief idea of how I reached and stated Cone's thesis of the operatic singer-composer. For it is, naturally, on my own version of that thesis that I want to build.

In my previous essay I suggested that there

were two reasons to feel uncomfortable, not with Cone's conclusion itself, but with the way it was reached. The first reason was that Cone's method requires obliterating the distinction between realistic and operatic song, since he argues, alternatively, that the intimacy of expression in realistic song makes us want to say that it is really operatic song, and, contrariwise, that the prevalence of realistic singers in opera makes us want to say, in effect: all operatic singing is really realistic singing. This two-pronged attack on the distinction between realistic and operatic song is Cone's pathway to the conclusion of the operatic character as composer-singer. But for those, like myself, who might want to have Cone's conclusion, while hanging on to the distinction between realistic and operatic song, an alternative to Cone's distinction-obliterating argument is an obvious desideratum.

Secondly, in obliterating the distinction between realistic and operatic song, as well as in asking us to imagine operatic characters all as "composers," Cone widens the gap, already difficult for many listeners to tolerate, between the real world and the world of opera. A world where speech is song is difficult enough for some to accept as an artistic convention. But a world where all characters are "composers," and where our ordinary distinction between speaking and singing no longer holds, compounds the felony. Might there not be a way of making out Cone's conclusion while *narrowing* rather than broadening the gap between our world and the world of opera which *it*, after all, is meant to represent? That is what I attempted to do in my previous essay.

My argument took off from R.G. Collingwood's thesis that "art," "expression," and "language" are co-extensive; and I took as my epigraph his remark: "Every utterance and every gesture that each of us makes is a work of art."[9] I made it clear in my earlier essay, and I want to reaffirm it here as well, that I do not endorse Collingwood's philosophy of art. Rather, I was, and am making a variation on a Collingwoodian theme. And as I can assume here, as I could not there, that my readers are well acquainted with the details of Collingwood's system, I will not need to dwell at length on the theme, but can move quickly on to the variation.

For Collingwood "expression" (as he used the term) is not a process in which one first determines what it is he wants to express and then casts about for a ready means to express it. It is, rather, always an innovative process, a "creative" process, if you will, in which you feel the need to express you know not what, you know not how, and in the process of coming to know the latter you at the same time come to know the former: in other words, in finding "expression" for what you vaguely feel you must express, you come to know what it was that you felt. But if "art" ≡ "expression" ≡ "language", then even ordinary speakers of English (or any other natural language), when they succeed in expressing, must have succeeded in making works of art; and that is what Collingwood is acknowledging in his paradoxical and dark saying: "Every utterance and every gesture that each one of us makes is a work of art."

Now, of course, Collingwood knew well that this saying had an air of paradox about it. Taken literally it was not true, even on his own principles, and in order for it to be we would have to suitably qualify both "gesture" and "utterance" so as to get the authentic Collingwoodian statement: "Every [successfully expressive] utterance and every [successfully expressive] gesture that each one of us makes is a work of art"—unless, of course, "utterance" and "gesture" are being used in the same Collingwoodian sense as "language": to wit, "language" (properly so-called), "utterance" (properly so-called), "gesture" (properly so-called), already assuming success of expression in the concept (properly so-called). Collingwood, of course, was not saying that "Please pass the salt," when uttered at table, with obvious intent, is a work of art. But nor was he saying that it is "language" (properly so-called). For on Collingwood's view only when what people ordinarily call "language" is "innovative," is truly "expression" in the proper, Collingwoodian sense, and not merely cliché, language ready-made, and hence by definition not "expression," is it "language" properly so-called. And only when it is "language," properly so-called, is it art.

Without in the least endorsing the philosophical theory, or the dubious philosophical method which produces it, I find Collingwood's remark, that "Every utterance and every gesture that each one of us makes is a work of art," a suggestive metaphor. For it can serve to remind us of a remarkable fact about language: its ability, even in the hands of the minimally competent, to respond on the spot to the novel and the unexpected; to, in other words, operate successfully in human conversation, which is, by nature, unpremeditated, spontaneous, "improvisational." Of course we all possess ready-made conversational schemata, and few of us are, like Dr. Johnson, linguistic innovators, true conversational artists in our every-day speech. But to a certain extent every conversational situation, when "the ball is in our court," constitutes a novel and unpredicted one. Whatever I expect my conversational partner to respond, I cannot ever know exactly, nor do I usually "plan ahead"; and yet, without premeditation, on demand, I respond intelligibly. That is something remarkable about the spoken language that I am not, of course, original in commenting upon. And it is that remarkable "inventiveness," that each one of us must evince in conversation, that makes it true, in even a more extensive way than Collingwood had in view, that our every utterance and gesture is "a work of art," and each of us a linguistic "artist"— the "authors" of our words. This is my variation on Collingwood's theme.

I do not for a moment suggest the above as a philosophical thesis or a "theory" of language. I suggest it, rather, as an "imaginative exercise." See your world, for now, in this somewhat Collingwoodian way, as one in which you and your co-conversationalists are "authors" of your conversational thrusts and gambits, engaged in the grand "improvisation" of colloquy. We are *all,* in this imaginative, but *not fictional* way of looking at ourselves, minimal linguistic "artists"; for we have to, in conversation, "make it up for ourselves" as we go along.

But if we see ourselves in this way, then perhaps we will not seem as distant from the denizens of "opera land" as we seemed heretofore. For we share with them the role of "conversational artist": only in their world the "art of conversation" is the art of song, and they the "composers" of their expression, as in Shakespeare's world the "art of conversation" is poetry, and its conversationalists "poets on demand." This, then, is my way of reaching Cone's conclusion that operatic characters, in the image of Orpheus, invite us to see them as composers and singers of songs. It was this point that I had reached in my previous essay on the subject; and I now want to push it forward, for it will not withstand critical scrutiny without emendation and elaboration.

III

Let me introduce, at this point in the argument, the hard-nosed operatic "metaphysician," who will not let matters stand as so far stated. Here is his (or her) complaint.

"Your suggestion that we imagine the denizens of 'opera land' as 'composers' of their conversations, as we are the 'authors' of ours, is a pleasing conceit, but a total misrepresentation of the 'metaphysics of fiction.' For if you ask, for example, what Hamlet is doing when he says his speeches, the answer is not that he is reciting Elizabethan blank verse, of which he is the 'author,' but that he is speaking Danish prose, of which he is the 'author.' (He is, after all, a Danish prince.) And if, similarly, you ask what the Countess is doing, when she sings 'Dove sono,' the answer is that she is not singing at all but, presumably, speaking seventeenth-century Spanish, of which she is the 'author' (for seventeenth-century Spain is where Mozart and Da Ponte have set The Marriage of Figaro)."

The metaphysician's complaint cannot be gainsaid: it is, ontologically speaking, squeaky clean. Yet, one is compelled to ask, what is seventeenth-century Spanish to me, when I experience The Marriage of Figaro? Or medieval Danish when I experience Hamlet, for that matter? If what the metaphysician says is completely irrelevant to my artistic appreciation of these works, then it does not have aught to do with Cone's and my thesis, which is about, I take it, just that very thing: the appreciation of opera as an art.

Well, such a grumpy, high-handed dismissal of the metaphysician's complaint may be appropriate for some others who write about the opera; but it cannot be appropriate for one, like myself, who writes of it as a philosopher of art. For if I am not to heed the arguments of the metaphysician, who is, after all, a card-carrying member of my tribe, with considerable seniority, my own philosophical credentials could surely, and with reason be called in doubt. Answer the metaphysician I cannot: I have already con-

ceded the correctness of his claim. But accommodate him I think I can; and to do so we must pursue the metaphysics of operatic utterance a trifle further.

What is the ontological status then of the singing, in The Marriage of Figaro, if what the characters are doing in the fictional world of that work is speaking seventeenth-century Spanish? The obvious, and correct answer would seem to be that it is the medium of representation. That is to say, we must think of seventeenth-century Spanish speech as being represented by eighteenth-century music. The music is the medium. In like manner we must see Elizabethan blank verse as the medium of representation for medieval Danish prose in Hamlet, and English with a German accent the medium of representation for German speech in Hollywood war movies of the 1940s.

With that established, we can now introduce the familiar concept of the transparency of the medium. And this is best accomplished by turning, for a moment, to the visual arts. If I set my gaze on Seurat's Grand Jatte, I am acutely aware, at all times, of the tiny daubs of paint with which the painter represents his subject; these splotches are Seurat's medium, and it is a singularly untransparent medium because it never ceases to be prominently in the gazer's awareness as he or she experiences the work. On the other end of the spectrum are trompe l'oeil paintings in which the fruit and game are so "realistically" depicted as to tempt one to reach into the "space" of the canvas to touch the objects therein. Here, we are tempted to say, medium has become transparent to perception, is seen through without refraction, to the representational content within. It may indeed be true, as Arthur Danto argues, that: "The medium ... is of course never really eliminible. There is always going to be a residuum of matter that cannot be vaporized into pure content."[10] Nevertheless, even though complete transparency is not an achievable (or, for that matter, desirable) goal, that there are works and styles where medium is more or less transparent than others is an important aspect of our aesthetic experience. And that comparative judgment, that perception of degrees of transparency is all I require for present purposes.

Let us revert, now, with the transparency of medium concept in hand, to more relevant territory. The metaphysician will tell us that in the world of *Hamlet* the melancholy Dane is speaking medieval Danish prose, and that, in the world of *Death of a Salesman,* Willy Loman is speaking 1940s American-style English. And he will tell us, further, that the medium in which Hamlet's speech is represented is Elizabethan blank verse.

What is the medium of Willy Loman's conversation? Well that might stump the metaphysician for a moment, because, I want to suggest, the medium in which the dialogue of Arthur Miller's great play is depicted is far more transparent to us than the medium of Shakespearean drama and, therefore, we tend not to notice it, which is to say, we tend not to notice that there is a medium interposed between us and the content at all.

But it is, clearly, a metaphysical impossibility for there not to be an artistic medium of representation of Willy Loman's conversation; for if there were no medium, Willy Loman would not be a fictional character, just as if the "flowers" were not paint, they would be *flowers,* which is, of course, absurd. And a moment's reflection will reveal that the representational medium of Willy Loman's 1940s American-style English just is that very thing: 1940s American-style English—which is why, of course, it is so transparent a medium.

Once, however, we become aware of the medium in which Willy Loman's speech is represented and attend to it more closely, we see, of course, that it is not *exactly* 1940s American-style English at all. For it has received the impress of the artist's hand. No one succeeds, in life, in expressing his or her thoughts and feelings that perfectly, that powerfully, in the native tongue. Conversation without glitches does not happen in real salesmen's homes. Emotional climaxes, self-revelations, and insights do not occur at just the right (or just the tragically *wrong*) moments, if, indeed, they occur at all, in the ordinary course of human affairs. In other words, the medium, *artistically transformed* 1940s American-style English bears all of the *expressive,* all of the *aesthetic* properties that, as Danto argues, only the medium of representation, not the content itself can intelligibly be described as having.[11]

Nonetheless, given that the medium in which speech is represented, in *Death of a Salesman,*

has not, as Danto would put it, "vaporized into pure content," which would have been the case if its medium had achieved full and perfect transparency, it surely makes sense to say that this medium is *more* transparent (say) than that of *Hamlet,* where medieval Danish prose is represented in Elizabethan English blank verse. In a perfectly obvious sense, we will never cease being aware, *strongly aware,* that when we attend to a performance of *Hamlet,* we are hearing a *recital of poetry.* To borrow a phrase (if not the concept) from Richard Wollheim, we will never "hear in" the medium of *Hamlet* medieval Danish prose, for all that the metaphysician may say, as we will "hear in" the medium of *Death of a Salesman* ordinary, 1940s American-style English.[12] The medium of *Hamlet* is too thick, too opaque for that.

With that being said, it is now time to return to our subject, the opera, and to apply what we have learned. It will be clear, straight-away, that the operatic medium is very far from the transparency end of the spectrum, further, indeed, even than Elizabethan tragedy. For if we cannot "hear in" Shakespearean verse medieval Danish prose, we cannot, *a fortiori,* "hear in" Mozart's music seventeenth-century Spanish prose. Nowhere are we more perceptually aware of medium, and less of content, than in opera and music drama.

Charles Burney called opera "the *completest concert.*"[13] He knew full well that it was also *drama-per-musica.* But in calling it a concert he revealed how pervasively *he* thought the medium of opera obtrudes into our experience of it. For as a concert, opera is a recital for voices; and when we hear it thus we are, of necessity, at the fullest possible remove from the metaphysical center, which is *speech* represented *in* music. We are, in effect, totally involved in the medium: we are listening to *singing.*

Now, of course, opera, even the *opera seria* of Burney's time, which has been charged with being so, is *not* merely a concert in costume. And anyone who experienced it merely as a voice recital, even when in concert performance, would be seriously misreading it, whether in the obvious case of Wagnerian music drama or in the more "concert-like" case of Handelian *opera seria.* Yet the fact is that, particularly in "number" opera, but not solely there by any means, the "concert attitude," if I may so call it, is very much intermingled with what one might call the "representational attitude." We do, after all, go to the opera to hear beautiful music beautifully (we hope) performed.

What all of this, then, adds up to, it appears, is that when we experience (say) the opening scene of the second act of *The Marriage of Figaro,* we are in a mode of attention that is both—and very *strongly* both—one of attending to a singer giving a "performance" (remember how the action comes to a full stop for the applause!), and attending to a character in a drama making an expressive utterance. Further, both the "concert attitude" and the extreme "opacity" of the representational medium, which, indeed, mutually reinforce each other, make it impossible for us to "hear in" the Countess's "soliloquy" anything like what the metaphysician (quite correctly) tells us is being represented, namely, seventeenth-century Spanish conversation.

What, then, *do* we hear when we hear the Countess as a character, given the opacity of the representational medium and the ever-present "recital attitude"? Well, we hear, I would suggest, a world in which the character is a "composer" of her vocal expression, as, in my world, I am the "author" of mine. And in concluding that, we now have our sought after accommodation with the hard-nosed operatic metaphysician. The metaphysician has spoken of how things *are,* we of how things *are experienced.* The opacity of the operatic medium, except perhaps in such cases as recitative, *stile rappresentativo,* or a musical fabric like that of *Pelléas et Mélisande,* where we really can hear speech "in" the representational medium, is such that what we hear is characters expressing themselves not in speech represented by the medium of music but expressing themselves in the medium, the *music* itself. That is the truth of

Cone's and my conclusion: not an "ontological" truth but an experiential one. Or, to wax metaphorically Kantian in conclusion, the operatic metaphysician has spoken of the operatic *ding an sich,* we of the operatic "phenomena." And at the operatic end of the spectrum from relative transparency to relative opacity of representational medium, the phenomena are all that we have. The reality—that the Countess is speaking seventeenth-century Spanish, or Elektra ancient Greek—is merely a metaphysical shadow, although, indeed, a metaphysical truth.

1. Edward T. Cone, "The World of Opera and Its Inhabitants," in Edward T. Cone, *Music: A View from Delft: Selected Essays,* ed. Robert P. Morgan (University of Chicago Press, 1989), p. 129.

2. Ibid., pp. 127–128.

3. Ibid., p. 135.

4. Ibid., p. 131.

5. Ibid., p. 129.

6. Ibid., p. 134.

7. Ibid., p. 138; italics mine.

8. Peter Kivy, "Opera talk: A philosophical 'phantasie,'" *Cambridge Opera Journal* 3 (1991): 385.

9. R.G. Collingwood, *The Principles of Art* (Oxford: The Clarendon Press, 1938), p. 285.

10. Arthur C. Danto, *The Transfiguration of the Commonplace: A Philosophy of Art* (Harvard University Press, 1981), p. 159.

11. Ibid., pp. 158–159.

12. Richard Wollheim, *Painting as an Art* (Princeton University Press, 1987), pp. 46–47, et seq.

13. Charles Burney, *A General History of Music,* ed. Frank Mercer (New York: Dover, 1957), vol. II, p. 676. I have discussed this passage at greater length in *Osmin's Rage: Philosophical Reflections on Opera, Drama and Text* (Princeton University Press, 1988), pp. 133–136.

STEPHEN DAVIES

Musical Understanding and Musical Kinds

Suppose someone, call her Cecilia, is keen to understand the music composed by Mozart after 1778. She listens carefully and repeatedly to the first movements of the Symphonia Concertante for Violin and Viola in E-flat Major (K. 364 of 1779 or later), Symphony No. 36 in C Major ("the Linz," K. 425 of 1783), the last of the Piano Concertos in C Major (K. 503 of 1786), Symphony No. 41 in C Major ("the Jupiter," K. 551 of 1788), and the Clarinet Concerto in A Major (K. 622 of 1791; the first movement was written in G for Basset Horn in 1789). She reads (from the record notes) that each of these movements is in sonata form and she listens to them with that in mind.[1] In time she knows of each movement how it is put together. Does she understand the music composed by Mozart after 1778?

Understanding comes in degrees and in various modes. The previous question might make more sense if it is posed in terms of understanding how, what, that, or why. Let me begin the process of clarification by laying aside some possible versions of the question. The question is not one about Cecilia's abilities as a performer; I will suppose she lacks the practical knowledge and skills required to perform or to direct others to perform in a way which might reveal her view of the work. My question is one about an understanding of the music which is to be revealed, if at all, through the descriptions which she will offer of the works. But, just as the query is not one presupposing Cecilia's mastery as a performer, neither is it one presupposing on her part a detailed, technical knowledge of music theory or analysis. A final warning: the question is highly specific. I feel this discussion will have achieved a great deal if it says something useful about the understanding

invited by the kind of music mentioned, which is central to the Classical tradition, even if the dangers of generalizing beyond this case are only too apparent to those whose affection focuses on other kinds of music.

What does Cecilia know of these works so far?—roughly, how they are put together (in the sense of understanding how many bits there are and where the joins are to be found). She knows that some tune begins here and ends there, that later it is repeated, that parts of it are recalled in the bits between the main tunes, that it has an expressive character which distinguishes it from the other main themes though it is more hesitant and equivocal in some of its statements than others, and so on. Sometimes one hears complaints against dry, academic formalism. If these are objections to a mechanical, formulaic, rigid approach to musical structure, or to an obsession with technical labels, they might have some point (even if, equally, there is a point in describing the broad outlines of structural types which are common to many works). But if they reject as irrelevant to Cecilia's goal of understanding the given pieces a concern with their structure, then the objection strikes me as mistaken. If, after a number of listenings, one can't hear the tunes, or distinguish one melody from another, or recognize that a melody is being repeated, or hear some difference where the key shifts from major to minor, or sense the instability of a passage passing through a series of transient tonal centers, or feel surprise in face of an unprepared modulation to a distant key, then it is far from clear that one can qualify as an appreciator of the work in question, for there must be doubt that one can distinguish the given work from any others. The recognition of musical structure, such as Cecilia now has achieved, just is an awareness of the overall pattern of such events. It is the recognition of repetition, similarity, instability, emphatic closure, and so on (but not necessarily of the technical devices by which such results are achieved), and more generally of patterns which emerge from successions of such events, which amounts to the recognition of musical form.[2]

According to a common view of musical understanding, to know how a piece is put together is to advance a long way toward understanding it.[3] I disagree with this view, for I think that Cecilia might achieve a much deeper appreciation of the works which interest her were she to consider matters which never are mentioned by those who press the "common view." Her understanding is like that of the butcher who draws dotted lines where the cuts most conveniently are to be made. The butcher need not know why beasts are put together as they are in order to do his job; he need not ask why the legs are found at the corners. The physician or the zoologist will consider form with respect to function, as is appropriate when regarding a living animal rather than a corpse. Cecilia will find more to interest her in Mozart's works of post-1778 if she approaches them more as a doctor than a butcher. She needs to ask not just "how are these works put together?" but "why are they put together as they are?" This latter question, asked as one about function, involves a consideration of how the particular work differs from others of its kind, and that in turn requires a grasp of what it is that distinguishes one musical kind from another.[4] I find that such matters are almost entirely absent from the work of philosophers who have published on musical understanding.

So far Cecilia has an idea of how each first movement of each work is assembled. She knows that each movement differs from every other, and that all fit the pattern of sonata form, loosely characterized. As yet she has no way of sorting significant from incidental differences. What more must she do if she is to attain the fuller understanding which this skill presupposes? First, she must listen to a sufficient number of Mozart's symphonies and concertos to reach a judgment about if and how Mozart's treatment of these genres differ. Then she must ask *why* they differ as they do, expecting thereby to learn what (in Mozart's view) distinguishes

the musical purpose or function of the symphony and the concerto. (Or one might put the issue this way: what "problem" was acknowledged by Mozart in trying to compose a work of the given type such that what was written was an answer to it?)

The important question is not "how is it put together?" but "why is its being put together this way rather than that significant to its being a concerto as opposed to being a symphony?" As I have said, questions of this second type are ignored by most philosophers who discuss the nature of musical understanding. This surprises me, for I do not see how Cecilia can understand the particular works which interest her unless she is in a position to answer it. If the work is a concerto, knowing how it is put together will tell her next to nothing about whether it succeeds as a concerto unless she has some idea of what concertos are supposed to be for and what difficulties are presented to the composer in meeting that function within the broad confines of a sonata form framework. Moreover, though she might know what features of the movement belong to it in virtue of its being in sonata form, without some idea of the treatment of sonata form appropriate to a concerto (as opposed, say, to a symphony) Cecilia cannot be sure which features of the work depend on its being a concerto and which belong to it as the particular concerto it is. Not all similarities between concertos need result from their being concertos; some such similarities might be coincidental, others might depend on the composer's individual style, or depend on the fact that both concertos are written for fortepiano. Without a view on which similarities between concertos are essential to their being concertos, and which are not, Cecilia cannot be sure whether she is understanding the work merely as an instance of its type, or for the sake of its individuality, or for its success in combining and reconciling the two.

Of course, Cecilia is not likely to pose the question so bluntly as I did above—"why is its being put together this way rather than that significant to its being a concerto as opposed to being a symphony?" After she has listened to the first movements of Mozart's symphonies and concertos (of post-1778), I would expect Cecilia to ponder the following: "why do the concertos have more tunes than the symphonies and why do those tunes come where they do?" (That is: what is it about the concerto that it needs more tunes if it is to do what it should within the framework of sonata form?)

The opening movements of Mozart's post-1778 symphonies present a number of thematic ideas in different keys and play these off against each other, sometimes developing the possibilities of one or more at length and exploring a range of keys, until a modified version of the thematic material returns, firmly anchored in the home key. The symphony seems to be intended to reveal the musical possibilities of the material presented, aiming for the generation of interest and diversity from limited resources, so that economy, integration, and unity are no less important than is contrast. By contrast, the concerto gives special prominence to textural contrasts in that it aims to present a soloist as an individual (or a group of soloists as a unit) standing over and against the orchestral background. Sometimes the tutti (full orchestra) opposes itself to the voice of the soloist; at other times material is shared in a conversation between the soloist and groups within the orchestra, with the former elaborating and decorating the ideas or commenting on them. Because the first statement of the exposition is reserved for the orchestra,[5] in order to establish the individuality of the soloist it is necessary to hold back important thematic material until the second exposition. As a result, the two expositions differ and so too will the recapitulation, in which material exclusive to each of the expositions must be integrated. The broad outlines of sonata form can be adapted to accommodate the rather different projects embodied in the symphony and the concerto, and Mozart applies consistent principles to this adaption, so that, as soon as one becomes interested in detail, the first movements of the symphonies and the concertos can be heard to belong to distinct structural types.

In some of the symphonies in question Cecilia finds that a slow introduction begins the first movement (K. 425, 504, 543). In all cases she finds that two subject groups are presented in the exposition. They contrast tonally, and/or thematically and/or in their expressive character. Roughly speaking, the first subject group is in the tonic and the second subject group is in the dominant major (or in the relative major if the tonic is minor). The second subject group frequently has a cantabile (singing) style, features chromatic decoration and allows more prominence to the wind instruments as soloists. Each subject group might end with a codetta. The two groups are separated by a bridge passage which is modulatory. The key of the second subject group usually is preserved in a following bridge and coda. The coda and codettas often are related and share a strongly cadential character. The various bridges sometimes are related to each other. Sometimes these bridges develop material shared with the subject groups; sometimes they contain sequential passage-work of no thematic distinction; sometimes they contain new thematic ideas with sufficient character to stand on their own. The exposition is not always repeated in the performances Cecilia hears, but she reads that it is marked with a sign which means that it is to be repeated. (K. 319 and 338 are the last of the symphonies from which the notated repeat is absent.) The following section usually is half the length of the (unrepeated) exposition and sometimes alludes to or develops earlier material, as well as containing modulations. In the earlier symphonies this section functions as a transition to the recapitulation; from K. 504 onwards the development of material is more extensive, with contrapuntal passages and the like. Occasionally the first subject is announced as if the recapitulation has begun, but subsequent events reveal this not to be the case. Sometimes the recapitulation is prepared by a pedal on the dominant; the recapitulation always heralds a return to the tonic. Changes between the recapitulation and the exposition usually are confined to these: the modulatory passage which precedes the second subject group is modified so that the key remains in the tonic; there may be some extension of the final coda; the second subject group and the music which follows usually is in the tonic key—where the movement's key is major, frequently this involves no more than transposition. Cecilia reads that, in some symphonies (one version of K. 385, as well as K. 504), it is indicated that the combination of development and recapitulation should be repeated, though she notes that this instruction is not respected in the performances she hears. (While most of Mozart's symphonies after 1778 conform readily to the

Exposition													
1	9	24	37	49	56	62	68	71	75	81	89	94	101
Fx2	C1	B1			S					B2			C2
		x	x'		m	m	n	p	p'	q	r	r'	
C			G							C	c	C	G

Exposition													
1	9	24	37	49	56	62	68	71	75	81	89	94	101
Fx2	C1	B1			S					B2			C2
		x	x'		m	m	n	p	p'	q	r	r'	
C			G							C	c	C	G

Development
121

Recapitulation													
189	197	212	226	237	244	250	256	259	263	269	277	282	289
Fx2	C1	B1'			S					B2'			C2'
		x"	x'		m	m	n	p	p'	q'	r	r'	
C	c	Bb	G	C					F	f	F	C	

FIGURE 1. Symphony No. 41 in C, K. 551—The "Jupiter"

general model, Cecilia notices that the first movement of Symphony No. 38, K. 504, does not.)

I offer only two examples.

The first movement of Mozart's last symphony provides a copybook example of the structural type (see Fig. 1). The bridge to the second subject (B1) elaborates elements of the first subject in some detail. The recapitulation of this bridge uses a subtle touch in presenting material from the first subject in the tonic minor. (Cecilia observes that Mozart frequently slides briefly to the tonic minor, shading with darkness even the most cheerful of the works in major keys.) The second subject group involves internal repetition and development. Despite its fluid character and a certain amount of chromaticism, plainly there are motivic relationships between the first and second subject. The bridge to the coda begins in a startlingly powerful manner and introduces without preparation the tonic minor. The transposed version of this passage in the recapitulation is modified, with a shift from the minor to the major on the subdominant. The coda begins with a thematic idea of some distinction which, because of its character, sounds rather like a second subject.

My other instance is the "Linz" symphony of 1783 (see Fig. 2). The first movement of this symphony differs in minor respects from that of the "Jupiter." It begins with a slow introduction and shows some tonal variety in the second subject, the first part of which emphasizes the relative minor of the dominant in the exposition and of the tonic in the recapitulation. The shortness of the development section is not unusual for the earlier symphonies.

The first movements of Mozart's post-1778 concertos display a richer, more complex form than is found in his symphonies' first movements. There never is a slow introduction. The first, that is "orchestral," exposition presents the first subject (F) and the orchestral second subject (OS) in the tonic. (This orchestral second subject is absent in K. 415 and 459; in K. 413 and 449 it appears in the dominant rather than the tonic, and in K. 466 a shortened version is stated in the tonic's relative major.) In two concertos (K. 467 and 491) the first subject returns before the close of the orchestral exposition. The second, that is "solo," exposition sometimes is separated from the first by a bridge (K. 415, 450, 466, 482, 491, and 503) which introduces the solo instrument; otherwise the soloist enters with or alongside the first subject. In a number of works (K. 365, 450, 467, 482, 491, and 503) the orchestral second subject (OS) is replaced by a "solo" second

Introduction	Exposition								
1	20	30	42		72	88	106 111	120	
I	F	F'	B1		S		B2 C		
								x	
C				G a	G e G e G				

Exposition								
20	30	42		72	88	106 111	120	
F	F'	B1		S		B2 C		
							x	
C			G a	G e G e G				

Development
123

Recapitulation							
163	173	185		218	234	252 257	103
F	F'	B1'		S		B2 C'	
							x'
C		F C		a C a C			

FIGURE 2. Symphony No. 36 in C, K. 425—The "Linz"

subject (SS); the second subject (OS or SS) appears in the dominant (or relative major where the tonic is minor) and is shared between soloist and orchestra, with the winds often prominent. In addition, the solo exposition usually includes a theme, sometimes in the minor, given exclusively for the soloist's use (L). Typically the second exposition is about a third as long again as the first. The development generally is half or more the length of the second exposition. Often it features sequential passages from the soloist rather than thematic development as such. The recapitulation repeats the second exposition, but interpolates material which has not been heard since the first exposition. If the orchestral second subject was replaced in the second exposition, it returns along with the solo second subject in the recapitulation (except in K. 365). In the recapitulation the codetta which closed the second exposition is followed by the cadenza and the movement is brought to an end by a coda which derives usually from the first, rather than the second, exposition. Because it contains material exclusive to each exposition, the recapitulation is longer than either, and the cadenza usually adds a further twenty bars or more to its length.

As examples I offer both K. 364 and 503 (see Figs. 3 and 4); it is instructive to observe how similar are these two given that the first marks the early days of Mozart's maturity, whereas the second is among his last concertos. In K. 364 the first subject is truncated and decorated in the second exposition; in the recapitulation it includes elements from the versions in both expositions as well as the bridge which leads to the soloists' version. The solo subject (L) first appears in the relative minor of the tonic and is recapitulated in the relative minor of the subdominant before returning to the tonic. The orchestral second subject (OS), which is announced in the tonic, is replaced in the second exposition by a solo second subject (SS) which is presented in the dominant; both themes return in the tonic in the recapitulation. The final coda combines bridging material first heard in the orchestral exposition (B1) with material which served as a codetta to the soloists' statement of the first subject (C2). (All of the codetta passages are related.) Mozart heard the famous orchestra at Mannheim in 1777 and elements of Mannheim style are apparent, especially a crescendo (MC—from which B1 is derived) which features both in the orchestral exposition and in the development.

K. 503 differs structurally from K. 364 in only a few respects: the treatment of the first

First Exposition/Tutti						Solo
1 4	13	25 27	38	46	58	70
F		C1	OS	MC	B1	B2
a b	c	d				
Eb						

Second Exposition					Tutti	
78	90 93	106	126	133		158
F'	C2 L	B3	SS	B4		C3
a d a d'						
Eb	c	Bb				

Development/Solo
168

Recapitulation/Tutti					Solo					Tutti	
223	229	237	249 252	265	285	293	301	328	CAD 25 bars	364	376
F"	B2	F'	C2 L'	B3	SS	OS	B4	C3		B1	C2
a b'											
Eb			f Eb	Ab Eb							

FIGURE 3. Sinfonia Concertante for Violin and Viola in Eb, K. 364

subject is more orthodox (though the subject itself is more adventurous in that it merges with the bridge and includes a shift to the tonic minor); the bridge between the two expositions (B1) does not return; the solo subject (L) is in the relative major of the tonic minor; the tonic minor is hinted at constantly in the expositions and makes a noteworthy appearance at the end of the first subject (motive "a") and in the first statement of the orchestral second subject (OS); the orchestral second subject (OS) is repeated in the tonic major in the first exposition, but is stated only once (in the tonic major) in the recapitulation; the development is worthy of the name and is given over entirely to the orchestral second subject (OS); the final coda is based on the coda of the first exposition (C2); most of the bridges are closely related to, and develop material found at, the close of the first subject (motive "a").

The first movement of Mozart's final concerto (See Fig. 5), K. 622, is a cruiser to K. 503's battleship. The orchestral exposition does not include a second subject (a device restricted to K. 415 and 459 among the piano concertos), but does develop the first subject in a manner which is recalled in the second exposition and recapitulation (B1). The development concentrates on the first subject and on the bridges based on it. In the recapitulation, the solo subject (L) follows the solo second subject (SS) and is presented in the relative minor of the key in which the second subject appears. The cadenza arrives unexpectedly early. A version of the codetta of the bridge (C2) introduced in the orchestral exposition is inserted before the movement's final coda.

Summary: Mozart's concertos of the period are much more complex in structure than are his corresponding symphonies in that they introduce more thematic ideas and, in doing so, distinguish the expositions from each other and from the recapitulation. All this plainly results from the attempt to provide the soloist with new material (L and SS), so it stands out as an individual, rather than having it simply repeat material presented by the orchestra in the first exposition. There is no similar reason for differentiating the expositions and recapitulation of the symphony, while the goals of economy and precision also count against a proliferation of themes. (Cecilia will notice, though, that in K. 503 and 622 the close relation between themes and bridges makes for a unity and intensity which bears comparison with the symphonies.)

The comparison of the first movements of the concerto and the symphony in terms of Cecilia's question ("why does the concerto have/need more themes?") was fruitful. A close lis-

First Exposition/Tutti								Solo
1	19	25	41	51	66	71	83	91
Fx2		C1		OS	C2			B1
	a	m	n		p	q	r	
C	c	C		G	c	C		

Second Exposition									Tutti	
112	130	136	143	149	157	170	187	193	214	219
Fx2		B2	C2	L	B3	SS	B4		C1'	
	a'						a"	s	m'	n'
C	c	G		Eb		G				

Development/Solo
229

Recapitulation/Tutti			Solo									
290	308	314	321	327	335	345	365	372	378	399	CAD	411
Fx2		B2	C2	L	B5	SS'	OS'	B4		C1"		C2'
	a'						a"	s		m"		p' q' r
C	c	G		Eb		C						

FIGURE 4. Piano Concerto in C, K. 503

tening to the works reveals a connection between details of their structure and the different functions served by each musical type. With that understanding, Cecilia now is capable of much finer discriminations than formerly, so that she hears Symphony No. 38, K. 504 (the "Prague") as complexly structured (for a symphony) and K. 622 as comparatively simple (for a concerto), though the "complex" symphony contains fewer thematic ideas than the "simple" concerto. She can distinguish those aspects of structure which belong to the work qua concerto or symphony and those which mark the particular work as an individual of its type.

As I said, the method was fruitful in one case, but is it generally useful as an approach to musical understanding? I believe so and illustrate this now by considering a new example. I develop the contrast between the first movement of the symphony and the opera overture.

What is the function of the opera overture? It should introduce the opera, lasting long enough to allow the audience to settle but not so long that impatience sets in before the rise of the curtain. It should set the tone of the work, establishing not only the work's key, if it has one, but also a suitable mood. Finally, it should, if it can, establish a connection of some intimacy

between itself and the body of the work (whereas it is not at all usual in Mozart's case that an explicit connection be established between the various movements of a sonata or symphony). What aspects of symphonic treatment within sonata form count against the pursuit of these goals? In the symphony the first and second subject groups often contrast in their melodic and/or tonal and/or expressive character, and the emphasis and reconciliation of these differences gives the movement much of its character. By contrast, the opera overture usually should aim to present a consistent, uniform mood. Also, the argumentative, dialectical style of the symphony makes demands on the listener's attention and concentration which might not be appropriate in the context of the opera overture. Even if the overture should present a musically viable form, it cannot always do so merely by imitating the symphonic movement, though it shares with the symphony's first movement a general commitment to sonata form. One can predict that the formal model will be adapted to avoid undue contrasts (for example, in the second subject) and complexities (for example, in the development).

Cecilia listens to the overtures of the operas completed by Mozart after 1778:[6] *Idomeneo,*

First Exposition/Tutti

1	17	24	44	49
Fx2	C1	B1	C2	C3
A	E	A		

Second Exposition/Solo   **Tutti**

57	75	95	100	116	128	155	164
F+F*	B2	C4	SS	L	B1'	C1'	C5
A		a C	e E	c#	E		

Development/Solo

172

Recapitulation/Tutti   **Solo**   **Tutti**

251	269	283	288	304	316	344	347	352
F+F*	B2'	C4'	SS'	L	B1' (CAD)	C1'	C2'	C
A	aCda			A	f# A			

FIGURE 5. Clarinet Concerto in A, K. 622

King of Crete (K. 366 of 1780), *The Abduction from the Seraglio* (K. 384 of 1782), *The Impressario* (K. 486 of 1786), *The Marriage of Figaro* (K. 492 of 1786), *Don Giovanni* (K. 527 of 1787), *Così fan Tutte* (K. 588 of 1790), *The Magic Flute* (K. 620 of 1791), and *The Clemency of Titus* (K. 621 of 1791). She discovers a wide range of approaches, but it is possible to hear in many cases that the symphonic proportions and style of sonata form are modified for the operatic context. (One obvious change is in the absence of a repeat of the exposition.)

The overtures to *Impressario* and (especially) *Titus* allow for an orthodox development section, but the unsatisfactoriness of this approach in Mozart's mind is evident elsewhere. In *Giovanni, Così,* and *Flute* the development is relatively truncated. In *Idomeneo* and *Figaro,* the development section is no more than a bridge connecting the exposition to the recapitulation. In *Seraglio* the development is replaced by the theme from Belmonte's aria (No. 1), presented in the minor rather than the projected major. These modifications require others if the formal balance of the overture is not to be upset. The overtures of *Giovanni, Così,* and *Flute* involve slow introductions, reducing accordingly the length devoted to exposition, development, and recapitulation. The developmental treatment of material is shifted back into the exposition in the overtures of *Così* and *Flute.* The arrival of

the second subject group is delayed in *Idomeneo, Flute,* and *Figaro*—especially so in the latter case where we arrive *at* the dominant in the expected place, but do not reach the second subject group until later, where a firm A major cadence announces that we are *in* the dominant. This "squeezing" and "stretching" of the formal parameters has the effect of down-playing the development, so that the style is not argumentative.

The importance and distinctiveness of the second subject also is reduced, resulting in a tendency toward uniformity rather than contrast. In the overtures of *Seraglio* and *Così,* the second subject is derived directly from the first, and in *Flute* elements of the first subject remain present in the accompaniment of the second. As mentioned above, the extension of bridging passages postpones the arrival of the second subject in *Idomeneo, Figaro,* and *Flute,* so it seems like an afterthought. In *Figaro, Giovanni, Così,* and *Flute,* the second subject retains the expressive character of the first. In both *Idomeneo* and *Seraglio* the second subject group is excised altogether from the recapitulation.

The overtures show an affinity for their respective operas. Each overture establishes its opera's key. And in every case the emotional tone of the overture matches that of the work as a whole—skittish humor in the *opera buffa* (other than *Giovanni*) and majesty and pageantry in the *opera seria.* Chromaticism in the overtures of *Idomeneo* and *Giovanni* anticipates the sinister tragedies which are to follow; the fugal treatment of material indicates the underlying seriousness of the drama in *Flute;* the "Turkish" music of the overture in *Seraglio* draws attention to the exotic setting and prefigures the musical style associated with Pasha Selim and his followers. In *Seraglio* and *Giovanni* the overture leads directly into the first number, which in the latter case involves a modulation from the overture's home key. In *Titus* the order of the first and second subjects is reversed in the recapitulation, so the overture closes with flourishes suitable to the scene on which the curtain opens.

The most intimate connection between overture and work will be established by quotation, but there are obvious difficulties in the approach. The melodies of arias are of a length which would interrupt the flow of the overture if they are quoted; besides, without words the dramatic context which gives point to the aria is absent. Mozart replaces the development of the overture of *Seraglio* with a statement (in the minor) of the aria with which Belmonte begins the opera. (In this case the audience need not wait long before the significance of the melody is revealed.) More often, the overture shares with the opera not more than a motive or fragment. Only one brief figure is common to the overture of *Figaro* and the work as a whole (see bars 7–9 of No. 14); motives from the overture of *Idomeneo* return within the body of the work (note especially the chromatic figure in the first subject group which returns in No. 21, and parts of the second subject group which are hinted at in No. 8); flourishes first heard in the overture return in Act 2 of *Titus.*

Perhaps the most satisfactory approach to the thematic integration of overture and opera is that achieved in *Giovanni, Così,* and *Flute.* In these works a motive or idea, rather than a fully-fledged theme, is highlighted in the slow introduction of the overture and later takes on dramatic significance—in *Giovanni* it is the sinister, chromatic figuration which accompanies the arrival of the avenging statue; in *Così* it is the "così fan tutte" motive which returns with those words in No. 30; and, in *Flute,* it is the three chords which are associated with the three temples of Tamino's initiation (No. 9A). In the overtures of *Così* and *Flute,* the

motives return within the overture—in the former at the beginning of the coda and in the latter before the start of the development. In these cases the shared material is rather brief but highly recognizable. The introduction of the quotation in the overture does not compromise the overall structure, as is the case in *Seraglio,* for the motive appears before the exposition and, if restated, is interpolated between formal sections.

It has been useful to take guidance from structural differences between the overture and the symphony's first movement as indicating their different functions and, thereby, to come to a deeper understanding both of that function and of what it is in a given piece which marks it as an overture, as well as the individual overture it is. Encouraged by this, and with a deeper interest in music, Cecilia extends her careful listening of Mozart's music to other movements, and to other musical types. She wonders if there are consistent differences between trios, quartets and quintets, between serenades and piano sonatas, and so forth. She compares Mozart's dance music with the minuets of the symphonies. She returns to the concertos, wondering if there are differences between the concertos for fortepiano and the remainder. She returns to the overtures also, looking for distinctions between those for *opera seria, opera buffa* and *Singspiel.*

After all this, has Cecilia achieved a profound understanding of Mozart's music and the concertos and symphonies with which she began? It is not clear that she can be expert, for as yet she has no basis for comparison between Mozart and other composers of the period, so that she cannot sort features of Classical style from those individual to Mozart. She must broaden her horizons, comparing Mozart's last symphonies with Franz Joseph Haydn's "London" symphonies, and Mozart's "Haydn" quartets with Haydn's Op. 33, 50, 54, 55, 64 sets, and so on. Perhaps she could have the fullest grasp of Classical style only if she could find within it the seeds which were to flower into the Romantic movement. So she might turn her attention to Beethoven, whose early symphonies, quartets, sonatas and piano concertos imitate Mozartean structures.

Again, has Cecilia then achieved a profound understanding of Mozart's concertos and symphonies? Not yet. She knows nothing of the influences which shaped Mozart's personal style; neither is she familiar with the structural types from which the concerto and the symphony sprang. She regards the works as musical bastards, having no awareness of the lines of breeding which shape their forms. When she turns to works written by Mozart before 1777, Cecilia hears music influenced not by Franz Joseph Haydn and the Mannheim school, but by J. C. Bach, Michael Haydn and the Italian style. In structure, these earlier works owe far less to sonata form than to older, Baroque formal types. The form of the Galant concerto, for example, depended more on the alternation of sections for the full orchestra (tutti, or ritornello) with those featuring the soloist than on thematic development or patterns of tonal change. The overall structure of Mozart's earlier original concertos might better be heard not in terms of sonata form, but as Tutti (first exposition), Solo followed by Tutti (second exposition), Solo (development), Tutti followed by Solo and closing with a Tutti (recapitulation). Where the development is little more than a bridge or transition, such a work will come nearer to possessing a binary (TST/TST) than ternary (exposition/development/recapitulation) structure. Aspects of the early concertos which seem crude and puzzling when heard as aspiring to sonata form now will make more sense when heard as arising from the concerto grosso. And this way of approaching the music will carry over into a consideration of the later concertos too, for now Cecilia will hear the form not so much as a departure from the symphonic ideal caused by the exigencies of writing for a solo instrument, but as the healthy issue of a successful marriage between the Baroque concerto and the Classical symphony. (She might also like to reconsider the first movement of K. 504, the "Prague," in light of this idea.) Similarly, when she learns that the symphony arose from the *sinfonia* which in the early Baroque introduced the opera, she will be less inclined to view the operatic overture as a trivialized symphonic movement and more likely to hear both as the natural children of a common ancestor, each taking the course it does in response to its environment.

Earlier I emphasized that the "problem" of the concerto arises from the fact that the first exposition is the preserve of the orchestra, so that the solo instrument has to establish its individuality in the second exposition. One way of solving this "problem" would be by dispensing with a double exposition. Cecilia could not appreciate why this option was not available to Mozart without recognizing that he was heir to styles and conventions which the composer might modify and enrich, but which he was not free to reject out of hand. Until she considers the precedents against which Mozart works, she treats the structures of his works as created *ex nihilo* and does not understand where Mozart was working with musical givens.

A grasp of the conventions with and against which Mozart worked is crucial if one is to appreciate not only the successes, but also some of the failures. Early in the final, fourth act of *Figaro* both Marcellina and Basilio sing grand arias. The dramatic impulsion of the work, built up and sustained over more than two hours, here is halted and dissipated. But if the arias are cut (as now they commonly are), the final act lacks the length and weight needed if it is to balance the mighty second act. Why did Mozart and da Ponte write those arias rather than something else? The answer, of course, is that they were bound to include those arias, whatever the price. They wrote within a tradition which emphasized (yet more than now is the case) the star-status of the singer. Many of the conventions of the genre were dictated by the singers' importance. Each major character had to be given at least two "exit" arias. (The exit from the stage promotes applause and provides the opportunity for bows and encores.[7]) Each secondary character with more than a walk-on part was to receive at least one, large, exit aria. Those who sang the parts of Marcellina and Basilio had to be given their due—there could be no choice in the matter. In effect, Mozart and da Ponte had painted themselves into a corner; they had run out of plot before all the musical debts had been paid.

Mozart was aware of the manner in which the conventions worked against the marriage of music and drama and he did much to alter the practice of the time, but there could be no alternative to working with and through the established tradition. The conventions provided the vehicle, the framework, which, with da Ponte, he set in motion. Mozart's aim was to bring the characters to life in the music.[8] This can be achieved only if the action takes place in the "numbers," rather than being confined largely to *secco recitatives*. Where the action takes place in the numbers, pace and timing, characterization, expression, humor and dramatic/musical structure all fall under the composer's, rather than the librettist's, control. Mozart's progress as an opera composer might be charted through a consideration of the ways in which he attempted to achieve the goal of containing the dramatic action within the numbers. The accompanied recitative becomes prominent and often is merged with a following aria; there is a general tightening up of the introductions to arias and ensembles; arias tend to become shorter and less ornate; in some cases the aria is integrated into an ensemble. Where possible the aria involves action rather than reflection; vocal display, if used, serves a dramatic point. Ensembles become a focus of action—the ratio of arias to ensembles falls steadily. In particular, the finales (comprised of continuous music uninterrupted by recitative) become longer (extending toward the middle of the act rather than prolonging it).[9]

Mozart subverted, without rejecting, operatic conventions with the point of glorifying the singer in his attempt to create a satisfactory dramatic form from a musical one. This is most evident in *Figaro*. Beaumarchais's play, adapted by da Ponte, was banned for its criticism of the aristocracy. The opera concerns the attempt of Count Almaviva to have first "use" of Susanna on her marriage to Figaro, though the Count officially has renounced the *droit du seigneur,* and with the attempts of Figaro to thwart the Count's plans. The battle is between an aristocrat and his servant. As one might expect, this political conflict is highlighted in arias sung by the protagonists—Figaro hopes to play the tune to which his master will dance (No. 3) and the Count rails against his servant's cheek (rather than out of sexual frustration) (No. 17). That is to say, the political message is foregrounded by Mozart in his use of standard operatic techniques. But there is another agenda driving the action, and this is revealed no less clearly (though more subtly) in the music and the opera's structure. The opera is mistitled—it should have been called "The Marriage of Susanna."

Susanna dominates the action, but does not occupy the spotlight in doing so. The plans she hatches with the Countess win the day—Figaro's plans all founder. Susanna controls the action through her relationships with others and not, as in the manner which is standard in opera of the day, through her arias. In fact, one way or another, her importance is masked throughout. She deals with others on a one-to-one basis (as in the duets), or she seeks the relative anonymity of shadows, or she disguises herself to present the public identity of others. But her importance is ever-present in the music—she is above all Mozart's creation.

As a major character Susanna is entitled to two arias, but neither is a set-piece conforming to the standard model. The first concerns the dressing of Cherubino as a girl; usually Susanna kneels by the stage while the page steals the limelight. The second, a declaration of love, is brief and typically indirect in that, teasingly, it is addressed to the eavesdropping Figaro who takes it, as he is meant to, as intended for the Count. Susanna's pivotal role is revealed in the ensembles. The opera contains six duets and Susanna appears in each. (Only Figaro shares more than one duet with her.) She is featured also in each of the two trios, as in all the other ensemble pieces. The first duet, between Susanna and Figaro, models the dramatic structure of the work; both Figaro and Susanna introduce their own thematic material, but by the end of the duet Figaro has joined with Susanna in singing her music. In several cases (Nos. 7 & 18) her music impels the action forward through the introduction of tonal contrasts. In the finale to the second act, it is Susanna's appearance which heralds the move to the dominant major which commits the finale to the circle of fifths which drives it to its conclusion.

Susanna's part in the work cuts across the divisions of class in focusing on a more fundamental division between the sexes. Susanna mocks the men irrespective of their class-status. She amuses herself at the Count's expense with feigned slips of the tongue (No. 16), just as she mocks Figaro with his own vengeance music ("Di qua non muovo il passo" in the Finale of Act IV). Meanwhile, she co-operates as an equal with her "class enemy," Rosina, the Countess. Those who view the opera as political while missing the centrality of her role do not take their analysis far enough in that they fail to appreciate the sexual politics in accordance with which all women, who derive their outward status only from their husbands, comprise a social class the status of which is lower than that of a male servant.

In *Figaro* Mozart operates within the context of conventions and forms which were known to the performers and audience, and with a plot which draws on familiar themes from the *commedia dell'arte,* all of which establishes the foreground of dramatic action. But the opera has a more subtle structure, which is no less a musical than a dramatic form, created by Mozart. This form places Susanna at the opera's heart. It is the interplay between, and reconciliation of, these two structures which makes *Figaro* what it is. Cecilia could understand the opera— that is, could appreciate why it has the strengths and weaknesses that it does—only if she had an awareness of the conventions which provide the scaffold from which the composer works and of the historical (and social) context which gave those conventions their life.

The moral is simple: If a piece's being a quartet as opposed to a symphony, say, makes a difference to how it should be written which will be audible to the attentive listener, then the listener will need to have some notion of the relevant respects in which quartets and symphonies are distinct. (What I take to be the same point can be put this way: If the quartet poses the composer problems—of form, instrumentation, or whatever—which differ from those raised by the symphony, then one cannot recognize the solutions for what they are unless one has some idea of the problem and its significance.) Learning what it is that makes a symphony a symphony in a given period involves a great deal of close listening, reflection on what has been heard, and some idea of the social place and function of such music. While most philosophers who write on musical understanding emphasize the importance of close attention to the music with an ear to its macro-structure, they say next to nothing about the knowledge and experience required if the listener is to interpret the musical significance of that macro-structure. This is a serious deficiency in their views.

We live in an age in which it is regarded both as offensive and as false to suggest that there is not democratic equality among all kinds of music

in their artistic value and among all listeners in their understandings of music. It also seems to be widely held that understanding comes simply as a result of one's giving oneself over to the music (as if there must be something wrong with a work if it does not appeal at first hearing). The idea that there are worthwhile degrees of musical understanding which might be attained only through years of hard work, and that there are kinds of music which yield their richest rewards only to listeners so prepared, smacks of an intellectual elitism which has become unacceptable, not only in society at large, but in the universities. "Anti-democratic" ideas are rejected not just for music, of course, but across the social and political board, but the case for musical "democracy" is especially strong since almost everyone loves and enjoys some kind of music. Nevertheless, the arguments I have developed above suggest to me that many music lovers are mistaken in equating the enjoyment they experience with the pleasure afforded by the deeper levels of understanding.[10]

1. The title of the structure is misleading, for it is a form found within individual movements rather than a way of uniting movements in an entire sonata; also, it is a form found in most extended movements, whether the work be overture, sonata or symphony. At times the structure also is called "first movement form," but this is not an improvement, for the form is used quite extensively in other movements.

Sometimes one hears it said that Mozart and Haydn did not know what sonata form is, because they composed prior to the technical specification of the formal type by musicologists. I regard this view as silly. Mozart and Haydn lacked the *terminology* which later was codified, but they certainly knew the structural *functions* performed by the various parts of the music they wrote, and I take that to be what justifies claims about their writing in sonata form.

2. It should be apparent that, in discussing the work's form, I have in mind audible, macro-musical chunks, like themes. The education of the ear, the concentration of the listener, the familiarity with the music, and many other considerations affect what an individual might find audible, but most of the features I mention in the example analyses are plainly audible, I think. Many inaudible features might

give rise to audible, artistically important effects. A person aware of the causal influence of these features might, nevertheless, be unable to *hear* them doing their work. This is one reason why music analysts sometimes concern themselves with uncovering musical relationships which cannot be heard. Cecilia is not seeking this kind of understanding; she aims to enrich her experience of the work as sound so far as possible and to understand that experience. For my view of the importance of factors which are not readily audible, see Stephen Davies, "Attributing Significance to Unobvious Musical Relationships," *The Journal of Music Theory* 27 (1983): 203–213. For further useful discussion see Mark DeBellis's "Conceptions of Musical Structure," *Midwest Studies in Philosophy* 16 (1991): 378–393.

3. See Monroe C. Beardsley's "On Understanding Music" in *On Criticizing Music: Five Philosophical Perspectives*, ed. Kingsley Price (Johns Hopkins University Press, 1981), pp. 55–73; Michael Tanner's "Understanding Music," *Proceedings of the Aristotelian Society* Supp. Vol. 59 (1985): 215–232; Malcolm Budd's "Understanding Music," *Proceedings of the Aristotelian Society* Supp. Vol. 59 (1985): 233–248; Roger Scruton's "Musical Understanding and Musical Culture" in *What Is Music?: An Introduction to the Philosophy of Music*, ed. Philip Alperson (New York: Haven Publications, 1987; Pennsylvania State University Press, forthcoming); Peter Kivy's *Music Alone: Philosophical Reflection on the Purely Musical Experience* (Cornell University Press, 1990); Jerrold Levinson's "Musical Literacy," *The Journal of Aesthetic Education* 24 (Spring 1990): 17–30; Wayne D. Bowman's "The Values of Musical 'Formalism,' " *The Journal of Aesthetic Education* 25 (Fall 1991): 41–59. I agree with much that these authors write—and in this might differ from Nicholas Cook's *Music, Imagination, and Culture* (Oxford: Clarendon Press, 1990)—it is what they leave out which concerns me. In fairness I should note that some (such as Levinson and Tanner) leave out less of what I value than do others.

4. As will become evident, I believe that, because their identities and features depend very much on their historical/cultural location and their artistic categories, one can have the fullest understanding of a given work only if one has a similar understanding of all the works and conventions which establish its context, and these will include prior and subsequent pieces, as well as contemporary ones. Contextualism of this sort seems to generate a paradox: one cannot understand x without understanding y and z, but one cannot understand y without understanding x and z, and one cannot understand z without understanding x and y,

and so on as the number of instances multiply. It seems as if understanding never can begin. At least part of the solution to this paradox depends on realizing that understanding comes in degrees; understanding can be partial. One reason for thinking that the paradox must be soluble is this: the reasoning which generates the paradox also shows that no first language could be invented, and that no individual could acquire a language.

5. The soloist plays along with the tutti, but should not be conspicuous in doing so. A solo violin would play along with the first violins, a fortepiano would accompany the 'cellos' bass-line and might act as a continuo instrument.

6. Because the overtures were written last, the operas which were not completed do not have overtures.

7. At the second performance of *Figaro* five numbers had to be repeated, at the third, seven. Emperor Joseph II, in a note to Count Rosenberg on 9 May 1786, wrote as follows: "To prevent the excessive duration of the opera, without however prejudicing the fame often sought by opera singers from the repetition of vocal pieces, I deem the enclosed notice to the public (that no piece for more than a single voice is to be repeated) to be the most reasonable expedient. You will therefore cause some posters to this effect to be printed." *Mozart: A Documentary Biography*, ed. Otto Erich Deutsch, trans. Eric Blom, Peter Branscombe, and Jeremy Noble (London: Adam & Charles Black, 1966), p. 275.

8. By no means is this the only approach which might be taken to opera. The masque, from which opera evolved, was concerned with spectacle rather than drama. The element of spectacle retained its importance in later times—especially in the French tradition, where long ballets were included in the opera, for example.

9. Peter Kivy writes of *Così*: "Its 'characters' therefore are not Fiordiligi, Dorabella, Gugliemo, Ferrando; they are *the* soprano, *the* mezzo-soprano, *the* heroic tenor, etc. They are instruments in a *sinfonia concertante*, instruments with proper names. ... [L]ike the characters of *opera seria*, the characters of *Così fan tutte* are as close to being character types as they can be without ceasing to be characters at all." *Osmin's Rage: Philosophical Reflections on Opera* (Princeton University Press, 1988), p. 259. I can see how one might arrive at this view if one approached the work as if it were isolated from Mozart's earlier operas, but, given the pattern of development apparent in those works and its continuation in *Così*, either Kivy is mistaken or his claims need much more detailed support than he offers.

10. I am grateful for helpful discussion of an earlier draft of this paper with Robert Nola.

JAMES MANNS

On Composing "By the Rules"

The present paper aims to provide insight into the relationship between particular musical works and the rules of composition toward which such works are oriented. We sometimes feel prompted to ask: Do compositional rules constitute formulas for good music? Are they, that is to say, something akin to hypothetical imperatives of artistic conduct; or do they possess no more coercive force than, for instance, a museum guide book, which one follows closely at the outset but discards after developing a sense of the layout of the place?

The moment this question is posed, however, a couple of others, more fundamental yet, clamor to be answered: (a) Just what *is* a rule of composition? and (b) When can a composer be said to be following a certain rule or set of rules? These are not easy questions to answer. There exist, for example, Baroque treatises that delineate the proper procedure involved in fugal construction, yet subsequent scholarship has been known to step in quite unabashedly, void these writings, and offer in their place an account of the "real" rules pertinent to that form.[1] And we are not always lucky enough even to have any contemporary treatises. It was Carl Czerny, after all, not Haydn or Beethoven (or even Stamitz or Clementi) who first laid claim to having formalized the compositional procedure we now know as sonata form, and he did so in 1840—thus making explicit the paradigmatic Classical form at a point in time entirely subsequent to the Classical period.

I proceed in this paper by taking on this latter pair of questions first, so that we might reach agreement on what the rules are and who, over the centuries, has been obedient to them. Once this is accomplished, we will be in a position to judge how closely the rules have been followed by the best of composers and the worst of composers. More specifically, I give critical consideration first to the approach which regards the rules of any era as those practices which are adhered to *universally* by composers. Secondly, I evaluate a position which regards rules not as general formulas such as one might find in a textbook, but as generative principles indissolubly linked to individual works. Thirdly, I offer my own interpretation as to what should be taken to be the rules of composition. This turns out to be an endorsement of the type of formulas the textbooks offer, although this endorsement has to be coupled with the acceptance of an important distinction, namely, that between being *obedient to* a rule and being *mindful of* it. And fourthly, with some concept at last in hand as to what a rule actually consists in, I scrutinize the logical behavior of this concept, in light of the actual careers enjoyed by certain rule systems and would-be rule systems.

I

There is no shortage of theorists who contend that in order to count as a rule, a given principle must be adhered to by all legitimate practitioners in any era. The two theorists whose ideas I present here—Graham George and Adele Katz—are similar in that both look to the tonal aspect of music in their search for foundational principles, though their accounts of what ultimately constitute such principles turn out to be quite different in character.

A. George claims, in his book *Tonality and Musical Structure,* that if we focus on music of the period stretching from Baroque through Romantic times, it is only in terms of a process he calls "tonal opposition" that we can comprehend works of this period.[2] "Sonata form," as the textbooks characterize it, hardly fits any of the music we still listen to which supposedly adheres to that form; and all we can say of any of Bach's fugues, he claims, apart from indicating certain patterns of tonal opposition, is that after the exposition is over, anything, thematically speaking, can happen.[3] And this is not saying much. He concludes:

> To insist on pigeon-holing every musical process is an infallible way of paralyzing the capacity for aesthetic perception. *Yet every piece of music must derive its shape from a principle governing the relationship of its parts,* and we cannot appreciate—or even apprehend—subtleties until we have grasped the commonplace possibilities inherent in the operation of the parent principle.[4]

This "parent principle" of tonal opposition consists, he contends, in the alternation of a fundamental key with "bright side" and "dark side" harmonies, bright side harmonies being those to the "sharp" side of the fundamental key, dark side harmonies those to its "flat" side. Such an alternation creates what he terms a "tonal rondo," the basic pattern of which would be "tonic-bright side-tonic-dark side-tonic."[5] Of course, within this pattern much variation is permissible, and it is not the only pattern possible—for example, Bach preferred, according to George, a "home-dark-middle-home" scheme. But whatever patterns might be discernible, they nevertheless can be seen to derive from the fundamental process. And it is this process alone to which composers were faithful during a most fertile century and a half or more. Those textbook rules which supposedly dictated the basic "shape" of a work were often, and easily, suspended in deference to tonal opposition.

B. Adele Katz, spokeswoman for that most influential of theorists, Heinrich Schenker, appeals to the notion of a primordial harmonic-melodic structure to account for a great diversity of compositional practices, some of which seem at times to be quite irregular.[6] She too rejects the traditional formal models as thoroughly uninformative regarding the true compositional process. If one looks at the works of Bach, Haydn, or Beethoven in terms of such models, she claims, they appear almost incoher-

ent; but this apparent incoherence can be shown to vanish if we scrutinize the manner in which these composers elaborated certain fundamental tonal formulas which can be said to *underlie* the variegated surfaces of their works. Such tonal formulas, therefore, can be taken to be regulatory principles under which particular instances—the works themselves—can be assimilated.[7]

Seen in this light, Katz argues, the harmonic ambiguities that have been detected in one of Bach's versions of the chorale "Herzliebster Jesu" easily resolve themselves into the working out of the basic harmonic progression.[8] And similarly, the vague introduction to Beethoven's C-major Quartet (Op. 59, No. 3) does not "wander, as in the dark," but exhibits a definite harmonic direction, when related to the depth structure of the movement as a whole.[9] And these are but two of a great number of examples she cites, each of which is called upon to illustrate one or another of the basic patterns whereby a tone is elaborated (prolonged) into an entire piece. One must, on her account, turn to the works of Schoenberg or Stravinsky in order to find any widespread abuse of basic principles, but certainly not to any of the masters from the Baroque through the Romantic period.

Here, then, we have two theories, each of which aims to construe the rules of composition in a fashion that would, so to speak, regularize even the most seemingly exceptional works from a rather broad segment of the history of Western music. In order to demonstrate that both of them aim wide of the mark, let me begin by drawing an analogy with another art form—painting.

Tonality, I suggest, has enjoyed a position in Western music of the past few centuries comparable to that of representation in traditional Western painting. Neither tonality nor representation is a necessary condition in the absence of which we would withhold from an entity the label "painting" or "musical composition," yet both are fundamental constituents of artistic perspectives that projected themselves through the centuries (longer, obviously, in the case of representation). The important point in this comparison is that an Italian apprentice, let us say, was not taught *to* represent the world pictorially: he was taught *how* to produce such representations. As no alternative presented itself it makes no sense to say that a painter of this era who painted representationally was *as such* obeying the rules. Similarly, regarding most of the period in music's history during which compositions were invariably tonal, it becomes vacuous to claim that because a fundamental adherence to the aim of orienting tones around a center can be discerned in a composer's works, therefore that composer, whatever other eccentricities his or her works might have manifested, was still composing in a lawlike manner. So long as no thought of doing otherwise ever occurred, the composer can in no meaningful sense be judged to have been constrained by or obedient to rules. A further comparison, that between the musical rule and the civil law, is appropriate here. The need for legislation only arises when certain citizens give indication that they might not behave in a socially desirable fashion. But a community in which respect for the property of others goes unquestioned has need of neither locks nor laws to guard against theft.

Might not the fact that Katz, Schenker, and George are all twentieth-century theorists lend a measure of corroboration to this contention? This, after all, is the century in which *alternatives* to tonality were first forwarded; so it is only natural that some theorists should now come to think that the time-honored procedure was (and perhaps is) in fact regulatory. Only at the edges of the expanse of time during which tonality reigned—as the practice was firming up around 1600, that is, and as it was coming apart, earlier in our own century—is it reasonable to view tonality as a regulatory system.[10] These edges, however, are not at all where George and Katz are looking. (The question of the life span of a rule is dealt with more thoroughly in Section IV.)

The lesson I would derive from this discussion, then, is that a rule thrives on the threat of contrariety—on the possibility that a practice which seems to have proven successful will be (unwittingly or intentionally) contravened; inevitably, so some believe, to the detriment of the composition. But where there is no such possibility, there is no need to crystallize practice into principle, and no grounds for ascribing anything as strong as "obedience" to a composer faithful to the practice.

II

Let us examine in this section an approach to rules of composition which aims to be more narrow than the one adopted by George and Katz, and which would have the further advantage of specifying how it is that *great* music is regulated. I refer to the position articulated by D. F. Tovey throughout his numerous and profound critical writings.

Now it is no secret that what have come to be regarded as the standard textbook rules prescribing how to construct a fugue or a sonata-allegro movement have frequently been broken, even during the time when they supposedly held sway, and frequently to good effect. Bach, the unsurpassed master of fugal composition, is equally unsurpassed in the liberties he seems to have taken with that form: recall George's claim, cited above, that "after the exposition is over, anything, thematically speaking, can happen." In a similar vein, J. A. Fuller-Maitland, in the *Oxford History of Music,* remarks that "the laws of fugue can be more clearly deduced from the works of the older, more conventional composers than from those of Bach."[11]

A similar liberty with sonata form is observable on Beethoven's part, increasing in intensity as his career progressed, while the mature Mozart never did manage to compose a "classical" piano concerto, though the ones he in fact wrote during that period stand to this day as quintessential specimens of Classical concerto writing. If the "standard text-book procedures" describe the rules of a particular form correctly, then a great many immortal works seem to have placed themselves outside the law. Therefore, should one be squeamish about calling the great composers lawless, the clear alternative is to reconceive the manner in which rules of composition function. This is precisely what Tovey does, by developing a notion of *artistic form* which "regularizes" many of the most seemingly eccentric works.

Tovey calls the more "traditional" accounts of compositional procedure "the perky generalizations of textbooks by writers who regard the great masters as dangerous, and who deduced their rules from the uniform procedures of lesser composers,"[12] and elsewhere refers contemptuously to "people who talk *a priori* nonsense about the sonata forms, as if these forms were stereotyped moulds into which you shovel your music in the hope that it may set there like a jelly."[13] Instead, he asserts, "every individual work must be judged on its own merits,"[14] claiming, for example, that "Beethoven's work developed so rapidly that he seems to be driven to invent a new technique for almost each composition."[15] More specifically, he urges that "we shall never make head or tail of the Ninth Symphony until we treat it as a law unto itself,"[16] and observes of Mozart's C-major Piano Concerto (K. 503) "all that we can be sure of is that nothing will be without its function, and that everything will be unexpected and inevitable."[17] Furthermore, he offers to provide analyses of each of Beethoven's late works, if need be, to demonstrate that "Beethoven's forms become more and more precise in his later works, and if thereby they become less and less like each other, this is what anybody who understands the nature of artistic forms as compared to living forms ought to expect."[18] Tovey's notion of "artistic form," therefore, not only permits an individual work to be formally unique yet formally proper: it *demands* that it be.

Such a view might at first glance appear quite appealing, releasing great works from any obligation to live up—or *down*—to those dreaded "textbook glosses." I believe, however, that closer scrutiny reveals its inadequacies both as a barometer of artistic value and as an account of the rules of composition capable of "making sense" out of a tradition.

First, let us consider the question of artistic value. It is evident that Tovey wishes his position to do explanatory justice to great music or great art, for invariably the works he cites are those which we hold in the highest regard, and it is they, likewise, which fit the traditional formulas most uncomfortably. I contend, however, that he fails to offer any real guidance in this area, and as Susanne Langer once observed, "an analysis to which the artistic merit of a work is irrelevant can hardly be regarded as a promising technique of art criticism."[19]

The fact seems to be that not only can a great composition be regarded as a law unto itself— so too can the not-so-great and the positively paltry. To the extent that Beethoven's Ninth contains elements which internally dictate the nature of its formation, so too does Neil Sedaka's "Calendar Girl." Call a mediocre artist's work boring, and he or she might well reply "I was striving to capture the very essence of boredom"—a job well done, in that case. Judge of a work that it just makes no sense, it doesn't hold together at all, and expect to be told: "Precisely! Neither does life!" And of course there is a certain measure of truth to the maxim which holds that it is only the mediocre who are always at their best.

In short, every composition accomplishes what it accomplishes, and if our estimate of "what it ought to accomplish" derives directly from our sense of what it in fact accomplishes, it is hard to see how either critic or composer could go wrong. Yet this seems to be precisely what Tovey has done: he has lived with certain works long enough to be told by them where they were going—they revealed, as it were, their "inner necessity." Unfortunately, his sense of this necessity is hopelessly grounded in the actuality of the work itself, and this is not the direction our modal inferences ought to go.

As with any theory having organicist leanings or commitments, Tovey's view suffers from its *retrospective* character: it judges of the inevitability or necessity of certain elements within a work after hearing them and only them in the context of that work. But what is the case is that each phrase, each gesture within any work (whether good or bad) is alive with alternative modes of continuation and completion. A composition can be viewed as a series of choices: a good composer makes interesting choices, while a mediocre one opts for the humdrum; neither option, however, is necessitated. Indeed, we can only wonder how many of Bach's "inevitable" gestures were penned over in later versions which have been lost to us! Talk of the inevitable in music, I contend, really boils down to asserting (a) I approve of X the way it is, and (b) I lack the creativity to conceive of any alternative which would be more effective. This is perhaps the reason a view such as Tovey's attaches itself so readily to great music, for it is in the great music that the techniques employed and the results produced quite outdistance the creative capacities of even the most imaginative of critics.

The above considerations accept that a composition could be a law unto itself only for the sake of reducing such a notion to vacuity. In truth, I would argue, no reasonable conception of "law" allows for individuals to be laws unto themselves. It may be contingently true that a rule, once enacted, is actually obeyed but once; yet in virtue of its being a rule there must exist the possibility that others—or even just one-self—*could* obey it at other times. Were this not the case, there would be no way to distinguish a rule from a whim. How would "vowing (i.e., laying down the law to oneself) to do X this one time only" be in the least different from just . . . doing X? As Tovey would have it, though, the law governing the formation of a work is inextricably bound to just that work, which, in turn, tumbles inevitably from the law of its formation. Viewed in this fashion, the notion of "law" seems quite expendable.

III

As different individually as they might be, the three interpretations of rules we have considered here do share a few telling similarities. First, they seem, quite unsurprisingly, to reflect a general agreement as to what music is most valuable, most *worth* accounting for—Bach, Beethoven, and Mozart are names which recur relentlessly in their analyses. Secondly, they all look with disfavor on the standard textbook accounts of musical forms, due to the poor correspondence between what these accounts prescribe and what the great works actually involve. And thirdly, each attempts to reformulate the rules of composition in a manner better capable of "accounting for" these great works. George and Katz do this by casting their nets so wide, so to speak, that no work, however guileful, can escape; Tovey, on the other hand, attempts to weave a net which will allow all but the great works to slip through it. Both approaches have been shown to be deficient.

In this section I should like to argue in support of those much maligned "textbook glosses," precisely for their ability to account for the great works as well as the not-so-great ones. Clearly, my argument turns on the manner in which the notion of "accounting for" a work is to be interpreted, so let us begin by examining this question.

It is obvious that all the above theoreticians regard it as the duty of analysis to supply a principle or principles capable of *exhaustively* accounting for what occurs in a musical composition. What is not obvious is *why* they should hold such a belief. It is likely that they are uncritically accepting a paradigm of explanation which would be appropriate within the natural sciences, for there, surely, it is proper to expect theoretical gaps, holes, and loose ends to be, respectively, bridged, plugged, and tied together. But art is not nature; hence, understanding or explaining art is not the same as understanding or explaining nature. While Tovey scoffs at the pusillanimity of those theorists who "regard the great masters as dangerous," he himself does not seem to be able to summon up the courage to allow for the possibility that certain practices (of which we approve—in which we delight) might properly be deemed *irregular*.

To be sure, it is easy to deviate from rules: ignorance of them or indifference toward them is all that is needed. Our own century has provided us with no shortage of pseudo- or would-be-artists whose creations were irregular for such reasons as these, as well as for even more pernicious ones such as brute iconoclasm or the urge for notoriety. It was perhaps out of their (justifiable) aversion to genuine artistic aberrations that Tovey and the others were led to adopt an inappropriate explanatory paradigm. I believe, however, that between the slavishly rule-bound and the aberrant lies a very fruitful middle ground, and I suggest we enter into it by distinguishing between being *obedient to* rules and being *mindful of* them.

When Mozart, in his A-major Piano Concerto (K. 488), devotes his entire development section to a theme which never appeared in the exposition, we can appreciate the new material to some extent by itself, but we will be considerably more appreciative if we know what should have occurred at that point in the composition, but didn't. Mozart knew, of course—he was *mindful* of the standard practice, and thereby knew what others would have done and what he was expected to do. What is special about his work, however, is the manner in which it refuses to fit the expected mold. And yet to refuse a demand openly is to give open acknowledgment of its existence.

How often do Beethoven's works invite comparisons with works of his lesser contemporaries! His Ninth Symphony has such an eerie, indefinite opening, but is it not heard in this manner after one has become accustomed to the firm, foursquare openings of symphonies by Spohr or Albrechtsberger, or Haydn in one of his less inspired moments? If all one knew of symphonies was the Ninth, there would be no reason to regard its opening measures as anything other than perfectly normal and straightforward. Likewise, do we not hear the majesty of its development section against the backdrop provided by any number of mechanical, perfunctory developments?

In short, those composers can be said to be mindful of a practice who allow it to contribute to the shaping of their musical ideas, *even if* in the end their ideas do not take on precisely the shape prescribed by that practice. And an audience is mindful of a practice when their expectations are guided by the patterns specified in that practice, *even though they might well find gratification in music which deviates strikingly from these patterns.*[20] I submit, then, that the proper goal of musicological analysis with respect to rules of composition is not to seek out rules which encompass all cases, but rather, to determine when and why obedience to them is effective, and when and why deviance from them is desirable.

Viewed from this perspective, those procrustean textbook practices provide a valuable service to composer, listener, and analyst alike, though it is clear that this perspective requires that we drop the qualifier "procrustean." It is when, for example, rules are taken in a procrustean sense that disputes can arise over such a question as whether the recapitulation section of a sonata is announced tonally or thematically. In fact, the two elements "should" coincide, but they are under no obligation to do so, and it can well be quite exciting when their return is "staggered." We will *listen* for their simultaneous occurrence, but we may take delight in the disconfirmation of our expectations. The irregularities discernible in the works of the great composers, in short, stand out clearly and significantly when these works are held up for comparison against the much maligned textbook procedures, while their importance— their "difference"—was quite obscured by the analyses of George, Katz, and Tovey. Given this more flexible interpretation of rules of composition, let us now look more closely at the logi-

cal and ontological dynamics which they exhibit.

IV

In pursuing these considerations, I find it helpful to orient my analysis to Max Black's by now classic essay "Notes on the Meaning of 'Rule.'"[21] Two points in particular are of concern here.

First, Black suggests that a rule becomes a rule simply by virtue of one's stating it as a rule: "And though it be the case that no one ever has or will ever play [read 'compose'] according to that rule, it is a rule for all that. It would be absurd for someone to murmur 'I wonder if there is any such rule?' for my answer supplied the rule."[22]

Secondly, a rule, in its central, regulatory sense, according to Black, can be said to have a "history."[23] Unlike the normal, past-directed sense of history, however, Black sees a rule's history as *commencing* with its *enactment,* thus stretching *ahead* in time from this point of enactment. Of these two points, I believe it is important to reject the first outright; and I should like to amend the second so as to make a special case of rules of composition. Let us begin by examining a rule's "history."

Rules of composition do, I believe, have histories of the sort that Black describes. They are not enacted, however, in the manner of civil statutes, but instead grow out of practices which precede them and thereby constitute their *real past.* This past, then, lays the foundation, not for the enactment of any such rules, but for their *articulation.* Normally, that is to say, any practice accepted as regulatory will likely be done so after a certain number of historical precedents have given testimony to its effectiveness. The principles of sonata form, for example, which governed music of the late eighteenth and early nineteenth centuries were not *enacted;* they were arrived at by a trial and error process, reflected in the music of K. P. E. Bach, Johann Stamitz, Josef Haydn, and others during the period from 1750–1770. Yet even so, it is my contention that we could not say they were rules unless practice *subsequent to* this trial and error period manifested some inclination toward obedience, which of course it did. It is this subsequent inclination toward obedience which corresponds to Black's sense of "history." But while a rule, according to Black, demands obedience only after it has become law, a rule of composition will become law *only after* a certain measure of obedience (in a weaker sense) has been manifested toward a certain practice.

As regards the first point above—that a rule becomes a rule simply by one's specifying it as such—this is not true of most kinds of rules, and certainly seems to be false concerning rules of artistic conduct. In making such a claim, Black was simply attempting to illustrate one important difference between rules and "things," namely, that if asked to give an example of thing x—an admiral, say—one supplies a name—Nelson—or a description—the man who defeated the French at Trafalgar—that will enable us to pick out an admiral, but when asked to give an example of a rule, no such intermediaries are involved; the rule is stated straightaway: "A pawn reaching the eighth rank must be exchanged for a piece."[24]

Now while the elimination of needless intermediaries or shadowy referents seems a laudable goal, Black steps across the bounds of good sense when he allows that *any* rule-like assertion, whether actual, such as the above, or fanciful, such as "A king can move two squares after both queens have been captured," capably fills the request for an example of a rule. For this latter sentence in truth states no rule; all it provides is an illustration of the grammatical form possessed by sentences used to express rules.

Black improves matters little by likening rules to questions and claiming that if one is asked to give an example of a question, a reply such as "Can termites sleep?" immediately fulfills the request. But here again all we have been offered is the grammatical form of a question, in which subject and verb are inverted and a question mark is placed at the end of the sentence. A real question, however, is an interrogative sentence which is thought or uttered at the threshold of inquiry; questions are not just stated, they are *posed, raised.*

Black seems to have taken what is only a necessary condition for the formation of a rule (or a question)—the grammatical shape it takes—as a sufficient condition for its exemplification. But there is another necessary condition which he has overlooked. A rule is not just a string of words of the form "It is mandatory that (in order to achieve result A) you do X"; it is a prescription (expressible in this form, obviously) which enjoys its prescriptive status within a *context* which generates and sustains it. A rule may be enacted, it may evolve, but in either case, the conventions governing its enactment or evolution are serious and strict and not at all as potentially whimsical as Black's contention makes it appear. To put these claims to the test, let us consider first the case of Anton Reicha, then that of Arnold Schoenberg.

In 1824 Reicha published a *Traité de haute composition musicale*,[25] in which he formulated certain "radical" ideas for the construction of a fugue, allowing, for example, for the possibility of thematic entries at all intervals, and not just the perfect ones. Coherent as they may have been, they suffered from one shortcoming, which did not go unnoticed to composers contemporary with and subsequent to him: they paid precious little heed to traditional procedures, being, it seems, an expression of Reicha's own ideas of what a fugue, or at least some fugue-like form, could or should be like. Quite likely as a result of this, there is no evidence that any composer who was then or is now regarded as significant (that is, whose works have "come down to us") paid any heed to Reicha's ideas.

In light of these considerations, would it not seem bizarre to judge that Reicha had articulated the—or even "a set of"—*rules* for fugal composition? Clearly it would be more appropriate to say that he forwarded certain *suggestions* as to how one might go about writing a fugue; but the very indifference of these suggestions to the past, and the further indifference of subsequent composers to them deprives them of any claim to regulative status, and reduces them to nothing more than an historically interesting curiosity.

A stronger test of this notion of a rule's temporal imbeddedness is posed by Schoenberg's dodecaphonic system of composition, which made its appearance precisely a century after the publication of Reicha's thought experiment. Actually, a certain degree of confirmation for the idea that a rule of composition properly emerges from a proximate past is provided by the very nature of the debate that was carried on between Schoenberg's supporters and his detractors, for both focus on whether his system had such a past, and both appear to have regarded it as important that it should. His critics claimed that the system in fact had no such past—that it constituted a radical break with previous practice—and that it was therefore artistically illegitimate. Supporters, on the other hand, including Schoenberg himself, argued that such a claim was false, that twelve-tone music emerged directly and with hardly a hitch from practices in use immediately preceding its formulation, and that this fact affirmed its legitimate authority.

Judging which side in this dispute is in the right depends on where we situate ourselves in the historical continuum. Critics contemporary with Schoenberg would seem to have the upper hand on him since, if we trace out the implications of his system, the schism with even the immediate past appears far more striking than the continuity. Whatever intimations of atonality one finds in Wagner, Mahler, or Debussy, they occur nonetheless within a basically tonal framework, and serve basically tonal ends— threatening the tonal order so that the return to that order will be all the more gratifying. Seen against this background, a system designed to avoid any implications whatever of tonal structuring, as Schoenberg's explicitly is, had to be termed radically novel, arbitrary, and thus utterly lacking in prescriptive power. And of course, whose musical conduct, apart from the designer's own, had been guided by it at the time of its inception? Its past was weak and its future was bleak.

But that was in 1923. As it turned out, the system, for a variety of reasons (not all of which were strictly artistic),[26] went on to develop a considerable following. Many composers of high repute began producing atonal works. Other musical parameters—rhythm, volume, even timbre—not just pitch, came to be serialized, with the result that Schoenberg's original adventure came to appear rather tame by comparison. We therefore seem obliged to conclude that *there came a time* when Schoenberg's twelve-tone system really did enjoy regulatory status. In its early years, as with Reicha's, it could hardly have been said to possess any more than suggestive power, but *unlike Reicha's,* a sufficient number of works actually did follow its suggestions, and these gradually crystallized

to form a "history" (in Black's sense), which endowed it with genuine prescriptive power.

Rules develop prescriptive status because, for a time, at least, they do genuinely provide effective compositional formulas. How *long* a time a given formula lasts will depend on how rich it is: a rectangular, transparent formula is likely to depart as quickly as it appeared, while a set of prescriptions such as sonata form, with its specifications as to thematic entries, key changes, its openness to various unspecified developmental possibilities, and the architectonic structure it imposes will enjoy much greater longevity.

The very acceptance of a formula *as* a rule, however, insures its mortality. The explicit formalization of a technique, that is, provides a framework for the production of any number of duplicate works, which will eventually begin to vibrate as one in the ears of the listening public. When this happens, the well-being of the formula in question becomes very precarious, although composers might well remain *mindful of* it, thus maintaining it in a state of animation considerably beyond the time when simple adherence to it would produce desirable results, for it can continually give rise to new ideas— ideas, again, which both presuppose and violate it. This too can be seen to have occurred with sonata form. In fact what we might regard as the most "fulfilling" moments in the career of a rule come at precisely those times when it finds itself being transcended.

In sum, then, I contend that a dictum in the musical realm which can show neither parentage nor progeny is no rule at all. A rule of compositional procedure in all likelihood will have emerged from a practice with a productive past; as a rule per se it will aim to dictate future practice; to be judged a rule of composition it must show us that it has to some extent fulfilled this aim. And the dicta which are most fruitfully and informatively taken to constitute such rules are the textbook procedures which the great composers regularly violate. After all, it is impossible to measure the flight of genius without some fairly definite idea about its point of departure.

1. See, for example, Ebenezer Prout, *Fugue* (New York: Haskell House Publishers, 1969). (First published in 1891.)

2. Graham George, *Tonality and Musical Structure* (New York: Praeger Publishers, 1970), p. 49.

3. Ibid., p. 94.

4. Ibid., p. 165. Emphasis mine.

5. Ibid., p. 49.

6. Adele Katz, *Challenge to Musical Tradition* (New York: Alfred Knopf, 1946).

7. The "tonic-dominant-tonic" pattern might be termed the ultimate one, but there are others nearly as ultimate: "Tonic-supertonic-dominant-tonic," "tonic-mediant-dominant-tonic," and "tonic-subdominant-dominant-tonic."

8. Ibid., pp. 42–48.

9. Ibid., pp. 172–177. The "wander, as in the dark" characterization comes from Adolf Marx's *Ludwig von Beethoven: Leben und Schaffen* (Berlin: O. Janke, 1863).

10. I thank one of my reviewers for calling my attention to this point.

11. J. A. Fuller-Maitland, *Oxford History of Music*, 7 vols.; Vol. IV: *The Age of Bach and Handel* (Oxford: Clarendon Press, 1901–1905), p. 5.

12. Donald Francis Tovey, *The Forms of Music* (New York: Meridian Books, 1964), p. 125.

13. Donald Francis Tovey, *Essays in Musical Analysis*, 7 vols.; Vol. II: *Symphonies 2* (London: Oxford University Press, 1972), p. 18.

14. Tovey, *Forms*, p. 125.

15. Ibid.

16. Tovey, *Essays*, Vol. II, p. 6.

17. Tovey, *Essays*, Vol. III: *Concertos*, p. 23.

18. Tovey, *Essays*, Vol. II, p. 15.

19. Susanne K. Langer, *Philosophy in a New Key* (New York: Penguin Books, Inc., 1942), p. 168.

20. The point of view I am developing here owes an obvious debt to the important work done by Leonard Meyer concerning the role of expectation in musical audition and appreciation. See *Emotion and Meaning in Music* (University of Chicago Press, 1956), and *Music, the Arts and Ideas* (University of Chicago Press, 1967).

21. Max Black, "Notes on the Meaning of 'Rule,'" *Theoria* 24, parts 2 and 3 (1958). Another interesting treatment of the concept of a rule is by Thomas M. Olshewsky, "On the Notion of a Rule," *Philosophia* (July 1976).

22. Black, p. 110.

23. Ibid., p. 137.

24. This and the citations occurring in the following paragraphs can be found in Black, "Rule," Ibid., pp. 107–110. My thanks to one of the reviewers for requiring this point to be developed.

25. Anton Reicha, *Traité de haute composition musicale*, 2 Vols. (Paris: Zetter & Cie, 1824–25).

26. By "strictly artistic" I mean something like "directly pertinent to the artistic medium." I wish to exclude such factors as forcefulness of personality, journalistic "advertising," and the like.

JERROLD LEVINSON

Evaluating Music

Wagner's music is better than it sounds.
—Mark Twain

If it sounds good, it is good.
—Duke Ellington

The above opposed epigrams about musical worth serve neatly to introduce the issues I want to explore. Is Twain right, in terms of what he implies about the grounds for evaluating music, or is Ellington? If they are both right, how can we reconcile the apparent conflict between the principles suggested by their respective observations?[1]

One possibility for reconciliation is that Ellington's epigram is to be taken straight, while Twain's is to be understood as tongue-in-cheek. Another is that Twain is alluding to secondary or sophisticated aspects of musical worth, while Ellington is focused on primary or elemental ones. A third is that their epigrams simply apply to different, and disjoint, spheres of music, Twain's to the classical tradition, and Ellington's to that of jazz. A fourth is that Twain's observation reflects the fact that, for some music, evaluations evolve over time, so that impressions formed on first exposure are replaced, on deeper acquaintance, by opposite ones, while Ellington's observation underlines that, for much music, the ear's first impression is a pretty reliable guide to musical worth.

I shall forbear trying to decide among these possibilities for reconciliation. I shall, however, assume there is some truth to Twain's remark underneath its display of wit. We shall see a reflection of this shortly in our discussion of whether all the value of music as music can be encompassed under the rubric of *how good it sounds*, or even that of *how rewarding it is to experience*.

I

When confronting the issue of musical value, two questions must be distinguished at the outset. One question is that of the value of music *generally*. Why is any music valuable, and how does music, of any sort, add to or enrich human life? A particular form of this first question asks what makes music *distinctively* valuable, as opposed to other arts; that is, what does music—more or less any music—offer that other arts or activities do not, or at least, not to the same degree?

A second question is that of the value of *particular* pieces, genres, or styles of music, and is more obviously inherently comparative in nature. What makes a given piece (genre, style) of music valuable, or alternatively, what makes this piece (genre, style) of music more valuable than that one?

In even pithier guise, the two questions are, in effect, (a) what makes *music* a good, or contributory to human good, and (b) what makes *this* music good, or better than other music?

Once these questions are roughly distinguished as above, an immediate concern is, What is the relationship, if any, between acceptable answers to them? Does knowing the answer to (a) help with the answer to (b), or vice versa? Is there a constraint in either direction, so that, for example, what makes music valuable generally is also essentially what makes particular pieces valuable? Or that what makes particular pieces of music valuable, writ large or in some way summed, is what makes music valuable generally?[2] One possible relationship might be that a work displaying in high degree the properties that make music valuable generally, or one fulfilling well the function fulfilling of which makes music of value generally, was therefore a relatively valuable piece of music. But is that so? It seems unlikely things are as simple as that.

In any event, a clear case of divergence between the value of music as a whole—of the phenomenon or practice of music—and the value of an individual piece of music would be the opportunity music affords to bring people together in a social setting for shared experience and interaction. Call that the *social* value of music. This appears to be a value of music generally without being a differentiating value of any individual piece of music. Other candidates for values of music generally that are not yet such as to add much, if anything, to the comparative value of an individual work of music, would be these: serving as a vehicle of relaxation; serving as a distraction from practical concerns; serving as an accompaniment to and facilitator of activities involving bodily movement, such as dancing, marching, exercise, or physical labor.

II

In a recent book devoted to the second of our questions, namely, that of the artistic value of individual works of art, the philosopher Malcolm Budd offers a completely general conception of such value, meant to cover all artworks in all artforms.[3] Budd aims to identify an artwork's artistic value in such a way as to differentiate it from other values it may possess, for example, as social record, religious artifact, financial investment, or totem of prestige. Budd's straightforward proposal is that the artistic value of a work of art, its value as art, is determined by or is a function of *the intrinsic value of the experience the work offers.*

By "the experience the work offers" Budd means an experience in which the work is fully and correctly understood, its individual nature grasped for what it is. By "the intrinsic value of the experience" Budd means the value of having such an experience for its own sake, rather than for the sake of any effects or consequences the experience may engender.

What is excluded from the artistic value of an artwork is thus (a) anything about the work not directly reflected in the right sort of *experience* of it; and (b) any value of such experience that is not purely *intrinsic* (i.e., is in some way *instrumental*).

Budd's proposal, applied to music, is thus in line with, if obviously a refinement of, Ellington's dictum that music's value lies, above all, in how it sounds when you listen to it. There is little point in gainsaying the healthy intuition behind both Ellington's dictum and Budd's proposal. Still, though Budd's proposal seems roughly acceptable, there are at least three grounds on which it might be challenged.

The first concerns the presupposition of a viable division between the *effects or consequences* of an experience, and the *parts or elements* of an experience, a division that may be difficult to sustain. The second concerns the restriction to the *intrinsic* value of the experience a work offers as the sole gauge of a work's value as art, a restriction that appears inadequately justified. And the third concerns the confinement of artistic value to that which is manifested in or through *experience* of a work, a confinement that seems at odds with certain firmly grounded judgments of artistic value. I elaborate on these in turn.

The distinction between an experience and its effects, though unproblematic on its face, has some tendency to dissolve under scrutiny. Experiences often have no unequivocal beginning and ending points. They characteristically do not start up with the sharpness of a pistol crack, nor do they characteristically close with a full stop. Many experiences have indeterminate beginnings, and take shape slowly. Often, rather than ceasing abruptly, they simply fail to continue developing or ramifying, though exactly where and when may remain elusive. This blurriness-around-the-edges is evident enough with traumatic experiences, such as losing a loved one, but attaches, if less blatantly, to many more ordinary experiences, appreciative ones among them. Turning to the case at hand, the endpoint of the experience of a musical work in audition, for instance, is fairly fuzzy, with no clear cutoff between the experience itself and what might be called, fittingly enough, its echoes and reverberations.

A second, more important, challenge to the formula Budd offers us is this: Even if we assume the artistic value of a work of music to lie wholly in the value of the experience, suitably demarcated, that the work offers, it may not be defensible to restrict that value to the *intrinsic*, as opposed to *instrumental*, value of the experience—that is, the value of the experience itself as opposed to its effects.[4] Granting for argument's sake the workability of the division in question—between effects of, and elements in, a given experience—there is insufficient reason to hold that only the intrinsic value of the experience a work offers is a measure of its artistic value, rather than what accrues in virtue of the experience's effects.

Suppose a given work of music is valued in part because it gives insight, when properly experienced, into the character of romantic love or the inevitability of suffering. If so, would this count as an intrinsic or an instrumental value of experiencing the music? The best answer would seem to be that it is both. It is, of course, intrinsically valuable to have such insights while listening, or in the course of subsequent reflection on the music. But it is also instrumentally valuable; the insights are thus, after all, acquired, something one can summon up for further use or benefit. If something counts as an insight, and if music affords it, then it is an enduring asset, something whose value goes beyond the confines of the experience in which it is acquired. The same could be said about music that gave one access to a point of view that had not been previously available to one; the value of this would seem to transcend the value of the experience of achieving such access through the music, and thus be partly instrumental.

It is also natural to consider here the possible moral effects of music.[5] If there are any such, and if they could be shown to issue with some regularity from the comprehending experience of certain music, then they would constitute an instrumental value of the experience of such music that would seem to be at least a candidate for inclusion in the music's artistic value.

But is there not a Catch-22 of sorts lurking in regard to the putative improving tendency of certain music? It seems that either you already have a refined human nature or developed moral sensibility allowing you to appreciate such music (in which case you will not be improved by it), or else you do not (in which case the music will not be rightly appreciatable by you, and so will fail to have its proper effect). In other words, that you appreciate such music presupposes you are a person of some moral capacity; thus, such music would seem to be powerless to transform you into that.

A partial answer to this is as follows: Even if you have to have certain minimal moral capacities in order to adequately appreciate great music, calling as it does on emotional repertoire and practical insight as much as on perceptual ability, exposing yourself to such music conceivably helps to *develop* or *reinforce* such capacities, in part through providing a controlled arena in which such capacities to respond are exercised in a specific way, serving as a kind of touchstone of what it is to be human. In other words, it is true that you might already have to be disposed, in some measure, to a moral form of life, in order for great music to be of benefit to you, but immersing yourself in it might still function, *ceteris paribus*, to make you more fully human than you were before—without, of course, guaranteeing any such result.

The example of Hannibal Lecter from the film *Silence of the Lambs* is usefully recalled here, for that unparalleled villain notoriously displays both the most malevolent cannibalism and the most cultivated appreciation of J. S. Bach. If one is so unkind as to observe that Hannibal Lecter is a fiction, and a meretricious one at that, it remains true that the coexistence of moral turpitude and aesthetic refinement in a given person is more than merely imaginable: Richard Wagner approached this, and many of the Nazis who later gloried in his music exemplified it rather fully.[6]

But such cases, fictional or actual, are largely a red herring with regard to claims of a moral dimension to music and the possible relevance of such to some music's artistic value. No one would claim that great music can, entirely on its own, make appreciators of it better people, nor that great music, however supplemented and seconded, is likely to make all appreciators of it moral. The most anyone can sensibly propose is that such music, properly grasped, exerts, through the attitudes or states of mind the music projects or the complexes of feeling it evokes, a humanizing and moralizing force (though one easily enough overridden or neutralized) and thus that, all things being equal, people exposed to such music tend to be morally better, more fully human, than they would otherwise be. Of course even this remains unproven, but it is not to be dismissed out of hand.[7]

In sum, it is perfectly reasonable to take a musical work to be greater, and greater as art, on the assumption that it has moral effects or tendencies of the sort postulated, among those who experience it fully and correctly, leaving aside whether it can be shown to have them. And this assumption constitutes a ground of value, or reason for valuing, distinct from that of the specific musical merits in virtue of which the work possesses such moral force as it does.

This is not, of course, to license every attestable benefit of the experience of a work as contributory to its artistic value. Being instrumentally beneficial in the ways I have been discussing (moral, cognitive, and emotional) is arguably a part of art's proper purpose or mission—unlike, say, the capacity of experience of a work to alleviate mental illness, induce sleep in the weary, or promote a sense of self-satisfaction. The instrumental benefits to which I draw attention are consonant with historically prevailing intentions of composers for their works, as well as being implicitly involved in received judgments about greatness in art. Such benefits rightly enter, it seems, into the assessment of a musical work's goodness as art.

There are surely other instrumental benefits of the experience of music that could reasonably be reckoned relevant to its worth as art. Music can be instrumentally valuable in virtue of providing, through its sounding form, a paragon or practicum of how to move or to be—how, in effect, to go on. Good music, adequately experienced, can serve as a highly abstract, though suggestive, "design for living."[8]

Some music, correctly appreciated, may be instrumentally valuable in virtue of the influence exerted on one's general outlook, enabling one to think or feel the world differently, thus enlarging one's life as a result. Such music does so by embodying a process of thought or a frame of mind, one that through attentive and sympathetic listening one is allowed to enter, and that might not be otherwise communica-ble—or at least, communicable in as vivid and effective a way.

Some music, finally, may be instrumentally valuable through contributing to the sense of self or to the formation of individual personality. Musical works can help to constitute and define the self that attends to them, internalizes them, and identifies with them.[9] Some music may even have the disposition to produce such effects on personality as to count as transfigurative—though of course this disposition will not be realized in every case.

III

I turn now to my third challenge to Budd's proposal about artistic value. Even if the artistic value of music is acknowledged to be centrally a matter of the value of experience of it, whether intrinsic or instrumental, that does not exhaust what such value comprehends. Why? Because certain things enter into an artwork's artistic value that are not reducible to the value of experiencing the work in the prescribed manner. The artistic value of a work of music, in other words, may quite reasonably outstrip its experiential value, even broadly understood.

An important component of musical artistic value is what may be called *influence-value*, the impact a musical work has for the better on the future course of music.[10] Examples of works in whose artistic value there is a significant component of influence-value include Beethoven's "Eroica" Symphony, Debussy's "Prelude to the Afternoon of a Faun," Schoenberg's Piano Pieces, Op. 23, and Stravinsky's "Rite of Spring." This component of the artistic value of music goes beyond the value, intrinsic or instrumental, of the experience it offers. It is reflected in the works of value that the aforementioned works have spawned, the new avenues of musical composition they have opened up, or the unforeseen sorts of musical experiences they prepare the ground for, but do not themselves afford. When we identify musical works as seminal, revolutionary, or ground-breaking, and praise them as such, we are in the realm of artistic value I am labeling influence-value.

It may be suggested, though, that *actual* influence-value is one thing, and *potential* influence-value another. The former would consist in actual positive effects on the future of music, whereas the latter, by contrast, would consist in being such as to give rise to such effects, conditions of reception being favorable. In other words, a work's potential influence-value would amount to its having the capacity to influence the future of music beneficially through its directly appreciable artistic features, to wit, its form, expression, or technique. Having distinguished actual from potential influence-value in this manner, one might then go on to suggest that only potential influence-value, which flows directly from a work's having "the right stuff," is relevant to claims of artistic value.

Yet it seems to me that, despite the validity of the distinction between them, *actual* influence-value, and not just potential influence-value, is properly accounted part of the artistic value of works of music, especially when such works are seen not in isolation, but as part of an ongoing tradition of music-making and musical thinking. No doubt having the right stuff, and at the right time, figures in a work's artistic value, but so, it seems, does what becomes of that work historically. Since actual influence on the history of music depends, as we know, not only on the nature of the work and the relations it bears to its antecedents, but on a contingent degree of receptivity to and uptake of what it offers, we may need to recognize a measure of artistic luck in how much artistic value accrues to a work. That is what actual, as opposed to merely potential, seminality, revolutionariness, and so on, require.

But what of influence that is freaky, undeserved, or even a result of repugnance—as when an inferior work, in an unpromising mode, prompts an artist angrily to create something superior in a wholly other vein? The sort of influence that would seem germane to artistic value is where earlier art prompts emulation, adaptation, or further exploration in the same or related directions—where it serves as an example and inspiration to later art, rather than merely a negative spur to it. Perhaps, then, what is defensible is only that *some* actual influence-value contributes to a work's value as art; perhaps only when such actual influence-value is coupled with, or rests on, a work's potential influence-value does it do so. Still, in those cases, contribute it does.[11]

But suppose that, contrary to what I have just been arguing, it is really *only* potential influence-value that can be held germane to artistic value, a work's particular fortunes in the subsequent history of music being discounted as irrelevant. The existence of such influence-value would still constitute a challenge to Budd's proposal. For a work's potential influence-value—its power or propensity to alter the stream of musical culture for the better—remains something over and above the features of the work in which that power or propensity inheres, and is distinct from and not reducible to the value, whether intrinsic or instrumental, of experiencing the work correctly.

Having said this much, influence-value may now rightly be qualified as a *secondary* sort of artistic value, though a real one nevertheless. The reason is as follows: Such value is clearly parasitic on primary, experience-based artistic value, in the sense that it is value that accrues to a work in virtue of its issuing in or paving the way for other works that have a value *beyond* influence-value—presumably, experiential value. To have led to the creation of other works, but ones without notable experiential value, or ones with only influence-value, would seem not to amount to artistic value of any kind. Influence-value is thus like a promissory note that needs to be redeemed by the exhibition of subsequent induced works of positive experiential value. But such notes *can* be redeemed, and have been, time and again.

Finally, are there other varieties of artistic value possessed by individual works of music, apart from influence-value, ones that go beyond the value, intrinsic or instrumental, of experiencing the work comprehendingly? Here are some candidates:

(1) Problem-solving value.   Part of the artistic value of a musical work might reside in the problems it solves subject to various constraints, formal or expressive.[12] It is true that the way a work answers to problems set by its predecessors might enter into how it strikes an informed ear, with awareness of such solutions being intrinsically rewarding to sustain, but the fact of constituting a solution to a preexisting artistic problem of some importance would seem to be a ground of value in itself, not reducible to the value of a listener's awareness of such a solution having been arrived at.[13]

(2) Originality-value.   Part of the artistic value of a musical work might lie in its original-

ity or innovativeness relative to its tradition. Now although this might again be encompassed in the experience the work offers to an informed ear—in that originality, a backward-looking characteristic, comes across when one holds a work up against its context of emergence, its prototypes and predecessors, while listening— the originality of a work vis-à-vis its background, a complex relational property, is of value in a way that goes beyond the value of appreciating such originality.

(3) Performance-value. Part of the artistic value of a musical work might be as a source of pleasure for performers in negotiating its difficulties, or as a vehicle for performers' displays of emotionality or taste. Clearly, music might be especially enjoyable to play, or pose challenges to execution that are exhilarating to overcome, or provide unusual opportunities for self-expression, without being particularly rewarding to listen to. Furthermore, some music might be said to be more valuable in virtue of allowing, more than most, for differently revealing interpretations from performance to performance, performances that work out differently the relation between the music's form and content.

So it seems that there certainly *are* other non–appreciative-experience-based sources of artistic value, apart from influence-value. I shall not, however, try to settle here exactly how many, or how important, those sources are.[14]

IV

My aim in the remainder of this essay is to explore the primary, that is to say, *intrinsic-experiential*, value of a piece of music for a listener. I want to pinpoint what that value fundamentally consists in, and what it might, most generally, be gauged by. As the preceding discussion has made clear, I hold that a significant part of the artistic value of a piece of music, that is, its value as art, may be *non*experiential, consisting in such things as originality, or influentiality, or being a solution to a standing problem in a musical tradition. In addition, I hold that the experiential value of a piece of music as art may in principle go beyond what is *intrinsically* valuable in such experience, and properly reflect extrinsic benefits of certain kinds. My target here, however, is precisely that

central dimension of music's value for listeners: namely, that which is intrinsic to the listening experience itself, wherein such experience is deemed worth having for its own sake.

Even if we agree that the artistic value of a work of music is primarily given by the intrinsic value of experiencing the work with understanding,[15] our criteria for assigning musical value are naturally apt to be considerably more concrete than that. Asked to defend the judgment that some piece of music was good as music, a listener will rarely, and certainly not only, submit that experience of it is of high intrinsic value. There seems surely to be a place for, or a role played by, various low-level criteria, such as attractive melody, interesting rhythm, intense expression, pleasing timbres, inventive harmony, intelligible overall form, and so on. Such criteria are, of course, invoked more frequently on the ground than is the inherent rewardingness of an understanding experience of music.

Yet clearly, such low-level musical merits lack generality, and fail to be even presumptively good-making, taken by themselves. Music can be good, and easily so, without attractive melody (for example, Stravinsky's *Rite of Spring* or Webern's *Five Movements for String Quartet*), without significant harmonic invention (for example, much of Palestrina or Handel), without substantial rhythmic interest (witness Satie's *Gymnopedie* No. 1), without pleasing timbres (witness Bach's keyboard music), without evident emotional expressiveness (as with Conlon Nancarrow's studies for player piano), and so on.

What is interesting is whether there are any defensible intermediate principles, so to speak, ones less abstract than that of the intrinsic rewardingness of the experience of listening, but not so concrete or so limited as those just recalled. Between the most abstract condition that might be taken to analyze the core of music's artistic value—that experience of it be intrinsically worthwhile—and the most concrete experientially satisfying merit features appealed to in casual justification of verdicts of goodness of music (e.g., attractive melody, varied orchestration) may lie *midlevel principles* that capture the ground on which such verdicts and justifications rest, while providing a specification of general validity of what experiential musical value centrally consists in.

One approach popular in philosophical aesthetics for almost forty years (though it has somewhat wilted of late under attacks from particularists about evaluation) is to identify general properties of works of art that invariably conduce to or underlie artistic goodness across the arts—and presumably do so because such properties are inherently satisfying to experience, alone or in combination, under appreciative conditions. The modern source of this tradition of theorizing is Monroe Beardsley, who proposed that there were three "primary canons of criticism": unity, intensity, and complexity.[16] The claim is that insofar as a work exhibits one of these features it is ipso facto better as art than it would otherwise be, and that any of its features that appear to contribute to its value as art can be shown to be forms of, or to rest on, those three primary criteria.

But there has been significant skepticism over whether those three are always, in all circumstances, positive-tending features; whether there aren't sometimes interactive effects among them, ones that prevent an increase in one such dimension from always being value enhancing; whether those three are all the independent positive-tending features with regard to artistic goodness; whether there is any effective way to sum such criteria, so as to justify comparative rankings of works exhibiting the three primary criteria to different degrees; and whether the presence of such features, even in high degree, is ever sufficient by itself to support a judgment of high comparative artistic value.[17]

So rather than attempt rehabilitation of that approach,[18] I want to pursue another tack, one that tries to bring into relief the distinctive grounds of value for individual musical works, as opposed to works of art generally, while at the same time hewing more closely to the intuition that artistic value is centrally a function of the worthwhileness of the experience it offers. What I have in mind are proposals that might naturally be regarded as specifications of that intuition as it applies in the musical case.

v

Consider these two approving responses to music: (a) "I like how it sounds"; and (b) "I like how it goes."

While neither of these responses (which, strictly speaking, are simply subjective judgments of approval) constitutes an adequate basis for judgments of the artistic value of a piece of music, (b) both says more than (a), and also comes rather closer to being such a basis than does (a). And that is because (b) captures a feature fundamental to music's being good, at a level less abstract than that of experience of it being intrinsically rewarding.

Someone offering response (a) commits himself only to approving, first, the mere sonic appearance of the music, and second, an aspect of the music manifestable in the smallest perceivable doses. Someone offering response (b), on the other hand, has gotten nearer to the musical heart of the matter, since such a response reflects enjoyment taken in musical progression, in how music evolves from point to point, whose most obvious manifestation is perhaps rhythm, and the way music's parts, and especially those of small span, are joined together from moment to moment. "I like how it goes" is a more telling specification of "I find experience of it intrinsically rewarding" than "I like how it sounds," because the latter, strictly speaking, indicates nothing of the essentially kinetic nature of music's basic appeal. "I like how it sounds," one may observe, would apply equally well to an imaginary art of short-duration sound bursts, carefully synthesizer-designed for aesthetic delectation. The appeal of the products of such an art overlaps only slightly, I would claim, with the appeal of music, which is indicative of why "how it sounds" is less apt as an epitome of what makes music good than "how it goes."

"I like how it goes" connects with the absolutely crucial notion of *following* music. There is in fact a rough equivalence between "I like how it goes" and "I find the experience of following it intrinsically rewarding." To take satisfaction in some music is, above all, to enjoy following it, and its value as music is plausibly quite centrally its enabling an experience of following its evolution over time that is intrinsically rewarding.

Leonard Meyer's central idea on the topic of musical worth is very much in this vein. It is that music is valuable insofar as it sets up expectations in the listener for how it will proceed, and then consequently fulfills or frustrates those expectations in various ways, to varying degrees, and with more or less delay. The most valuable music, for Meyer, provides a structure in which there is delayed, but not indefinitely postponed, fulfillment of expectations, the gratification that results ultimately being the more valuable for the delay involved in attaining it.[19]

Clearly this is a further concretization of the idea that music is valued insofar as one relishes how it goes, or takes satisfaction in following it, one that gives it more specific content still. Unfortunately, and especially as it seems to privilege the unlikely or deviant continuation, it may be too specific, too limiting, to cover all ways that music may "go"; that is, unfold or develop over time, that people find intrinsically rewarding. Sometimes a continuation that just seems right, beautiful, or cogent, may not be particularly unexpected—may not, in terms Meyer favors in a later formulation, impart a large amount of information relative to alternatives.

A related suggestion, in this middle terrain between the conceptually unassailable and the empirically false, which concretizes further the idea of enjoying following music as the key to its central experiential artistic value, was offered by Edmund Gurney.[20] The idea is that music, or at least music of the sort Meyer has labeled teleological (i.e., giving an appearance of purposiveness or goal-direction) has experiential value almost entirely in virtue of *the satisfyingness of its individual parts experienced sequentially* (i.e., in virtue of the satisfyingness of its small-scale evolution or progression, from moment to moment).

Now another such suggestion, on roughly the same level of concreteness, would bring in, finally, that on which I have so far been silent, namely, the expressive side of music, and locate the experiential value of music centrally in the *satisfaction of apprehending and responding to music's expressive aspect*. If the previous suggestion aims to capture most comprehensively what music offers on a *formal* level, as a process uninterpreted in other than musical terms, then the present suggestion aims to capture most comprehensively what music offers on the level of *content*, or as a process interpreted in terms of human life. For surely much of the interest of music is wrapped up in what it intimates of human gesture, feeling, and agency.

But a principle more adequate than either of these may be arrived at by, as it were, putting them together. More than merely enjoying following the music in its concrete particularity or finding satisfying precisely how it goes, and more than enjoying perceiving and responding to the gestural, affective, and agential qualities that emerge as the music unfolds over time, what one finds intrinsically rewarding in the experience a good piece of music offers, and what perhaps most importantly determines its artistic value, is its very particular *wedding* of its form and content. That is to say, with a good piece of music one enjoys "how it goes," to be sure (its individual, temporally evolving form) and again one enjoys "what it conveys"[21] (the attitudes, emotions, qualities, actions, or events it communicates). Above all, however, one enjoys and finds intrinsically rewarding the *fusion* of how it goes and what it conveys, the precise way in which what it conveys is embodied in and carried by how it goes.[22]

If we equate the "how it goes" of a piece of music with its configurational (or kinetic) form, and the "what it conveys" with its expressive (or interpretive) content, then the "what it conveys in relation to how it goes" of such a piece might reasonably be identified with its form *or* its content, more comprehensively viewed—that is, with its *significant* form, or *immanent* content. Call this picture of things "Model 1."

Model 1

1. How it goes: how note follows note, chord chord, motive motive, phrase phrase, and passage passage: configurational/kinetic form.

2. What it conveys: gesture, action, feeling, mood, emotion: expressive/interpretive content.

3. What it conveys in relation to how it goes: significant form/immanent content.

Of course, marking off configurational/kinetic form from expressive/interpretive content in this manner is not meant to suggest that these are standardly distinguished as such in concrete listening experience. Usually one attends to *content-infused form*, or *formally-embodied content*, rather than either form or content per se, though it remains possible, with effort, to focus abstractly on such form or content as such. The progression or movement of music is usually heard as *both* configurational *and* expressive, with those aspects fused together. Indeed, the boundary between purely intramusical relations, motions and tensions grasped at the level of configuration (or kinesis) and gestural, affective, or actional contents grasped at the level of expression (or interpretation), is perhaps essentially blurred. The above model, then, just makes explicit the two poles, so to speak, of the object on which musical appreciation properly focuses.

What is here proposed as the main focus of musical appreciation—that is, what music conveys vis-à-vis how it goes—helps explain why the prevailing attitude in relation to music one loves is the desire to experience it repeatedly and fully in actual hearing. Only through such experience, or the simulacrum of it that mental simulation can provide, can one access the specific fusion of human content and audible form my working formula points up. Merely abstractly recalling the form, or even reviewing it concretely but unrespondingly, does little to satisfy the distinctive hunger for a sorely missed piece of music. Even less does abstractly recalling the music's content, referenced in some manner or other, without retrieving and rehearing its specific sonic embodiment.

The above model, and the formula from which it is derived, is perhaps most adequate to the experience of music on the basic or ground level, as a succession of events of relatively short duration, each with a significance of its own, more or less absorbing. But another, more complex, model also recommends itself to us, in which it is acknowledged that what I have designated the side of content *itself* admits of form—that is to say, a "how it goes"—at a higher level, which form then generates in turn a further dimension of content, thus providing ultimately for the relationship between that content and its underlying form. Call this "Model 2."[23]

Model 2

1. How it goes on an expressive level: how an episode of one expressive character follows an episode of another such character, and the pattern of this succession as a whole: expressive form.

2. What it conveys in virtue of how it goes on an expressive level: dramatic content.[24]

3. What it conveys dramatically in relation to how it goes expressively: (global) significant form/immanent content.

To complete the picture we would need to recognize that relationships between higher-order forms and contents and those on the ground level might also enter into the appreciation of music; that is, serve as potential foci of intrinsically rewarding attention. Thus, if from Model 1 we have three elements, configurational form, expressive content, and their resultant low-order significant form/immanent content, and from Model 2 three elements as well, expressive form, dramatic content, and their resultant high-order significant form/immanent content, then in theory there are another nine relationships that become candidates for musical apprehension or contemplation, and hence, loci of evaluative assessment. Of those, the relationships between expressive and configurational form, and between dramatic and expressive content, would seem the most relevant. But at this stage of reflection we surely begin to lose our grip on what the experiential value of music mainly consists in. Thus I think we may safely ignore any further relationships of this sort, and rest with the two models already articulated, in which the central object of musical appreciation is identified as the relationship of content to form, on lower and higher levels, with such form and content themselves functioning, as well, as secondary and supporting objects of attention.

VI

Confining our sights to Model 1, the simpler and more fundamental of our two models, it might seem that there is an asymmetry between the component labeled "how it goes" (configurational form) and that labeled "what it conveys" (expressive content), as potential loci of musical value. For the former (musical form) appears to have an independent claim on listeners, that is, is of interest to apprehend on its own, while the latter (extramusical content) may appear, taken by itself, to lack any such claim. Budd, for example, adopts such a viewpoint: "our experience of the expressive aspect of music is not separable from our experience of the music, and we value the expressive aspect not in itself but *as realized in the music.*"[25] In other words, that a work of music has a configurational form that is absorbing, expressive meaning aside, is already a ground of musical value, such form being an appropriate, if limited, object of musical appreciation; but not so, it seems, that a work has this or that expressive content, identified apart from the musical form that realizes it.

But is this really so? I think not. What is true is that there is an asymmetry in *degree*—in that a work's expressive meaning abstractly identified is of *less* artistic interest, and *less* contributory to artistic value, than the quality of its configurational form or the manner in which the expressiveness emerges from said form. It is false, however, that such meaning, considered apart from its vehicle, is of *no* such interest, or that its nature has *no* bearing on the artistic value of a work. Unusual, rare, subtle, deep, profound targets of expression, if attained, make a musical work better, because such contents are themselves more rewarding to contemplate, engage with, or respond to. For instance, a musical work expressive of bittersweet melancholy, or communicating the gestures of resignation, is arguably artistically more valuable, all things being equal, than one expressing simple cheerfulness or conveying an ordinary sort of anger.

Recall that for Budd, the question about a musical work's artistic value is simply this: Is the experience the work offers *intrinsically valuable*? The questions I have highlighted in this section, by contrast, are rather, What is the *nature* of the experience musical works typically offer, so far as the intrinsic value of such experience is concerned? And what, more specifically, are the *dimensions* of the experience in which such value resides? I have ventured to generalize about the value-relevant dimensions of the experience of music, and have concluded that they are irreducibly three: experience of configurational or kinetic form, experience of expressive or interpretive content, and experience of the embodiment or realization of the latter in the former. So if the experience a work offers possesses intrinsic value, this will be because the work is found inherently rewarding expressively, or configurationally, or in terms of its fusion of the expressive and the configurational, or in all three ways. Thus we can, if we like, now identify three fundamental, if formulaic

criteria of experiential goodness in music: (1) how rewarding it is to experience how the music goes, that is, how rewarding it is to follow as tonal process; (2) how rewarding it is to register or respond to what it conveys; and (3) how rewarding it is to experience what it conveys in relation to, or as embodied in, how it goes.[26]

VII

How do the formulae and models of experiential value proposed above fare when held up against a piece of unquestionable and surpassing musical worth? By way of conclusion I choose, for brief examination in this light, Schubert's Piano Sonata in A major, op. posth. D. 959. I suggest that this sonata's experiential value, that is, its central value as music, fits comfortably under the umbrella provided by those formulas and models. In short, its goodness as music is a matter of how satisfyingly it goes as a purely musical process, of how satisfying it is to engage with the content it conveys, and above all, of how satisfying it is to experience the way in which what it conveys is embedded in, intertwined with, and borne by how it very precisely goes.

But let us try to identify, in regard to this particular musical composition, some of what, in particular, makes it so good. Now the schematic midlevel answer to the question, Why is Schubert's sonata musically so good? is that the experience it affords, on a configurational level, on an expressive level, and on the level of their interrelation, is so inherently satisfying or worthwhile. On the purely kinetic level, it is highly absorbing to follow, in its small-scale and large-scale movement; from beginning to end the ear is regaled with beautiful, cogent, and original forms, or ways of sounding in time. On the level of content, what it expresses or conveys is distinctive, intense, and well worth engaging with. And on the level of fusion, the specific manner in which the work musically conveys its content seems wholly compelling, exhibiting throughout an elegance and rightness of means to ends.[27]

Still, it will not be amiss to go into somewhat more detail in regard to the expressive and dramatic dimensions of Schubert's musical essay. I begin with the former. The sonata possesses an intensity and variety of emotional expression quite out of the ordinary, covering almost the full range of human feeling. It displays perhaps the greatest range of moods and affects of any of Schubert's works, yet manages to tie them all together into such a satisfying whole that listening to it is like living a human life in microcosm. What, then, are some salient loci of expressive goodness in this sonata? The following are four instances of distinctive expression, distinctively achieved, in most cases through music that is, in addition, itself entirely satisfying on a configurational level:

The uneasy stasis, suggestive of restless anxiety or obsession, at the beginning of the first movement's development, achieved through harmonic oscillation between C major and B major—as opposed to the more usual nonreversing journey from key to key.[28]

The unique nostalgia of the first movement's coda, in which the movement's opening rhetorical theme is recollected as if through a haze—its vital, almost peremptory force drained off, but its essential identity intact.

The unparalleled violence, approaching chaos, of the slow movement's middle section, a remarkable evocation of someone going desperately out of control.[29]

The charming perkiness of the scherzo movement's main theme, which charm is based in part on the piano writing's suggestion of string pizzicati.

I turn now to dramatic, or global expressive, content. A striking example is afforded by the intense, soul-searching dialogue in which the music's persona is engaged at the climax of the second episode of the sonata's rondo finale (see Fig. 1). In this passage the music's persona seems to pose, then reluctantly answer, questions it would rather not face, but that can no longer be avoided. And a sympathetic listener cannot help feeling they are the life-and-death questions of his or her own existence as well. As for the source, structurally speaking, of the passage's dialogic quality, it is the stark alternation of treble and bass in the sounding of the passage's sharply etched, individually expressive motifs.

Another example of dramatic content in this sonata is almost impossible to put into words:

the impression a listener receives during its first movement, and perhaps most pointedly, its opening statement, of being addressed by an adult and as an adult, of reflectively and unhurriedly being given the benefit of someone's wisdom and maturity. This is one of several quite singular attitudes of mind somehow communicated by this sonata in the large, attitudes that give it the sort of moral force I earlier speculated may belong to certain pieces of music.

A final example of dramatic content in this sonata concerns a special sort of unity that some pieces of music attain. One kind of most valuable music is that which displays unity in such manner and degree as to stand as a powerful emblem of the unification of opposites and the reconciling of the diverse, not through the subduing or overpowering of one element by another, but through the evincing of a deeper relatedness despite superficial differences. Call unity of this sort *transcendent* unity, in contrast to the merely *formal* unity that is, in most cases, its substantial underpinning. Such emblematicity of wholeness as I have in mind is not just an abstract relationship one reflects on intellectually, but rather something one registers feelingly in the course of listening.

Schubert's sonata displays that sort of unity, if any piece of music does. There is a striking thematic, rhythmic, and harmonic unification effected in subtle ways throughout the sonata, despite the rich surface variety of its four movements, which helps to generate the piece's pronounced transcendent unity. Here I shall just note some aspects of the sonata's formal unification, ones that seem to play some part in its achievement of the other sort of unification.

The opening six bars of the first movement are echoed, in loose retrograde, by the closing eight bars of the fourth and last movement; the first movement's development section is derived almost entirely from the opening figure of the movement's second theme; there is a clear reminiscence of the agitation of the slow movement's middle section in the interpolated repeated-note triplet figures in the reprise of the slow movement's main theme; the tensions resident in the first and second movements reappear in the second half of the scherzo movement's main section, employing a variant of the figure from the first movement's development; the opening motif of the trio section of the scherzo

FIGURE 1. Schubert, Sonata in A major, op. posth., D. 959, fourth movement.

is a loose inversion of the first movement's opening motif; rising or falling semitone motion is an important element in the main themes of the first, second, and fourth movements, and includes the mysterious alternation of A-major and B-flat arpeggios at the very end of the first movement; and there is a clear locus of harmonic gravitation in the sonata constituted by keys a third up from the tonic. Of course elements of formal unity in a musical composition, even when pervasive, do not inevitably issue in the sort of global expressiveness I have labeled transcendent unity (whose ultimate mark is a sense of transfiguring oneness in the listener), but I submit that in this case, they do.

It would be quixotic to think that this selective survey of sites of goodness in one very fine musical composition can conclusively establish the validity of the schematic midlevel formulae proposed earlier for that in which musical value resides—to wit, configurational, expressive, and expressive/configurational satisfyingness, or at a higher level, expressive form, dramatic content, and dramatic content/expressive form satisfyingness—but at least it has turned up nothing that cannot easily be encompassed under them. In any event, it is only through such midlevel formulas, I think, that we may perspicuously bring together the view from above on this subject, in which musical value is understood in terms of the intrinsic rewardingness of experience of a work, and the view from below, in which musical value is seen in terms of familiar features—sound, melody, rhythm, or mood—directly cited by listeners as grounds for approving a work.[30]

1. These epigrams are not, of course, *strictly* inconsistent with one another; Twain's epigram does not even entail that Wagner's music is good. But suppose, for the sake of argument, we take Twain's remark to have the force, that there is music that is good, but does not sound good. Even so, there is no conflict per se with Ellington's dictum, but only with its converse: to wit, if music is good, it sounds good. However, if we construe Ellington as implicitly committed to the biconditional, which seems reasonable, then a contradiction emerges.

Otherwise put, if we elaborate the principle behind Ellington's remark to be "music is good just insofar as, and to the degree that, it sounds good," and that behind Twain's remark, taken straight, to be "music is not always good just insofar as, and to the degree that, it sounds good," then the logical opposition of these principles is plain.

2. See Stephen Davies, *Musical Meaning and Expression* (Ithaca: Cornell University Press, 1994), pp. 275–76.

3. See Malcom Budd, *Values of Art: Pictures, Poetry, and Music* (London: Penguin Books, 1996).

4. It may be that the broader value these instrumental goods contribute to—that a *life* is a certain way, or possesses certain features—is intrinsic, even if they remain instrumental goods of the *experience*.

5. Two recent essays on this topic are Colin Radford, "How Can Music Be Moral?" *Midwest Studies* 16 (1991): 421–38 and Donald Walhout, "Music and Moral Goodness," *Journal of Aesthetic Education* 29 (1995): 5–16. The topic is also explored at length in Kathleen Higgins, *The Music of Our Lives* (Philadelphia: Temple University Press, 1991); Higgins makes a good case for recognizing a moral dimension to music, though her focus is on plausible ethical effects of whole genres and practices, as opposed to individual musical works.

6. The examples of Hannibal Lecter and Nazi doctors enjoying their chamber music in the evening strike us so forcefully, I suggest, precisely because they *are*, in fact, exceptional. They violate an empirically grounded norm of artistic taste comporting with some degree of moral awareness. While it seems almost natural for purveyors of gangsta rap to be engaged in immoral and antisocial activities from time to time—what would one expect, given the content of such music and the implausibility of fobbing it all off onto a persona unrelated to the rapper?—it is rather astonishing when professional pianists and symphonists are. The exception—of immoral or inhuman behavior from devotees of fine music—calls attention to the presumptive rule, that there is likely some degree of connection, some *ceteris paribus* association, between aesthetic refinement and moral awareness. (Kant, of course, thought this link was of a transcendental sort, but we need not embrace any such suggestion.)

7. At the least, good music may help to remove barriers to moral education by increasing an individual's awareness of the subjectivity of others, which is clearly prerequisite to treating others as ends in themselves and taking their interests into account in deciding how to behave. Appreciation of good music may plausibly lead to a more vivid imaginative grasp of the mental life of others, a necessary condition for regarding those others in a morally appropriate manner.

But does great music simply inform us of morally relevant data or acquaint us with morally relevant perspectives, thus supplying a necessary condition of acting morally? Or does it in addition motivate us, to some extent, to act morally? If it does not, then it will not be, even *ceteris paribus*, a morally improving force, but only something that lays the groundwork for acting in a moral way. However, I think there is reason to believe that some music, at any rate, is not only of epistemic value, but also motivating, in relation to moral life.

Much more could be said on the mechanisms of moral improvement through art, especially for art of an abstract sort. The following, at least, seem relevant: increased ability to inhabit in imagination other subjectivities or points of view; increased grasp of narratives, in terms of which lives are lived, and on which moral instruction may rest; and presentation of desirable models of wholeness or integrity.

8. This is not unrelated to Monroe Beardsley's suggestion that music might reasonably be held to symbolize or exemplify general patterns of continuation, growth, or development. See his "Understanding Music," in K. Price, ed., *On Criticizing Music* (Baltimore: Johns Hopkins University Press, 1981).

9. See Leonard Meyer, "Some Remarks on Value and Greatness in Music," in *Music, the Arts, and Ideas* (Chicago: University of Chicago Press, 1967): 22–41; Anthony Savile, *Kantian Aesthetics Pursued* (Edinburgh: Edinburgh University Press, 1993), chap. 6; and Kathleen Higgins, *The Music of Our Lives*, chap. 6.

It is important to note that the *objective* value of a piece of music in this respect is distinct from its *personal* value in that respect to a given individual. Both are comparative, but only the latter is relative in a strong sense. The former concerns a piece's power or potential, among works of music generally, to contribute to self-definition and the like in virtue of its formal and expressive qualities; the latter concerns the actual historical contribution of a given piece of music to shaping some person's identity. The latter may be owed, in part, to the former, but there are usually idiosyncratic factors at work as well. That some piece of music had a profound effect on Sam, and became a touchstone of his emotional and intellectual life thereafter, means that it is, unchallengably, a piece of music with personal value for Sam. But it may not, for all that, have much objective value in this regard; that is, it may lack significant potential to so affect prepared listeners generally.

10. I am ignoring, for simplicity of discussion, positive effects on *other* arts or spheres of culture. But in principle there is no reason to exclude these as irrelevant to an assessment of artistic value. Also, in speaking of influence-value I shall, unless otherwise indicated, have in mind *positive* influence value, that of influencing the future of art for the better.

11. Note also that influence-value, of either sort, might very well reside naturally in a *set* of pieces, rather than any particular one of the set, though those individual pieces would then share or participate in the influence-value of the whole. A good example would be the last ten or so of Mozart's piano concertos.

12. See Stephen Davies, "Musical Understanding and Musical Kinds," *The Journal of Aesthetics and Art Criticism* 52 (1994): 69–81, and reprinted in this volume; Anthony Savile, *The Test of Time* (Oxford: Oxford University Press, 1982).

13. A similar brief might be lodged for *constructional* features of a musical work that are not appreciatively accessible, yet are partly causally responsible for features that are—though I would be less confident of such a brief. One would have to make the case that there was value here that outstripped both that of the features made accessible to the ear and that derived from appreciative reflection on the role played by such constructional features.

14. Another sort of value that might seem to figure in artistic value may be denominated *composer-value*. The composer-value of a musical work would reside in its functioning as a model for other composers of forms, techniques, or procedures for realizing valuable artistic ends. However, such value would appear to be pretty clearly para-

sitic on the value of works for listeners and performers, the intended recipients of music. That is to say, a musical work will be valuable in virtue of guiding and motivating other composers to further composition only insofar as it itself embodies value of some sort for listeners or performers; otherwise, that it prompts and enables further composition along the same lines would be, if anything, to its discredit.

15. Note that this might rightly be taken to include, in addition to apprehension of music as it sounds, retrospective reflection on or contemplation of music after audition is complete.

16. These were first enunciated in his *Aesthetics: Problems in the Philosophy of Criticism* (New York: Harcourt, Brace & World, 1958).

17. Some writers, notably George Dickie, have expressed this skepticism by doubting whether there are any "strong," as opposed to "weak," principles of criticism involving such criteria. "Weak" principles get one only to judgments to the effect that a work has *some* artistic value—which is, of course, compatible with its being a *bad* work of art. See his *Evaluating Art* (Philadelphia: Temple University Press, 1988).

18. But see Frank Sibley, "General Criteria and Reasons in Aesthetics," in J. Fisher, ed., *Essays on Aesthetics* (Philadelphia: Temple University Press, 1983); and John Bender, "General but Defeasible Reasons in Aesthetic Evaluation: The Particularist/Generalist Dispute," *The Journal of Aesthetics and Art Criticism* 53 (1995): 379–92.

19. See Meyer, "Some Remarks on Value and Greatness in Music."

20. See his major work, *The Power of Sound* (London: Smith, Elder, & Co., 1880: reprinted New York: Basic Books, 1966).

21. I here make use of "conveys" as a blanket term for music's relation to its content, broadly speaking; that is, anything beyond the properties it possesses as merely a sequence of sounds. "Conveys" is thus intended to cover "expresses," "exemplifies," "represents," "symbolizes," "signifies," "suggests," even "evokes"; that is, it is being used synecdochically to stand for the whole array of meaning-relations music may exhibit. Much the same, by the way, is true of "expressiveness" and "expressive," as those terms figure in later formulations; they too should be understood synecdochically, as covering dimensions of musical meaning beyond that which can strictly be denominated "musical expressiveness," as I would analyze that notion (see my "Musical Expressiveness," in *The Pleasures of Aesthetics* [Ithaca: Cornell University Press, 1996]).

22. Of course this is a familiar idea in the annals of aesthetics, if not put in precisely these terms. Certainly Croce, Collingwood, and Dewey defended versions of the intimacy of form and content in art, and Budd endorses the idea at several points in his *Values of Art*. A congenial development of the idea can be found in an essay of Richard Eldridge, "Form and Content: An Aesthetic Theory of Art," *British Journal of Aesthetics* 25 (1985): 303–16, though it is there elevated—in my view, mistakenly—into an account of the notion of art itself. For related discussion see also the first two essays in my *Pleasures of Aesthetics*.

23. For simplicity's sake I am leaving out the fact that high-order, or dramatic, content depends on and emerges out of not only high-order, or *expressive*, form but also large-scale *configurational* form (that is, the *architectonic*

structure of a piece of music). But to acknowledge that in this model would reduce its transparency even further. For more on such complications, and a defense of the primacy, nevertheless, of *small-scale* configurational form, see my *Apprehending Music* (Ithaca: Cornell University Press, 1997).

24. "Dramatic," it must be conceded, is not an ideal name for all varieties of global expressive content, but "dramatic" here, like "conveys" and "expressive" earlier, is intended broadly, so as to cover all sorts of content of a global sort that music may convey, in virtue of its overall form and relationships existing among the local expressivenesses of individual passages.

25. Budd, *Values of Art*, p. 152.

26. Does it then follow that a work that rates highly in all three dimensions of the experience it affords is thus necessarily better than a work that rates highly in only two such dimensions? For instance, that a work with a distinctive representational content that exhibits a musically absorbing form and weds the two in a successful manner is necessarily better than a work with a more commonplace expressive content exhibiting musically absorbing form successfully wed to that content?

The answer, I believe, is that it does not follow. This is because of the possibility, even likelihood, of interaction or interference between the dimensions of such experience. For example, it may typically be the case that works of markedly representational character, even when musically absorbing and exhibiting good integration of the representational and configurational, do not afford an experience on the whole so inherently rewarding as much music of non-representational and only middling expressive character. The value of the appreciative experience of such a work is not the sum of the values of the three dimensions of appreciation considered in isolation; in trying to realize them all in a single appreciative experience one finds that attention to the representational dimension negatively competes with attention to the configurational, more so than when music has extramusical but not representational content.

Still, though the value of musical experience will not, if this is right, be simply the sum of the value of the three dimensions of such experience I have identified, those dimensions would seem to be the ones in which all such value resides, and satisfyingness in those dimensions taken separately the only prima facie reasons to regard a work as musically good.

27. The means here would include the configurational form basis of the music's local expressiveness, and the expressive form basis of the music's dramatic content, or global expressiveness. Some expressive forms (e.g., patterns of expressiveness) are less satisfying than others, whether as forms per se, or in virtue of the sort of the higher-order content they generate (or else fail to generate).

28. I owe this observation, as well as some others below, to Charles Rosen's discussion of the sonata in *Sonata Forms* (New York: Norton, 1988).

29. The specific image of a man distraught to the point of tearing out his hair is, for me, almost inescapable.

30. I am grateful to Stephen Davies, Stan Godlovitch, Mitchell Green, Fred Maus, Roger Shiner, Robert Rynasiewicz, Alicyn Warren, and Susan Wolf for their helpful comments on earlier versions of this essay.

JOHN ANDREW FISHER

Rock 'n' Recording

The Ontological Complexity of Rock Music

There was even a time when I asked Paul McCartney to dub in a note on a record, and he said he didn't want to because he thought it was cheating. I told him: "We've all been cheating all the time." And he did it.

—George Martin[1]

"None of them along the line know what any of it is worth." This line from Bob Dylan's "All Along the Watchtower" could serve as a trenchant summation of the response of the discipline of aesthetics to rock music. In spite of the fact that rock is the dominant form of music in the second half of the twentieth century, very little has been written about rock by philosophers or music theorists.[2] No doubt this reflects an unstated judgment about the relative worth of rock music compared to classical music. This unstated value judgment is, in my view, closely connected to the fact that what has been written about rock by academic theorists tends to assume that the conceptual scheme that fits classical music is adequate to understand rock. Placed within that scheme, the questions that have been asked tend to treat rock principally as a social phenomenon, a medium of folk poetry, or a genre of songs that are musically more complex than you might have thought.[3] Much is missed by this approach; it is a limiting framework that inevitably discovers a limited musical form.

Rock does not just challenge traditional assumptions of taste—although it certainly does do that—and it is not a simplistic musical medium. It is really best viewed as a separate type of music.[4] Its mode of existence is significantly different from classical or even earlier pop music. Failure to see this can be explained by a general disregard of the question of the ontology of rock musical works. Academic and even critical writing on rock is endemically vague concerning what rock musical works are. In such writing it is never made clear what exactly rock musicians create. The working assumption seems to have been that we can understand rock on the model of pop songs, and these in turn, on the model of classical music, which is the only musical form whose ontology has been extensively investigated.[5] But this assumption, I shall argue, is mistaken.

Moreover, it is a mistake with significant aesthetic consequences. The assimilation of rock to pop song and classical musical works leads thinkers to focus on the wrong features of rock music, insofar as they notice it at all, and to disregard whole domains of aesthetic interest that exist in rock music.[6] Given the rudimentary and predictable nature of rock's tonal structures, allegiance to traditional musical standards forces any search for rock's special character to shift to the power of live performance over its youthful audience and the social role of rock music in their lives. But this leaves out much that is special about the character of the music as heard.

To work out a complete reconceptualization of rock music would require a thorough rethinking of such central concepts in the philosophy of music as scores, works, and performances as these apply to rock. In this essay I shall focus on the concept that is key to understanding the changes in all the other central concepts of music as applied to rock: to understand the nature and history of rock music, as well as to understand why the aesthetics of rock music significantly differs from classical music, one must recognize the centrality of recording in rock music. But how central and in what way?

This centrality could be stated in many ways, some more radical than others—all, however, emphasizing a different relationship between music and recording than exists in other genres of music. In *Rhythm and Noise: An Aesthetics of Rock*, Theodore Gracyk argues that rock "employs recording as its *primary medium*."[7] Elsewhere, I have made the claim that rock musical *works* are recordings.[8] Donald Meyer claims both that "the producer is now the primary *auteur* of rock music," and that "the record (or CD) has become the *musical object*, now consumed in the car, at work or at home rather than in the concert hall."[9] Robert Ray asserts, "What distinguishes rock & roll from all the music that precedes it—especially classical, Tin Pan Alley, and jazz—is its elevation of the record to *primary status*."[10]

These claims are far from equivalent, nor are they transparently clear; they need philosophical scrutiny. If these thinkers are right, we must now add the concept of a recording to the fundamental concepts in the philosophy of music, if we wish to understand rock music. Accordingly, the details of how to formulate the central claim concerning rock music and recordings, why we should regard it as true, what a recording is, and what aesthetic consequences follow, will be sketched in what follows.

I. THE STANDARD ACCOUNT OF MUSIC

The account of musical works prevalent among philosophers and music theorists is founded on three interconnected concepts: work, score, and performance. The musical work is determined by the musical score, but is not to be identified with the score. Performances are instances of the musical work, which itself is commonly regarded as having the ontological status of a universal or a type, as individual 1987 Honda Accords are instances of the abstract type: 1987 Honda Accord.[11] Although, of course, the sensual pleasure of hearing the music can be achieved only if individual performances are produced, they otherwise have no bearing on the properties of the musical work per se. The differences between performances, in particular, are not of special theoretical interest, as all performances are conceived to approximate the ideal sound structure or pattern described by the score.

One of the claims implicit in most theoretical work on the ontology of music, whether Platonistic or nominalistic, is that this standard account, itself prior to any ontological theory,

describes the nature of *all* music. It is commonly implied that it applies to musical works in general, not just to the set of works these theorists particularly care about, namely, the classical music canon from 1700 to 1950. And even if the standard account fits Native American music or Tibetan rituals rather awkwardly, its proponents no doubt believe that at least it adequately describes Western music of recent centuries. I believe, however, that not even this is true. There is an extremely familiar and all-pervasive type of music that is not fully or adequately described by the standard account, and that is rock music.

II. ROCK MUSICAL WORKS AND RECORDINGS

Undoubtedly, the field of rock music, from the mid-1950s to the present, is enormously varied. Still, I believe that we can usefully begin to understand rock musical works by noting two points: first, that rock musicians of any stature first and foremost make recordings;[12] and second, that their hit recordings are their most important product. In itself this may not seem remarkable. After all, classical and jazz musicians of any stature also make recordings. One might even grant for the sake of argument that their recordings too are in some ways their most important product. This admission, however, does not appear to require reconceptualizing the familiar triad of work, score, and performance. This is because the recording may be viewed simply as a documentation of one important live performance of the work. What is "primary" in rock, according to this perspective, is either the song or the performance of the song. Adherents of this perspective will hold that rock pieces (i.e., songs) are independent of recordings and that recordings document performances of rock pieces, pieces that can be and are performed on many other occasions as well.

But this assimilation of rock recordings to pop or classical recordings, and with it of rock pieces to classical musical works, rings false to anyone familiar with rock music. If we reflect upon favorite rock pieces, we immediately sense that recordings stand to rock musical works in a different relation than recordings of classical music works stand to those works: for example, that the Beatles' recording of "Lucy in the Sky

With Diamonds" (on *Sgt. Pepper's Lonely Hearts Club Band*) stands to the work "Lucy in the Sky With Diamonds" in a more definitive relation than Monteux's recording of *The Rite of Spring*, however authoritative, stands to *The Rite of Spring*. Indeed, I join Gracyk and others[13] in proposing that instead of bracketing rock with the multiply-instanced arts of classical music and literature, that we regard it as primarily a recorded medium and we bracket it with film and printmaking (which are also multiply-instanced, but in an autographic way). Just as the final cut of a film is not just a recording of one performance of that film, but rather the definitive version of *the film* in all its detail (ditto for a lithograph plate), so a rock recording is, with the exception of "live" recordings, the definitive version of that musical work in all its detail.[14]

But unlike movies, rock music does involve live performance and sometimes even scores. So the intuition that rock records are somehow primary and analogous to movies will require much analysis and clarification. Before we can make any progress in that analysis, we need first to develop an adequate account of what a recording is.

III. ONTOLOGY OF RECORDINGS

There is a fundamental ambiguity at the heart of how we think about recordings. We think of them both as temporally ordered sets of sounds and as physical objects, for instance, as LPs, tapes, or CDs on the shelf. This ambiguity is reflected in the very meaning of "recording," which is ambiguous in much the way the term "book" is. In such utterances as "Is the *Philosophical Investigations* on the shelf?" "That's a heavy (or worn-out) book," and so forth, we are referring to physical objects that encode the book in its other and primary sense, that is, as a more abstract item, defined in the case of books/texts in terms of words, word order, and punctuation. Similarly, in such utterances as "How many records do you have in this room?" "These records are heavy," or "The *Sgt. Pepper* CD is a lot smaller than the old *Sgt. Pepper* record," we are referring to recordings as physical objects. In this, the material sense, recordings have little aesthetic importance.

But examine any discussion of recordings,

whether classical, pop, jazz, or rock, and you will hear a discussion, not of the physical properties of tape or disc but of sounding properties and events, whether of the musical work (for classical music), or of the performance, or of the mix or ambience. The very sounds we hear are the subject of discussion; what is *not* being talked about are the physical properties of tapes or discs. I shall call the temporal sequence of sounds we hear on a recording, the "extended sound event." This includes all the sounds one hears when the recording is played back. (I shall not try here to work out the units of this extended sound event. I do not, however, assume that these can be described always or adequately as tones in standard notational systems.) At any rate, to attend to the extended sound event is to attend to the exact speed of the music at any moment, the exact timbre of instruments, the exact balance of instruments, exact distortion of instruments, and any other sounds (found, sampled, generated) that are introduced. Thus, Glenn Gould's recording includes his humming as well as the exact frequencies from his piano (tones we crudely describe as bright or dull, sharp or flat, and so forth), his tempo fluctuations, the exact quality of his attack on each note, and so on. Here are some examples of features of the sound events on rock recordings: the exact way Paul McCartney's bass is mixed up over the vocal in "Got to Get You Into My Life"; the exact ways that the two backup vocals are mixed with Levon Helm's lead vocal on the chorus of the Band's "The Weight," each with a distinctive character that the recording highlights (even to mixing up the wordless vocalizations of the highest voice); or the exact juicy, squishy, reverb sound of the bass drum on that same cut (a sound whose descending first four notes, in contrast to the gentle folk guitar introductory chords, does so much to define the song);[15] more generally, the exact speed and the ways the tempo fluctuates on any given cut; or the exact feedback distortion and sounds (not just the particular notes—if he even hits conventional notes) that Jimi Hendrix gets out of his guitar on his extended guitar solo (from 4'25" to the end at 6'49") on "Third Stone From the Sun" (*Are You Experienced?*) as well as the sound of his highly processed and distorted voice on the same cut, which is mixed with electronically distorted found sounds; or the studio sounds, coughing, noodling on their instruments, and the voice counting: "One, two, three, four, one, two" at the beginning of "Taxman" (*Revolver*)—and so on, through an indefinite number of examples of properties that rock recordings have as extended sound events.

For some types of music, especially electronic and rock, we have learned to go beyond conventional musical nomenclature in order to describe the sounds that are heard, for example, in our understanding and description of electric guitar sounds ("feedback," "fuzz," "wah-wah"). For rock an eclectic vocabulary has to be used that borrows from ethnomusicology, electrical engineering, and performance criticism (e.g., in describing vocal sounds). In some cases, the best way to describe sounds and sonic properties may be to refer to how they are produced, as in "phase shift," "sine wave," or the sound of a saw tooth generator.

There is an obvious objection, however, to taking the recording as a sequence of sounds: *Which* sequence of sounds shall we regard as *the* recording?[16] Played back on tiny speakers a piece will sound very different·from the way it sounds played back on big speakers with a powerful amplifier. And the reissue of a recording on CD may sound different from the way it sounded on the original 45s, even more so if the reissue is in simulated stereo whereas the original was in monaural (a once common practice). Such tremendous variability of the sound events, depending on format and circumstances of playback, might tempt one to associate the recording with the unchanging master tape; in its stolid determinateness and causal priority it appears to be the fundamental determinant of the identity of the recording, whereas the tape or LP purchased in the store and the sounds generated therefrom seem mere epiphenomena by comparison.

However, there are insuperable problems with identifying the recording with the master tape. The master tape is the wrong *type* of thing. It doesn't have the same types of properties as a recording does in the sense in which we discuss the latest recordings of the Beatles or Cecilia Bartoli. The tape is so many feet long, whereas the recording lasts 3'42". The tape weighs so many pounds whereas the recording does not weigh any pounds. And so on. The tape

has the *capacity* to produce music upon appropriate playback, but in itself it does not begin loudly or with a F-sharp played on the organ.

Moreover, the recording is unique, whereas the master tape is not. Typically at least two master tapes are made and it is possible to make even more copies of it and for the recording to continue to exist even though the original master tape is destroyed.

The same argument that eliminates the master tape because of the lack of shared types of properties between a recording and the master tape also undermines any attempt to identify the recording with the physical LPs, tapes, and CDs produced when the recording is released. Besides, some of these may be defective. But absent appeal to the master tape, what sensible standard could establish which are defective?

It is natural to react to these problems by identifying the recording with the extended sound event *produced by* tapes, CDs, or LPs. This is on the right path but we need to solve some problems, the most important of which we have already seen: we will hear different sound events depending on which format we choose and how we choose to play it back. Assuming there is just one recorded entity, must we not choose one format and one right sound on playback? On what basis do we make such choices? And if we do make such choices, how can they be reconciled with a central way we think about recordings, namely, that the *same* recording exists in different formats?

IV. RECORDINGS AS NORM-KINDS

To accommodate these points, I propose an account that, while acknowledging the priority of the master tape, holds that the sort of entity we want is the extended sound event with its sonic properties. To frame such an account of what a recording is, I shall begin with the notion of norm-kinds, a notion due to Nicholas Wolterstorff and developed by James Anderson to account for the ontology of classical musical works.[17]

The idea of norm-kinds is simply the idea that there are kinds of thing that can have defective instances. Anderson gives the example of animal species: for example, the Lion; there can be properly and improperly formed lions. The kind Red Thing on the other hand, is not a norm-kind, "for there cannot be an improperly formed red thing, *qua* red thing" (44). The properties that define the norm-kind K are said to be "normative within a kind," and these are defined as properties that it is impossible to lack and still be a *properly formed* example of K. Now, Anderson points out that to every norm-kind there is a descriptive-kind that is defined as the kind of thing that *exactly* possesses all of the set of properties that define the norm-kind, for example, the descriptive-kind Perfect Lion. He uses these two notions to give an account of norm-kinds brought into existence by human activity (unlike animal species), such as musical works: "Perhaps the best way to understand the activity of creating a norm-kind is as an intentional operation on a previously existing descriptive-kind. . . . A humanly-created norm-kind, then, is a descriptive-kind made normative by a person at some time" (47). In the account Anderson proposes of the classical musical work the previously existing descriptive-kind is the sound structure defined by the score. This sound structure is made normative by the composer's publication of the score. And this is Anderson's point. He realizes that norm-kinds can be created by human activity, and thus he sees a plausible way to explain how composers can genuinely create their musical works, even though their works are in some sense identical with timeless sound structures.

Applying the notion of a norm-kind to recordings, I propose that the *descriptive-kind* that underlies the recording is the extended sound event (the sequence of sounds) produced by a studio-quality standard playback (circa the time of creation) of a master tape. There is no absolute precision here. If there are two master tapes, they might vary slightly, as might episodes of playback in the studio, even if governed by industry technical standards: for example, different speakers would produce slightly different sounds. But this fuzziness is built into the identity of the recording, I claim, just as a similar if lesser fuzziness is built into the identity of a film.

The *norm-kind*, which *is* the recording, is brought into existence, at least for commercial recordings, by the recording artists releasing or at least authorizing or approving a master tape;[18] this amounts to an extended sound event being made normative by industry and musical con-

ventions. Industry conventions govern the production of physical recordings (discs, tapes, LPs) to ensure that they approximate this sound when played back in the intended way.

To further capture our concept of a sound recording it is necessary to require that instances of the extended sound event be produced by a causal process emanating in the right way from the original master tape. This is because we regard even an exact *copy* of a recording's sound, if it is made by other musicians and engineers on a new master tape, as inauthentic; in rock, where such copies have been produced frequently, they are regarded as fakes. For example, in rock music we do not regard best-of-hits copies by other artists as authentic instances of the original recording, however accurately the copying artists mimic the sound of the original. This point is reflected in copyright law: although the sound of the recording is copyrighted, other musicians are free to make another recording that mimics that sound. Such a copy produces instances of the song but does not produce an instance of the original recording and would, therefore, not be regarded as an infringement of copyright.[19] It is a new recording. The failure to require a causal tether from an originating master to instances of a norm-kind is a significant gap in Anderson's account of norm-kinds. Its absence from an account of recordings would disguise the fact that recordings are autographic, and thus that musical works that are recordings, such as electronic music (and rock music; see below), are autographic artforms.

Anderson treats the relation between descriptive- and norm-kind as analogous to the relation of simple set inclusion in that *any* entity that instantiates most of the properties of the descriptive-kind would be an instance of the norm-kind. But it is doubtful that this is sufficient, even, in the case of a lion. A particular type of causal history of a putative lion is clearly being assumed. If a "lion" does not gain its properties by generation from a lion zygote, we will not be sure that it is really a lion. This is equally true for classical musical works, which are regarded by Anderson as abstract tonal structures made normative by composers. As Jerrold Levinson has shown, for a sound event to be a performance of a classical musical work—and there cannot be *instances* that are neither performances nor recordings of performances—some causal relation between sound production and original compositional indication of the sound structure has to exist.[20]

To summarize then, we can say that an instance of a recording must be produced by playback of a copy of a pressing master causally descended from the master tape. Causal processes are implicated at two stages then in our understanding of recordings; they also play a role in defining the norm-kind itself: it is the sound produced by appropriate playback of the master tape (or digital substitute) in the studio, where appropriate playback is clearly a notion that is governed by conventions in the music world and the record industry. An implication of this is that the precision or fuzziness of the norm kind could then change over time as the conventions vary in their requirements for studio playback.

On my account, then, instances of recordings have two types of salient properties: an essential causal condition and normative sonic properties. The essential condition of being an instance of the norm-kind Sound Recording is that it be the result of a playback of a properly caused physical recording—that is, a causal descendent from the master tape—whatever format that might be (tape, CD, LP), and even if it is a pirated copy.[21] The normative properties, against which playback is measured, are determined by the properties of the extended sound event heard in studio playback. So, if your tape recorder plays a tape of "No Expectations" at an incorrect or varying speed, it is still a playback of "No Expectations," but a defective one (in which, say, the pitches of the instruments are off).[22] If you equalize the playback in an exotic way, eliminating the bass and amplifying the higher frequencies, for instance, that is also a defective instance of the norm-kind.[23] If your record produces pops or thuds from a scratch, you are still hearing the recording but with additional sounds.

Now, Anderson claims that "[t]he essential characteristics of a norm-kind remains the same . . . such a kind is a kind for which correct and incorrect instances are possible."[24] It seems to me that recordings diverge in a significant way from both sorts of cases that he focuses on, that is, biological species and performances of classical music. In contrast to species and perform-

ances of classical musical works, where it is typical to correctly instantiate the norm, almost all instances of the norm-kind Recording only *approximate* to a certain degree the descriptive-kind defined by the studio playback.[25] Because of this difference, I suggest that we call Recordings and other entities that typically only approximate a norm, *approximate* norm-kinds. There is also another difference, tending in the opposite direction: instances of a recording (i.e., playback episodes) will be more similar to each other, considering their nonrelational properties, than are instances of natural kinds. Species, for example, can have all sorts of variable non-normative features such as hair and eye color or size. By contrast, the main variable quality for instances of recordings is absolute volume.

Although I regard recordings as similar to movies, prints, and photographs in being both autographic and norm-kinds, these other art-forms do not appear to be approximate norm-kinds. Movies, for instance, must be projected in a standard way (this standardized causal process defines the norm-kind). For example, there is nothing for movies quite like the freedom to change loudness and equalization that is so characteristic of playing a recording. Recordings are played back on millions of variable and adjustable playback systems. In this privatized setting, playback is only partly standardized. Nor are the differences introduced in this way irrelevant to our experience of the music. On the contrary, the variable features of playback events, especially for rock records, directly and relevantly affect our musical experiences in a way that, say, reading a book with very large or very small type should not affect our aesthetic experience of the book.

Let's briefly examine the application of this account to some recordings. Glenn Gould's first recording of the *Goldberg Variations* is the norm-kind whose normative properties are defined by the sounds produced by the master tape he and Columbia Records produced in 1955; his last recording of the *Goldberg Variations* is the norm-kind whose normative properties are defined by the sounds produced by the master tape he and Columbia Records produced in 1982. If the original was recorded in monaural and then released in fake stereo, then such stereo records are instances of the norm-kind although universally defective in one regard. Defective physical records are explained by this account, since they produce sound event instances defective relative to the descriptive-kind. If the recording is released in different formats, it may well sound different when played back in these different formats. But again, the notion of norm-kinds accommodates this: all of the resulting recordings produce instances of the work when played back even though they sound discernibly different from each other and some may be more defective than others. But what if, as happens in rock, a record is mixed differently for different formats? For playback on tinny portable phonographs, 45s may have been mixed in a way to boost their bass frequencies, for example; and dance club mixes are notoriously different in sound from the other versions of the same recordings. In such cases, we have to say that the work exists in different versions, since in effect there are different master tapes, just as a movie may exist in different versions, for example, in different "final" cuts.[26] On the other hand, a total remix, as in pieces on the recent *Blondie Remix Project* ("remixed, remade, and remodeled for the 90s") creates a new if derived work because it adds and alters material so as to stray significantly from the original extended sound event heard in the studio when the recording was originally produced.

IV. CONSTRUCTIVE RECORDINGS

The idea that rock pieces are recordings or that recordings are or can be musical works are not new ideas, but they have not until recently been taken seriously.[27] In part this may be because we have not previously had a clear notion of the ontology of recordings. But to get at the idea that a recording can be an *artwork* we need more than this. We need to make a distinction among recordings because not all recordings of music ought to be regarded as themselves musical works. That required distinction is between veridic and nonveridic or "constructive" (as I shall call them) recordings. Veridic recordings—or those regarded as true-to-performance—are those that are guided by two regulative ideas: (1) the notion of an independently existing live performance that the recording documents, and (2) a notion of how the live performance should sound, as established by some set of conventions for listening to per-

formances of that sort. Examples of musical subject matters whose recordings are standardly regarded as veridic are classical music, ethnic and folk music, classical jazz, and live rock music.[28] Such recordings played back are meant to sound as much as possible as the live extended musical event would sound, and they are, accordingly, regarded as the product of a neutral registration process in the same way that photography is often regarded (naively, to be sure) as a neutral recording of what things look like. Indeed, we tend unreflectively to think of *all* recording as necessarily veridic, but that is not correct.

If constructivity is a status based on how a recording is regarded, in most cases this status is honestly earned because of the type of causal process involved in producing the final recording. The total process of making a sound recording contains many points at which truth-to-performance can be undermined—put another way: many points where creative addition, subtraction, and alteration of the sounds can be accomplished. We may schematize the total recording process into inputs, mixing, processing, and mastering. Since this process is practiced on electronic, and therefore manipulable and degradable signals, it involves tremendous effort and skill, in fact, to produce a recording at the end of the process that is true to a performance played into microphones at the beginning. (If there is such a performance, as there is not for many recent rock recordings if we require that a "performance" involves the musicians playing together at the same time.)

Now, it will be clear that I am claiming that many rock recordings are constructive. This was much less true at its beginnings in the mid-1950s, but became more true as the recording technology developed sufficient complexity and power by the mid-1960s. Signals are input from sources other than microphones (e.g., electronically generated sounds and found-sound tapes). Signals are altered by various electronic devices to produce alteration in the wave forms and to add or subtract information through the use of processes such as feedback distortion, wah-wah, reverb, echo, aliasing, flanging, chorus, compression, and devices, such as harmonizers, ring modulators, enhancers, and so forth. With multiple tracks, signals are recorded at different times and places—thus removing the objective reality of an actual performance being recorded—and they can be mixed together in an indefinite number of ways. When a medium takes advantage of these possibilities, as rock music has, then it has certainly entered the realm of constructive recording. There likely will not be any actual, and there may not even be a possible performance that the recording reproduces (other than a "performance" consisting of a reproduction of the recording). The lack of a possible live performance is often invoked as an explanation of why some groups, such as the Beach Boys and the Beatles, ceased performing. The constructive nature of rock recording is also why, although a "live" recording of classical music is very similar to a studio recording of the same music, a "live" recording of rock music is usually very different from studio products.

We are now in a position to formulate the notion that recordings have a unique centrality in rock music. Here are two salient claims that one might make concerning any given recording:

1. The recording is (itself) a musical work.

2. The recording is the *primary* musical work brought into existence when the record is created.

Note that (1) is necessary but not sufficient for the truth of (2). Note, also, that typically, neither (1) nor (2) are true of veridic recordings. But while there seems no reason to regard veridic recordings as artworks in their own right no matter how important they may be for a given genre of music,[29] there is substantial reason to regard constructive recordings as artworks, indeed, musical works.

Recordings that are highly constructive because of their causal genesis (we might dub this subcategory "causally constructive") are compelling candidates to be regarded as musical works in their own right.[30] Recall that a recording is an extended sound event or sequence of events. In a recording that is causally constructive to a high degree this sound event is largely a product of the way electronic signals are generated and mixed within the recording process. The final result is created in the way that a sculptor might assemble a complicated sculpture. For example, to get the fantastic hurdy-gurdy sound on "Being for the Benefit of Mr. Kite," George Martin, the producer on *Sgt. Pepper*, made tapes of recordings of Victorian steam organs, cut the tapes into sixty small sections, mixed them randomly, and spliced them together, thus creating "a whole amalgam of carousel noises." As Martin describes it: "It was an unreal hotchpotch of sound, arrived at without rhyme or reason; but when it was added as a background 'wash' to the organ and harmonica track we had already made, it did give an overall impression of being in a circus."[31] Practices at least as causally constructive as this have become entirely typical in the recording studio since then. Certainly for such recordings it is plausible to hold that the musicians and producers and engineers have created a new type of musical work: together they have intentionally produced an extended sound event, tokens of which are produced when one plays their record. They have just as much claim to have produced a musical work as a classical music composer who composes electronic music on a record.[32]

Causal-constructivity is a matter of degree. While many records are far removed from any originating live performance, others are closer. Especially in rock until the mid-1960s, and for many groups since, the recording begins with musicians playing and producing sounds in the studio. The sounds on the recording, although certainly altered from the sound of live performance, still reflect the sound events of studio performances.

Even in such cases in which the recording process has only modest but definite influence, we can still regard the recording as constructive in the appreciative sense that it is not regarded as a veridical documentation of a live performance. Gracyk argues for this status for many rock and roll records, starting with Elvis's Sun session recordings of 1954. Gracyk, Greil Marcus, Peter Guralnick, and Robert Ray all point out the crucial nature of the sound of those Sun recordings. Guralnick writes: "The sound was always clean, never cluttered, with a kind of thinness and manic energy." Marcus adds: "There is that famous echo, slapping back at the listener. . . . The sound is all presence, as if Black and Moore each took a step straight off the record and Elvis was somehow squeezed right into the mike." And as Gracyk says, "the

Sun recordings were records first rather than recordings of musical performances," while Ray adds, "the performances that began rock & roll, Elvis's Sun recordings, could not be reproduced in any live situation except in a very small and empty (to permit reverberation) room."[33] Critics, knowledgeable listeners, and just plain fans all pay attention to the sound of rock records. It is the object of critical discourse and appreciative attention. Gracyk concludes that the Sun recordings "embodied a new *sound* as an essential quality of the musical work." Thus, even though only modestly causally constructive, these recordings became appreciated as constructive (nonveridical) as soon as they were released. This mode of listening was rapidly to become the common way of appreciating rock recordings, indicating why records have played a constitutive role in the development of rock music.[34]

We can now formulate two theses relating constructive recordings and rock music. The first is that, since rock records for the most part have been constructive, they have been musical works (in their own right). More strongly, I suggest that since the mid-1960s (for most rock recordings) the recording has been the *primary* musical work brought into existence with the creation of the rock record. I turn now to developing the idea of the recording as the primary work by comparison to other musical entities *also* generated in the creation of rock recordings.

V. THE ONTOLOGICAL MULTIPLICITY OF ROCK

Saying that the recording in rock is the primary musical work involves the idea that the sounds of the recording cannot be regarded adequately merely as a performance of a song—in the traditional sense of "song"—in the way that pop and folk recordings in the past have often been correctly regarded as recordings of performances of songs. Rather, the sounds that compose a rock recording constitute a work in themselves. Plus, they are the primary target of both the artists's intentions and the listeners' attentions. To be sure, there is a common use of the term "song" in which it refers both to the hit recordings of rock music and to the song proper instanced on the recording. That song proper is

an entity that can be performed by an indefinite number of people in an indefinite number of ways. The criteria for the identity of a song qua song are quite minimal. It is merely a melodic structure and a verbal text. Recognizability is the main condition defining an instance as a particular song.[35] A song can be arranged in an indefinite number of ways. In itself it does not have to have any particular instrumentation or speed or loudness or phrasing. It is extremely schematic, as any comparison of what is common to all of the covers of any Beatles song clearly shows.

Take, as an example, a recent recording of the Beatles' psychedelic masterpiece "Tomorrow Never Knows" (*Revolver*) by guitarist Michael Hedges.[36] Through the use of extensive overdubs and tape-loops, the original plunges the listener into a whole universe of screaming gulls and people, hysterical trumpets, distorted and apocalyptic electric guitars, with symphony orchestra and cheerful honky-tonk piano in the background. In decided contrast, Hedges arranges the song for acoustic guitar and fretless bass. His version takes the song at a relaxed medium tempo, producing a mellow, laid-back, pretty piece of music in the acoustic folk tradition. He uses overdubbing and distortion only near the end of the cut. Hedges also takes great liberties with the notes and phrasing of the song, removing the hypnotic and edgy quality of the narrow up-and-down oscillation of the melody. The result is surely the song "Tomorrow Never Knows," but it is rather like performing a Schubert song substituting an entirely different piano part from a different musical era and leaving out half of the vocal part. In the classical tradition, such a rearrangement would be regarded as, at best, a new work. Hedges's arrangement dismantles the original relation of the music to the words from the Tibetan *Book of the Dead* and Timothy Leary: it alters almost every expressive and aesthetic property of the original music. What properties? Mark Lewisohn describes "Tomorrow Never Knows" as

a heavy metal recording of enormous proportion, with thundering echo and booming, quivering, ocean-bed vibrations. And peaking out from under the squall was John Lennon's voice, supremely eerie, as if it were being broadcast through the cheapest transistor radio from your local market, and delivering the most bizarre Beatles lyric yet, including one line taken directly from Dr. Timothy Leary's version of the Tibetan *Book of the Dead.* [37]

Although songs proper are thus ontologically "thin," to use Gracyk's terminology,[38] they are important. As I have already suggested, the names of rock musical works are used in a systematically ambiguous manner both for the song and for a particular recording. "Tomorrow Never Knows" refers to a song as well as to a famous recording. There is, in fact, a clear dualism of creation in rock recordings. They exhibit the creation of two main items: the song proper and the recording (and in fact a third item, the arrangement). My thesis is that the principal object of appreciation, the entity with the best claim to be the rock musical work itself, is the recording.[39]

Arrangements of songs need to be considered as well. They can involve various levels of specificity from the crudely schematic ("head arrangements") to those fully notated in standard musical notion. Such a precisely scored arrangement is in many ways parallel to a classical musical work. However, even precise scores of the sort we get in classical music will not include all the relevant information that goes into determining a recording. In any case, the creation of a rock recording usually represents the creation of at least three musical objects.

We can contrast song, arrangement, and recording by imagining a score of the arrangement of the Rolling Stones' "No Expectations," in which were notated the particular bass line that Bill Wyman plays, with its very striking swooping attacks on the two high bass notes played on the words "to pass" (at 57″). These notes and the way they are played are definitive of the recording but inessential to the song (as demonstrated by their striking absence in the last chorus). But in spite of the greater completeness of the imagined score, the point I insist on is that even a scored arrangement in standard musical notation cannot fully capture the particular extended sound event that we hear when we play a paradigm rock record such as "No Expectations," since the exact mix, and many other features of the extended sound event are not part of the scored work. The exact way

Wyman attacks those notes *each* time he plays them as well as the way the bass is mixed up for those two notes and then mixed down at other times is not part of the conceptual scheme of standard musical notation, which does not comment on recording mix. Nor should it comment on exact recording mix. Far from dictating an exact sound, it is an essential feature of standard musical notation that it leaves open the possibility of nuanced variation of performances of scores within norms of performance practice.[40] The difference between the many ways Wyman might have played those notes on different takes of his track all would have been consistent with a score in standard notation (even one with standard expression marks).

Along with the incompleteness of a standardly notated score is an equally significant fact about rock recordings: the absence of a preexisting score. This absence is a critical conceptual feature of the rock recording. Because of this absence, the definitive nature of the rock recording cannot be thought to be the result of its being a particularly significant performance of a work specified by a preexisting score, as we might regard a recording of Rachmaninov playing one of his own piano works or the recordings by Britten and Stravinsky conducting their own orchestral works.[41] So, even though scores of arrangements underlying rock pieces are sometimes produced after the fact by transcribing the recording, these scores are in a curious limbo. Insofar as they are meant to be scores to be performed—and this seems to be the standard case—they will conform to standard musical notation, and accordingly diverge (often quite radically) from the sound heard on the recording, leave instrumentation partially open, and allow for variation in performance.[42] If, however, they were an attempt to capture as exactly as possible the notes played on the recording, they would be only a guess about what possible imaginary arrangement the band instantiated, a guess not underwritten by conventions of authorship and publication in the way that the publication of a score for a classical musical work authoritatively determines that work.

Every musical creation requires the invocation of conventions for bringing the work into existence—the publication of a score, for instance. In rock the release of the sound recording is the act by which the work is brought into existence,[43] and this has consequences for the nature of the rock musical work. While the *song* can be recovered from the recording, it is much less clear that a specific authoritative score of an arrangement can be recovered or that it is relevant to recover it. Indeed the after-the-fact production of a score does nothing to show that the recording was a performance of that scored work, and not, by contrast, a wayward performance of a different score.[44] This underlines the point that the preexisting classical score is normative for performance whereas an after-the-fact rock score is essentially descriptive and could not be normative for future performances.

(What is normative for performance? This is a complex topic. Let me say here, only that we ascribe to the original artists and only to them the ability to produce authentic re-creations of the rock musical work in live performance. Both these authentic instances as well as the ubiquitous fakes—that is, covers—are directly guided by the sound of the hit recording.)

To return to my main thesis, support so far has come from the nature of the record production process and from the observations just made concerning conventions and the absence of scores. There is a further argument for the thesis. We very naturally ascribe the properties of the recording to the work: for example, that in *Exile on Main St.* the voice is, as Christgau says, "submerged under studio murk."[45] And many of the properties one naturally ascribes to the work turn out to be properties of the recording, not of the song nor even an arrangement of the song. Consider the very common practice of fade-outs and cutoffs. R.E.M.'s "What's the Frequency, Kenneth?" (*Monster* [1994]) begins with a tape cut in the middle of the full band sound, giving this work an incredibly abrupt beginning. On the same album, "I Don't Sleep, I Dream" ends with another tape cut in the middle of the full sound of the band. The sudden cutoff is inevitably *shocking*. So, "What's the Frequency, Kenneth?" begins abruptly and "I Don't Sleep, I Dream" has a shocking ending. But the properties of having an abrupt beginning or a shocking ending are not properties of the song (strictly defined) or even of any *possible* arrangement of the song, since in live performance of a standardly notated arrangement[46]

the sound of the instruments cannot be suddenly turned on or cut off.

VI. AESTHETIC CONSEQUENCES

I shall briefly conclude with some consequences of the account I have put forth. One consequence I do *not* think follows is the reduction of rock music to the recording. Obviously, live performance is very important in rock. But we tend to give it undue weight in our theoretical accounting. The extreme valorization of rock stars encourages us to romanticize their live performances over the more "technical," collaborative, and distanced events in the recording studio. If the present account is correct, we must add producers and engineers to the group of creative artists who bring the rock musical work into existence.[47] As Mark Lewisohn remarks of "Tomorrow Never Knows," "It would be wrong to assume that the Beatles alone were responsible for this remarkable recording, or for the progressiveness which would be the hallmark of much of their future output."[48] A recording that is a musical work is, like a movie, the product of a collaboration.

Moreover, knowing about the nature of that collaboration is essential to a proper appreciation of the musical work, once we accept that the recording itself is the primary musical work. Knowing about the alternative takes, what was included and what was discarded, is as relevant for rock records as knowing the musical sketches of classical composers is to their works. Moreover, knowing how sounds were produced and combined to make a recording is essential even to knowing *what* one is hearing. Is that a real chicken or an electric guitar at the beginning of the reprise of "Sgt. Pepper's Lonely Hearts Club Band"? (In fact, it is both: the sound of a clucking chicken is so mixed as to turn into the opening guitar note of "Sgt. Pepper.") In short, knowledge of how the recording was made affects and should affect appreciation. It is as relevant as contextual information concerning the creation of artworks is to other art forms.

We have seen that the relevant aesthetic properties of rock musical works are different, more wide-ranging and complex than those of the song sound structure or even than those of the particular conventional arrangement exemplified on the recording. It follows that we cannot seriously propose that, say, *Sgt. Pepper* or *Surrealistic Pillow*, or any of the songs on these albums, are among the great musical works of the second half of the twentieth century if we do not focus on what *Sgt. Pepper* or *Surrealistic Pillow* really are—or conversely, if we consider only a highly schematic description of them as aesthetically relevant. We can, for instance, make legitimate and illuminating comparisons between the power of the climax, the last twenty-four bars, of "A Day in the Life," and the most powerful moments in classical musical works. But to do so it is necessary to have a full and unblinkered understanding and experience of all the elements that go into that sound sequence (the rising sound of the symphony orchestra overdubbed four times, each out of phase, the final overdubbed "crash" chord, the final 45-second decay of the sound while the microphones increased sensitivity to include all the ambient sound).[49] The theoretical framework necessary to achieve this understanding is one that focuses on the recording, and thus includes *all* of its sounds.

The complexity of the recorded rock work is not such as to be captured by standard musical notation, nor does it involve the harmonic development of classical music. Nonetheless, it has its own compelling dimensions, such as timbral, rhythmic, and sonic effects, often much more intricate and powerful than those of classical music. This is why it is important to sort out the ontology of rock. It is premature to focus on the style of rock music, as has been done up until now, before we identify the main types of musical objects associated with it and their properties. This set of musical objects comprises at the least the recording, the song (in the strict sense), and that rather shadowy entity, the arrangement. I have shown here why, from this set of musical objects, we should regard the recording as the primary "rock musical work." Not only is it a new kind of musical object, it has been the dominant force in the development of rock music. After the mid-1960s, recording became, to use George Martin's words about the recording of *Sgt. Pepper*, "something which will stand the test of time as a valid art form: sculpture in music, if you like."[50]

1. George Martin, *All You Need Is Ears* (New York: St. Martin's, 1979), p. 78.

2. An important exception to this generalization has recently been published: Theodore Gracyk's *Rhythm and Noise: An Aesthetics of Rock* (Durham: Duke University Press, 1996). Other significant exceptions include Richard Shusterman, "Form and Funk: The Aesthetic Challenge of Popular Art," *British Journal of Aesthetics* 31:3 (July 1991): 203–13, and Bruce Baugh, "Prolegomena to Any Aesthetics of Rock Music," *The Journal of Aesthetics and Art Criticism* 51:1 (Winter 1993): 23–29.

3. Examination of academic writing on rock music reveals, unsurprisingly, that the two most popular subjects for attention are rock lyrics (as literature) and the social causes, functions, and implications of rock music. A distant third place goes to the occasional attempt to apply formal music analysis to rock songs.

4. It is beyond the scope of this essay to tackle the complex question of how to define "rock" music. I take rock to be a generic form of music that includes subgenres, such as rap, reggae, punk, (some) blues, heavy metal, and so forth. It grew out of, and in many ways includes rock and roll, which was born in the early 1950s. I agree with Gracyk and Moore that it ought not to be defined essentially as a musical style (in terms of form, harmonies, rhythms, instrumentation, and so forth). It has to be admitted, however, that there is also a common use of the term for a particular style that is only a subspecies of the generic category. Limiting the notion of "rock" music to this subgenre, however, would have the paradoxical effect of ruling out many (perhaps most) of the recordings regularly regarded as among the greatest in the history of rock music: for instance, most of the cuts on *Sgt. Pepper*, a third of the cuts on *Rubber Soul*, and so on. See Gracyk, *Rhythm and Noise*, and Allan F. Moore, *Rock; The Primary Text: Developing a Musicology of Rock* (Buckingham and Philadelphia: Open University Press, 1993).

5. This is by now a very large literature. See Jerrold Levinson, "What a Musical Work Is, Again," in his *Music, Art, and Metaphysics: Essays in Philosophical Aesthetics* (Ithaca: Cornell University Press, 1990); Peter Kivy, *The Fine Art of Repetition: Essays in the Philosophy of Music* (Cambridge: Cambridge University Press, 1993); Roman Ingarden, *The Work of Music and the Problem of Its Identity* (Berkeley and Los Angeles: University of California Press, 1986); and Lydia Goehr, *The Imaginary Museum of Musical Works: An Essay in the Philosophy of Music* (Oxford: Oxford University Press, 1992).

6. This claim is argued with great vigor by Gracyk in *Rhythm and Noise*. Culture critics of rock music—for example, Allan Bloom, *The Closing of the American Mind* (New York: Simon and Schuster, 1987); Theodore Adorno, *Aesthetic Theory* (London: Routledge & Kegan Paul, 1983); and Mark Miller, *Boxed In: The Culture of TV* (Evanston: Northwestern University Press, 1989)—invariably focus on the "wrong" features of rock music. That is, they focus on dimensions (such as harmonic development), that are not important to rock, or else on features (such as rock's often sensuously overwhelming "noise") that *are* important for rock but that in rock are not the mistakes or failings they would be in classical music. For a rebuttal to such critics, see Shusterman, "Form and Funk."

7. Gracyk, *Rhythm and Noise*, p. 13; emphasis added.

8. "The Ontological Complexity of Rock Music," paper delivered at the American Society for Aesthetics convention, Saint Louis, Missouri, October 1995. Gracyk makes a related but clearer claim: "While the song appears on the fifth track on *Born to Run*, that track (the recording) is a distinct musical work [emphasis added] in its own right" (*Rhythm and Noise*, p. 17).

9. Donald C. Meyer, "The Real Cooking is Done in the Studio: Toward a Context for Rock Criticism," *Popular Music and Society* 19:1 (Spring 1995): 9; emphasis added. Concerning the question of who is the artist in rock, Charlie Gillett has argued "that the artist on a phonograph record can very well be the producer, not the performer." Charlie Gillett, "The Producer as Artist," in H. Wiley Hitchcock, ed., *The Phonograph and Our Musical Life: Proceedings of a Centennial Conference* (New York: Institute for Studies in American Music, 1977), p. 51.

10. Robert Ray, "Tracking," *South Atlantic Quarterly* 90:4 (Fall 1991): p. 781; emphasis added. Jonathan Tankel puts it an even different way. About at least some recordings he says, "The recording itself *is* . . . rock music"; "The Practice of Recording Music: Remixing as Recording," *Journal of Communication* 40:3 (Summer 1990): p. 41.

11. Although Nelson Goodman's nominalist account of the ontology of musical works in *The Languages of Art: An Approach to a Theory of Symbols* (Indianapolis: Hackett, 1976; originally published, Bobbs-Merrill, 1968) blocks him from thinking of the musical work as a type or universal, in other respects his account is a model of the standard one.

12. I realize that (a) a rock group develops and plays *something* prior to recording—though over the last twenty years that "something" less and less resembles a completely arranged song for many groups—and that (b) there may be rock "pieces" that are never or at least not yet recorded. To account for these entities requires a complex discussion of live performance that must be reserved for a larger project of which this essay is a part. Roughly, we may regard such entities on the margins as analogous to sketches (case a) or to song arrangements (case b). See below where it is acknowledged that rock music comprises multiple entities.

13. Gracyk says that in "rock, musical works with a status 'like that of a film' are perfectly common" (*Rhythm and Noise*, p. 17). Gillett, in "The Producer as Artist," argues that the producer is analogous to the director of a film.

14. Accordingly, I believe that Nelson Goodman's claim that music *in general* is an allographic art is an invalid generalization. To show this in any detail, however, goes beyond the bounds of this paper and needs to take into account some of Goodman's qualifications about "marginal" musics (such as electronic music) being nonallographic. In rock it is a familiar fact that there are accurate copies that are not the authentic works—namely, covers—that are both recorded and live; see section IV below, and see also Gracyk, *Rhythm and Noise*, chap. 1.

15. Indeed, these subtle differences are so important in rock recording that contemporary producers of rock records can choose from literally thousands of sampled drum sounds to get just the right drum sound on the record.

16. This problem was emphasized to me by Dale Jamieson.

17. See Nicholas Wolterstorff, *Works and Worlds of Art* (Oxford: Clarendon Press, 1980), and James Anderson, "Musical Kinds," *British Journal of Aesthetics* 25:1 (Winter 1985): 43–49.

18. Recordings can exist even though unreleased. This follows from such facts as that a scholar can study an unreleased recording or that artists can sue the recording company to have the recording released. But because many recordings are "constructive" (see below) it may not always be so clear whether unreleased material amounts to a recording. In part, this confusion results because "approval" or "authorization" is such a complex fact. It comes in many forms. For example, Coleman Hawkins said of his best take on Max Roach's "Driva' Man," during which he makes a prominent squeak, "No, don't splice. When it is all perfect, especially in a piece like this, there's something very wrong" (Max Roach, *Freedom Now Suite*, Columbia JC 36390). Another factor is the type of music involved. For instance, a putatively veridical recording such as the recently discovered but previously presumed lost Byron James recording of *Pictures at an Exhibition* clearly existed even if James did not get a chance to approve it. This is especially so because of his practice of recording in one long unedited take. I would contrast this with the Beatles' never released, nearly complete album *Get Back*, compiled and mixed by Glyn Johns in 1969. The Beatles album (marked: "Keep—do not scrap") may be regarded as never having been fully brought into existence as a complete work (or collection of works); see Mark Lewisohn, *The Beatles: Recording Sessions* (New York: Harmony Books, 1988).

19. See J. Gunnar Erickson, Edward R. Hearn, and Mark E. Halloran, *Musician's Guide to Copyright* (San Francisco: Bay Area Lawyers for the Arts, 1979; rev. ed., New York: Scribner, 1983). Note there the attempt to make the distinction by using the expression "the actual sounds": "infringement takes place whenever all or any substantial portion of the *actual sounds* that make up a recording are reproduced . . . by any method. . . . Mere imitation of a recorded performance by means of a separate, independent sound recording does not constitute a copyright infringement" (p. 39; emphasis added).

20. See Jerrold Levinson, "Autographic and Allographic Art Revisited," in his *Music, Art, and Metaphysics*. The problem that the casual requirement is designed to deal with is to differentiate structurally identical but otherwise different musical works—in other words, indiscernible counterparts. See John Andrew Fisher, "Is There a Problem of Indiscernible Counterparts?" *Journal of Philosophy* 92:9 (September 1995): 467–84. In rock and roll almost indiscernible counterparts of recordings have been common but up until now knowledgeable listeners have been able to tell takes and later covers by the same artists from the original hit.

21. See Erickson, Hearn, and Halloran, *Musician's Guide to Copyright*, p. 39.

22. For example, the premiere of Varèse's *Poème Electronique* in New York in 1958, although a disappointment because it was a greatly flawed playback, was an instance of the work. The work, composed as three tape tracks, was originally played on three banks of specially designed and positioned speakers in Brussels at the World's Fair, whereas in New York it was played over a single set of speakers. See Peter Manning, *Electronic and Computer Music* (Oxford: Oxford University Press, 1985; 2d ed., 1993), p. 86.

23. With with exception of *HPSCHD* by John Cage and Lejaren Hiller (1970), which mandates for each copy of the physical record a different set of specific changes in volume, treble, and bass settings for the left and right channels to be made every five seconds over the course of the 21-minute work.

24. Anderson, "Musical Kinds," p. 47.

25. Of course, a sufficiently defective playback or physical recording will lead to an unrecognizable playback, and this will not be an instance of the norm-kind. This is not a problem. We no more have to decide ahead of time exactly what counts as a nonversion of the recording—that is, where along all the relevant sonic dimensions to draw sharp lines, than we have to decide how many wrong notes (or ignored expression markings) constitute a nonperformance of a classical musical work or how many missing anatomical features constitute a noninstance of an animal species.

26. What of a recording of a recording (e.g., a tape recording of a CD)? Does this also encode the work? If there is an analogy between recording and printmaking, and a copy of a print (e.g., a very good photograph of it) is not the work, then a copy of a physical recording should also not be the musical work, that is, the recording. But the parallel breaks down here. We allow a reproduction process to be iterated in the case of sound recordings, and on my account these will count as examples of the recording.

27. For example, twenty years ago Charles A. Schicke put it this way: "As one commentator on the record scene has astutely noted, 'The record is the song.' " *Revolution in Sound: A Biography of the Recording Industry* (Boston: Little, Brown, 1974), p. 159.

28. In the case of classical music recordings the assumptions of veridicality to an actual performance is something of an illusion. For one thing, rarely does a recording in fact register a single take; rather, it is a mixture of takes. For the exception that proves the rule, see the *New York Times* (11 December 1994) article on the presumed-lost recording by Byron Janus of *Pictures at an Exhibition* done in a single take, "A Fresh Relic of a 'Lost Generation.' " Still, a recording is meant to represent a possible performance.

29. Paul Berliner, in *Thinking in Jazz: The Infinite Art of Improvisation* (Chicago: University of Chicago Press, 1994), argues that recordings have had a tremendous influence on the development of jazz, for instance. Recordings have enabled jazz musicians to hear and learn influential performances, many of which were improvisations. Still, these recordings document a performance and they are typically listened "through"; that is, they are regarded as transparent records of what a live performance sounded like.

30. For this reason, there are many examples of musical works that exist solely as recordings. For example, many works of electronic music—those that involve no live performance—are essentially recordings: Charles Dodge's *Earth's Magnetic Field*; Pierre Henry's *Variations on a Door and a Sigh*; Luening and Ussachevsky's *Sonic Contours*; Edgar Varèse's *Poème Electronique*; and so on. There are also other genres of music in which musical works are created primarily in the form of recordings: various new-age/environmental records (e.g., ocean with synthesizer, Enya), and many pop recordings, especially those by such studio masters as Esquivel and Les Paul.

31. George Martin, *All You Need Is Ears*, p. 205.

32. With a new type of artwork comes a new art medium. The favored term for this medium is "phonography." See Evan Eisenberg, *The Recording Angel: Explorations in Phonography* (New York: McGraw-Hill, 1987).

33. All quotes from Gracyk, *Rhythm and Noise*, p. 15.

34. This was partly a *social construction*, caused by the mass-produced phonograph record. Given that in rock, each group performs its own distinctive songs (proper), does not often produce multiple recordings of the same song, and is relatively unavailable for live performance, the recording is bound to take on a life of its own even without the further impetus of causal constructivity. How many of us ever heard or could have heard Booker T and the MG's or the Meters live? They were studio creators and creations, even though they did perform live.

35. In the law, copyright infringement of songs requires only tonal similarity between the two musical works and "lack of originality," which means that the similarity is the result of derivation of the later from the earlier work.

36. Michael Hedges, *Oracle*, Windham Hill (1996).

37. Lewisohn, *The Beatles: Recording Sessions*, p. 72.

38. Gracyk, *Rhythm and Noise*, pp. 19–20.

39. Although this thesis is made initially plausible by considering such electronic creations as "A Day in the Life," its scope, as has already been indicated, goes beyond such music to include even recordings from the beginnings of rock and roll, such as those that originated in the studios of Chess and Sun Records; see Robert Palmer, "The Church of the Sonic Guitar," *South Atlantic Quarterly* 90:4 (Fall 1991): 649–73. That is why I have called attention to characteristics of recordings of other less electronically oriented musicians, such as The Band and the Rolling Stones.

40. I take it that there is convincing evidence that each performance of the same arrangement or classical music score will differ from every other, even performances by the same performers; see José Bowen's "Connecting Performance, Interpretation, and Meaning: When Is Beethoven's Fifth Heroic?" paper delivered at the American Musicological Society convention in Minneapolis, October 1994. That's why different interpretations (i.e., performances) of classical music are so interesting, because they differ in all sorts of important ways, but within norms for performing scores. While a given recorded performance is only definitive of one particular performance of a classical music work, in rock it is definitive of the piece itself.

41. No matter how interesting or significant such recordings are, they do not amount to a binding interpretation of the score that subsequent performers must copy. And for good reason, as the composer is free to decide to perform the work a different way subsequently.

42. Meyer, "The Real Cooking Is Done in the Studio," notes defects in Wilfrid Mellers's analysis of Beatles recordings resulting from inappropriate reliance on transcriptions: "I questioned why the harmonic analysis of some songs was given in a different key from that of the harmony on the record, but it became clear that Mellers was contemplating the sheet music version of the songs rather than the records. Scholars like Mellers, it seems, would rather address a secondary realization of the music—the transcription rather than the record—since it bears the comforting similarity to the score in classical music" (p. 3).

43. This is a simplification. There is a curious limbo for

unreleased recordings such as the Beatles' album *Get Back.*
Consider Prince's unreleased *Black Album.* It was recorded
in 1987 but only released in 1994. Prince ordered all copies
destroyed in 1987. So did it exist from 1987? A necessary
condition, surely, is that the album be completed. However,
this may not be determined decisively until it is released.
Thus the Beatles' *Get Back* metamorphosed into *Let It Be,*
and so forth; see Lewisohn, *The Beatles: Recording Sessions.*

44. There are no conventions to determine an answer
here, as far as I can see. And wherer there are no conventions, an answer requiring conventions cannot be right.

45. Robert Christgau, "The Rolling Stones," in Jim
Miller, ed., *The Rolling Stone Illustrated History of Rock &
Roll* (New York: Random House, 1976), p. 188. This is not
a defect of the recording as it would be of a recording of,
say, *Exsultate Jubilate.*

46. This qualification is required because live performance has come to resemble a recording session in its use of
electronic processes and prerecorded material to mimic studio effects. Thus sudden starts and stops might be possible,
in a small room at least, through the use of electronic means
on amplified sounds.

47. This has already been asserted for some famous producers, such as Phil Spector. For instance, Lewisohn claims:
"Almost all of Spector's output carried the stamp of a domi-
nating and forceful producer; they were perhaps more his
records than the actual artist's" (*The Beatles: Recording
Sessions,* p. 197).

48. Ibid., p. 70.

49. Martin writes: "Geof had his faders—which control
the volume input from the studio—way down at the moment
of impact. Then, as the sound died away, he gradually
pushed the faders up, while we kept as quiet as church mice.
In the end, these were so far up, and the microphones so
live, that you could hear the air-conditioning" (*All You Need
Is Ears,* p. 212).

50. Ibid., p. 214. This article grew out of two papers delivered at meetings of the American Society for Aesthetics. I
read "The Ontological Complexity of Rock Music" in Saint
Louis, Missouri, in October 1995, and I read "The Ontology
of Recordings: A First Pass," in Asilomar, California, April
1996. I thank my commentators on those occasions, Patricia
Herzog and Stephen Davies, for helpful discussion. I also
thank Christopher Shields, Jason Potter, and Richard Cameron for reading various versions. Above all, I thank musicologist, rock performer, record producer, and ancient
instrument performer, Mark Davenport, for giving me the
benefit of his superior knowledge. Thanks are also due Tom
Peard, who insightfully discussed the argument of this essay
with me several times. That argument is much clearer because of his influence.

NOËL CARROLL

Cage and Philosophy

The influence of the late John Cage extends in many directions, affecting not only musical practice and the theory of composition, but postmodern choreography, poetry, performance art, and even philosophy. In this brief note, I intend to explore Cage's relevance to philosophy. To this end, I shall examine Cage's own philosophy of music and conclude with some remarks about the significance of Cage's project for the philosophy of art in general.

Cage, of course, has left us a large body of writing. Even if he did not think that his music "said" anything, he surrounded it with a great deal of doctrine, freighting his experiments with aesthetic, moral, and political relevance. Much of the writing is polemical, animated by a philosophical conception of music, or, as he would prefer to call it, of the "organization of sound."[1] Of sound, Cage asserts:

A sound does not view itself as thought, as ought, as needing another sound for its elucidation, as etc.; it has not time for any consideration—it is occupied with the performance of its characteristics: before it has died away it must have made perfectly exact its frequency, its loudness, its length, its overtone structure, the precise morphology of these and of itself.[2]

For Cage, what we call music ought to be sound as such, bereft of anything we might be tempted to call "meaning."

He says that "I imagine that as contemporary music goes on changing in the way that I'm changing it what will be done is to more and more completely liberate sounds from abstract ideas and more exactly to let them be physically uniquely themselves."[3] And along with eschewing the association of abstract ideas, Cage explicitly rejects attributions of themes or pur-

poses to his compositions.[4] Cage's philosophically motivated musical practice, in turn, was to rivet aesthetic attention to sound as such. That is: "New music: new listening. Not an attempt to understand something that is being said, for if something were being said, the sounds would be given the shapes of words. Just attention to the activity of sounds."[5]

Of the programmatical importance of emphasizing or foregrounding sound as such as the object of audience attention, Cage claims:

... I said that since the sounds were just sounds, this gave people hearing them the chance to be people, centered within themselves where they actually are, not off artificially in the distance as they are accustomed to be, trying to figure out what is being said by some artist by means of sounds. Finally I said that the purpose of this purposeless music would be achieved if people learned to listen; that when they listened they might discover that they preferred the sounds of everyday life to the ones they would presently hear in the musical program; that that was alright as far as I was concerned.[6]

Put in the idiom that is increasingly popular nowadays, Cage construes what the tradition identifies as *musical* sounds to be "privileged." He, in response, is concerned to dethrone them. Moreover, this ambition seems underwritten by the sense that the distinction between music and sound (or noise) portends a deeper division, namely one that divorces the listener from the world. Here it is useful to contrast Cage's view with Schopenhauer's. It was Schopenhauer's conviction that music was the highest art just because it bore the least relation to the everyday world of appearances. But for Cage, insofar as the distinction between music and noise is another instance of the dichotomy between art and the world, it warrants dissolution.[7] Thus, he approvingly quotes Jasper Johns's remark that "I can imagine a society without any art at all, and it is not a bad society."[8]

One of Cage's key strategies for dissolving these homologous dichotomies is to foreground noise—sometimes naturally occurring noise, sometimes musical (but decontextualized as in *Hymns and Variations*). In *Imaginary Landscape No. 4,* the "instruments" are twelve radios, tuned according to random procedures. This results in a mélange with neither discernible structure nor comprehensive sense, thereby putatively reducing attention to the humanly produced sounds as just sounds. Likewise, in the self-explanatory *Demonstration of the Sounds of the Environment,* three hundred people silently follow an itinerary generated by aleatoric procedures derived from the *I Ching.* Of course, Cage's best-known piece in this genre is his *4'33"* in which silence is used as a notational device, i.e., as a way of framing circumambient sounds. In it, the performer opens the score, but plays nothing, compelling the audience—by subtraction, so to speak—to attend to whatever sounds happen in the interval of "silence."

In all these cases, Cage's goal is to design a context in which *ex hypothesi,* the audience is, in a manner of speaking, encouraged, if not coerced or reduced, to attending to the qualities of the sounds themselves for the simple reason that the events have been constructed in such a way that there is nothing else to which one could attend. On some occasions, Cage's polemical justification of these strategies reminds one of the sloganeering of the early Russian formalists. That is, his defamiliarizing strategies, such as the use of chance composition and silence as a notational device, enable us to listen to the world afresh.[9] By being confronted, in other words, by sounds in a new way, we attend to qualities that heretofore went unnoticed. But at other times, Cage is also apt to characterize the importance of foregrounding sound as such in the language of classical aesthetic theory. By reframing sound via notational silence, we are granted access to generally unheeded beauties. Thus, at times Cage motivates attention to sound as an adventure in the perception of qualities that are customarily

ignored, while, at other times, he is wont to speak more generically of beauty.[10]

Part and parcel of Cage's brief against the musical tradition of the West is his insistence that the sounds that he foregrounds neither say anything nor do they have a purpose. Cage appears to believe this is because chance operations pre-empt the direct operation of the will on his material. This makes its interpretation in terms of authorial intention impossible, for the artist no longer has the means to express herself or to realize intended purposes. Paraphrasing Susan Sontag, an aesthetician obviously under the influence of Cage, we might say that the composition just is; it does not convey a meaning to be interpreted; it exists as a sensuous presence that engages our attention, rather than our interpretive capacities.[11]

According to Sontag and Cage, Cage's sounds and Cage-inspired works such as those of Yvonne Rainer in dance, and of Robert Morris and Larry Poons in fine art are on an ontological par with ordinary sounds, ordinary movements, and ordinary objects, like bathroom sinks. Not only are they indiscernible from mere real things, but they are said to lack what Arthur Danto calls *aboutness.*[12] That is, Cage and his followers maintain that the objects and events in question are semantically mute in precisely the way that mere real things and events are not *about* anything. Ordinary objects and events just are. And according to Cage, this is also the condition of his sounds. Therefore, if these compositions are in fact on a par with everyday sound events—primarily in virtue of their lack of meaning—then there will be no principled way of drawing a distinction between them and everyday sound events. Thus, there will be no way in which to place them in separate ontological categories like art or music.

So the crux of the matter hinges on whether or not Cage and aestheticians like Sontag are right in claiming that the works in question are mute, that they say nothing, that they are, even in an extended way of speaking, meaningless. Surely, the intervention of automatic procedures of construction makes these works problematic as examples of art under classical expression theories of art.[13] And it at least thwarts certain types of psychoanalytic interpretations of the works. However, there are other ways in which these works can be thought to bear meaning such that we will argue that Cage's sounds can be differentiated from mere real events.

Initially, I think that if we take Cage seriously—which I maintain we should—then we must insist that the sounds Cage foregrounds in works like *4'33"* have a semantic dimension. For part of Cage's project is to bring it about—by means of his composition—that we become attuned, so to say, to the richness, perhaps even the aesthetic richness, of noise. But Cage's noises, then, are not like everyday noise. They have a semantic function. They are, to use Nelson Goodman's terminology, exemplifications of everyday noise—i.e., samples of everyday noise—indeed samples which within a certain musicological context are supposed to illustrate the latent potentials of noise.[14] They are framed—in some cases by notational silence—and that framing within the context of musicological debate gives them a point. Pointedly, they are symbols of noise, not abstract symbols, but symbols as samples.

Ordinary noise in this sense is not a symbol because ordinary noise is not framed. Ordinary noise does not refer to anything. But Cage's noise, given its staging, does refer to something: it refers to itself and in referring to itself in the way and in the context it does, it functions as a sample of ambient noise in general. It possesses certain properties or qualities which it exemplifies in a way that calls—and on Cage's accounting is supposed to call—our attention to congruent properties in other noises.[15] Cage's noises are, in other words, illustrative. Thus, they have a semantic content or function that the ordinary noises to which they allude lack.[16]

One objection to Goodman's notion of exemplification is that Goodman seems willing to apply it in cases where the artworks in question seem to merely possess certain properties.[17] Thus, given Goodman's overall defense of the cognitive status of art,[18]—i.e., its role in mapping the world and its properties—exemplification sometimes seems like a catchall symbol of last resort. But, it is argued, something does not exemplify, and, therefore, does not symbolize simply by possessing a property: some referential (or self-referential) machinery must also be in place.

Nevertheless, even if this general criticism of Goodman's deployment of the concept of exemplification is accurate, it does not compromise my invocation of exemplification with respect to Cage. For in the case of Cage, through his strategies of framing, the referential requirements for exemplification are clearly met. Moreover, the concept of exemplification seems perfectly to match Cage's stated intentions. Thus, despite his polemics to the contrary, the seminal works of Cage and of many of the artists he influenced (especially in the sixties) are symbolic. They are exercises in exemplification.[19]

Cage's noise, then, does, given its pragmatic context, say something and it does have a purpose: it illustrates something about sound and its potential—something of especial autobiographical significance for Cage, given his avowal of his love of sound in his earliest childhood memories.

Of course, by emphasizing the importance of context for the intended operation of Cage's noise, I have in mind not only the immediate circumstances of his performances, but also the historical context in which they are situated. One reason that I think that contemporary philosophers would disagree with Cage's claim that his music is meaningless is that many of them have become convinced of the Wittgensteinian notion that meaning is a function of the use of a word or a gesture within a context that has a structure. When I raise my hand in a classroom, that signals that I have something to say, not because raising one's hand has a natural meaning but because in the context of the classroom, given its rules, one uses hand raising to signal that one has something to say.

Now the artworld is not as structured in terms of rules as a classroom is. However, it does provide a context—specifically a tradition—in which certain gestures take on meaning. For example, at a time when verisimilitude was thought to be objective, a logical space was opened in which figural distortion could call forth associations of subjectivity. That distortion should go with subjectivity, rather than, say, democracy, is a function of the frameworks and constraints placed on our associations by the pre-existing artistic context. A certain choice, when made in a given art-historical context, is going to get its point by being used in a context that itself has already been structured by history. And that point, broadly speaking, is its meaning; that point is the sort of thing that we mobilize interpretations to isolate.

Clearly, in this sense, Cage's work bears interpretation. It is purposive and it has a point, one that depends on it being meaningful or purposive activity within a certain context of debate. Earlier I discussed aspects of that context of debate, as has Cage in writings like "The Future of Music: Credo." But, we do not need to read Cage's writings in order to figure out the point of his work, if we are already familiar with the context in which it serves eloquently as a call broadening the range and richness of auditory experience. Likewise, where, as a participant in our musical culture, one is apprised of the almost inescapable pervasiveness of the concept of artistic expression, one easily comprehends the polemical thrust of aleatoric techniques as contextually poignant gestures of repudiation.[20]

If one doubts the semantic content of Cage's noise, one need only recall the degree to which these works depend on affronting entrenched musical ideas. Using what might be called bourgeois taste as a straightman, Cage's aleatoric techniques taunt; the ensuing outrage makes the presence of communication unmistakable. Nor is the indignation inarticulate in the way that a response to a slap on the face might be. Those offended know precisely what is at stake theoretically. This is apparent when they say, "But anyone could do *that*."

In virtue of their historical context, Cage's compositions have a subject. Indeed, they have more than one. They are about something, in part by way of exemplification, and in part by contextual (art-historical-conversational) implicature in conjunction with exemplification. For example, they are about ordinary sound and the contrast between ordinary sound and (traditionally) musical sound. Indeed, through his ingenious intervention in the tradition of music, Cage may well have created a new aesthetic category, that of *ordinariness*. Whereas before Cage, the ordinary object figured in aesthetic discourse negatively—as a foil to the art object—Cage's noise functions to introduce a positive aesthetic predicate, *ordinariness,* which focuses attention on a newly discovered realm of value.[21] That is, Cage's compositions provide us with a new symbol with which to organize the world. They are not only meaningful in the sense of having a purpose; they are meaningful in the sense of being symbols, sym-

bols, indeed which show us a new world, or which show us the world in a new light, or, perhaps, more aptly, sound us the world in new tones.

Cage was certainly right to challenge the view that art is divorced from the world. However, he need not have gone so far as to argue that in order to do this, his compositions had to be completely shorn of meaning. He did succeed in severing his particular sounds from authorial intention in one sense. But it is not clear that he severed his compositions from intentionality altogether. For his compositions remain situated in a cultural space, one which imbues gestures within it with purposes, and, as we have seen, with semantic content and meanings, at least in a broad sense. The cultural context, that is, provides a matrix of meanings, which carry intentionality—a tradition which both constrains moves within it, and invests genuine actions within it with meaning. If Cage says that his works like *4'33"* lack meaning, it is because the compass of meaning that he has in mind is narrower than that countenanced by many contemporary philosophers of art.

On the other hand, it is exactly the perplexities of the Cagean aesthetic that forced contemporary philosophers to begin to rethink the accepted boundaries of meaning and interpretation. Furthermore, if my analysis is correct so far, it may also be instructive about changes in the temper of theoretical activity between the fifties and sixties, on one side, and the seventies and eighties, on the other side. Today, in many areas of thought, not only philosophy, we are impressed by the extreme degree that most of what we encounter is culturally charged and, in that sense, meaningful. In the fifties and early sixties, attentiveness to the cultural and historical envelopment of virtually every aspect of human activity was not in the forefront of our thinking in the same way. The difference that I have marked between Cage and recent philosophy of art bears testimony to the way in which we now find it difficult to conceive of culture, history and cultural meaning as not having bearing on almost everything we produce.

I say this not in order to disparage Cage. That his philosophy of music is a creature of its moment is something that we should expect. But, at the same time, through his practice, he paved the way for a more contextual philosophy of art by challenging the conception that artworks exist in splendid isolation from the world. Cage's work opened art to the environmental surround, which, in turn, prefigured an appreciation of the cultural and historical surround. As well, without bold conjectures like Cage's that his sounds said nothing, it would have been less likely that philosophers would have struggled with questions of how such artworks manage to have meanings, to be about things, to speak to us. Thus, in the recent dialectic within the philosophy of art, John Cage alerted the community to some of our most important issues.[22]

1. John Cage, "The Future of Music: Credo," from his *Silence* (MIT Press, 1970), p. 3.

2. Cage, "Experimental Music: Doctrine," from *Silence,* p. 15.

3. Quoted in Michael Nyman, *Experimental Music: Cage and Beyond* (New York: Schirmer Books, 1974), p. 42.

4. Cage, "Experimental Music: Doctrine," p. 17.

5. Cage, "Experimental Music: Doctrine," p. 10. In a recent article, Daniel Herwitz questions whether the utopian goal of attending to sound as such is possible. See Daniel Herwitz, "The Security of the Obvious: On John Cage's Musical Radicalism," in *Critical Inquiry* 14:4 (Summer 1988): 784–804.

6. In *Die Reihe* 5 (1959): 116. Quoted in Paul Griffiths, *Modern Music: The Avant Garde Since 1945* (New York: George Braziller, 1981), p. 124.

7. In *M: Writings '67–'72,* Cage, always the leveler, writes "*Classification ... ceases when it's no/longer possible to establish/ oppositions. ...*" See p. 10.

8. John Cage, "Forward," from his *M: Writings '67–'72* (Wesleyan University Press, 1973), n.p.

9. See, for example, Victor Shklovsky, "Art as Technique," in *Russian Formalist Criticism: Four Essays,* eds. Lee T. Lemon and Marion J. Reis (University of Nebraska Press, 1965), especially p. 12.

10. For example, Cage writes: "Beauty is now underfoot wherever we take the trouble to look. (This is an American discovery)." See "On Robert Rauschenberg, Artist, and His Work," in *Silence,* p. 98. Also, note the undeniably Kantian inflection of the following: "And what is the purpose of writing music? One is, of course, not dealing with purposes but dealing with sounds. Or the answer must take the form of a paradox: *a purposeful purposelessness or a purposeless play*" [Emphasis added], *Silence,* p. 12. Cage also makes autobiographical remarks about his own love of the beauty of sounds as a child.

Furthermore, I should add, that insofar as Cage continues to use the language of beauty, I am not convinced that he is as radical as Daniel Herwitz claims and, therefore, I am not persuaded that Cage's supposed skepticism merits the refutation that Herwitz deals it in his "The Security of the Obvious."

11. See Susan Sontag, "Against Interpretation," in her *Against Interpretation* (New York: A Delta Book, 1966). For criticism of Sontag's view, see Noël Carroll, "Trois propositions pour une critique de la danse contemporaine," in *La Danse au Défi,* ed. Michèle Febvre (Montreal: Parachute, 1987).

12. See Arthur Danto, *The Transfiguration of the Commonplace* (Harvard University Press, 1981), especially Chapter 1.

13. It is interesting to note that Louis Mink has sketched a way in which work like Cage's might be accommodated within the framework of a *new* sort of expression theory. See his overlooked article: "Art Without Artists," in *Liberations: New Essays On The Humanities in Revolution,* ed. Ihab Hassan (Wesleyan University Press, 1972), pp. 70–86.

14. See Nelson Goodman, *Languages of Art* (Indianapolis and New York: The Bobbs-Merrill Company, 1968), pp. 52–71; and Nelson Goodman, *Ways of Worldmaking* (Indianapolis: Hackett Publishers, 1985), pp. 63–70.

15. The jargon of properties, here, is, of course, my own and not Goodman's since Goodman ultimately rejects property-talk.

16. It is interesting to note that Cage begins *Silence* by saying that "My intention has been, often, to say what I had to say in a way that would *exemplify* it; that would, conceivably, permit the listener to experience what I had to say rather than just hear about it" [Emphasis added]. What I, of course, wish to claim is that this penchant for exemplification is a major underlying strategy in much of his work. See *Silence,* p. ix.

17. See, for example, Monroe C. Beardsley, "Semiotic Aesthetics and Aesthetic Education," in *The Journal of Aesthetic Education* 9:3 (July 1975): 5–26.

18. For example, Goodman, *Languages of Art,* pp. 255–265.

19. I have always been surprised by the fact that Goodman's notion of exemplification did not gain more critical currency than it did. For whatever philosophical difficulties Goodman's use of it may raise, it seems not only unproblematically but appositely suited to elucidate critically a great deal of contemporary art.

20. For a discussion of the notion of repudiation in the preceding paragraph, see Noël Carroll, "Art, Practice and Narrative," in *The Monist* 71 (1988): 140–156.

Also, I should explain that the reason that I refer above to Cage's gestures of repudiation as "poignant" is that I believe them to be ultimately self-refuting. The problem here that confronts Cage's attempts to say nothing by way of his noises is analogous to the problems that beset the artist J. (for Jasper?) in the first chapter of Danto's *Transfiguration of the Commonplace.* Ironically, Cage, like J., winds up saying something while trying to say nothing. And, again ironically, Cage, like J., says something in virtue of the art theory he holds, which theory itself is contradicted by the very works he produces—works which are about something in the teeth of a theory that claims they have no semantic content.

Though Cage's noise says quite a lot by my accounting, I

do not believe that it can be thought of as propounding or advancing a theory. At best, Cage's noises emblematize or exemplify theories, or, perhaps, introduce putative counter-examples to antecedently existing theories. For further arguments supporting this conclusion, see Noël Carroll, "Contemporary Avant-garde Art and the Problem of Theory," in *The Adventures of the Avant-garde: from Dandyism to Postmodernism,* eds. Pellegrino D'Acierno and Barbara Lekatsas (Westport, Ct.: Greenwood Press, forthcoming).

21. This idea is related to Arthur Danto's idea of a style matrix, though I part company with Danto's suggestion that artists may bring it about that past artworks acquire new properties. Cage, himself, on the other hand, might endorse the possibility, suggested by Danto and T.S. Eliot, of backwards causation in art history. After all, Cage seems to like DeKooning's boast that "The past does not influence me; I influence it." See Arthur Danto, "The Artistic Enfranchisement of Real Objects: The Artworld," in *Aesthetics: A Critical Anthology,* eds. George Dickie and R.J. Sclafani (New York: St. Martin's Press, 1977), p. 34; John Cage, "History of Experimental Music in the United States," in *Silence,* p. 67; T.S. Eliot, "Tradition and the Individual Talent," in *Twentieth-Century Literary Theory,* eds. Vassilis Lambropoulos and David Neal Miller (State University of New York Press, 1987), p. 146.

22. An earlier version of this paper was delivered as a talk on 2/24/88 at Wesleyan University as part of a conference honoring Cage's achievements. I would also like to thank Peter Kivy for his suggestions regarding this article.

LYDIA GOEHR

Political Music and the Politics of Music

I. OVERTURE

On September 24th, 1947, a composer with "an international reputation" became the first Hollywood artist to be called before the Committee on Un-American Activities [HUAC]. The charge against him was that his music had aided the Communist infiltration of the motion-picture industry.[1] A significant part of his defense consisted in his claim that he was only a musician and thus not responsible for any part of a Communist conspiracy. What is peculiar is that he almost got away with this unlikely defense, unlikely because he had spent much of his life developing a political music consistent with the ideals of Communism. In the end, the Committee caught him out on technical grounds: it found a history of inaccurate statements in his visa applications. The composer was deported. It was the second exile of his life: the first had been from Germany ten years earlier.[2]

The composer's name was Hanns Eisler. Born to a Jewish philosopher and a Christian "worker" in 1898, he was educated in Vienna. Moving to Berlin, he studied composition with Arnold Schoenberg. For many years he collaborated with Bertolt Brecht. Involved in avant-garde groups as well as political music organizations, he composed revolutionary music—songs, theater pieces, and choral works—in addition to what on the surface looks like a more traditional repertoire of chamber works. He also wrote scores for numerous films and documentaries made in Europe and America (e.g., for Brecht's "Hangmen Also Die," Steinbeck's "Forgotten Village," Sartre's "The Witches of Salem," and Odets's "None But the Lonely Heart"). After being deported from the United States he made his home in East Germany. For that country he composed a national anthem. He died in 1962.

Eisler wrote abundantly on music and politics. He endorsed two political causes: the emancipation of the proletariat and the fight against fascism. Music, he wrote, should not turn a "deaf ear" to the conflicts of the times. Following the Marxist line that revolution involves the radical transformation of the old into the new, Eisler aspired to develop a political musical language out of what, in his view, had become a thoroughly apolitical one.

Though he adopted Schoenberg's atonalism as his model, he adapted it. Schoenberg's compositions, he believed, were encouraging modern music to become ever more inaccessible, overspecialized, and elitist. "Modern composers are of the opinion," Eisler bemoaned, that "'absolute music' ... music without words, cannot express anything definite at all, and certainly nothing about 'the urgent issues of our day.'" They think "[t]he purpose of music is only to be found in music itself. Music for music's sake."[3] But they are wrong. "A music which loses its sense of community loses itself: music is composed for the people by the people."[4]

Eisler's idea was to abolish the reigning bourgeois and fetishistic view of music, and to replace it with a view of music as inseparable from politics. "The crisis in music has been caused by the general crisis in society," he wrote in 1935: "In music it appears concretely in the technique of composing."[5] Eisler thus moved to create a social art through formal innovation. This involved putting traditional formal techniques to work for new musical functions, a process which would result in internal changes in musical language—in the creation of new purely instrumental and text-based forms. Revolutionary music, he asserted, is the music of critical argument. New forms can be used simultaneously to negate one set of ideals and affirm another. They can be used dialectically to represent the contradictions of society. "The history of music will be written by Marxists," Eisler proclaimed, and "[w]hoever does not understand that, is a blockhead."[6]

Eisler rejected the traditional format of the concert. Performers should no longer merely interpret music; they should be revolutionized. Listeners should no longer sit as passive audiences; they should participate in the performances. Eisler censured the view that music be used like a narcotic, offered to audiences to arouse "effects." Instead, music should transform the consciousness of an active community of people. The bourgeois musical concert was to be transformed into a political meeting.[7]

Eisler experimented with new media and technology, believing the latter could penetrate every level of society in a way the traditional concert could not. Adopting film techniques of montage, fragment, and commentary, synthesizing popular and classical forms, Eisler sought to produce a mass-music, a "useful" or "applied" music, a popular music of wide appeal.

Influenced, finally, by fin-de-siècle criticisms of decadence, Eisler maintained that his development of a truly political music required the purification of musical language for, otherwise, truth would be in danger of succumbing to ideology.[8] Truthful and sincere communication is the essential function of music. Truthful music hides neither behind ornament and complexity, nor behind a denial of the political. In precision and conciseness resides the most effective political force.

Given these well-known facts about Eisler's life, one would think that the HUAC would have had no problem at all in establishing that Eisler was a communist, or at least a revolutionary, or at the very least a composer interested in politics. But it did. Faced with the accusation by Eisler's paranoid sister Ruth Fischer that Eisler was "a communist in a philosophical sense," the Committee found themselves unknowingly confronting the possibility that Eisler's music might itself be only communistic "in a philosophical sense."

The Committee had begun its interrogation by trying to pin Eisler down to "active" or "real" membership in various communist organizations, but Eisler had simply denied any such active membership. "I was not active in political groups," he contended: "I was not a member in any real sense. ... [M]y relations to the Communist Party was [sic] such a loose thing."[9] The Committee then turned to the political character of his music, especially to his music with words. Having had one's songs and choral works performed at openly revolutionary meetings surely sustained a concrete alliance between music and revolutionary politics. This time, Eisler responded by disclaiming responsibility for how and where his music had been performed. "I made no objection if somebody want[ed] to play my music," he recalled.

Unswayed but now annoyed, the Committee asked Eisler whether he was responsible for the content of his political songs, songs which had undeniably subversive titles—"Red Front," "Red Wedding," and "Abortion is Illegal"— and equally subversive lyrics. Eisler answered that he was responsible only for the music. He could not be blamed for the words; they weren't his words. Had he read and agreed with the words when composing the music?, the Committee asked sardonically. Eisler seemed to elide the question by stressing that the words were being used in a poetic, artistic, and philosophical, but not in a real context. "This is poetry and not reality," he said. The Committee, unsurprisingly, was not convinced.

Eisler's general strategy seemed to be single-minded: he was trying to retreat into the domain of the purely aesthetic, and when he could, the purely musical. "My life is wholly devoted to music," he was contending. "I am not an organizer. I am a composer. ... I stick to my music, I don't know about politics." Of all people, Eisler seemed to be trying to convince the Committee that being a musician meant that one was necessarily uninvolved in politics. And despite the fact that Eisler had spent his entire life openly committed to the development of a truly political music, the Committee found that they could not easily prove Eisler's responses untrue, even though they clearly didn't believe them. What was the difficulty? In a nutshell, the Committee found it hard to establish a sufficiently demonstrable link between Eisler's music and his politics.

Why was Eisler's strategy effective in this

regard? How could he even have thought the Committee would take seriously his response that he was *only* or *merely* a musician? What background of assumptions was he importing into these troubled hearings that prompted him to use phrases such as "This is only music, and nothing else." or "I am not a hero. I am a composer." or "I see everything from the musical point of view." so centrally in his defense? It was in trying to answer these questions that I was led to write the following paper.

II. THE PROBLEM

In what relation does music stand to society? Is all or any music politically committed and, if so, how?[10] Though these questions have arisen in regard to other types of music—both classical and popular—it is within the domain of Western art music that they have arisen in their most challenging and long-standing form. Of all types of art and music, theorists have found it most difficult to describe how classical music, especially music without words, could have meaning beyond or outside itself given that it is, in the accepted view, non-referential, non-discursive, non-representational, and non-conceptual.

Were I to treat my questions regarding music's relation to society at the most abstract level, I would have to consider some of the logical problems involved in delimiting the boundaries of the musical domain, boundaries which are used in the literature to demarcate the musical from the so-called extra-musical domain. But I have already addressed these particular problems elsewhere.[11] In this paper, I shall confine myself to exploring the difficult issues which stem from trying to answer this question: In determining the meaning and nature of musical works, to what extent, or according to what principles of selection, should we take extra-musical factors into account?

Contrary to the "purist" or "formalist" tradition, in which theorists (musicological and philosophical) have tried to account for everything significant or essential in music by appealing to purely musical factors, many recent theorists, especially those of postmodern or poststructuralist persuasions, have begun to emphasize heavily the influence of the extra-musical. Their claim is that something essential is lost in our musical understanding when we ignore the extra-musical conditioning of music. That which is lost is most often understood to be the political or social character of music. To understand music in all its dimensions, theorists thus argue, it no longer suffices to analyze the form and content of musical works in isolation; we must investigate as well the institutional context in which the composition, performance, and reception, the production, exchange, and distribution of works take place—the context in which the works assume their full meanings. In fact, theorists say, it is *only* by describing this context, that one can actually show how musical works that have no audible, apparent, or explicit political or social content can still be seen to have a political or social character.

Behind the current tendency to socialize or politicize music lies a strong impulse: to pull music down from its romantic pedestal—to deromanticize it—to treat music of Western high culture as we do any other kind of music or any other kind of cultural artifact. This leveling down has been inspired by at least three different forces. The first is the democratic trend towards pluralism and tolerance, in which attention is given to differences rather than to universal samenesses. The second comes from recent ethnomusicology and cultural studies. Their combined effect has been to persuade classical music theorists that if non-Western and popular forms of music can safely wear their social and political natures on their sleeves, perhaps Western high art music can do this too. The third force derives from what is now just called "theory"—from European-influenced and post-Marxist processes of deconstruction and archaeology. These processes have focused on unmasking the ideological forces that have been concealed, as the story goes, behind Western high culture's posturing that its claims are disinterested, objective, moral, and true.

Against the first impulse, however, a quite different but equally strong impulse has arisen—to find for music a form of protection *from* the political *once* music has been deromanticized. Unmasking the politics of music has generated a desire to protect music from being reduced merely to what Adorno once called "social cement." The desire here is to pre-empt the reductionist view that music is always and only in service as a form of ideological expression, a "prostituted" endorsement of reigning "interests." The desire to find a "dispensation" or "safe-haven" for music has almost inspired some theorists to retreat back into the purely musical, into the "sanctity" of the aesthetic. (The religious metaphors are not accidental.)[12]

This impulse has been felt all the more urgently within the recent resurgence of censorship and the consequent challenge to free expression in the Western, "free" world.[13] In this regard, the desire expressed within the musical world to delimit the political is not so different from that currently identifiable in the academy at large. In the present climate we want to determine how the academy of "free floating intellectuals" can acknowledge their political responsibility, yet resist falling prey to the censorious verdicts of the thought-police, or be controlled by what Trotsky so aptly called the "mediocrities, laureates, and toadies."

Between the desire to reduce music to politics, on the one hand, and to preserve the purity of music, on the other, lies a delicate middle position. This position asks us to reconcile two seemingly opposed desires: the demand that we be true to the *political* in music while also remaining true to the *musical* in music. It is the purpose of this paper to seek an adequate description of this middle position. Though I shall say little more about this (because it will show itself fairly evidently), I understand my purpose to be historically and philosophically related to the desire to describe the relationship in which individuals stand *as* individuals *to* society. Both accounts depend upon one's working out a satisfactory conception of autonomy.[14]

The concept of "autonomy" with which I am concerned has its origins in the Greek city-state: "*autos*" translates as self, "*nomos*" as law. According to Gerald Dworkin, "a [Greek] city had *autonomia* when its citizens made their own laws, as opposed to being under the control of some conquering power."[15] Autonomy connotes freedom, independence, self-sufficiency, and self-determination. In modern political philosophy, the concept of autonomy comes to be employed with respect more often to individual persons than to cities as a whole. A central question is how free individuals can, and under what conditions they should, subject themselves to the laws of their society without that

subjection compromising their freedom of thought and action.

In the literature on aesthetics and the arts, two different solutions to the problem of autonomy have been offered. The first I shall call the *crude* (i.e., the vulgar, naive, or pre-reflective) solution; the second the *critical* (i.e., the reflective) solution. Briefly, the crude solution suggests a neat formula: a given musical work is either autonomous or it is political, but it cannot be both. The critical solution suggests a different formula: only a work which is autonomous is truly political. Set against the crude solution, the critical one looks contradictory. How can an autonomous work be truly political if autonomy is defined as non-political? To say that truly political works are non-political, and that what we normally call political works—programmatic works, national anthems, protest songs, military marches, etc.—are not truly political appears to be utterly incoherent. As one would expect, the apparent contradiction dissolves when the phrases "truly autonomous" and "truly political" are elucidated in a non-standard way.

For the rest of this paper, I shall describe the crude and critical solutions respectively. Having taken the two solutions as far as they go in the literature, I then proceed to develop the critical one so as to give it a more acceptable form. I argue, however, that though the critical solution can be made to look quite acceptable, it fails ultimately to describe adequately the basic relation that holds between the musical and extra-musical. In the light of this criticism I draw a rather unexpected conclusion.

III. THE CRUDE SOLUTION

The crude solution is situated at the difficult intersection between theories about aesthetic and political ideals and concrete realities. Thus, within the solution, an "iron curtain" has gradually been drawn forcing theorists to affiliate their theoretical options with unrefined political camps, with the left or right, with communism or capitalism, with liberalism or conservatism. As a general (Western) public, we've learned to see the production of pure art and aesthetics as coming out of the Western world, and the production of tendentious or propaganda art ("if we can even call it art!" the Western world will say) as coming out of the former Soviet system.[16] Crude Westerners suggest that only the social and political conditions of their free society encourage the production of pure art. Crude East-bloc theorists, by contrast, teach that the production of free art is only possible in a communist society. In this society, individuals, including artists, are not alienated as they are in capitalist society, and they choose in freedom to serve the society as "musical citizens." Remember, these views are the crude ones.

At their root lies a quite specific and consistent reading—perhaps even a misunderstanding—of the concept of autonomy. This reading has been responsible for allowing Western theorists to conclude that classical music is autonomous music and thus, by definition, apolitical, and East-bloc theorists to conclude that music should be political and therefore not autonomous. The reading, however, originates in, and resonates with, what turns out to be one of humanity's deepest religious and philosophical impulses—to transcend the ordinary world of human imperfection.

Moving momentarily away from crude conceptions, consider how this impulse motivated the rise of romanticism around 1800, and the concept of aesthetic autonomy that romanticism articulated as a way to separate out the fine arts from other human productions. Then recall the view, held from that time on, that romanticism could serve as a secular surrogate to Christianity and as an extension of the transcendent life of philosophical contemplation. The creation, performance, and reception of the fine arts, activities reconceived around 1800, could meet needs formerly met in religion and still met in philosophy. German writings from Herder to Schopenhauer amply demonstrate the continuities of religion, philosophy, and aesthetics.

Thus, within romanticism, we are asked to distinguish what is universal and necessary from what is particularized, contingent, and arbitrary; what is elite and specialized from that which is common, popular, and vulgar. Other contrasts are best represented in two lists.

Transcendent	*Ordinary*
truth, knowledge	belief, opinion
civilized, cultured	base, animalistic
thought	behavior, feelings
contemplation	participation
controlled	instinctual, uncontrolled
the ivory tower	the real world
separation, distance independence	involvement
beyond	within
abstract	concrete
dignity	compromise
self-expression, individuality	conformity
pure, clean, "germ free"	"dirty hands"
useless, functionless	useful, functional
non-practical	practical
disinterested, non-conceptual	interested, empirical
high	low
art	craft
music for music's sake	music for the people[17]

The differentiation between the transcendent and ordinary worlds has reinforced the crude solution by solidifying the difference between Western and East-bloc perspectives. According to the Western perspective, art music falls on the side of transcendence, that of "popular" or "folk" music—as well as the entire domain of politics—on the side of the ordinary. The Western view instructs us that art music (like religion and philosophy) should stay quarantined from the ordinary world, and thus from politics. Inadvertently perhaps, the poet Heine offers us a rationale for this crude view. "The world," he tells us, "is a great cowshed which is not so easy to clear out as the Augean stable because, while it is being swept, the oxen stay inside and continually pile up more dung."[18] For us, if not for Heine, the general idea is that we should keep something as dirty as politics out of the musical world and keep something as clean as music out of the political world. On the ordinary side, we must, so to speak, keep our hands in the dung; on the transcendent side, we must elevate ourselves as far as possible above the dung. (The dung metaphor stops here.) Thus, rather than seeing the two worlds, or more specifically the worlds of music and politics, as connected by an "and" clause, crude theorists use a strong "versus" clause to render music in opposition to society and politics—to see music as standing not only *against* the world, but also as not being *of* the world.

The placing of art-music within the transcendent world has been fully supported by the complex institution of the concert hall and by the ascendancy and valorization of purely instrumental music—the most purely musical music of all musics. It has also been supported by what has generally been considered a legitimate desire to resist involvement with the political. The worse the ordinary world, the more beautiful music has asserted the right to maintain its separation from it. Operating hand-in-hand with this desire has been an assumption that activities undertaken in a free Western society can move beyond political concerns to attend to their essential concerns. Everything is or has to be political only in an unfree society.[19]

The crude East-bloc perspective, by contrast, transfigures the Western one. Thus, with the distinction between the two domains acknowledged, the entire domain of transcendence is rejected on the grounds of its being bourgeois and alienated. The argument has sophisticated premises but a crude conclusion. Marxists have argued that too strong a separation of the worlds of transcendence and the ordinary has negative consequences both for the domain of art and for "the real world." "The effort to set art free from life," Trotsky once wrote, "to declare it a craft self-sufficient unto itself, devitalizes and kills art."[20] And to cut off the domain of truth from the real world leaves the world in the potentially evil hands of ideology without recourse to its "own interior laws," or "internal evolution."[21] Too great a stress on separability at the expense of involvement is a symptom, Trotsky believed, of a general cultural decline. Marxists argue that it is a deeply ideological and not a truthful position to say that autonomous music is not political.[22]

In the early years of this century, having developed increasingly modernist and abstract forms, much modern classical music was criticized for having produced a set of formal musical languages that were cut off from the real world and of no appeal to general audiences. This music had become too autonomous and formalistic. It had become elite and specialized, too concerned with purely technical or musical innovations. Even if it still claimed to have transcendent meaning, of what real value, Marxists asked, was it in the world if so few people could understand it?

From claims regarding the absence of ordinary meaning and value, Marxists quickly moved to claims linking absence of meaning to political subversiveness. Rejecting the crude Western claim that music had transcendent but not ordinary meaning, theorists began to suspect music of being secretly subversive in its purist and apolitical intent. A proclaimed lack of worldly meaning was a sure sign of a degenerate music.

Having rejected the crude Western desire to quarantine music from the ordinary world, East-bloc theorists were left with a choice. They could either rethink the relation between music and society entirely—this is what sophisticated theorists did; or they could offer exactly the opposite view to the Western one— this is what crude theorists did. Thus, crude East-bloc theorists took the critique of bourgeois autonomy, and concluded from it that, despite its claims, no music is in fact autonomous. All music, they said, should be placed completely within the ordinary domain and should serve the state. In this view, music had its links to transcendent values completely severed and its links to ideology concretely reinforced. (Of course, Marxists weren't the only group to be thinking about music in this way, but they were one such group.)

Behind this crude conclusion seemed to lie an age-old anxiety. Ever since Plato produced his forceful argument in the *Republic,* we have witnessed numerous expressions of a deep-seated desire on the part of governing bodies to regulate those parts of human behavior and those human activities whose effects are so great but which we so thoroughly fail to comprehend. The control of music has long been pervasive, ranging from determinations of acceptable modes or scales to regulation of composition, reception, and criticism. In modern times, despite its purely instrumental form and its apparent absence of ordinary meaning, critics have continued to fear music's ordinary effects. They have thus denied music its autonomy.

To the present day, this crude and complex discourse demarcating the Western and East-bloc perspectives has been sustained by Cold War anxieties and internal, national paranoias. Generally, it seems, when theory becomes linked to *realpolitik,* sophisticated positions that break down false dichotomies are silenced in public discourse. That does not mean that their expression ceases—on the contrary, their theorists just write "between the lines" or "underground." Only in our general understanding, for the supposed sake of "domestic defense," do they get ignored. With the iron curtain now down, perhaps we can re-educate our general understanding.

IV. THE CRITICAL SOLUTION

The critical solution cuts straight across crude, iron curtain dichotomies. Though it also originates in Plato's *Republic*—suggesting the problems at stake are universal rather than historical—it must be stressed that, like the crude solution, the critical one has also been shaped profoundly by the last two centuries of political and aesthetic thought. Thus, it emanates out of romantic aesthetics, Hegelianism, Marxism, and critical theory, phenomenological existentialism, as well as the liberal tradition of political philosophy. All these traditions, despite their major differences, have tried to articulate satisfactory conceptions of autonomy.

Like the crude solution, the critical one accepts that romantic aesthetics emerged amidst the development of bourgeois and capitalist society, the connection crystallizing and thus coming most clearly into view around 1800. And it, too, acknowledges that, within this process, a separation crystallized between the aesthetic and the political. But, unlike the crude, the critical solution stresses that, though aesthetics is separable from politics, the ideals regulating each should be neither reduced one to the other, nor formed in isolation from one another. The separation recognizes functional and categorial differences but avoids mutual isolation or exclusion.

As is well known, there were widespread increases in classifications and distinctions around 1800—in academic disciplines, public institutions, and in human capacities and practices. But never was it intended that these things be differentiated so sharply that we would lose our sense of the totality. Not even Modernism, the once proclaimed age of fragmentation and disunity, lost its sense of the whole. Thus, within both Western liberal and sophisticated Marxist theories, the view has continually been sanctioned that music and politics, art and morality, the transcendent and the

ordinary, are each and all inextricably connected. Kant urged such connections in his understanding of the "bridging" relation between his three *Critiques,* as well as in his specific reminder that the Kingdom of Ends must be brought about in our midst—in the practical realm of human action.

> The moral law as the formal rational condition of the use of our freedom obliges us by itself alone, without depending on any purpose as material condition; but it nevertheless determines for us ... a final purpose towards which it obliges us to strive; and this purpose is the *highest good in the world* [*mögliche Gut in der Welt*] possible through freedom.[23]

Thus, when the critical solution separates out the aesthetic from the political, it does so only as the first step. The second is to demonstrate that this separation is necessary for art to fulfill its function, to serve in its aesthetic freedom the cause also of political freedom. In its original articulations around 1800, the doctrine of art for art's sake and the subsidiary "formalist" doctrine of music for music's sake rested on two claims: [1] that the fine arts had at last been released from their hitherto servile and ritualistic, courtly and religious, roles; and [2] that, now in their freedom and newly emancipated state, the fine arts could help bring about political freedom in the world. When Sartre reminded us in this century that it would be impossible to write a great novel in support of fascism, he was reiterating a view held a century earlier. Though beauty is an end in itself, it nonetheless still serves as a "symbol" or "analogue" of morality and of the political good. Contrary to crude interpretations, there is no contradiction in holding both claims. The claim to autonomy thus has a history separating aesthetics from politics and morality, but also a history that reconnects aesthetics back to politics and morality once separated.

The critical solution works with two distinct conceptions of the political and accords more importance to the second. The first focuses on the external and contingent relation that holds between particular musical works and concrete political messages. The crude solution works with this conception only. The second conception focuses on an internal, essential, and abstract relation that holds between the musical and the political. This relation establishes that autonomous music is necessarily political.

The critical solution not only admits the possibility, but also makes it a basic requirement, that music should fall under both descriptions of the transcendent and the ordinary. Music is connected to society by an "and" as well as a "versus." The solution recognizes in fact that musical autonomy is double-sided, two-directional, Janus-faced, dialogical, or dialectical: that music can be purely musical *and* politically committed without contradiction—"formally perfect" and "heroically struggling" as we often identify the dualism in a Beethoven symphony.

To claim that music is politically committed must not, then, amount to denying music its freedom. Quite the opposite: music's involvement in the world is regarded as indispensable to its own freedom. Adorno captures the dialectic when he writes: "[p]recisely that which is not social in [art] should become its social aspect." Benjamin captures it similarly when he writes, in this case of literature, that "a literary work can only be politically correct if it is also literarily correct."[24] A "vice versa" is needed here, because a literary work can only be literarily correct if it is also politically correct.

The critical solution works with a relational or a "relative" conception of autonomy.[25] Music functions in relation to that which it is not, to something against which it constantly asserts its independence. That something is the dictate or the social conditions of the status quo; it is the social conditions in which music is produced. Music responds to its conditions of production by resisting them. Music's freedom is essentially a form of resistance, a constant assertion of difference, a negation of that which it constantly posits as "Other." Whether or not music actually achieves this distance is irrelevant. What is important here is that music's freedom must always be a "freedom from." Were it free in the sense of its being isolated, or having no connection to the ordinary world, it would cease to have value. Again, from the critical perspective, music's meaning and freedom *is possible* only *in* the world.

Of all the arts, music is most able (or at least paradigmatically able) to serve fine art's political function. Why? Because it completely lacks representational or conceptual content. It is the art whose content is least likely to be confused

with ideological "causes." Music is the art of pure sound and pure motion, and thereby of pure emotion and pure thought. The "thereby" needs explaining. In providing this explanation critical theorists have found themselves appealing in non-crude ways to principles of transcendence.

The explanation, again, has two parts: first, it explains in what sense music is separated from society; then it shows how music is reconnected back to society. Thus, music is able to contribute to the political world. Ideally, music's function is to help bring about a better world, by presenting the world as it is and by manifesting an alternative vision of the world. To fulfill this function, music must first manifest or depict the status quo, the situation as it is, and then resist the status quo, so that it can embody a vision beyond it. "Music is prophecy," Jacques Attali thus writes in his recent book *Noise*:

Its styles and economic organization are ahead of the rest of society because it explores, much faster than material reality can, the entire range of possibilities in a given code. It makes audible the new world that will gradually become visible, that will impose itself and regulate the order of things; it is not only the image of things, but the transcending of the everyday, the herald of the future. ... Music ... is intuition, a path to knowledge. A path? No—a battle-field.[26]

That music has no referential content should make readers wonder how music has any chance at all of fulfilling what seems to be an entirely conceptual and representational mission. It was just this wondering that led Sartre to claim that only literature can be politically committed because the so-called "pure" arts cannot articulate political visions. But what Sartre came slowly to understand, and what composer Rene Leibowitz worked hard to explain to him, was that the way music articulates a vision of a better world is not through concrete representation at all. The articulation, instead, is abstract.[27]

Thus, the appeal to abstraction normally assumes a distinction between two sorts of commitment, one abstract, the other concrete.[28] Music can be composed "representationally" or "concretely" to support a particular and partisan cause, but it can also be used to embody, within its purely musical form, abstract political ideals. "The identification in art with the proletariat requires more than simply writing for the proletariat," Eisler once told his audience. One has, rather, to develop from within art a truly revolutionary art. "The basic attitude," Brecht then added to Eisler's thought, "is revolutionary in the highest sense."[29] Their purpose was to show how precisely in its abstraction, music succeeds in being truly political, and, also, how precisely in its transcendence music succeeds in being truly ordinary. Thus, an abstract conception of the political is not devoided of concrete content or worldly implication; in its abstraction, it is not, in other words, devoided of all political content, for otherwise it would cease to have any meaning at all. Recall, transcendence works, in these views, within the ordinary, and not apart from it. Adorno attempts to describe the complex relation in these terms:

Music is nonobjective and not unequivocally identifiable with any moments of the outside world. At the same time, being highly articulated and well-defined within itself, it is nonetheless commensurable, however indirectly, with the outside world of social reality. It is a language, but a language without concepts.[30]

That theorists generally find it extremely hard to describe the relation of musical form (or the internal logic of music's formed-content) to political ideals and social relations does not undermine their conviction that some such relation exists. Indeed, they try hard to describe it correctly. In this endeavor they travel across the entire range of metaphors. Thus, we hear of music (its logic or form) standing to society in a relation of expressing, mirroring, crystallizing, encoding, enmeshing, highlighting, enacting, confronting, intervening, transfiguring, signifying, symbolizing, transforming, prophesying, and foretelling—and this is by no means an exhaustive list.

Despite the difficulties of accurate description, the basic idea is that purely musical form stands in an antagonistic though internal relation to the social relations and dominant codes of society at large. "The chief task," Adorno writes, "is ... to discover how the entirety of a society, as a unity containing contradictions, appears in a work; in which respects the work remains true to its society, and in which it tran-

scends that society."[31] Music's antagonistic relation to society—its ability, for example, to resist society's desire to produce perfect and complete aesthetic unities—allows music to unsettle the status quo, to make, in Hegelian terms, the familiar disturbingly unfamiliar. Such disturbances help motivate social change. "The greatness of works of art," Adorno writes further, "lies solely in their power to let those things be heard which ideology conceals."[32] And yet elsewhere he writes:

Music will be better, the more deeply it is able to express—in the antinomies of its own formal language—the exigency of the social situation and to call for change through the coded language of suffering. It is not for music to stare in helpless horror at society. It fulfils [*sic*] its social function more precisely when it presents social problems through its own material and according to its own formal laws—problems which music contains within itself in the innermost cells of its technique.[33]

In the critical solution, the abstraction characterizing music is often described as manifesting itself in silence. "Without mentioning anything [it] can say everything," Ilya Ehrenburg once said of Shostakovich's Eighth Symphony.[34] In the same period, Schoenberg was expressing his own form of silence in the world: "We, who live in *music*," he wrote, "have no place in politics and must regard it as foreign to our being. We are a-political, at best able to aspire to remain silently in the background."[35] Was Schoenberg expressing a crude or critical view about music's relation to the world? It is not entirely clear.[36] He could be expressing the crude view that musical interests should be kept completely separate from political interests; he could also be expressing the critical view that, by denying involvement with the political, musicians might be playing out in the music their most effective political role—in silence, in abstraction, in transcendence. As Adorno suggested, the less music blinks in the direction of society the more it represents it.[37]

In general, abstraction or transcendence has been seen to be achieved in the employment of creativity, imagination, and contemplation, in what nearly two centuries ago was referred to as the "free play of the faculties." It can be achieved through the mimetic capacity of the fine arts to stand at a distance from reality, through the ability of those arts to interpret that reality.[38] Finally, and again in Kantian terms, it can be achieved by defending subjective freedom or agency (represented in the fine arts by creativity and formal discipline) against the objective law-governed necessity of nature.[39]

At the core of the critical solution lie two desires that must always go together: first, the desire to maintain the autonomous development of musical composition by *not* conceiving it as a mere consequence of social developments at large; second, the desire to find within that autonomous development the source of music's freedom to manifest the political. It helps to characterize the first form of freedom as "freedom from" and the second as "freedom to": "freedom from" is the condition by which music develops on its own purely musical terms; in "freedom to" music finds its freedom of expression—an abstract expression that has transcendent political force in the ordinary world. But lest one fear that these two concepts of freedom miss the essential tension and connection that exists between the purely musical and the truly political, and between the transcendent and ordinary worlds, I recommend adding the explicit requirement that "freedom from" plus "freedom to" must always amount to "freedom within."

Making this requirement explicit affords me the opportunity to take the critical solution a step further than theorists have traditionally taken it. In fact, I want now to move away from the almost entirely modernist terms in which I have thus far described the critical solution to see if any postmodernist updates (if that is what they are) are illuminating. I move in this direction not, however, to find discontinuities between modernism and postmodernism, but, if I can, continuities. I shall simply begin by asking what light my requirement throws on music's relation to society or, in a slightly different light, on musical meaning and value.

One advantage of the "freedom within" requirement is that it tells us how music, or art more generally, can have value and meaning beyond its immediate context of production. (Why is Beethoven's music still meaningful to us today?) One of the dangers of politicizing music is crude relativism: relativizing musical significance to specific cultural and historical locations. My requirement avoids this relativism not because it moves us into absolutism or universalism but because it moves us to a position of difference. Music only needs to be different from that which is to have value or meaning beyond the status quo, to have a value or meaning that may encourage social change. Of course, difference can never be an end in itself. So the critical solution has to say more. What it usually says is that music must also strive to be truthful in its difference if it is to guarantee that the social change it promotes will be the sort of change we should want—whoever the "we" is. In aesthetics, there is, apparently, a "will to truth."[40]

Indeed, the critical solution assumes that the production of great art is contingent upon the imperfections of humankind. Like legal or moral systems, the production of art is necessary because humanity is imperfect—and art production can help make the world better. It assumes that just as legal and moral systems strive towards truthful regulation of our world, so art strives also. Whether art, like moral or legal systems, would still be necessary in a perfect world now becomes a difficult question whose answer clearly depends upon what one puts forward as a perfect world.

This question prompts another: is great art more likely to be produced in a less or in a more perfect world? In the critical solution, one must think deeply about the relation between the freedom of art and that of society to determine whether and to what extent the condition of a society determines that of its artistic production. One can no longer simply assume that the best art is actually produced within the context of a free society—again, whatever the best art is and whatever a free society is.

As I said, this entire understanding of the role of art depends upon one's vision of a truthful world. In the tradition, truth has been linked to perfectibility, which, in turn, has been linked to a Utopian vision. But truth does not have to be so linked. Recall the argument presented by Isaiah Berlin in his seminal essay "Two Concepts of Liberty."[41] His argument, I believe, cuts straight across one modernism/postmodernism divide. It recognizes basic values but accommodates difference.

Berlin argues that the very idea of a perfect society is linked to the Utopian Enlightenment tradition that has now, in his view, exhausted itself. In its place, he offers a theory of pluralism that accommodates difference without relativism. He conceives of a society which is marked by a wide divergence of values and conceptions of the good, so wide a divergence that the values cannot all be endorsed at the same time. Some values have to take priority over others; some have to be chosen even if that means denying others. Berlin asks us to acknowledge that, since we cannot have a perfect society whose values are all in harmony with one another, we must learn to be content with pluralism, a pluralism that tells us there are genuine alternatives regarding the good. Such pluralism, in Berlin's view, is quite healthy, for it leaves us with a robust and permanent uncertainty about whether we have ever chosen "absolutely the right set" of values. This uncertainty, in turn, persuades us always to be open to new discussion of our values, to constant reconsideration of our most basic beliefs and standards.

The critical solution can usefully draw on Berlin's non-Utopian pluralism. The resistant stand which music takes against the status quo never reaches a final resolution or reconciliation. The conflict remains constant insofar as music might challenge the status quo at any point. The health of the conflict varies. Music is most threatened when it has to fight against a society that, in its own unfreedom, denies music its freedom. Music is most healthy when society allows both for differences within it and the constant discussion, in part through the production of music, of its values. The latter is a society that allows domains of freedom to exist within it, and allows music to occupy one of those domains in music's essential state as at once separate but connected to society. This is the essence of the conception of musical autonomy as "freedom within." Of course, it still remains a question whether a healthy rather than an unhealthy antagonism between music and society produces the best music.

What about "the best music"? The first thing to say about the best music is that, though many if not most critical theorists can more or less easily be identified with liberalism or leftism, it is possible for the critical solution to accommodate "conservative music" or musicians who would like to "conserve" rather than to over-

throw or revolutionize a political or a musical tradition. Conservatism also requires that musicians take a stand, that they have a critical distance from the status quo or the tradition within which they live. For the notion of critical distance more importantly suggests understanding and reflection than it does rejection and rebellion.

Secondly, as an utterly ironic twist to my entire paper, it could also be that the best music, or the most effective political music, comes not from the domain of classical music at all, but from popular music instead. This conclusion would follow from recent postmodernist thinking which, as I intimated earlier, takes popular culture as manifesting, much more explicitly than classical music culture, theories of difference and pluralism.[42] Though this position finds a lot of support nowadays, postmodernists know that they would not be the first to turn the traditional classical/popular divide on its head. Some modernists also tried to undermine the divide—notably Eisler and Brecht. And, as is well known, their influence on American popular music was by no means negligible.

Were one to move in a postmodernist direction, would the entire question of autonomy and how we locate the political in music have to be revamped? I do not think so, despite appearances to the contrary. It is true that within postmodernist considerations of popular culture the traditional distinction between ideology and truth has been challenged, a distinction that helped modernists describe the way classical music could achieve distance from the status quo. It is also true that postmodernists want to show that the political is situated in a dynamic web of relations—and in the forms of representation through which those relations are mediated—all of which connect music to words, to singers, to musicians, to settings, to audiences, to industries, and so on. Any description—either of classical or of popular music—should attend to what Susan McClary likes to call the "socially-circumscribed discourses" in which all types of music find their full meanings. Of course, the attempt to describe the content of music within a socially-circumscribed discourse only further encourages the perception that musical expression has been reduced to ideological expression.

But, as I see it, these sorts of positions certainly do not force postmodernists to hold crude views. Their content-in-context or content-in-discourse arguments, and their stress on media and representation, can be made consistent with the critical solution regarding the truly political nature of autonomous music. Calling music autonomous, for example, is not the same as calling it purely instrumental. For autonomy captures any music's relation to society; it does not, as has often been thought, just describe classical music's formal or "purely musical" content. Popular musics also have "forms," "styles," and "logics." Furthermore, the artistic engagement with media and forms of representation can be thought of (à la Benjamin) as helping to re-produce or transfigure those media and forms, and thus, indirectly, society itself.

Postmodernists can also studiously avoid reducing descriptions of the truly political character of autonomous music merely to ideological descriptions of ideological contexts. They can do this, for example, by developing a theory of "truth within" that runs along much the same lines as the theory of "freedom within." To illustrate the point quickly, consider the words of popular music theorist Simon Frith: "Transcendence," he writes "is as much a part of the popular music aesthetic as it is of the serious music aesthetic; but ... in pop, transcendence marks not music's freedom from social forces but its patterning by them." "Of course," he adds, "the same is true of serious music."[43] Had Frith only written that "transcendence marks music's patterning *within* social forces and not *by* them," he would have suggested that music can resist the ideology of the status quo while remaining situated within social forces—thus giving a less ambiguous meaning to his own commitment to transcendence; he would also have captured quite perfectly music's relation to society as being a transfigurative relation of freedom within.

V. CODA

Now I could easily stop here and conclude that the critical solution and its "freedom within" requirement adequately captures the most basic political function of music. I could also point out how my framing of the problem of autonomy within an old modernist debate naturally ended up suggesting some postmodernist themes.

But to conclude in this way I would have to ignore what remains the central problem in the critical solution, namely, that the internal relation that connects the purely political function of music to autonomous musical form cannot adequately be described. In confronting this problem I find myself offering an unexpected ending to my paper.

Skeptics who remain utterly dubious that any relation exists between musical form and politics at all, might find themselves sympathetic to Eisler's general response, that music is only music. Of course, Eisler did not believe this: he devoted his life to composing political music. Perhaps, in the Hearings, Eisler did tend towards the view that music is not political, but it's hard to tell. His responses could have expressed either a crude or a critical view of music. Perhaps he wavered between the two. The Committee, however, focused on the crude view and that's why it couldn't establish the relation between Eisler's music and politics. They were looking, mistakenly, for a concrete relation and though there were clearly examples of such a relation, Eisler found it easy to deny or undermine them. His music was, as perhaps only he knew, political "in a philosophical sense."

Back now to the skeptic's feeling that music is only music. The feeling is confused. To deny music any function other than a purely musical function is one thing; quite another is to draw this conclusion from the fact that the relation between music and the extra-musical cannot adequately be described. Persons who claim that "this is only music" are often being disingenuous or defensive. Music's meaning and value might come solely from within itself as a product of its purely musical form and content, but it has meaning only for human beings who live in a human world. To assert utter separability from the ordinary world without involvement in it is just as dangerous as asserting that music must be reduced to involvement without any form of separation. Both deprive music of its meaning.

The fact, however, that musicians have so consistently been able to get away with the extreme separability response still tells us something important about music, namely, that the description of music's relation to the extra-musical always falls short of being convincing. This failure might be due to a variety of reasons, say, to the prominence in the Western world of visual and spatial description at the expense of adequate auditory description. Perhaps, however, the failure is less contingent than this: perhaps it is metaphysical.

I am reminded here of one of Wittgenstein's arguments. "Logic," he wrote in the *Tractatus,* "is not a body of doctrine, but a mirror-image of the world (6.13)."[44] Our access to logic's relation to the world comes not via description, for that would situate the relation within the world, but, rather, through an intuitive or revelatory experience (6.233). Whatever the experience is, it is *not* cognitive (5.552/6.41). Logic's relation to the world cannot be spoken about, Wittgenstein argued, it can only be shown. Perhaps, I now want to suggest, something like this view is true also of music's relation to the world.

"The sense of the world must be outside the world," Wittgenstein continues (6.41). From this he goes on to say that, in a legitimate philosophical sense, the *Tractatus* is an unreadable text for, with its metaphysical claims, it attempts to say things which can only be shown. Perhaps music or any text about music, which attempts to say things which can only be shown is also unreadable. Attali, for example, seems to want to say both these things. First, he describes music as an "instrument of understanding," and the world as not "for beholding," but "for hearing." The world, he writes, is "not legible, but audible." Second, he writes that his intention is "not only to theorize *about* music, but to theorize *through* music."[45]

For Wittgenstein, however, the point of writing unreadable philosophical texts is to help us climb up the ladder of understanding. When and if we reach the top, we can throw the ladder away. In regard to music I do not think we are yet at the top of the ladder. For first we have to understand that if what is truly political in music is an essentially unsayable relation that internally connects music to subjectivity, then all concrete concerns about where we actually locate the political character of music within a socially circumscribed discourse are theoretically irrelevant even if materially interesting.

So my conclusion. The critical solution is far preferable to the crude one, and its associated doctrine of "freedom within" has all the features I desired it to have. The critical solution also suggests many elements of the Tractarian

metaphysics. But since, at a crucial point, it ignores the consequences of that metaphysics and tries to say what cannot be said, it leaves us, as philosophers are often left, able to say much more about the problem than we can say about the solution—although clearly we can say something even if it is not the crucial thing. Usually when we discover that our problems beg for less talk rather than more, and at a certain point, no talk at all, the best thing we can do is just stop talking.[46]

1. "Hearings regarding Hanns Eisler," Hearings before the Committee on Un-American Activities, House of Representatives, Eightieth Congress, Public Law 601, United States Government Printing Office (Washington, 1967). Material on Eisler has been gleaned from the Hearings, from Albrecht Betz's excellent book, *Hanns Eisler* (Cambridge University Press, 1982) and from Eisler's writings collected in *A Rebel in Music,* ed. M. Grabs (New York: International Publishers, 1978).

2. For background behind the Committee's decisions, see Betz, *Hanns Eisler,* pp. 194–207.

3. *A Rebel in Music,* p. 108.

4. Ibid., p. 197.

5. Ibid., p. 107. Cf. Benjamin's discussion of technique in his "The Author as Producer," repr. and trans. in A. Arato and E. Gebhardt eds., *The Essential Frankfurt School Reader* (New York: Continuum, 1982), pp. 255 ff.

6. *A Rebel in Music,* p. 197.

7. Ibid., p. 33.

8. Throughout this essay I will be thinking about ideology in terms of complexes of signifying practice and symbolic formations which serve: (i) to give out lives within a society a particular range of meanings; (ii) to legitimate the particular interests of a particular group or a range of groups; and (iii) to reinforce the power of a particular group (or range of groups) by legitimating their interests at the expense of the interests of any other group. (Cf. Terry Eagleton's *Ideology: An Introduction* [London: Verso, 1991], Ch. 1.)

9. Hearings, pp. 13 & 43. Note that Eisler's responses were not so dissimilar from those made by other musicians and artists called before the Committee. See, for example, Robin Denselow, *When the Music's Over: The Story of Political Pop* (London: Faber, 1986), Ch. 1.

10. Throughout this essay, "politics" and "the political" should be understood broadly; oftentimes, one could use the terms "social" and "moral" interchangeably with "political" without affecting the argument. All refer to so-called "extra-musical" dimensions of music.

11. "Writing Music History," *History and Theory* 31 (1992): 182–99.

12. Cf. Adorno's mention of an aesthetic dispensation in

his essay "Commitment," repr. in *Aesthetics and Politics,* ed. F. Jameson (London: Verso Pubs., 1980), p. 183.

13. See my "Music has no Meaning to Speak of," in M. Krausz ed., *The Interpretation of Music: Philosophical Essays* (Oxford: Clarendon, 1993), pp. 177–90.

14. For a statement of this analogy and relation, see Adorno, "Lyric Poetry and Society," repr. in S. E. Bronner and D. M. Kellner eds., *Critical Theory and Society* (London: Routledge, 1989), pp. 157 ff. See also the excellent essays (especially the first four) of Rose Rosengard Subotnik collected together in her *Developing Variations: Style and Ideology in Western Music* (University of Minnesota Press, 1991).

15. See G. Dworkin, *The Theory and Practice of Autonomy* (Cambridge University Press, 1988), p. 12.

16. Not irrelevantly, underground art produced in the unfree world has been understood as aspiring to the free conditions of the Western world.

17. These contrasts are often used nowadays to distinguish the modernist from the postmodernist aesthetic. Bakhtin also captures these differences when he contrasts poetic with dialogical language; see Ken Hirschkop, "The Classical and the Popular: Musical Form and Social Context," in C. Norris ed., *Music and the Politics of Culture* (London: Lawrence and Wishart, 1989), p. 287.

18. Quoted in Betz, *Hanns Eisler,* p. 246.

19. Cf. K. Hirschkop, in C. Norris ed., *Music and the Politics of Culture,* p. 289: "The bourgeois view of music separated *music,* cultivated sound, and its listeners ... from sounds which were insufficiently refined or vulgarly connected to everyday needs."

20. Trotsky, *Art and Revolution: Writings on Literature, Politics, and Culture* (New York: Pathfinder, 1970), p. 39.

21. Adapted from "Historical Objectivity and Artistic Truth," *Art and Revolution,* p. 93.

22. As Boris Schwartz has written more recently: "Music, *per se,* cannot be ideologically right or wrong—it must be judged on its own, purely musical terms ... a statement of ideology if ever there was one!" quoted in Malcolm Barry's "Ideology and Form: Shostakovich East and West," in C. Norris ed., *Music and the Politics of Culture,* p. 172.

23. *Critique of Judgment,* [AK. 450] Part II, Appendix, §87, Of the Moral Proof of the Being of God, trans. J. H. Bernard (London: Macmillan, 1931), p. 380. Recall here, also, Trotsky's statement that to remove art from life deprives art of the possibility of its being meaningful.

24. Adorno, "Lyric Poetry and Society," p. 160; Benjamin, "The Author as Producer," p. 256.

25. See Trotsky, *Art and Revolution,* p. 13.

26. *Noise: The Political Economy of Music,* trans. B. Massumi (University of Minnesota Press, 1985), pp. 11 and 18.

27. Sartre, *What is Literature? and Other Essays* (Harvard University Press, 1988), pp. 25 ff.; also Sartre, "The Artist and his Conscience," (a response to Leibowitz), in

Situations, trans. B. Eisler (Greenwich, Conn.: Fawcett Pubs., 1965), pp. 142–55. See also a discussion of this debate in Paul Robinson's "Sartre on Music," *Journal of Aesthetics and Art Criticism* 31:4 (1973): 451–57, and in Christina Howell's "Sartre and the Commitment of Pure Art," *British Journal of Aesthetics* 18:2 (1978): 172–82.

28. See Adorno, "Commitment," pp. 177–95.

29. *A Rebel in Music,* p. 17.

30. *Introduction to the Sociology of Music,* trans. E. B. Ashton (New York: Continuum, 1988), p. 44.

31. "Lyric Poetry and Society," p. 156.

32. Ibid., p. 157.

33. "On the Social Situation of Music," quoted in Martin Jay, *Adorno* (Harvard University Press, 1984), p. 136.

34. Cf. Claire Polin's "Why Minimalism Now," in Norris ed., *Music and the Politics of Culture,* p. 231.

35. Quoted in Betz, *Hanns Eisler,* p. 44.

36. Eisler thought Schoenberg said these sorts of things just to make himself interesting. See Betz, loc. cit.

37. *Introduction to the Sociology of Music,* p. 211.

38. This is the feature of art Arthur Danto likes to stress. See, for example, his "Dangerous Art," in his *Beyond the Brillo Box: The Visual Arts in Post-Historical Perspective* (New York: Farrar, et al., 1992), p. 193.

39. Cf. Christina Howell's "Sartre and the Commitment of Pure Art," pp. 172–82.

40. Cf. Terry Eagleton, *The Ideology of the Aesthetic* (Blackwell, 1990), pp. 350 ff.; also Martin Jay, *Adorno,* p. 159: "The need to lend a voice to suffering is a condition for all truth. ... If there is a positive moment in aesthetic truth, it is evident only in those works that strive for the utmost autonomy from the present society, defying immediate accessibility and popular impact."

41. *Four Essays on Liberty* (Oxford University Press, 1969/1990), pp. 118–72. Note that Berlin's two concepts of freedom are rather different from but not incompatible with mine.

42. See Angela McRobbie's "Postmodernism and Popular Culture," in Lisa Appignanesi ed., *Postmodernism: ICA Documents* (London: Free Association Books, 1989), pp. 165–80.

43. "Towards an Aesthetic of Popular Music," in R. Leppert and S. McClary eds., *Music and Society: The Politics of Composition, Performance, and Reception* (Cambridge University Press, 1987), p. 144.

44. See *Tractatus Logico-Philosophicus,* trans. D. F. Pears and B. F. McGuinness (London: Routledge and Kegan Paul, 1961), pp. 58 ff.

45. *Noise,* pp. 3 and 18–20.

46. Many thanks to my seminar students of Fall 1992, to participants in the Center for the Humanities Fall Seminar "Making and Selling Culture," at Wesleyan University; to Brian Fay, Tom Huhn, James Kavanagh and Sanford Shieh for their extremely valuable comments on the text; to Steve Gerrard, Indira Karamcheti, Amélie Rorty, and Paul Schwaber for their help in conversations.

Autonomist/Formalist Aesthetics, Music Theory, and the Feminist Paradigm of Soft Boundaries

The importance of new paradigms, or models of thought and action, has been a frequent theme in feminist aesthetics, and in revolutionary movements in general.[1] The particular value of a feminist aesthetic paradigm lies in its ability to go beyond the liberal feminist vision of equal representation in the mainstream institutions and canons of the arts, and to challenge the underlying exclusionary framework of values and practices that produce and maintain gender inequality, both in and outside of the artworld.[2]

Since the rise of the discipline of aesthetics in the eighteenth century, those exclusionary values and practices have developed around the autonomist/formalist position, i.e., the view that art is ideally created and appreciated in a "disinterested" structurally-oriented manner, apart from any considerations of cultural context or function.[3] The autonomist/formalist position may be seen as an extension into the aesthetic realm of the general logocentric tendency in Western thought to contain, categorize, and hierarchize experience, such that the physical, emotional, and cultural aspects are viewed apart from the intellectual/verbal aspects, and devalorized as irrational or primitive. Although this tendency was recognized before the development of feminist theory, it has since been identified by many feminist scholars as a masculinist tendency, because the aspects of experience that it devalorizes have regularly been associated with women or "the feminine."[4]

There are three main elements to autonomist/formalist aesthetics: (1) the definition of art as a distinct activity, apart from other cultural practices; (2) the isolation and reification of "artworks" (i.e., the physical objects of art), away from their origins and symbolic meanings in human experience; and (3) the use of formalist, or structurally oriented, concepts as universals for judging and hierarchizing the value of artworks. Only the first two of these elements were present in the aesthetic writings of early romantic philosophers and critics of art, for the romantics explicitly rejected many of the formalist concepts and judgments of eighteenth-century aesthetics in favor of a more organic approach to art and art criticism. Since the early nineteenth century, however, the elements have typically appeared together, as, for example, when Clive Bell assigned the highest aesthetic value to primitive sacred icons because of their "significant form," or when Eduard Hanslick defined and judged music entirely on the basis of its "tonally moving forms."[5] In part because of the seemingly abstract, non-representational character of musical sounds, the autonomist/formalist position has reached its height in application to the art of music, producing a profusion of structural concepts and analytic procedures commonly known as music theory.

Notwithstanding its denial of cultural connections, the autonomist/formalist position itself arose in a cultural context, that of the "museum culture" of the arts.[6] Although the practice of preserving and exhibiting artifacts in museums had its roots in the Middle Ages, it wasn't until the latter part of the eighteenth century that museums became the major mode for the exhibition of art, as artistic patronage passed from the upper to the middle class, and from aristocratic chambers to public museums, concert halls, and other large-scale institutions of art. Despite presumptions of neutrality, the institution of the museum served to impose a radical new context on art and its public, in which people had to perceive separate artworks in conjunction with each other, according to themes and layouts determined by the museum personnel (or in music's case, the concert performers or organizers), and to do so in silence and physical and emotional restraint. The denial of the artworks' relatedness to culture and to physical and emotional engagement created a vacuum that could then be filled by formalist analyses and judgments.[7]

In short, the rise of autonomist/formalist aesthetics with the museum culture of art served to encourage formalist intellectual judgments of isolated artworks, while devaluing and de-emphasizing the physical, emotional, and cultural experience of art. In so doing, it not only discouraged individuals from those vital aspects of artistic experience; it also disenfranchised communities, whose roles in forming and experiencing the cultural meanings embodied in artistic practices and artworks were ignored. Instead of envisioning a broad community of artistic participants, autonomist/formalist aesthetics promoted fragmentation into isolated "high" and "low" art subcultures, proliferation of separate professional art specialties, and a hierarchization of art participants that assigned all proprietary rights to a singular artist/creator.[8]

Not incidentally, the ascendancy of the museum and its associated institutions of training (i.e., conservatories and departments of the arts) corresponded to a period of greater social exclusion and subordination for women—a move from patriarchal to masculinist culture as Barbara Ehrenreich and Deirdre English de scribe it—which affected the institutions themselves, in their practices of educating men and women artists and exhibiting their works on an unequal basis.[9] Such exclusionary practices in turn led to an increased concentration of women's artistic activity in domestic, utilitarian arts such as pottery, weaving, genre painting and song, arts that require little institutional support, but that were discounted under autonomist/formalist aesthetics. As a result, the canons of the arts, compiled mainly since the onset of the museum culture, have evolved to show a dearth of women artists, or "great" women artists, that has compared unfavorably to the genealogies of "great" men.[10]

As mentioned, liberal feminism, with its emphasis on equality, has lacked the means to challenge the exclusionary framework of autonomist/formalist aesthetics, although feminist scholars have drawn attention to the more glaring canonical exclusions. However, new feminist paradigms have challenged the autonomist/formalist framework, quite successfully in some cases. For example, the feminist paradigm of "genderized perspective" in the visual arts, and particularly the concept of the "male gaze," has helped to deconstruct the autonomist/formalist assumption of the gender neutrality of artists and spectators and the autonomy of images, and to refocus interest on gender and power relationships exhibited in the artworks and among the patrons, artists, and models who participated in their making.[11] The concept of the "male gaze" has clearly succeeded in changing the terms of the debate, so much so that art historians and philosophers must now learn the concept and its literature in order to dispute it and to keep up with their fields. The resulting widespread dissemination of the concept and the paradigm has allowed for the exploration of more complex theoretical ground as the debate progresses. It is no longer necessary for feminist theorists of the visual arts to reinvent the wheel of their critique in every academic outing.

Given the recent appearance of feminist scholarship in musicology,[12] I believe the time has come to consider a new, feminist paradigm for the understanding of music, to challenge the highly formalistic framework of concepts and judgments that have developed around that art. Given music's largely non-representational character, the paradigm of genderized perspective has a more limited application to music than to the visual arts; thus something more in the way of a challenge to the framework is needed. The paradigm I am proposing is that of "soft boundaries."[13] Like the paradigm of genderized perspective in the visual arts, soft boundaries aims to challenge a key element in the autonomist/formalist position. In this case, what is challenged is the covert valuation of "hard" or distinct boundaries in the concepts that have been used to define and judge music as an autonomous, intellectually-based art—concepts such as the musical work, movement, section, period, phrase, chord progression, motive, interval, and pitch. As I will show, these hard-boundaried concepts have served to exclude or diminish the physical, emotional, and cultural experience of music, placing that experience in a subordinate position to the practice of theory, mainly within the institutional framework of the discipline of music theory. With the paradigm of soft boundaries, the valuation of hard boundaries in music-theoretical concepts, analyses and judgments is balanced by consideration of the relatedness of music and musical entities across soft or permeable boundaries, including relatedness to the physical, emotional, and cultural, as well as to the intellectual or cognitive experience of music.

The connection of soft boundaries to feminist aesthetics is less explicit than that of genderized perspective, but just as important. The connection stems from the alliance of feminist theory in general to issues neglected under masculinist theoretical frameworks, including careful and continuing attention to all aspects of experience, appreciation for detail (attention to specific, rather than only universal features) and allowance for pluralism, i.e., the possibility of a multiplicity of valid concepts and judgments. (By contrast, autonomist/formalist aesthetics, and logocentric thinking in general, tends to produce universal concepts and unitary judgments on the supposed "main elements" of what is analyzed.)[14] At the same time, soft boundaries is not a radical feminist or essentialist paradigm, for it does not disallow the value of forming concepts and judgments about music. It simply calls for a readjustment in the roles of theory and experience, such that theory does not dominate or exclude experience, but is continuously affected in its concepts, definitions, and judgments by the evidence of experience. In other words, the soft boundaries paradigm calls for theory itself to have soft, permeable boundaries.

I. A CLOSER LOOK AT MUSIC THEORY

As previously mentioned, music theory is the discipline in which structural concepts and analytical judgments for music are formulated and taught, so it is music theory that one must address in order to effect any real change in academic musical discourse. Curiously, music theory occupies a very different status and role in music than does theory in the other arts (where theory generally is incorporated into historical and practical study). Theory in music is a separate discipline, with little direct connection to

the seemingly related disciplines of music philosophy (which functions institutionally as a branch of philosophical aesthetics), and musicology (including music history and sociology). It is the relative isolation of music theory that has made it so vulnerable to domination by the single aesthetic position of autonomist/formalism, at a time when the other arts have shown much more theoretical diversity.[15] Moreover, because two to three years of music theory study are required of all students who wish to study music academically on an advanced level, music theory has been able to assert its autonomist/formalist views over virtually everyone in the academic music world. A brief review of the institutional history of music theory may help to explain the control that music theory exercises on the dissemination of information and understanding about music in our society, and how much a soft-boundaried paradigm is needed.

Music theory's separate status and power goes back to ancient Greece, where it was music theory, not history or sociology, which was the focus of academic musical study and discourse. As Renée Cox has shown, Greek theoretical writing on music had as a hidden agenda the subjugation of some of the gynocentric musico-cultural practices the Greek tribes had encountered in their conquest of the Aegean region, and the advancement of musical practices that were considered more masculine.[16] Accordingly, Greek music theorists, such as Pythagoras, proposed universal concepts for music, rather than concepts relating to contemporary or historical musical practices. Medieval church theorists continued the universalist focus of the Greeks to aid in their agenda of discouraging popular cultural practices of the Germanic and Nordic tribes, while preserving music as a realm of pure speculation, suitable for otherworldly expressions of Christian worship.[17]

The rise of humanism and historicism, beginning in the Renaissance, gradually led to a more balanced inclusion of historical and practical knowledge in the academic study of music, while music theory came out of the clouds and into the hands of musicians, usually composer-performers, who were as interested in explaining contemporary practice as in speculating on universal forms.[18] Jean-Philippe Rameau, for example, was a noted music theorist, and also a keyboardist and opera composer; accordingly his theoretical treatises introduce and discuss speculative universal concepts, such as the fundamental bass, alongside practical issues of composition and accompaniment.[19] At the same time, contemporaries of Rameau were the first practitioners of musicology, initially the comparative historical study of musical composers, styles, and periods, and later including issues of music sociology.[20]

Unfortunately, the greater balance and connection of music theory, history, and performance achieved in the eighteenth century was strained in the nineteenth century by the fragmenting effects of the rising museum culture, wherein the formerly joined practices of composition, conducting, instrumental performance, and theoretical discourse began to emerge as separate, institutionalized professions, each with specialized skills and language beyond the knowledge and abilities of the general public. As composition became separate from performance, composers were increasingly isolated from the public within a romantic "aesthetic of originality" (as Carl Dahlhaus puts it), which led them to forego pleasing audiences with familiar styles, in order to maintain the autonomist/formalist dedication to "l'art pour l'art."[21]

By the early to mid-twentieth century, composers of "high" art music were mostly so estranged from the public that they had to seek economic sustenance in the universities, where they were generally assigned to teach composition and music theory, which then consisted mainly of taxonomy, i.e., music notation and chordal identification. To the extent that music theory was a research discipline, it functioned under the umbrella of musicology. Meanwhile, the universities themselves were affected by rising professionalism and positivism, as individual disciplines within the arts and humanities each aspired to the systematic technical language and tools associated with the most prestigious fields of the natural sciences. In music, many academic composer-theorists (as well as composers outside of the universities) turned to mathematical explorations of set theory for the organization of musical tones, and to electronic and computer systems for the generation and analysis of musical works.[22] This was also a turn away from identification with

musicologists and the history of musical styles; study of style, after all, involved the relativization of the composers' own creative activity, and it also required music-historical expertise that was often outside the knowledge or interest of creative artists.

By the late 1950s, the composer-theorists began to break away from general musicology circles to found their own journals, organizations, and graduate programs. David Kraehenbühl's foreword to the first *Journal of Music Theory* well expresses the isolationist, ahistorical spirit of the new theory specialists, as it makes an academically respectable connection of purpose between their speculative enterprise and that of the early Greek and Medieval music theorists:

In centuries past the formulation of laws regarding the practice of music was regarded as the highest aim for a musician. ... But in our own time it is the rare musician who knows how his art offers a key to universal understanding. Music theory has become a discipline in stylistic definition or, still less, a system of nomenclature and classification that offers no valid laws even regarding music. It is [to] the restoration of music theory as more than a didactic convenience, more than a necessary discipline, as in fact, a mode of creative thought that this journal is dedicated.[23]

The two most prominent figures in the "restoration" of music theory were Allen Forte and Milton Babbitt. Beginning in 1959, Forte taught at Yale, where he edited the *Journal of Music Theory* through much of the 1960s, and guided several generations of theory doctoral students who later proceeded to prominent teaching positions at other universities. Forte's intellectual focus throughout his career has been on the advocacy, development, and application of universalist systems for the analysis and formulation of pitch structures: first as an advocate of Schenkerian layer analysis, then as a formalizer of pitch class and interval class sets for analysis of twentieth-century serial music, and most recently as the advocate of a linear analytic method combining elements of Schenkerian and set theories.[24] From 1977–82, he also presided over the first years of the Society for Music Theory, the founding of which signaled the final institutional split of music theory from musicology.[25]

Milton Babbitt, on the other hand, inspired a generation of students at Princeton University (including the aforementioned Boretz and John Rahn), where the journal *Perspectives of New Music* was founded in 1962. Although less universalist in his stance than Forte, Babbitt has been more extreme in his isolationism and in his alliance to scientific system. Babbitt calls for "musical theory" [*sic*] to drop its ties to music and the arts and ally itself with scientific theory, and to produce only statements and musical compositions whose terms are verifiable.[26] His analysis of Schoenberg's deeply religious, humanistic opera *Moses und Aron* demonstrates this approach; it deals only with the location of the 12–tone pitch structures of the opera, apart from their significance in the plot, let alone the overall meaning of the epic, and without discussion of any musical features besides pitch.[27] Babbitt's followers, although less extreme in their renunciation of cultural connections, have nonetheless pursued his program of developing a more scientific music-theoretical language, based on observable primitives of time and pitch. Unfortunately, such language can lead to a particularly fragmented version of autonomist/formalism, as, for example, when John Rahn recommends thirty-one isolated hearings of the first 11 bars of Webern's *Symphonie* opus 21/movement 2 in order that the structural relationships be appreciated properly.[28] The narrowness of focus promoted by such "close reading" (as Rahn elsewhere describes the Princetonian approach[29]) makes balanced consideration of the experience of the full symphony all but impossible, not to mention consideration of its cultural context and meaning. Moreover, it leads to the exclusion of non-theorists from the critical discourse (and of the music from their discourse), as well as the exclusion of all music from critical consideration but the most systematically-constructed kind—which is just what Babbitt had hoped.[30]

Unfortunately, the increased separation and professionalization of music theory in the last thirty years has had more effect on music than the mere increase of speculative theories and analyses would suggest. Rather, due to the separation of theory specialists in graduate-level curricula and post-graduate research and professional interaction, they no longer share a strong intellectual or institutional connection with musicologists, which might otherwise serve to promote communication and correction of imbalances for both disciplines. They also lack contact and shared knowledge with philosophers of music; indeed the occupation by music theorists of the philosophical, or pseudo-philosophical, role in academic departments of music serves to separate musicologists from music philosophers as well, to the probable detriment of all groups.

The most disturbing effect of this isolation is not on music theory scholars, who may have the intellect to surmount it, but on musical education at the lower levels, as promulgated by the narrowly-trained specialists. For example, the isolation of music theory from music history results at the undergraduate level in the naive presentation of theoretical concepts about how music works, separate from the context of the history and performance of the music, and from historically-oriented issues of musical style.[31] The focus is almost entirely on formalist analysis of harmony (i.e., pitch structures), to the neglect of melody, rhythm, tone color, and large scale structure—all of which are more clearly related to culture and more accessible to listeners. This restricted form of presentation, extended over the two to three years which music theory occupies in the curriculum, leaves the misleading impression that the harmonic concepts presented have universal or at least normative validity. This impression is strengthened by the monolithic program and course title "music theory" (as if there is only one), and by textbook declarations that the concepts are basic, fundamental, and comprehensive, or that, as Forte puts it in his *Tonal Harmony in Concept and Practice,* "they stand at the very foundation of the art and reach forth to include its most elaborate expressions."[32]

Actually, if anything, the reverse is true. Most undergraduate theory textbooks present a decontextualized miscellany of nineteenth- and twentieth-century harmonic concepts, many of which are inapplicable to a great amount of music within Western culture as well as outside of it. In order to make the concepts appear relevant and comprehensive, textbooks (and teachers) focus on short, carefully chosen or newly-composed phrases. This is a claustrophobic approach that can lead to a narrow, distorted view of the music under consideration, and an extraordinary misuse of academic time and energies.[33] A similar approach to the college-level study of the art of literature would have students spending most of their academic time and energy applying textbook norms of one narrow aspect of writing style—say, rhyme—to isolated lines of Shakespeare, Milton or Dickinson, instead of reading and interpreting the full plays and poems. Unfortunately, when it happens in music, it's a worse distortion than it would be in literature, because students receive so little academic exposure to our musical heritage, that they are necessarily less aware than literature students might be of what a narrow and distorted view they are getting of the world of musical art.

In addition to the false universalism of the concepts of music theory, there is the problem of the underlying autonomist/formalist assumptions in the procedures of music analysis, including: (1) music consists of separate musical works, which can and should be isolated from their cultural contexts and analyzed; (2) analysis should deal with the structural organization of pitches inside the "musical work," as determined by the musical score; and (3) there are universal, or at least normative, standards of value with which musical works can be judged and compared.

These assumptions are so standard that they may appear reasonable, but they do not stand up to the test of trans-historical and trans-cultural evidence. Lydia Goehr has argued against the first assumption, showing that the concept of the musical work is part of the romantic model of the arts, which tends to distort the non-romantic music to which it is frequently applied, whether it be to Vivaldi or Duke Ellington.[34] The second assumption is similarly dubious. Understanding music (if that's the goal) depends at least as much on rhythm as pitch, precisely because rhythm is so tangibly physical, emotional, and cultural. Even if rhythm were not generally excluded from the picture, the practice of analyzing from the notated score is highly questionable, because, as Nicholas Cook points out, the notation is not itself music, but merely an analogy which developed and continues to evolve around the teaching of music-theoretical concepts.[35] Moreover, the practice of analyzing from the score ignores strong historical evidence that composers are not solely responsible for their musical works. Rather, performers are usually to some extent the co-creators of musical structures, not to mention musical experiences, in ways which depart from the notational indications in every musical parameter, including the fundamentals of duration and pitch.

The third assumption is easily disproven by the history of music theory itself, i.e., the proposal of different universalist theories, by Rameau, Schenker, Meyer, Forte, and others, which are not in retrospect universal at all, but rather reflect their formulators' frames of reference. (This assumption does not apply to theorists of the Babbitt school, who tend to regard each separate musical work as a theory unto itself.) Different as these and other universalist theories of musical value are, they have one thing in common: they lead to analytical procedures and data which center around the viability of the theories themselves, rather than the gathering of information about, or appreciation of, the music being analyzed. Frequently the theories function in circular fashion, with carefully chosen canonical works or passages serving both to help formulate and to prove the theory.[36]

Universalist theories and judgments, and autonomist/formalism in general, can be dangerously seductive in their simplicity, especially in an era of declining cultural literacy in art music. So, although some music theorists have recently begun to explore other critical approaches from interdisciplinary sources,[37] these explorations are institutionally disadvantaged in their competition with autonomist/formalism at all but the highest level of research, unless and until the paradigm changes. Moreover, as long as the pedagogy of theory and analysis remains fixed on the hard-boundaried paradigm, it is almost impossible for musicians trained under the current curriculum to free themselves from the autonomist/formalist assumptions and challenge the exclusionary practices in their own disciplinary corners of music, including the teaching and performance of an exclusive canon of white European male composers. It is also almost impossible for non-music majors to take upper-division courses in music history, as they might in art history or literature, without undergoing prerequisite years of training in music theory, a requirement which further isolates music from other academic departments and the wider community. As a consequence of the isolation, music receives little or no discussion in general humanities and social science courses and curricula which otherwise benefit from interdisciplinary integration. The same omission occurs in cultural criticism; that is, music is omitted from discussion in cases where it is obviously relevant, such as film reviews, or mentioned only superficially. In the case of many films, omitting critical consideration of the music is not unlike analyzing *Tristan and Isolde* without discussion of Wagner and his musical style. Nonetheless, it happens all the time.[38]

II. SOFT BOUNDARIES IN MUSIC THEORY

That is the general scope of the isolation maintained by the autonomist/formalist practices of mainstream music theory. The question is, what can the feminist paradigm of soft boundaries do to alleviate the isolation? The paradigm calls for the formulation and application of music-theoretical concepts and judgments only on the basis of the actual experience of music in a cultural context, avoiding any hard-boundaried preferences for intellectual experience, and avoiding the logocentric subordination of experience to theory. This is by no means a completely original suggestion. Under the influence of ethnomusicology, Marxist aesthetics, hermeneutics, and post-structural theory, many musicologists and some theorists concerned with musical style have increasingly turned to culturally-related concepts in the 1980s, in the belief that, as Judith Becker states, "evaluation is only viable within a culture, particularly within a genre."[39] In fact, so much more music analysis of a culturally-related nature has appeared in the last few years than in previous decades, that a paradigm shift may already have begun.[40] Of course, in bringing feminist theory into play, one risks alienating and closing more minds than are opened to the positive possibilities of a new paradigm. Yet, once feminist theory passes the hurdles of acceptance in an academic discipline, it has its advantages, for it speaks to a general human fascination with our own acculturation in gender and other social constructions. Thus, articulation of a feminist paradigm and rationale for changing the practices of music theory research and pedagogy may be more effective in breaking through the hard boundaries of mainstream theory and analysis than diffuse references to interdisciplinary theoretical models have been.

If applied, the paradigm would reorient music theorists toward the development and use of a far wider range of experience-related concepts in their own analyses, and in their teaching of theory and analysis to others. Music theory of this kind potentially would be accessible and interesting to many people, because it would help to explain their own experience with the music, rather than superimposing a complex formalist analysis of no apparent connection to their experience. (For this reason, analyses and judgments based on intellectual experience alone would be discouraged, though not prohibited, under the soft-boundaries paradigm.) As a result, the current isolation of music theory and music majors could be softened by the wider involvement of students from other disciplines, and by the softer boundaries that would develop within music departments between currently separate fields of music philosophy, history and sociology, and performance. Music theory could continue to play a central role in the formation and application of concepts for music analysis, but its role would be less isolated from that of music history, sociology, and philosophy, and more like that of theory in the visual and literary arts—where specialists in theory alone are rare. Like recent theorists of the visual arts, music theorists would find themselves relying more on historical and sociological information about the music they examine in order to formulate concepts and judgments about it. Possibly as a result, the status of music theory as a separate discipline with separate graduate programs, journals, and societies would wane. Most important, the current hegemony of music theory over the shape of musical education in our society would be lessened, as would the isolation and fragmentation of our academic and general musical cultures—without lessening our social needs or abilities to engage in critical discourse and understanding about music.

From where would the experience-related concepts come? They could come from the ways in which the music under consideration was composed, performed, heard, taught, danced,

moved, worked, or prayed to. They could include terms, preferably in the language of the
period, for sequences of bodily gestures which
were associated with dancing or playing the
music in question, or for the organization of accompanying texts, dramatic representations,
sacred rites, or work functions. Something very
like phrases would probably remain valid for
lots of music, because of the analogous structure of accompanying poetic lines and dance
motions in each case. But many other supposedly
normative concepts which occupy the great majority of music theory classtime—the altered
6th-chords, functional progressions, mediant
modulations, and so forth—would move from
the normative column into narrower application
in context with music composed under their
influence. Harmonic analysis of Bach chorales
according to Ramellian or Schenkerian concepts would be out; consideration of the source,
text, and religious function of the chorale, and
consideration of the meaning of Bach's particular harmonizations and melodic colorations in
comparison with other settings would be called
for in their place.

In cases of musical repertories for which evidence of theoretical concepts and procedures
are thin or lacking, the history of music writing, including notational practices, could act as
a guide: deconstructing supposedly universal
concepts of pitch, rhythm, harmony, tone color,
and dynamics by revealing music-historical
periods and repertories in which they were differently conceived or absent and reconstructing
ways in which the music was actually experienced and thought about. In the case of ninth-
century plainchant, for example, knowing that
the notation indicates the direction of liturgical
phrases, not individual melodic notes, should
discourage formalist melodic analysis of the
chant repertory.[41] Analysis instead of the way
directionality functions in chant would probably be much more illuminating. In the case of
eighteenth-century *adagios*, knowing that the
notation is an incomplete melodic and harmonic framework for the performers to elaborate, rather than a finished composition, should
discourage formalist analysis there as well.
Instead, theorists may be able to help us understand better when and why improvisation is
used.

The emphasis on experience-relatedness of

notation in music theory classes would likely
serve to enliven the course material and allow
students to contemplate by extension what our
current notational practices suggest about our
musical culture and ourselves—a form of critical thinking too often missing from classrooms
of music theory and analysis. Chances are that
contact with the historical contingencies of
music writing and notation would similarly
stimulate the thinking of the music theorists
themselves, as they are forced to deal with how
and why they should do a harmonic analysis of
a musical movement, such as a Baroque *adagio*,
whose pitches and rhythms (let alone dynamics,
tone colors, and other features) cannot be quan-
tified or verified. In such cases, the theorist that
would choose nonetheless to fix the pitches and
rhythms in a reified version which could be
analyzed, would be exposed under the new
paradigm as doing so not for the sake of understanding the music, but for the sake of an analysis which in its very nature had obscured
understanding.

In addition to the above suggestions, experience-related concepts could also come from
general aspects of a culture such as dress or
speaking style, wherein a culture's semiotic
codes for symbolic representation of emotions
or beliefs in color, shape, or sound might be
read in a non-musical context and applied analo-
gously to the culture's music. Susan McClary
demonstrates this approach by finding musical
gestures used in opera to illustrate eroticism,
for example, in contemporary, untexted or
"absolute" music.[42] McClary's finding of
meaning in absolute music goes against almost
two centuries of the claim, asserted during the
contemporaneous rise of German symphonic
music with German transcendental idealism,
that music is not representational in the sense of
the other arts but rather transcendent, or as
Schopenhauer saw it, a direct copy of the will.
However, the tendency to deny the representational aspect of music, while naively accepting
its presence in the visual and verbal arts, simply
reflects the privileging of verbal and visual
symbolism in our culture, a bias considered by
some feminists to be inherently masculinist. Is
Debussy's *Afternoon of a Faun* unrepresenta-
tional of that sensual, sexual subject, compared
to a picture of a faun, or Mallarme's poem?
Indeed, it would seem that music is more capa-

ble of representing some types of experience than are words or images.

The key to unlocking the meanings of supposedly autonomous structures of sound is probably rhythm, because it has the strongest ties to music's physical and emotional impact, and the weakest ties to formalist analysis. It's obvious that musical rhythm is related to dance, and other socially-constructed patterns of movement, and that such patterns themselves have cultural roots and functions. Use of the rhythms of a dance outside of its cultural context—as when Haydn uses minuets and Mahler uses Ländlers—involves the carryover of the cultural associations of the dance that in turn contribute to artistic meaning. Even where dance steps and other socially-constructed patterns of movement are not literally present, it should be possible for historically-informed music analysts to consider the meaning of different rhythmic motifs and styles, such as those of ragtime, blues, minimalist music, and even the formalist-organized rhythms of the concert hall—just as critics of the literary and visual arts consider the cultural meanings of non-representative features in those arts. By comparison, the universalist, formalist theories and analyses of rhythm which Grosvenor Cooper and Leonard Meyer (among others) have proposed appear to be empty exercises in isolation, judgment, and hierarchization, not at all oriented toward the understanding of the music.[43]

Under the new paradigm of soft boundaries, psychoanalytic models for interpreting artistic meaning may also be applied to music, much more successfully once the false universals of mainstream music theory have been cleared away, and the conscious meanings of musical gestures have been more openly explored. The particular value of the psychoanalytic approach is that it gets beyond the hierarchical focus on greatness, and into the analysis of the underlying meanings of artistic symbolism for the creative artist and the wider community. Walter Abell has suggested a mixture of Freud's emphasis on the personal unconscious of the creative artist, along with Jung's emphasis on the collective unconscious of the larger community, as a means to establish a "unified field theory" of interpreting meaning in art.[44] Applied to music, Abell's suggestion would involve comparison of musical gestures as used by a particu-

lar composer or performer, with the gestures common to the culture, in order to better understand the art, the artist, and the community. Given the symbolic nature of art, the ability to interpret artistic gestures and experiences could lead to a better understanding of our cultural ills and needs, just as psychoanalytic interpretation of dreams leads to personal diagnoses and recommendations.

Equally important to what the paradigm of soft boundaries will do in terms of music theory and analysis is what it will not do. For example, it will not produce theories and analyses which determine the comparative merit of different musics and musical works. This will no doubt disappoint many, for hierarchization is an honored practice in our culture, particularly in academic circles. Its honored status often leads us to imagine that hierarchization is essential to understanding, when in fact the understanding it provides is usually slight to nil—similar to the sort of enlightenment received when American Bandstand critics give a song an "88" for a good beat.

Too, the paradigm will not produce a clear rule as to which of the possible experience-related concepts are best to use in the understanding of a particular example of music, or a measuring standard as to when an analysis has been successful. A sense of increased understanding and appreciation of the music will be the only guide as to the validity of the analysis, just as it is in criticism of literary and visual arts. Another thing the paradigm of soft boundaries and relatedness will not do is promote theories and analyses which are ends in themselves, or which function in circular fashion. By forcing theorists to start with experience-relatedness as the basis of their analytical concepts, the paradigm of soft boundaries and relatedness necessarily reframes the analytical project as one in which understanding musical experience becomes an end in itself, rather than a means to the end of demonstrating a theory.

I foresee one serious objection to the paradigm and its particular application to music theory and analysis, having to do with the feasibility of increasing the complexity of music theory, which the paradigm will to some extent do. That is, how will students, who often have difficulty in understanding the simplistic concepts of traditional music theory, be able to cope with multiple, experience-related concepts?

This is a difficult question, to which there are several relevant answers. First, the current pedagogy, even if one considers it successful (which I do not), comes close to academic fraud. One does not learn in college-level physics that Newton's laws are universal and unchallenged, though that would be simpler for ill-prepared students to understand. Why then, is it acceptable to teach false universals in music? (If the comparison seems inappropriate, it may be because our society's respect for meaning and purpose in the arts is so much lower than that for the sciences.) Second, the difficulty students have in understanding traditional music theory results in part from the poverty of pre-college musical education, which neglects virtually all aspects of music except for service-oriented ensembles of band and choir. This too is a kind of educational fraud which should be addressed, rather than adapted to with increasingly simplistic approaches to music at the college level.

Third, the false universals and norms of music theory may be relatively simple in the context of music theory coursework but because they oversimplify musical practice, they make other courses, especially those in music history, more difficult. It may be, too, that the reason students currently have trouble with music theory is that they sense the falseness of the concepts and procedures while they are in school, and they find limited application of them to the music they experience outside of the classroom. Although multiple, experience-related concepts and procedures would introduce more complexity, it is possible that their greater connection to the cultural, physical, and emotional experience of music by the students would make the concepts, and academic musical study in general, actually easier to absorb and retain.

A final question about the paradigm of soft boundaries comes from the feminist side of the debate. That question is, what will the paradigm do, if anything, to improve the standing of women in the arts, past and present? This is a question with an underlying liberal feminist stance, according to which women and their advancement are taken to be the central focus of feminism. The paradigm of soft boundaries takes a more radical view of the feminist project, and aims to challenge the whole framework of exclusionary assumptions and practices in the arts, as mentioned at the outset. The focus is shifted to include not only the question of how many women are represented in the canons and institutions of the arts, but also how the canons and institutions are constructed, and why. Yet, use of the paradigm would likely gratify liberal hopes here as well, by reclaiming efforts of women artists that were devalued under the old autonomist/formalist aesthetics.

In the broadest sense, the paradigm of soft boundaries challenges the isolation of the arts from culture, and along with it, the focus on autonomy and individual greatness, by which the canons of mainly male composers have been promulgated. At the very least, from the feminist standpoint, the paradigm will serve to balance the genealogies with corrective emphasis on the activities of performers and other participants of music, as well as composers of popular music, female and male. At best, it will promote change in the exclusionary framework of our musical culture, lessen the isolation of academic music and music professionals, and perhaps by extension alleviate the isolation and devaluation of the arts in general. The result of such an alleviation would be a major improvement in our society's appreciation of and participation in the arts, in our understanding of the needs for educational and institutional arts funding, and in our overall appreciation of the importance of sensual pleasure and the reconnection of mind and body.[45]

1. For example, see Linda Nochlin, *Women, Art, and Power and Other Essays* (New York: Harper and Row, 1988), p. 146; and Mary Deveraux, "Oppressive Texts, Resisting Readers, and the Gendered Spectator: The *New Aesthetics*," *The Journal of Aesthetics and Art Criticism* 48:4 (Fall 1990), special issue on "Feminism and Traditional Aesthetics," pp. 337–48 (esp. pp. 339 and 344–46). Also see Remi Clignet, *The Structure of Artistic Revolutions* (University of Pennsylvania Press, 1985), who applies to art the analysis of paradigms in science of Thomas Kuhn, *The Structure of Scientific Revolutions* (University of Chicago Press, 1970).

2. See Christine Battersby, *Genius and Gender: Towards a Feminist Aesthetics* (London: Women's Press, 1989); Josephine Donovan, "Afterword: Critical Re-vision" in *Feminist Literary Criticism,* ed. Donovan (University Press of Kentucky, 1989), pp. 74–81; Gisela Ecker, "Introduction" in *Feminist Aesthetics,* ed. Ecker (Boston: Beacon Press, 1985), all of whom argue the need to challenge masculinist frameworks in aesthetics, as distinct from the views of liberal feminists and essentialists, the latter of whom advocate exploration of a "female" or "feminine" aesthetic; see, for examples, Heide Göttner-Abendroth, "Nine Principles of a Matriarchal Aesthetics," *Feminist Aesthetics,* pp. 81–94, and Renée Cox, "A Gynocentric Aesthetic," *Hypatia* 5 (1990): 43–62. Also see Cox, "Recovering Jouissance: Feminist Aesthetics and Music," in Karin Pendle, ed., *Women and Music: A History* (Indiana University Press, 1991), pp. 331–40, for a discussion of the different phases and aspects of feminist criticism and aesthetics since their beginnings in the 1970s.

3. Exemplified in Immanuel Kant, *Critique of Judgement,* trans. Werner S. Pluhar (1790; Indianapolis: Hackett Publishing, 1987). See Terry Eagleton, *Ideology of the Aesthetic* (Cambridge, MA: Basil Blackwell, 1990); and Janet Wolff, *Aesthetics and the Sociology of Art* (London: Allen and Unwin, 1983), for Marxist critiques of the underlying agenda of autonomist/formalist aesthetics.

Incidentally, the term "formalism" is used here in place of the more frequently used "cognitivism" in order to avoid confusion with the meaning of cognitive in psychology, as more inclusive of emotional and physical functions than in the philosophical use of the term.

4. For example, see Hélène Cixous and Catherine Clement, *The Newly Born Woman,* trans. Betsy Wing (1975; University of Minnesota Press, 1987), who initially wrote of the connection between logocentrism's binary oppositions, such as "Head/Heart," and the original couple, man/woman, pp. 63–4; and Sherry Ortner, "Is Female to Male as Nature is to Culture?," in *Woman, Culture, and Society,* Michelle Rosaldo and Louise Lamphere, eds. (Stanford University Press, 1974). For more recent discussions see Susan Bordo, "The Cartesian Masculinization of Thought," *Signs* 11 (1986): 439–56, especially pp. 448–55; Bordo and Alison M. Jaggar, *Gender/Body/Knowledge: Feminist Reconstructions of Being and Knowing* (Rutgers University Press, 1989); and Sandra Harding, *Whose Science? Whose Knowledge? Thinking from Women's Lives* (Cornell University Press, 1991). The question of whether women's supposed closer connection to non-intellectual experience is natural (due to child-bearing, for example) or cultural (due to discrimination and/or social construction) has not been settled, nor should it be as long as distinctions in social construction are so strong. In any case, criticism of feminist theory for its absence of consensus on this nature/culture question reflects the same logocentric binarism that feminist theory criticizes, as well as reifying the distinction between mind and body that feminist theorists tend to reject. My own view of the contribution of academic feminism in this area is that it has challenged not just the superiority of theory to experience under logocentrism, but the very separation of theory from experience. In fact, feminist theory recognizes that making and applying theory is experience, too.

5. See Clive Bell, *Art* (1911; New York: Capricorn Books, 1958), pp. 25–7; and Eduard Hanslick, *On the Musically Beautiful,* trans. Geoffrey Payzant (1854; Indianapolis: Hackett Publishing Co., 1986), esp. p. 29. Since World War I, autonomist/formalism has been most evident in the "New Criticism," whereby works of art are judged without reference to historical context or authorial intention.

6. Discussion of the museum culture of art goes back to the post-World War I era; see, for example, Paul Valéry, "Le Problème des musées" in *Oeuvres,* Vol. II, pp. 1290–93; and John Dewey, *Art as Experience* (New York: Capricorn Books, 1934), pp. 7–10, who also links the museum to the rise of bourgeois capitalism, nationalism, and imperialism. For more recent critiques, see André Bazin, *The Museum Age* (New York, 1967); and John Fisher, *Making and Effacing Art: Modern American Art in a Culture of Museums* (New York: Oxford University Press, 1991), esp. Part I, "The Work of Art, The Museum Culture, and the Future's Past," pp. 3–140.

7. Fisher, *Making and Effacing Art,* pp. 19–22. Also see Lydia Goehr, *The Imaginary Museum of Musical Works* (Cambridge: Oxford University Press, 1991), who argues that the rise of the musical museum of the concert hall has promoted the concept of the musical work.

Not surprisingly, the museum culture has given rise to the "institutional" theories of art, according to which art is defined and artworks identified by art institutions, critics, and teachers. See, for example, Arthur Danto, "The Artworld," *Journal of Philosophy* 61 (1964): 571–84; and George Dickie, *Art and the Aesthetic: An Institutional Analysis* (Cornell University Press, 1974). However, museums are at least as likely to destroy artistic meaning, as when the San Francisco Museum of Art exhibits a nineteenth-century piano with the sign "Don't touch the objects of art."

8. Also see Rose Rosengard Subotnik, "Individualism in Western Art Music and Its Cultural Costs," in *Developing Variations: Style and Ideology in Western Music* (University of Minnesota Press, 1991), pp. 239–64, who discusses the role of modern concepts of private property and individualism in disenfranchising people other than composers from music.

9. Barbara Ehrenreich and Deirdre English, *For Their Own Good: 150 Years of the Experts' Advice to Women* (New York: Doubleday, 1978), esp. pp. 15–20. Also see Linda Nochlin, "Why Have There Been No Great Women Artists" in *Art and Sexual Politics,* Thomas Hess and Elizabeth Baker, eds. (New York: Collier, 1971), pp. 1–39, for a classic discussion of institutional exclusion of women from painting in the nineteenth century. For a discussion of institutional exclusion in nineteenth-century music, see Nancy B. Reich, "European Composers and Musicians, 1800–1890," in Karin Pendle, ed., *Women and Music: A History* (Indiana University Press, 1991), pp. 97–122; and Eva Rieger, "Dolce Semplice? On the Changing Role of Women in Music" in *Feminist Aesthetics,* ed. Gisela Ecker, trans. Harriet Anderson (Boston: Beacon Press, 1985), pp. 135–49.

10. See Norma Broude and Mary Garrard, eds., *Feminism and Art History: Questioning the Litany* (New York: Harper and Row, 1982); and Marcia J. Citron, "Gender, Professionalism, and the Musical Canon," *Journal of Musicology* 8 (1990): 102–17, for further analyses of the institutional exclusion of women from the visual and musical arts.

Women in the literary arts were less affected, since writing skills were widely shared, and since exercising those skills takes little more than a room of one's own.

11. "Genderized perspective" is not a slogan in common currency, but a description of what many feminist aesthetic theorists have arrived at for analyzing the visual arts. See, for example, Gisela Ecker's "Introduction" to *Feminist Aesthetics*, pp. 15–22, which says that "feminist aesthetic theory must insist that all investigations into art must be thoroughly genderized" (22). Also see Mary Deveraux, "Oppressive Texts," and Laura Mulvey, *Visual and Other Pleasures* (Indiana University Press, 1989), for discussion of the "male gaze."

12. See especially Susan McClary, *Feminine Endings: Music, Gender, and Sexuality* (University of Minnesota Press, 1991); and Jane Bowers, "Feminist Scholarship and the Field of Musicology: I," *College Music Symposium* 29 (1989): 83–92.

13. In a previous article, I have discussed the relationship of the paradigm to feminist theory and other postmodern intellectual developments; see "Soft Boundaries and Relatedness: Paradigm for a Postmodern Feminist Musical Aesthetics," *boundary 2*, 19/2 (Summer 1992): 194–205.

14. See Hilde Hein, "The Role of Feminist Aesthetics in Feminist Theory," *The Journal of Aesthetics and Art Criticism*, special issue on "Feminism and Traditional Aesthetics" 48: 4 (Fall 1990): 281–92, who emphasizes the ties of feminist theory and aesthetics to experience (282), and to the avoidance of "totalizing," "overarching truths" of patriarchal thinking, but who warns against pluralism without rationality (289). Also see Naomi Schor, *Reading in Detail: Aesthetics and the Feminine* (New York: Methuen, Inc., 1987), esp. pp. 11–22.

15. See Joseph Kerman's *Contemplating Music: Challenges to Musicology* (Cambridge, MA: Harvard University Press, 1985) which discusses how the excessive isolation and positivism on the part of music theorists and musicologists has prevented the development of a serious music criticism, able to engage with the "latest chariots (or bandwagons) of intellectual life," including post-structuralism, deconstruction, and feminist theory (17). Also see Kerman, "How We Got into Analysis, and How to Get Out," *Critical Inquiry* 7 (1980): 311–31; and Lawrence Ferrara, *Philosophy and the Analysis of Music: Bridges to Musical Sound, Form and Reference* (New York: Excelsior Music Publishing Co., 1991), esp. p. 44, for critiques of the attitudes and approaches of standard music theory and analysis.

16. The Greek agenda of masculinizing music is reflected in Aristotle's preference for the "manly character" of the Dorian mode (associated with the Greek Dorian tribe) over the Phrygian mode that was associated with the gynocentric Phrygians they had conquered. Aristotle also denigrates musical performers, who were still largely female at the time, in consequence of music's long-term use in female ceremonies of goddess-worship. See Renée Cox, "A History of Music," *The Journal of Aesthetics and Art Criticism* 48:4 (1990): 395–409, who describes the Phrygian musical culture which the Greeks supplanted and to which Plato and Aristotle later referred (395–98).

17. Ibid., 398–400. Also see Julius Portnoy, *The Philosopher and Music: A Historical Outline* (New York: Humanities Press, 1954), who views the history of music philosophy as frequently opposed to cultural practices.

18. See John Hollander, *The Untuning of the Sky: Ideas of Music in English Poetry, 1500–1700* (Princeton University Press, 1961; Norton, 1970), for further examination of the more practical theoretical view of music starting in the late Renaissance.

19. See, for example, Rameau, *Treatise on Harmony*, ed. and trans. Phillip Gossett (1722; New York: Dover, 1971); two sections of the treatise are devoted to speculative, and two sections to the practical issues of composition and accompaniment. Rameau's famous innovative concept of the fundamental bass—an imaginary bass line of chord roots, preferably 5th-related, was both speculative and practical.

20. Warren D. Allen, *Philosophies of Music History: A Study of General Histories of Music, 1600–1900* (New York: Dover, 1939); and Kerman, *Contemplating Music*, for more institutional history of musicology. Kerman also explains the generally confusing issue of ethnomusicology's development: musicology initially did not extend to the study of non-Western musical cultures, leaving a vacuum filled in the twentieth century by anthropology-influenced "ethnomusicologists." Ethnomusicology's more sociological, cultural approach in turn has influenced musicology to study Western music with more attention to social issues.

21. Carl Dahlhaus, *Nineteenth-Century Music*, trans. J. Bradford Robinson (University of California Press, 1989), pp. 27–28.

22. See Matthew Brown and Douglas Dempster, "The Scientific Image of Music Theory," *Journal of Music Theory* 33 (1989): 65–106, for a critique of music theory's identification with science from a philosophical standpoint; see Susan McClary, "Terminal Prestige: The Case of Avant-Garde Music Composition," *Cultural Critique* 12 (1989): 57–81, for a musicological critique. Also see Bruce Wilshire, *The Moral Collapse of the University: Professionalism, Purity, and Alienation* (State University of New York Press, 1990), for a more general discussion of the underlying causes and the effects of academic professionalism, positivism, and specialization.

23. David Kraehenbühl, "Foreword," *Journal of Music Theory* 1 (1958): 1. Also see Kerman, *Contemplating Music*, chapter 3: "Analysis, Theory, and New Music," pp. 60–112, for more institutional history on the societies and other journals which the new theorists formed.

24. See for example, Allen Forte, "Schenker's Conception of Musical Structure," *Journal of Music Theory*; "A Theory of Set Complexes for Music," *Journal of Music Theory* 8 (1968): 136–83 and *The Structure of Atonal Music* (Yale University Press, 1973); and "New Approaches to the Linear Analysis of Music," *Journal of the American Musicological Society* 41 (1988): 315–48.

25. See Richmond Browne, "The Inception of the Society for Music Theory," *Music Theory Spectrum* 1 (1979): 2–5. Leonard Meyer, who has been involved with explorations of style and interdisciplinary theoretical models from psychology and linguistics, was the only theorist to express concern about the fragmentation from musicology, although he later joined the board of the organization. In his keynote address to the 1988 eleventh Society for Music Theory meeting, Meyer warned that "the time has come, this Walrus thinks, for music theorists and psychologists to consider seriously the claims of culture, and of history."

(Meyer, "A Pride of Prejudices: Or, Delight in Diversity," *Music Theory Spectrum* 13 [1991]: 241–51, 251.) But most theorists found the separation exhilarating. See, for example, Allen Forte, "Banquet Address: SMT, Rochester, 1989," in *Music Theory Spectrum* 11 (1989): 95–99, who makes an analogy to Schenkerian layers and finds musicology in the background, practical music in the foreground, and music theory in the middleground, "where all the action is" (99).

26. See Milton Babbitt, "The Structure and Function of Musical Theory," in *Perspectives on Contemporary Music Theory*, eds. Benjamin Boretz and Edward Cone (New York: Norton, 1972), pp. 10–21.

27. Babbitt, "Three Essays on Schoenberg: *Moses und Aron*," in *Perspectives on Schoenberg and Stravinsky*, eds. Benjamin Boretz and Edward Cone, rev. ed. (New York: Norton, 1972), pp. 53–60. There is an extraordinary distance between Babbitt's formalistic analysis and the literary-critical analysis of George Steiner, "Schoenberg's Moses und Aron" in *George Steiner: A Reader* (Oxford University Press, 1984), who discusses the opera's unique position in "the history of modern theater, of modern theology, of the relationship between Judaism and the European crisis" (234). Babbitt's approach would seem to indicate that following verifiability to extremes can lead to meanings not worthy of verification or communication.

28. John Rahn, *Basic Atonal Theory* (New York and London: Longman, 1980), chapter 1, pp. 4–18.

29. Rahn, "Notes on Methodology in Music Theory," in *Journal of Music Theory* 33 (1989): 143–54 (143). Rahn also includes non-formalistic approaches to analysis in "Aspects of Musical Explanation," *Perspectives of New Music* 17 (1979): 204–24; but they are all stated in the form of binary dyads, which invite the reader to marginalize the second, less scientific half of the dyad.

30. See Babbitt, "The Structure and Function of Musical Theory," p. 11: "I like to believe that a not insignificant consequence of the proper understanding of a proper theory of music is to assure that a composer who asserts something such as 'I don't compose by system, but by ear' thereby convicts himself of, at least, an argumentum ad populum by equating ignorance with freedom, that is, by equating ignorance of the constraints under which he creates with freedom from constraints." It follows, of course, that music of such composers does not merit analysis.

31. See Robert Gauldin and Mary Wennerstrom, "Pedagogy," *Music Theory Spectrum* 11 (1989): 66–73, who find that, notwithstanding the wide range of research activity during the first ten years of the Society for Music Theory, the pedagogy of theory has hardened, moving away from comprehensive, chronological, experimental, and integrated curricula towards maximal simplification and clarification, separate courses for each subject and skill, and a more limited repertoire of common-practice music. Also see Gunther Schüller, "The Compleat Musician in the Compleat Conservatory," *Musings: The Musical Worlds of Gunther Schüller* (New York: Oxford University Press, 1986), pp. 237–46, for discussion of the narrowness of musical education in colleges and conservatories.

32. Allen Forte, *Tonal Harmony in Concept and Practice*, 3rd. ed. (New York: Holt, Rinehart and Winston, 1979), p. 1. Also note the first sentence of the first article, first issue, and first journal of the Society for Music Theory, by David Beach: "The discovery, description, and codification of principles of pitch structure in music are and always have been of primary concern to music theorists." See Beach, "Pitch Structure and the Analytical Process in Atonal Music: An Interpretation of the Theory of Sets," *Music Theory Spectrum* 1 (1979): 7.

33. See Pieter Van den Toorn, "What Price Analysis," *Journal of Music Theory* 33 (1989): 167, who criticizes the "claustrophobic" approach with particular reference to the theory and analysis of twentieth-century music. Also see Gauldin and Wennerstrom, "Pedagogy," who mention falling cultural literacy in music and in general as a problem which is exacerbated by the fragmented pedagogy of current music theory.

34. Goehr, *The Imaginary Museum* and "Being True to the Work," *The Journal of Aesthetics and Art Criticism* 47 (1989): 55–67.

35. See Nicholas Cook, "Music Theory and 'Good Comparison': A Viennese Perspective" *Journal of Music Theory* 33 (1989): 117–41 (121).

36. Van den Toorn, "What Price Analysis," 167–68; and Richard Taruskin, "Review of Forte, *The Harmonic Structure of The Rite of Spring*," *Current Musicology* 28 (1979): 119, who explains that circularity is readily broken by external corroboration of details in the composition, performance, and transmission of musical works, i.e., in cultural detail.

37. See, for example, Nicholas Cook, *A Guide to Musical Analysis* (New York: George Braziller, 1987), for a demonstration of his more pragmatic, less formalistic approach; traditional, Schenkerian, psychological, formalistic, and semiotic approaches to analysis are all explored, each with reference to the historical context in which they arose. Also see Richmond Browne, "Report: The 1988 Oxford Music Analysis Conference," *Journal of Music Theory* 33 (1989): 228–36, who reports a turn to sociological factors in current music theory research; and Mary Louise Serafine and Wayne Slawson, "Interdisciplinary Directions in Music Theory," *Music Theory Spectrum* 11 (1989): 74–83.

38. Since film music frequently uses the Wagnerian technique of leitmotivic restatement and transformation, the comparison here is most apt. And while it's true that some film music is mentioned—e.g., Bernard Hermann's music for Alfred Hitchcock films, such mentions rarely extend beyond the name of the composer and a brief characterization of overall style, into the more significant issue of the symbolism of musical forms and motifs.

39. Judith Becker, "Is Western Art Music Superior?" *Musical Quarterly* 72 (1986): 341–59 (359).

40. See Joseph Kerman, "American Musicology in the 1990s," *Journal of Musicology* 9 (1991): 131–44, where he suggests the current presence of a paradigm shift (142), in part because of the rise of feminist scholarship in musicology. Also see Rahn, "New Research Paradigms," *Music Theory Spectrum* 11 (1989): 84–94; and Renée Lorraine [Cox], "Musicology and Theory: Where It's Been, Where It's Going," *The Journal of Aesthetics and Art Criticism* 51 (1993): 235–44.

41. See Leo Treitler, "The History of Music Writing in the West," *Journal of the American Musicological Society* 35 (1982): 237–79 (243–44).

42. McClary, *Feminine Endings*, chapters 1–3.

43. Grosvenor Cooper and Leonard B. Meyer, *The Rhythmic Structure of Music* (Chicago: University of Chi-

cago Press, 1960). But non-formalistic theoretical studies of rhythm are now on the rise, perhaps as part of the suggested paradigm shift; see especially Jonathan Kramer, *The Time of Music* (New York: Schirmer, 1988); and Lawrence Ferrara, *Philosophy and the Analysis of Music,* who emphasizes phenomenology and time in his "eclectic" approach to music analysis.

44. Walter Abell, "Toward a Unified Field in Aesthetics," *Aesthetics Today,* ed. Morris Philipson (New York: World Publishing Co., 1961), pp. 432–65. Literary critic Lawrence Kramer demonstrates this approach, commonly found in criticism of the literary and visual arts, in his "Culture and Musical Hermeneutics: The Salome Complex," *The Cambridge Opera Journal* 2 (1990): 269–94.

45. I would like to acknowledge the assistance received at the 1991 Institute on "Philosophy and the Histories of the Arts," sponsored by the American Society for Aesthetics and the National Endowment for the Humanities, in developing the ideas expressed in this essay. I also thank the referees and the editor of this journal for their helpful comments.

JOEL RUDINOW

Race, Ethnicity, Expressive Authenticity: Can White People Sing the Blues?

The idea of a white blues singer seems an even more violent contradiction of terms than the idea of a middle class blues singer.

Amiri Baraka (LeRoi Jones), *Blues People*

It is unlikely that [the blues] will survive through the imitations of the young white college copyists, the "urban blues singers," whose relation to the blues is that of the "trad" jazz band to the music of New Orleans: sterile and derivative. The bleak prospect is that the blues probably has no real future; that, folk music that it is, it served its purpose and flourished whilst it had meaning in the Negro community. At the end of the century it may well be seen as an important cultural phenomenon—and someone will commence a systematic study of it, too late.

Paul Oliver, *Blues Off the Record*

Can white people sing the blues? Can white people play the blues? On the surface, these may seem to be silly questions. Why not? What is Mose Allison, if not a white blues singer? Surely the performances of guitarists Eric Clapton and Stevie Ray Vaughan and pianist Dr. John must count as playing the blues. But the question "Can white people sing (or play) the blues?" is much more persistent, elusive, and deep than such ready responses acknowledge. The above passage from Paul Oliver exemplifies a tradition of criticism which distinguishes between the performances of black and white blues musicians, preferring those of black musicians and refusing to recognize as genuine those of white musicians.[1] This tradition raises questions of race, ethnicity, and expressive authenticity which go to the heart of the contemporary debate over multi-culturalism, the canon, and the curriculum. I derive my title, and take my theme, from the late jazz critic Ralph J. Gleason, who raised the issue definitively, at least for white liberals in the late 1960s, saying:

[T]he blues is black man's music, and whites diminish it at best or steal it at worst. In any case they have no moral right to use it.[2]

When I raise this issue in my Aesthetics classes, I find I must first get my students to appreciate it as a genuine and genuinely deep issue. They tend to dismiss it rather quickly by

simple appeal to their own musical experience. They tend to think that the mere mention of the name "Stevie Ray Vaughan" settles it. It doesn't. Nevertheless, there's something in this naive response. It reflects the central dialectic of the issue—the difficulty of appreciating its depth and significance in the face of its apparent implications. In an age of renewed and heightened racial and cultural sensitivity such a critical stance seems paradoxically to be both progressive and reactionary, and to stand in need of both clarification and critique. It seems to embody, as well as any, the problematic of "political correctness." The stance taken, as in the case of Gleason and Oliver, by white critics and scholars seems progressive in that it unambiguously credits African-American culture as the authoritative source of the blues as musical genre and style, something the dominant culture has by and large systematically neglected. And yet it seems reactionary—indeed, prima facie racist—to restrict access to the blues as a medium of artistic expression. Check through the "blues" racks at your best local roots record store. There you'll find quite a few white recording artists among the many black recording artists. Mike Bloomfield, Paul Butterfield, Dr. John, Mark and Robben Ford, Nick Gravenites, John Hammond, Delbert McClinton, Charlie Musselwhite, Johnny Otis, Roy Rogers (not the cowboy), Stevie Ray Vaughan, Marcia Ball, Lou Ann Barton, Rory Block, Angela Strehli, and so on. This would appear to make the affirmative case. Add to this list the non-black sidemen in the backup bands of many recognized blues artists—Jesse Edwin Davis (in Taj Mahal's early bands), Tim Kaihatsu (the Japanese second guitarist in Robert Cray's touring band), Albert Gianquinto (James Cotton's piano player for many years), to name only a few—and the thesis that the blues is a musical idiom which knows no racial or ethnic barriers begins to look pretty well confirmed. In the face of such evidence, what could have prompted our question in the first place? Is there some crucial difference between John Lee Hooker's blues and John Hammond's? What sort of difference could it be? Do the notes sound different when played with black fingers? If Leontyne Price can sing opera, and Charlie Pride can sing country, why can't Bonnie Raitt sing the blues?

I. A "RACIST" ARGUMENT?

Part of appreciating the issue is rescuing it from a racist reading. Let us first get clear about what would make the negative position "racist." "Racism" is widely discussed and many would say even more widely practiced, but it is rarely defined or clarified conceptually. For present purposes I will consider as racist any doctrine or set of doctrines which presupposes that there are "races" whose members share genetically transmitted traits and characteristics not shared by members of other "races" and which makes moral distinctions or other (for example aesthetic) distinctions with moral implications, on this basis alone.[3] Essentially racism seeks to establish a scientific, in this case biological, basis for differential treatment of human beings—a basis in the nature of things for discrimination.

Thus critiques of racism have attempted to establish that there is no genetic or biological (i.e., scientific) basis for *morally significant* classification of human beings into races, by arguing that those genetically determined gross morphological characteristics whereby individuals are assigned to racial categories (pigmentation, bone structure, and so on) are not morally significant and that those human characteristics which *are* or *can be* morally significant (intelligence, linguistic capability, and so on), though genetically determined, do not vary significantly with race. A more radical critique of racism would

undercut the concept of "race" itself as an artificial and harmful construct without objective foundation in science, arguing in effect that there is no foundation in biology or genetics for *any* system of classification of humans by "race." This might be based on the observation that the degree of variation, with respect even to gross morphological characteristics, within a given "racial" group exceeds that between "typical" members of different groups, and on the generally accepted finding in genetics that the probability of any particular genetic difference occurring between two members of the same "racial" group is roughly the same as for any two human beings.[4] We might do well to wonder whether, if either of these critiques has force, (and they both seem forceful to me), we can raise the issue of the authenticity of white blues musicians at all. Is there a way to enter into such a discussion without reifying "race" and investing it with moral significance? Doesn't the very question presuppose race as a morally significant human category with a verifiable basis of some sort?

Suppose we begin to answer this by distinguishing between race and ethnicity. Unlike race, let us say, which is supposed to be innate and in nature, ethnicity requires no genetic or biological foundation. Ethnicity is a matter of acknowledged common culture, based on shared items of cultural significance such as experience, language, religion, history, habitat, and the like. Ethnicity is essentially a socially conferred status—a matter of communal acceptance, recognition, and respect.[5]

Thus the negative position may *seem* racist since it may appear that nothing other than race is available as a basis for what is evidently both an aesthetic and moral distinction between black and white blues artists and performances. The negative position would *be* racist if, for example, it held that white people were genetically incapable of producing the sounds essential to the blues. Is there a difference between John Lee Hooker's blues and John Hammond's blues? Well, certainly. There are many. The diction, phrasing, and intonation of each as vocalist, as well as their techniques of instrumental self-accompaniment are distinctive and immediately identifiable (which shows that whatever differences there are are relevant *aesthetically*). If someone proposed to explain these differences on the basis of the genetically inherited expressive capacities and limitations of members of different races, and then went on to argue for some form of differential assessment of performances or treatment of artists on this basis, that would qualify as a racist account.

However, the question raised by the negative position is not one of genetically transmissible expressive or musical capabilities and limitations, but rather one of "authenticity." Again, the negative position would *be* racist if it held that music made by white people, however much it may resemble blues and be intended as blues, isn't authentic blues *simply because it is made by people of the wrong race.* But nobody says this. Nor does any serious adherent of the negative position hold that white people are somehow *genetically* incapable of delivering an authentic blues performance. What makes one blues performance authentic and another inauthentic? The question of authenticity is really a matter of "credentials."

II. THE AUTHENTICITY QUESTION

Authenticity is a value—a species of the genus credibility. It's the kind of credibility that comes from having the appropriate relationship to an original source. Thus authenticity's most precise, formal, and fully institutionalized application in the artworld is to distinguish from the forgery a work "by the author's own hand." When we authenticate a work in this sense, what we want to know is whether or not the putative author is who he or she is represented to be. In this application the "authentic/inauthentic" distinction is dichotomous, the alternatives both mutually exclusive and exhaustive, and the appropriate relationship is one of identity.

More broadly, less precisely, but in an essentially similar way, "authenticity" is applicable to the artifacts and rituals which are a culture's "currency," conferring value on those "acceptably derived" from original sources. So, for example, an authentic restoration of a turn of the century Victorian house might be one reconstructed according to original plans and specifications and perhaps using only the tools, techniques, and building materials of the period. An authentic Cajun recipe might be one traceable to a source within the culture using ingredients traditionally available within the region.

In such applications authenticity admits of degrees. A given piece of work may be more or less authentic than another. And the standards or criteria of authenticity admit of some flexibility of interpretation relative to purpose.

In the literature of musical aesthetics the authenticity question has been focused largely on the relation between performances and "the work"—or, because the work is conceived of as a composition, between performances and what the composer intended—and the criteria for authenticity have been understood in terms of accuracy or conformity with performance specifications which constitute the work. As applied to blues performances the authenticity question must be focused somewhat differently, for although we may speak of blues "compositions," what we thereby refer to consist of no more typically than a simple chord progression shared by many other such "compositions," with no definite key signature, no particular prescribed instrumentation, and a lyrical text which itself is open to *ad lib* interruption, interpretation, and elaboration in performance. As a musical genre, the blues is characterized by what we might call "compositional minimalism" and a complementary emphasis on expressive elements. The question of the authenticity of a given blues performance is thus one of stylistic and expressive authenticity, and our question becomes, "Is white blues 'acceptably enough derived' from the original sources of the blues to be stylistically authentic and authentically expressive within the style?" The negative position can now be understood as: white musicians cannot play the blues in an authentic way because they do not have the requisite relation or proximity to the original sources of the blues.[6] No one has made the case for the negative position more provocatively, eloquently, profoundly, and forcefully than Amiri Baraka (LeRoi Jones). In what follows I will consider that case, which I believe consists of two interrelated arguments, which I will call the "Proprietary Argument" and the "Experiential Access Argument."[7]

III. THE PROPRIETARY ARGUMENT

The proprietary argument addresses the question of ownership. Who "owns" the blues? Who has legitimate authority to use the blues as an idiom, as a performance style, to interpret it, to draw from it and to contribute to it as a fund of artistic and cultural wealth, to profit from it? The originators and the major innovative elaborators of the blues were in fact members of the African-American community. Women and men like Ma Rainey, Bessie Smith, Charlie Patton, Robert Johnson, Muddy Waters, Howlin' Wolf, John Lee Hooker, T-Bone Walker, Professor Longhair, and so on. The question arises, to whom does this cultural and artistic heritage belong? Who are Robert Johnson's legitimate cultural and artistic heirs and conservators?

The proprietary argument says in effect that the blues as genre and style belongs to the African-American community and that when white people undertake to perform the blues they misappropriate the cultural heritage and intellectual property of African-Americans and of the African-American community—what Baraka refers to as "the Great Music Robbery."[8] Baraka describes a systematic and pervasive pattern throughout the history of black people in America—a pattern of cultural and artistic co-optation and misappropriation in which not just the blues, but every major black artistic innovation, after an initial period of condemnation and rejection as culturally inferior, eventually wins recognition for superior artistic significance and merit, only to be immediately appropriated by white imitators whose imitations are very profitably mass produced and distributed, and accepted in the cultural mainstream as definitive, generally without due credit to their sources. Calling the blues "the basic national voice of the African-American people,"[9] he writes:

... after each new wave of black innovation, i.e., New Orleans, big band, bebop, rhythm and blues, hard bop, new music, there was a commercial cooptation of the original music and an attempt to replace it with corporate dilution which mainly featured white players and was mainly intended for a white middle-class audience.[10]

This is not an aberrant or accidental phenomenon, nor is it benign. Rather it is part and parcel of a subtle and systematic form of institutionalized racism which reinforces a racist socio-economic class structure.

The problem for the Creators of Black Music, the African-American people, is that because they lack Self-Determination, i.e., political power and economic self-sufficiency, various peoples' borrowings and cooptation of the music can be disguised and the beneficiaries of such acts pretend they are creating out of the air.[11]

Let's consider a possible objection, or set of objections, to this argument. The crucial claim is the ownership claim: that the blues as genre and style belongs to the African-American community. How is this claim warranted? Part of the warrant is the factual claim that the originators and major innovative elaborators of the blues were members of the African-American community like Ma Rainey, Bessie Smith, Charlie Patton, Robert Johnson, Muddy Waters, Howlin' Wolf, John Lee Hooker, T-Bone Walker, Professor Longhair, and so on. There is an interpretive tradition which holds, contrary to this, that the blues is an oral folk form with an ancient and untraceable pre-history, but in spite of this let us take the factual claim as true. But what is the principle or set of principles which connects this factual claim with the ownership claim that the blues belongs to the African-American *community*?

The crucial assumption underlying this as a *critical* question—as the basis for a series of objections—is the modern notion of intellectual property[12] as applied to the blues. On this assumption, an *individual* is understood to have certain rights regarding the products of his or her original creative work, including the right to control access to the work for the purposes of commercial exploitation, etc. So one could say that the musical literature of the blues rightly belongs to *certain members* of the African-American community like Ma Rainey, Bessie Smith, Charlie Patton, Robert Johnson, Muddy Waters, Howlin' Wolf, John Lee Hooker, T-Bone Walker, Professor Longhair, or their estates, legitimate heirs and assigns. But this list, even drawn up on the basis of a liberal reading of "legitimate heirs and assigns," even if *padded,* is not co-extensive with "the African-American *community.*"

Moreover, these rights can be alienated voluntarily and involuntarily in various ways. They can be purchased, sold, exchanged, wagered, and so on. So for example the rights inherent in

Robert Johnson's entire catalogue of recorded compositions now belong to something called King of Spades Music and the rights to the recordings of his performances of them belong to CBS Records, part of the Sony Corporation. In other words, on this assumption a number of individual and corporate ownership claims would seem to follow from the facts, but not the communal ownership claim central to Baraka's case.

Finally, the proprietary argument claims ownership of the blues as genre and style, so that musical and expressive elements as elusive as timbre, diction, vocal inflection, timing, rhythmic "feel," and their imitations become the subjects of dispute. For example, the rock group ZZ Top has obviously imitated or "borrowed from" elements of John Lee Hooker's distinctive style in several of their original compositions.[13] For Baraka this constitutes misappropriation—just another instance of The Great Music Robbery. But where in the notion of music as intellectual property can one find precedent for this? If anything, the history of music provides ample precedent for accepting such borrowings as legitimate forms of tribute and trade in ideas. The modern notion of intellectual property as applied to music can be used to support ownership claims concerning compositions but not musical ideas as ephemeral and problematic for purposes of documentation as these "elements of style."

Arguably this series of objections does very little damage to the proprietary argument. First of all, what the objection grants is important evidence in support of the proprietary argument. The modern notion of intellectual property, insofar as it is applicable to the blues, would seem to warrant at least an indictment of the American music establishment on the offense of Great Music Robbery, just as Baraka maintains. The means whereby the intellectual property rights inherent in the creative work of African-American blues musicians were alienated from the artists, later to turn up in various corporate portfolios at greatly appreciated value, were in many cases questionable, to say the least.[14]

But more important, though it may not be entirely inappropriate to apply an eighteenth-century English legal concept of intellectual property[15] to the blues—after all, the blues *is*

modern American music—it's not entirely appropriate either. Approaching the blues via such a conceptual route entails treating the blues as a collection of compositions, discrete pieces of intellectual property, convenient as commodities to the economic apparatus of the twentieth-century American music and entertainment industries, whereas attention and sensitivity to the social context of the music, its production, presentation, and enjoyment disclose phenomena rather more in the nature of real-time event and communally shared experience, in which the roles of performer and audience are nowhere near as sharply delineated as would be suggested by the imposition of the notions of creative artist and consumer upon them.

Stories, jokes, and music are all part of the blues performance. They flow together in small rooms filled with smoke and the smell of alcohol as couples talk, slow drag, and sing with the performer. ... During blues sessions the audience frequently addresses the singer and forces him to respond to their comments through his music. ... [T]he blues singer sometimes prevents fights by talking the blues with his audience and integrating their conversations between his blues verses. After he sings a verse, the musician continues instrumental accompaniment and develops a talk session. He may then sing another verse while participants remember rhymes and short jokes which they introduce at the next verse break. The singer always controls this talk through his instrumental accompaniment. ... [This] shows the limitations of using blues records in the study of oral tradition, for studio conditions completely remove the performer-audience dimension of blues. Listeners influence the length and structure of each blues performed and force the singer to integrate his song with their responses. ... [W]hat I first saw as "interruptions" were, in fact, the heart of the blues performance.[16]

Thus the question of how to derive communal ownership claims from individual intellectual property rights needn't detain us. Indeed it arguably misleads attention from the real sources of the communal ownership claim, namely that the blues as genre and style originated as a communicative idiom and practice within the African-American community.

Finally, in insisting on a contrast between musical compositions as documentable items of intellectual property and relatively problematic ephemera of musical and expressive style, the objection begs a complex set of deeply intriguing questions concerning the ownership and regulation of musical "fragments" as commodified abstract ideas—which, ironically, rap music (particularly in its employment of the technology of digital sampling) has lately elevated to the status of a pressing legal issue.[17] But even more to the point, far from being problematic ephemera, the elements of blues style, when understood within the context of the music's historical origins and the social context of its production, take on crucial semantic and syntactic significance.

On balance, the modern notion of intellectual property as applied to the blues seems little more than an elaborate red herring which in effect obscures crucial facts about the social circumstances of the music's production, appreciation, and indeed, *meaning*. This brings me to what I am calling the "experiential access argument."

IV. THE EXPERIENTIAL ACCESS ARGUMENT

Where the proprietary argument addresses the question of ownership, the experiential access argument addresses the questions of meaning and understanding as these bear centrally on issues of culture, its identity, evolution, and transmission. What is the significance of the blues? Who can legitimately claim to understand the blues? Or to speak authoritatively about the blues and its interpretation? Who can legitimately claim fluency in the blues as a musical idiolect? Or the authority to pass it on to the next generation? Who are the real bearers of the blues tradition?

The experiential access argument says in effect that one cannot understand the blues or authentically express oneself in the blues unless one knows what it's like to live as a black person in America, and one cannot know this without being one. To put it more elaborately, the meaning of the blues is deep, hidden, and accessible only to those with an adequate grasp of the historically unique experience of the African-American community. Members of other communities may take an interest in this experience and even empathize with it, but they have no direct access to the experience and

therefore cannot fully comprehend or express it. Hence their attempts to master the blues or to express themselves in the idiom of the blues will of necessity tend to be relatively shallow and superficial, i.e., inauthentic. Jazz players have an expression, a motto of sorts: Fake it 'till you feel it—the point being that authentic expression is expression derived from felt emotion. The experiential access argument in effect posits the experience of living as a black person in America as a precondition of the felt emotion essential to authentic expression in the idiom of the blues. Delfeayo Marsalis, in the liner notes to Branford Marsalis's 1992 release *I Heard You Twice the First Time,* writes:

Yes, one must pay serious dues in order to accurately translate the sorrow and heartache of the blues experience into musical terms. The great blues musician Charlie Parker once said, "If you don't live it, it won't come out of your horn."

And Baraka writes:

Blues as an autonomous music had been in a sense inviolable. There was no clear way into it, i.e., its production, not its appreciation, except as concomitant with what seems to me to be the peculiar social, cultural, economic, and emotional experience of a black man in America. The idea of a white blues singer seems an even more violent contradiction of terms than the idea of a middle-class blues singer. The materials of blues were not available to the white American, even though some strange circumstance might prompt him to look for them. It was as if these materials were secret and obscure, and blues a kind of ethno-historic rite as basic as blood.[18]

In the context of the kinds of questions raised here about culture, its identity, evolution, and transmission, the appeal to experience functions as a basis upon which to either establish or challenge authority, based on some such principle as this: Other things equal, the more directly one's knowledge claims are grounded in first hand experience, the more unassailable one's authority. Though there is room for debate about the centrality of experience as a ground of knowledge, as for example in current discussions of "feminist epistemology," such a principle as this one seems plausible and reasonable enough.

Nevertheless, stated baldly, and understood literally, the experiential access argument seems to invite the objection that it is either a priori or just dubious. The access that most contemporary black Americans have to the experience of slavery or sharecropping or life on the Mississippi delta during the twenties and thirties is every bit as remote, mediated, and indirect as that of any white would-be blues player. Does the argument subscribe to some "Myth of Ethnic Memory" whereby mere membership in the ethnic group confers special access to the lived experience of ancestors and other former members? It would be just as facile and fatuous for a Jewish-American baby boomer (such as myself) to take the position that only Jews can adequately comprehend the experience of the holocaust.

However the argument is susceptible of a more subtle and defensible reading, namely that the blues is essentially a cryptic language, a kind of secret code. Texts composed in this language typically have multiple layers of meaning, some relatively superficial, some deeper. To gain access to the deeper layers of meaning one must have the keys to the code. But the keys to the code presuppose extensive and detailed familiarity with the historically unique body of experience shared within and definitive of the African-American community and are therefore available only to the properly initiated.

There is a certain amount of theoretical and historical material, as well as textual material within the blues, available to support this argument. A general theoretical framework for understanding the development of cryptic devices and systems of communication under repressive circumstances can be found in the work of Leo Strauss. Strauss maintains that where control of the thought and communication of a subjugated population is attempted in order to maintain a political arrangement, even the most violent means of repression are inadequate to the task, for "it is a safe venture to tell the truth one knows to benevolent and trustworthy acquaintances, or ... to reasonable friends."[19] The human spirit will continue to seek, recognize, and communicate the truth privately in defiance of even the most repressive regimes, which moreover cannot even prevent public communication of forbidden ideas, "for a man

of independent thought can utter his views in public and remain unharmed, provided he moves with circumspection. He can even utter them in print without incurring any danger, provided he is capable of writing between the lines."[20] Unjust and repressive regimes thus naturally tend to engender covert communication strategies with "all the advantages of private communication without having its greatest disadvantage—that it reaches only the writer's acquaintances, [and] all the advantages of public communication without having its greatest disadvantage—capital punishment for the author."[21]

Evidence of the employment of such strategies within the African-American community is fairly well documented. For example, the evolution of "Black English," as well as a number of its salient characteristics, such as crucial ambiguity, understatement, irony, and inversion of meaning ("bad" means "good," and so on), may best be explained as the development of cryptic communicative strategies under repression.

Blacks clearly recognized that to master the language of whites was in effect to consent to be mastered by it through the white definitions of caste built into the semantic/social system. Inversion therefore becomes the defensive mechanism which enables blacks to fight linguistic, and thereby psychological, entrapment. ... Words and phrases were given reverse meanings and functions changed. Whites, denied access to the semantic extensions of duality, connotations, and denotations that developed within black usage, could only interpret the same material according to its original singular meaning ... enabling blacks to deceive and manipulate whites without penalty. This protective process, understood and shared by blacks, became a contest of matching wits ... [and a] form of linguistic guerrilla warfare [which] protected the subordinated, permitted the masking and disguising of true feelings, allowed the subtle assertion of self, and promoted group solidarity.[22]

Ethnomusicologists, working independently and apparently absent any familiarity with Strauss's work in political philosophy or sociolinguisitic studies of Black English, have arrived at strikingly similar conclusions regarding the origins, functions, and stylistic features of jazz and blues.[23]

Lyrically the blues are rife with more or less covert allusions to the oppressive conditions of black life in America. If Jimmy Reed's "Big Boss Man"

(Big boss man, can't you hear me when I call [twice]
Well you ain't so big, you just tall, that's all)

is overt, it is merely extending a more covert tradition central to the blues. As Paul Oliver observes:

An appreciation of the part African-Americans have played in United States society and of the rights and other aspects of living that were denied them is of major assistance in understanding the blues. But there are barriers to appreciation presented by the manner of delivery, of speech, and of form, and [even] when these are overcome the full significance of the blues to the black audience still remains elusive. ... Many black terms arose through the deliberate intention to conceal meaning. ... [I]nnocuous words were often given secondary meanings which were closed to all but the initiated and by their use the singer could be more outspoken in the blues than might otherwise be prudent. Some of these became traditional terms recognized and used throughout the states by blacks, for whom the colored man was the "monkey," the white man the "baboon." With comparative immunity Dirty Red could sing:

Monkey and the baboon playing Seven-Up,
Monkey win the money, scared to pick it up.
The monkey stumbled, the baboon fell,
Monkey grabbed the money an' he run like hell![24]

Similarly, the blues are full of covert and even overt references, both musical and lyrical, to the esoterica of African religions whose practice on this continent was prohibited and systematically repressed. When Muddy Waters sings:

I got a black cat bone
I got a mojo too
I got John the conqueror root
I'm gonna mess wit' you

we understand very little unless we recognize the references to the conjures and charms of the Dahomean religion which migrated to the Americas under slavery as vodun or "voodoo."

Similarly we lose whole realms of meaning in Robert Johnson's "Crossroads" if we miss the symbolic reference to the Yoruba deity Eshu-Elegbara. The prevalence of such references not only tends to confirm the Straussian hypothesis of a covert communicative strategy, but also begins to suggest what might be involved in a "proper initiation."[25]

Having said all this, it nevertheless remains apparent that neither the proprietary argument nor the experiential access argument quite secures the thesis that white people can not sing (or play) authentic blues. The experiential access argument has undeniable moral force as a reminder of and warning against the offense of presumptive familiarity, but it distorts the blues in the process by obscuring what is crucially and universally *human* about its central themes.[26] And it leaves open the possibility of the proper initiation of white people and other non-blacks, if not entirely into the African-American ethnic community, then at least in the use of the blues as an expressive idiom and so into the blues community. Obvious examples would include Johnny Otis[27] and Dr. John.[28] Given this, the force of the proprietary argument is also limited, since initiation into the blues community presumably carries with it legitimate access to the blues as a means of artistic expression.

This of course leaves the authenticity question still open on a case-by-case basis. Many white attempts at blues certainly come off as inauthentic, as no doubt do some black ones. However, if the authenticity question turns not on race but rather on ethnicity, which admits of initiation, and on the achievement and demonstration of genuine understanding and fluency, which are also communicable by other than genetic means, then it is hard to resist the conclusion that Professor Longhair's legitimate cultural and artistic heirs include Dr. John, and that Robert Johnson's legitimate cultural and artistic heirs include John Hammond. It is tempting to conclude on this basis that the answer to the question "Can white people sing (or play) the blues?" is: "Yes. Unless you're a racist."

V. CODA: HOW TO KEEP THE BLUES ALIVE

This isn't very likely to hold up as the last word, however—at least not yet. Some issues seem to persistently elude—and yet at the same time haunt—the discussion. Here I'm still bothered by the issues of race and racism despite my earlier attempt to set them aside. I wanted to say something in this paper about the authenticity of white blues without either descending into or inviting hateful discourse. And I'm afraid that, though the distinction I introduced earlier between race and ethnicity helps somewhat, it doesn't quite do the whole trick.

I can imagine someone objecting to the line of reasoning I've developed so far: "To dismiss black concerns about white cultural imperialism as 'racist'—to co-opt the notion of racism in this way—is the height of disingenuous arrogance. This so-called 'evolution' of the blues community and tradition is just another case of the Great Music Robbery. It's true that the racial makeup of the blues community has evolved over the years, especially if you count these white musicians as blues players (i.e., if you insist on begging the question). Just look at the contemporary blues audience: mostly white people who can't seem to tell the difference between John Lee Hooker (the real thing) and John Hammond (the white imitation)!" Such objections are not hard to come by. Charles Whitaker, in a recent *Ebony Magazine* article entitled "Are Blacks Giving Away the Blues?" goes even further when he notes with alarm the prevalence in the contemporary blues audience of "yuppie-ish white people who clap arrhythmically (*sic*)."[29] This seems prima facie racist, but is it? What if Whitaker said, "Of course I don't think it's a *genetic* thing, but they (white people) just haven't got it (rhythm). It's an *ethnic* thing." How much does this help? Is ethnocentrism a significant advance beyond racism? Certainly not when measured by the horrors and pointless suffering which have been inflicted over the years in the name of each. This is no way to keep the blues alive.

Of course not all talk of issues of ethnic heritage and authenticity need be ethnocentric. The fact that ethnocentric applications and uses of the concept of ethnicity are possible does not show that the concept itself is harmful or useless. There is a certain amount of truth in the observation that different ethnic groups use music in different ways and that members of different ethnic groups tend to make and respond to music in ways that are characteristic

of their respective communities. And to be fair to Baraka—to avoid suggesting *he* be read as a clumsy ethnocentrist—it must be said that he does recognize the possibility of (and even sketches an ordered progression of) initiation into African-American musics. He writes:

Jazz, as a Negro music, ... and its sources were *secret* as far as the rest of America was concerned. ... The first white critics were men who sought, whether consciously or not, to understand this secret, just as the first serious white jazz musicians ... sought not only to understand the phenomenon of Negro music but to appropriate it as a means of expression which they themselves might utilize. The success of this "appropriation" signaled the existence of an American music, where before there was a Negro music. ... The white musician's commitment to jazz, the *ultimate concern,* proposed that the sub-cultural attitudes that produced the music as a profound expression of human feelings, could be *learned.* ... And Negro music is essentially the expression of an attitude, or a collection of attitudes about the world, and only secondarily an attitude about the way music is made. The white jazz musician came to understand this attitude as a way of making music, and the intensity of his understanding produced the "great" white jazz musicians, and is producing them now.[30]

In other words, the essence of the blues is a *stance* embodied and articulated in sound and poetry, and what distinguishes authentic from inauthentic blues is essentially what distinguishes that stance from its superficial imitations—from *posturing.* I think that if we wish to avoid ethnocentrism, as we would wish to avoid racism, what we should say is that the authenticity of a blues performance turns not on the ethnicity of the performer but on the degree of mastery of the idiom and the integrity of the performer's use of the idiom in performance. This last is delicate and can be difficult to discern. But what one is looking for is evidence in and around the performance of the performer's recognition and acknowledgement of indebtedness to sources of inspiration and technique (which as a matter of historical fact *do* have an identifiable ethnicity). In the opening epigram Paul Oliver estimates the blues' chances of survival through these times of ethnic mingling as "unlikely." This kind of "blues purism" is no way to keep the blues alive either. The blues, like any oral tradition, remains alive to the extent that it continues to evolve and things continue to "grow out of it." The way to keep the blues alive is to celebrate such evolutionary developments.[31]

1. For convenient reference, I'll call this the "negative position," and distinguish it from the "affirmative position" represented so far by the above "ready responses."

2. Ralph J. Gleason, "Can the White Man Sing the Blues?," *Jazz and Pop* (1968): 28–29.

3. This follows Kwame Anthony Appiah's account in "Racisms," in David Theo Goldberg, ed., *Anatomy of Racism* (University of Minnesota Press, 1990), pp. 3–17. Racist attitudes and practices are no doubt more prevalent than racist *doctrines*. Following Appiah, I take racist doctrines as theoretically fundamental. To the extent that racist attitudes and practices can be rationalized at all, and thereby rendered accessible to rational assessment and critique, it is on the basis of racist doctrine. For a critical account of the concept of race presupposed by racist doctrine and practice ·thus defined, see Appiah's "The Uncompleted Argument: Du Bois and the Illusion of Race," *Critical Inquiry* 12 (Autumn 1985): 21–37.

4. See Appiah, "The Uncompleted Argument: Du Bois and the Illusion of Race," *Critical Inquiry* 12 (Autumn 1985): 21 and 30–31. Appiah notes that not all biologists are ready to accept, as an interpretation of the genetic data, that the notion of distinct "races" of human beings is an artificial construct without objective foundation in science, however attractive the idea may be for its egalitarian implications. The scientific debate is outside the scope of this discussion (and my competence). I am interested in its conceptual implications.

5. One important writer on these topics, W.E.B. Du Bois, attempted to reconceptualize "race" as a special case of ethnicity in order to avoid the irrational evils of racism while at the same time facilitating access to and expression of truths about peoples (such as the Negro people) united by common origins and struggles. See W.E.B. Du Bois, "The Conservation of Races," in *W.E.B. Du Bois Speaks: Speeches and Addresses, 1890–1919*, ed. Philip S. Foner (New York: Pathfinder Press, 1970), cited in Appiah, "The Uncompleted Argument."

6. Some may be tempted at this early stage to dismiss the negative position as an instance of the "genetic fallacy," which misconstrues an aesthetic property of the work or performance itself as a relational property arising out of the origins of the work or performance. However, I don't think this move would be fair. First of all, as I've said above, I think the negative position is right in taking authenticity as fundamentally relational. More important, the negative position, as we shall see presently, raises an issue of an essentially moral and political nature, and makes argu-

ments of sufficient depth and substance to merit assessment on their own terms.

7. See *Blues People* (New York: Quill, 1963) and *The Music: Reflections on Jazz and Blues* (New York: Morrow, 1987).

8. "The Great Music Robbery," in *The Music,* pp. 328–332.

9. "Blues, Poetry and the New Music," in *The Music,* p. 262.

10. "Jazz Writing: Survival in the Eighties," in *The Music,* p. 259.

11. "Where's the Music Going and Why?" in *The Music,* p. 179.

12. As understood, for example, in Article One, Section 8 of the United States Constitution, which gives Congress the power "to promote the progress of science and the useful arts, by securing for limited times to authors and inventors the exclusive right to their respective writings and discoveries."

13. Compare ZZ Top's "La Grange" or "My Head's in Mississippi" with John Lee Hooker's 1948 recording of "Boogie Chillun."

14. It's worth noting that the music industry, and entertainment industry more generally, are tough businesses, and blacks are not the *only* creative artists whose work has been stolen. This is not to deny the existence also of discrimination on the basis of race.

15. Intellectual property became a matter of English statutory law with the 1710 Statute of Anne, which gave exclusive copyright to the author for a renewable fourteen year period. Prior to this statute the "right of copy" was held by licensed printers as a matter of royal patronage and its function was not to secure compensation to the author of a work but to order and regulate publication in the interests of the church and the state.

16. William Ferris, *Blues From the Delta* (New York: Doubleday Anchor, 1978), pp. 101–103. Cf. Charles Keil, *Urban Blues* (University of Chicago Press, 1966), chapters 6 and 7, where Keil develops the notion of blues performance as ritual and the connection between the role of the blues singer and that of the preacher.

17. See Andrew Goodwin, "Sample and Hold: Pop Music in the Digital Age of Reproduction," in Simon Frith and Andrew Goodwin, eds., *On Record: Rock, Pop, and the Written Word* (New York: Pantheon, 1990), pp. 258–274; Bruce J. McGiverin, "Digital Sounds Sampling, Copyright and Publicity: Protecting Against the Electronic Appropriation of Sounds," *Columbia Law Review* (December, 1987): 1723–1745. There is even a rap group calling itself KLF (Kopyright Liberation Front).

18. *Blues People,* pp. 147–148.

19. Leo Strauss, *Persecution and the Art of Writing* (University of Chicago Press, 1952), pp. 23–24.

20. Ibid., p. 24.

21. Ibid., p. 25.

22. Grace Simms Holt, " 'Inversion' in Black Communication," in Thomas Kochman, ed., *Rappin' and Stylin' Out* (Urbana: University of Illinois Press, 1972), quoted in Richard Shusterman, *Pragmatist Aesthetics: Living Beauty, Rethinking Art* (Oxford: Blackwell, 1992), pp. 221–222.

23. See Ben Sidran, *Black Talk: How the Music of Black America Created a Radical Alternative to the Values of the Western Literary Tradition* (New York: Holt, Rinehart &

Winston, 1971). Cf. Roger Taylor's account of the origins
and significance of jazz, blues, and in particular the New
Orleans piano tradition in *Art, an Enemy of the People*
(Sussex: Harvester, 1978), chapter 4.

24. Paul Oliver, *Blues Fell This Morning: Meaning in the
Blues* (2nd ed., Cambridge University Press, 1990), pp. 265 ff.

25. The lyric is from Willie Dixon's "Hoochie Coochie
Man." For an exegesis and interpretive analysis of this and
other lyrical references within the blues see Oliver, op cit.
But see also Stanley Edgar Hyman's critique of Oliver's
interpretive analysis in "The Blues" and "Really the
Blues" in *The Critic's Credentials* (New York: Atheneum,
1978), pp. 147–182. For an introduction to the sources of
African-American art in African religious traditions see
Robert Farris Thompson, *Flash of the Spirit: African and
Afro-American Art and Philosophy* (New York: Random
House, 1983).

26. Hyman, op. cit.

27. A white American of ethnic Greek ancestry, whose
biggest hit was "Willie and the Hand Jive." As a rhythm
and blues bandleader for forty years, Johnny Otis gave
Little Esther Phillips, the Coasters, Little Willie John, and
Big Mama Thornton their initial breaks.

28. (Mac Rebennak), a central figure in New Orleans
music since the late fifties, a founding member (and the
only white member) of the black artists' cooperative AFO
(All for One) Records, and arguably the leading current
exponent of the New Orleans piano tradition.

29. Cf. Charles Whitaker, "Are Blacks Giving Away the
Blues?," *Ebony Magazine* (October, 1990).

30. Baraka, "Jazz and the White Critic," *Down Beat*
(1963), reprinted in *Black Music* (New York: Apollo, 1968),
p. 13.

31. This paper has been an embarrassingly long time in
gestation. I want to thank Bill Bossart, one of my first teachers in philosophy and aesthetics, for encouraging me to
think about topics like this one. This paper began to take its
present form as part of the syllabus for a course in Philosophy of Art and Contemporary Rock and Soul Music jointly
sponsored by the Department of Philosophy and the American Multi-Cultural Studies Department at Sonoma State
University. I am grateful to Stan McDaniel and Jim Gray,
the chairpersons of the two departments for supporting the
course proposal, to Cynthia Rostankowski for including a
workshop based on the course in the program of the American Association of Philosophy Teachers Conference on
Teaching Philosophy in a Multicultural Context, to Stan
Godlovitch and Michael Barclay for stimulating conversations, both musical and philosophical, on this and related
subjects, and for their gracious and insightful criticisms of
an earlier draft of this paper. Finally, I wish to thank the
students in the course for discussing these issues with me.
Two students in particular, Eric Charp and Sean Martin,
made especially helpful contributions to my work.

BRUNO NETTL

"Musical Thinking" and "Thinking About Music" in Ethnomusicology: An Essay of Personal Interpretation

I. INTRODUCTION

My assignment is to discuss the term or concept of "musical thought" from the perspective of ethnomusicology.[1] Whether, as Eduard Hanslick suggested,[2] the message of the musician is music, or whether instead, as recent publications by music historians argue, music expresses a subtext whose message is determined by extraneous issues such as culture, class, gender, and personality,[3] all this has been in the center of the issues debated by musicologists throughout the twentieth century. Ethnomusicologists, whose task it has been to study the world's musical systems from a comparative and culturally relativistic perspective, and to contemplate music as an integral domain of culture from an anthropological viewpoint, have tilted towards the latter view.[4] They have not really paid much attention to the concept of musical thinking as an activity distinct from other kinds of thought, or to the notion of music as residing in a particular portion of the brain, or indeed to the separateness of musical memory or talent as distinct from other kinds of cognition. Instead, they have deduced the thought processes of musicians in cultures foreign to themselves from analysis of musical compositions and performances; and ideas about music from anthropological participant-observation-style field work.

The history of ethnomusicology, however, has moved from an interest in musical thought, in finding out how different societies, as it were, "think" music, to an interest in ideas about music. Indeed, in the first part of the twentieth century, it was the conventional wisdom of ethnomusicologists that while members of all societies, including tribal cultures, engaged in musical thinking because they clearly composed, performed, and transmitted musical entities, only those societies which had developed "art" or "classical" music systems —the high cultures of Europe and Asia— thought and theorized about music and had ideas about it. At the basis of this belief was the assumption that societies that use music for explicitly aesthetic expression require a totally different view of music than those for whom music is principally "functional," that is, exists in order to accompany rituals and other nonmusical activities.

This viewpoint has now been totally abandoned. On the one hand, John Blacking's landmark work, *How Musical Is Man?*,[5] asks at least by implication whether musical thinking is a human universal. We are accustomed to asking whether an individual is or is not musical, and have developed, in our culture, the concept of "talent" as a measuring device. If you are musical, you have the capacity of musical thinking; to think *about* music does not necessarily require musicality. But Blacking asks how much musical talent humans have, whether they are musical, as a species, and, answering of course in the affirmative, suggests that musical thinking is a human universal.

Now, ethnomusicologists have determined that music is a cultural universal of humans. Not all human cultures would agree that they "have" music; the concept doesn't exist everywhere, and where it does, its shape varies. It's true that all societies have something that sounds to *us,* broad-minded, musical Americans and Europeans, like music.[6] And something that one can objectively distinguish from ordinary speech. Does this really mean that all people *have* music? And that they engage in musical thinking?

On the other hand, ethnomusicologists have come to believe that even those musics that exist, as it were, for the sake of art alone, the message of whose musicians is simply music, take their structure not merely from the genius of the composers but express important values of their culture.[7] Thus, for all musical scholars, but particularly for ethnomusicologists, the distinction between thinking music and thinking about music becomes increasingly complex as the understanding of music as a part of culture increases in sophistication. The ethnomusicological literature has changed in its scope from a body of work in which one documented the musical utterances of the world's peoples, taking for granted that this would inform us about their ways of thinking music, to work in which the ideas *about* music, expressed verbally, ferreted out from compositions, myths, forms of behavior, rituals, and taxonomies, play the principal role. There is a tension between these two approaches—they are parts of a chronology, but they also represent, respectively, the paradigmatic viewpoints of the "music" and "anthropology" components of ethnomusicology.

My purpose here is to look at two aspects of musical thought from an ethnomusicological perspective: the thinking of music, or "thinking music" by musicians, and ideas about music held by musicians and others in a society. I wish to discuss some of the ways in which these kinds of musical thought intersect with musical structure, musical behavior, and the central values of cultures, and how their study may be brought to bear on the understanding of music on a cross-cultural basis. Not qualified to talk about this on various levels that might be desirable, such as the perspectives of students of cognition and of physiological psychology, I cannot present a general theory. Instead, I want to make five brief excursions into cultures with which I have had direct experience, excursions in which the two kinds of musical thought interact, or in which the study of one may tell us importantly about the other.

II. THE BEAVER MEDICINE

A typical song of the Blackfoot people has the following structure: A short motif of five or six notes is sung at a high pitch level by the song leader, then repeated by a second singer. At that point, the entire group of singers begins what might sound like the same motif, but instead of completing it, moves to other melodic material, gradually descending in pitch until the initial motif is sung again, an octave lower, followed by a cadence of a repeated low tone. The portion of the song sung by the entire group is then repeated. This is the entire song, or at least one stanza of it, which may be repeated in its entirety four times.

In a classroom, the teaching ethnomusicologist might, while hearing the recording, write its form as follows:

A(1);A(1);A(2) B C A(3) (octave lower) X;
A(2) B C A(3) (octave lower) X.

This is in some ways, given its length, a complex song. If we were to try to dissect musical thought here, we would perhaps say two things: a) The song is easily divided into two, or possibly three, or perhaps four, or maybe even five or six sections, perhaps more, and these sections have rather specific relationships to each other. b) There is clearly a kind of hierarchy of materials; the beginning is a motif that generates parts of the rest of the song—a kind of theme that is succeeded by developmental and episodic material. It turns out that a very large proportion of Blackfoot songs follow roughly the same pattern, although the number of phrases and the interrelationship within the interior portion of the song may vary. Clearly, we have a pattern of musical thinking that can be described and explained in musical terms.

Asking Blackfoot singers about the shape of the songs yielded a few direct statements. For one thing, three singers analyzed the song in three ways: as a song whose last part is repeated; as one with four sections, as all Blackfoot songs ought to have four sections, even if they are of greatly differing lengths; and as a song with a good beginning, middle, and end.[8] Without going into detail: all three of these analyses tell important things about the way this song relates to Blackfoot culture, and all recognize the importance of dividing the song into sections. One would think, therefore, that these sections have some importance; for example, that one learns songs section by section, or that they may have lives of their own, moving from song to song, somewhat in the manner of the "line families" which I was able to identify in Czech folk songs.[9]

But not so. Because the other thing my singer/friends said was that one normally learns songs in one hearing.[10] This is maintained even though one can observe singers at powwows recording each other's songs, obviously to play them over at home to learn them. One hearing evidently isn't really enough. We may be tempted to chuckle about what seems to be a minor kind of hypocrisy, but two things help to convince us otherwise. First, the structure of the song militates towards the single-hearing theory. It's a complex form, but if you know the style well, you can, after hearing the first line, pretty much predict what the rest of the song will be like. If you can remember one line of music you don't have to remember too much else.

Well, this tells us something about musical thinking at two or maybe three levels, perhaps concentric circles that focus on the song itself, showing how its characteristics came to be as they are. Let me try one further circle, which tells us something about the way Blackfoot people think about music, what it has to do with culture, and why the relationship to culture may result in certain theories of music, and in turn, certain compositional forms.

Central to this illustration is a summary of an important myth, the story that tells the origins of the beaver medicine bundle.[11] This bundle is actually a group of perhaps close to 200 objects that are kept wrapped together and opened for ceremonial purposes. The objects are the dressed bird and animal skins of all the local wildlife, plus a few other objects and a large number of sticks representing the songs that accompany the bundle, as it were. It is associated with the beaver, who is a kind of lord of the part of the world below the surface of water; and thus it is one of the principal ceremonies of the Blackfoot religious system. Before the bundle is opened, the following story is told.

A great human hunter has killed a specimen of each animal and bird, and their dressed skins decorate his tent. While he is hunting, a beaver comes to visit his wife and seduces her, and she follows him into the water. After four days she returns to her husband, and in time gives birth to a beaver child. Affairs were unforgivable in Blackfoot society, but the hunter continues to be kind to his wife and the child. The beaver, visiting, expresses pleasure at this and offers to give the hunter some of his supernatural power

as a reward. They smoke together, and then the beaver begins to sing songs, each containing a request for a particular bird or animal skin. The hunter gives the skins, one by one, and receives, in return, the songs of the beaver and the supernatural power that goes with them, and thus, the principal Blackfoot ritual.

This myth imparts important things about Blackfoot music. Here are some: Music comes from the supernatural. Songs come as whole units, and you learn them in one hearing, and they are objects that can be traded, as it were, for physical objects. The musical system reflects the cultural system, as each being in the environment has its song. Music reflects and contains supernatural power. It's something which only men use and perform, but women are instrumental in bringing its existence about. Music is given to a human who acts morally, gently, in a civilized manner. It comes about as the result of a period of dwelling with the supernatural, after which a major aspect of culture is brought, so in a way it symbolizes humanness and Blackfootness.

What is musical thought? We have the thinking of the composer, the musical system as it is described by singers with its reference to forms and ideas about learning, and we have the myth, creation perhaps of medicine men, which explains what music does for culture, and how cultural values must be reflected in music. Which of these came first I'd hesitate to guess. Did the cosmologists shape their myths to account for the way music is formed, or did composers and singers shape their songs in order to make them fit a set of values promulgated in the mythology?

III. EXCURSIONS TO THE PERSIAN RADIF

My second foray is to the classical music of Iran. I went to Iran some 25 years ago because I understood that this music was improvised; and I wanted to know how, as it were, the musicians' minds worked. How the minds of European composers worked has been a subject for music historians for many decades. And one may indeed get a sense of what is perhaps with more dignity called "the creative process" by studying the structure of compositions. The musical mind, if I can put it that way, of Wagner can be read by studying his consistencies, and the way it differs from that of a Brahms or a

Verdi. One can study sketches, of course. But how does a musician think, as it were, on his or her feet?[12]

I thought the study of Persian improvisation would help tell me, at least for one culture. And I determined to go to Iran to study in two ways, first by trying to learn music as it is learned by an Iranian student, and second, to do a kind of controlled experiment, seeing how many musicians, and perhaps individual musicians on one occasion, would play, or improvise upon, one mode. It's like seeing how Ravi Shankar and Ali Akbar Khan play Rag Malkauns, or how several jazz musicians might play and develop, say, "Georgia on My Mind."

My teacher first said that I must learn the radif. This is a repertory of some 300 short pieces which in the aggregate require some eight hours to perform. The pieces require from a few seconds to some four minutes, the entire repertory is monophonic, the majority of the pieces are non-metric but some have meter while others alternate between rhythmic predictability and what is conventionally called "free rhythm."[13]

In some ways, the radif can be regarded as the theory of Persian music, perhaps something like a theory textbook that tells you the rules of composition. I asked whether one learned the radif, and then learned to improvise, and was told, No, once you learn it you *can* improvise. You use the radif as a basis for improvisation, and its structure and content teach you, as it were, how to improvise.

My teacher of Persian music in Iran once said to me, "You know, it is really something extraordinary and fine, something quite unique, this radif that we have created in Iran." And so, clearly, he regarded it not as a kind of tool, as we might have considered the textbooks traditionally used in music theory classes. Rather, it was the center, a kind of ideal, from which the real music emanated.

I began to study the structure of the radif, especially the interrelationships of its sections, and I'm still doing this, feeling that there is much more to be learned even though I—along with several other authors, Iranian, European, American, and Japanese—have written books about it.[14] What greatly impressed me was the many internal consistencies, the multifarious interrelationships by repetition, terminological

duplication, and rhythmic and melodic variation, all within the framework of twelve modes which are in some ways parallel and in others so different as to constitute genres. I also began to ask myself whether there were some basic principles of structure and emphasis.

The complexity of the radif struck me as parallel to other large forms known and long practiced in Iran: carpets, complex and book-length works of literature, compilations of poems. But the nature of the internal interrelationships did not become clear to me until I began to wonder also about the patterns of social behavior. Then I came to realize—I think I'm right in promulgating this theory—that similar patterns in music and social life could be identified. Without going into detail, I'll just say that Persians think of society on the one hand as a set of hierarchies; on the other a group of cells in which a group of people look to a single leader for authority and guidance; and in the third place, a group of equals, all humans being equal before God in Islamic theology. Also, Iranians think of themselves as individualistic, like to surprise each other, and relish the unexpected. And they have definite ideas as to what events and what people ought to precede and follow in a series of events. All of these interrelationships are found in the radif. The whole system is a set of hierarchies; the beginning of each section provides guidance in the sense of thematic development for what follows; in a sense, all 300 parts are equal, equally capable of becoming improvised music. Those parts of the radif that lend themselves to far-flung improvisation are valued; those that have predictability, such as the metric ones, are lower, following the value of individualism. The exceptional and unexpected is valued. There are further relationships,[15] and so, I had to conclude that what appeared to be musical thinking in the creation of the radif either followed, or developed parallel to, thinking and acting in Persian society and culture.

IV. EXTRACTING A THEORY TEXT

If all societies have musical thinking as well as thinking about music, do they all have a somehow articulated music theory? Many societies have, of course, articulated texts, treatises, and books. But what about non-literate societies? Would the things they say about music lend themselves to creating a theory text? Could the things they say about music be arranged into a system of articulated musical thought?[16]

Working with the Blackfoot people, I was often struck by their logical system of music, the way in which various components of musical sound, behavior, and ideas about music interlocked. That is why I related the myth of the beaver medicine. And I wondered about a culture that has such a neat musical system but no articulated theory, no theory text, and came to the conclusion that the myths might constitute such a text; after all, it is the function of myths to explain the world, of which music is a part. But, seeing myself as a kind of ethnomusicological extra-terrestrial emerging from a saucer in Evanston, if I were to try to find articulated forms of the theory of Western music I would perhaps try two approaches. One would be to examine formal presentations—treatises, textbooks, perhaps course syllabi, all more or less corresponding to the Blackfoot myths; and a second would be to observe how people talk about music, what kinds of statements they make, what they emphasize, and perhaps what statements are made repeatedly.

And so, having taken lots of notes and having made recordings of many interviews with learned and musical Blackfoot people who tried to tell me what their culture was all about, I decided to see what statements were made to me with a high degree of emphasis, what things might have been said repeatedly, what ideas and facts my teachers were particularly anxious for me to get right. I don't know whether I made the right choices from my materials, or whether, given a different schedule or set of contacts, I would have reached different conclusions; or whether somebody else would have had quite different experiences. But I decided to put together the selected statements to see if these could function, as it were, as a theory text. Let me read you the eighteen statements without further comment in the hope that you'll accept this as yet another way of approaching the problem of musical thought.[17]

The Concept of Music

1. The songs are some of the most important things we Blackfoot people have.
2. Our songs are different from white people's songs,

they are special; for one thing, they sound special, and they don't just have a lot of words.
3. Our songs came back to us (i.e., after 1950) when our Blackfoot feelings came back.
4. This Blackfoot song is one of the favorite songs of the tribe.
5. Our songs have a lot of stories that go with them.

Origins and History

6. The real songs of our tribe, our true songs, they mostly came in dreams.
7. Our songs (i.e., the style of our songs) are so old, they must go back to the days of Napi (the culture hero) (followed by a chuckle).
8. When I made up songs, dreaming had a lot to do with it.
9. Sometimes I hum a song, over and over, and that way I catch a new song.
10. We learned a lot of dances and songs from other tribes—like the Cree, Assiniboine, Gros Ventres— but then we changed them too.
11. Our tribe keeps getting new songs. There are always new songs coming into our reservation. But we try to hold on to the old songs too. Sometimes we can't, but we should.

Uses and Functions of Music

12. A good song is one that fulfills well the purpose of the song.
13. The right Blackfoot way to do something is to sing the right Blackfoot song with it.
14. We used to have a lot of different kinds of songs, you can't imagine how many kinds of songs.

Musicianship

15. A good song leader knows a lot of songs and has a good strong voice; he can get other singers to follow him.
16. Most Blackfoot people can sing a song after they have heard it sung only one time.
17. People used to have a better memory for songs than they do now. It's because they depend so much on reading and writing.
18. Our songs have a beginning, middle, and end. After beginning, somebody raises the leader, and then all sing.

V. THE FAMILY COMPOSER

In my life, Mozart has occupied something of a role of the family composer. My father devoted years of his life to research on Mozart's relationship to Prague, and to Masonry; my older daughter has choreographed to Mozart, and my younger one got married to his sounds, and if truth be told, the first piece of music I remember ever hearing my life was *Eine kleine Nachtmusik* (K. 525). And so I decided some years ago that even as an ethnomusicologist I too must write something about Mozart.[18]

What does an ethnomusicologist write about Mozart? Analyze his use of folk and non-Western music, his ability to manipulate Italian and German styles, Bach-like early music, Austrian folk themes, Turkish music, and all that? Look at the social views he presented in his works such as turning the world upside down in asking whether it was the men or the women who were really more perfidious in *Cosí fan tutte,* or what he meant when he had Tamino begin the *Magic Flute* screaming like a maiden in distress, only to be rescued by the little army of three ladies singing of their triumph in perfectly macho triadic fanfares; or as a social critic who has Monostatos and Osmin complaining about racial discrimination? Or perhaps provide a sociological analysis of musical life in Mozart's Vienna?

These are all worth doing. But most ethnomusicologists want to present the musical life of a society in which they work. The ethnomusicological E.T. arriving in Evanston or Urbana would quickly be confronted with certain figures, chief among them perhaps Bach, Beethoven, Schubert, Mozart, who are treated as both alive and dead. And I decided to look at the function of Mozart in contemporary art music society, a composer whose works occupy an enormous portion of the concert repertory, whose name is engraved on buildings, who is the subject of innumerable biographies, analytical studies, and even entire periodicals, and about whom as a person and artist people have certain ideas. It is these ideas which, I think, tell us something about musical thinking in our society; that they are often contrary to known historical fact is interesting but not necessarily relevant to the analysis of contemporary culture.

Indeed, what I might call the Mozart mythology tells us important things about our culture and our musical values. If I were to suggest those things most widely believed or empha-

sized about Mozart, they might be these: the concept of genius at its most extreme—a composer who didn't have to try, for whom everything was easy; a composer not appreciated by his own people, but more, perhaps, by foreigners in the distant city of Prague; a child prodigy whose childlike nature never left him; a composer for whom everything musical went right, who was good at everything, but for whom things in the rest of his life went wrong; the composer who wrote what we see as the most normal classical music, the standard against which to judge earlier and later; the composer whose work you can recognize within seconds. After all, Nicolas Slonimsky describes him as the "supreme genius of music,"[19] and Wolfgang Hildesheimer, as "perhaps the greatest genius in recorded human history."[20]

But we also know that the historical Mozart wasn't really like that. We know that he was a workaholic as a composer, was ambitious to try many kinds of things in music, was proud to be able to write in a variety of styles, dealt with varied degrees of success with the practical problems of his life. He set himself demanding musical problems and solved them, and he wrote extremely complex music, was thus regarded as a difficult composer in his time. He did some sketching, and there is evidence that he did careful planning, though to be sure his mind seems to have worked with lightning speed and his memory to have been flawless.

The contemporary mythology makes much of the differences between Mozart and Beethoven: Mozart, for whom everything was easy; Beethoven, the hard-laboring composer whose sketches show the intensity of his labors. A Levi-Straussian analysis would show various opposites: Mozart, the man about whose death there is mystery, who had problems with his father; Beethoven, with a mystery about his birth and origins, whose personal problems move in the other direction, to his nephew and son-substitute. Mozart, who wrote in much the same style through his life; Beethoven, whose style changed enormously. Mozart, the fun-loving lover of his wife, billiard-player, author of scatological letters; Beethoven, the man who eschewed women to save his art, avoided frivolity, kept to the moral high ground.

The two composers occupy roles of heroic types widely used in the myths of Western culture: the hard-working leader of humanity, and the genius (with supernatural qualities) who is misunderstood, betrayed, becomes a victim. It's Ulysses and Achilles, Hans Sachs and Siegfried, even—dare I intrude into theology—Moses and Jesus. It should not surprise us that humans in Western society think about musicians as they do about figures in other domains of culture, a culture in which duality and dichotomy plays a major role in structuring our way of classifying our universe, from good versus evil all the way to major and minor, and on to the typical pairing of composers from Leonin and Perotin to Bartók and Kodály. Interesting about the Mozart-Beethoven paradigm i the fact that it is related to two ways we conceive of the musical thought of composers, the difference between, put bluntly, inspiration and perspiration. Mozart is seen (again, we know he wasn't really *only* like that) as the inspired composer par excellence, and Beethoven as the man who worked things out, crafted them. It's clear also that we would all like to have inspiration and to avoid too much perspiration, and so we imbue Mozart with qualities that we like, more so than Beethoven. In *A Clockwork Orange,* Anthony Burgess[21] associated Beethoven with the destructive and sadistic Alex who can't escape a tragic fate, and Mozart, in another novel, *The End of the World News,*[22] with the escape of the fifty lone human survivors of a planetary collision in a spaceship, while listening to the strains of the *Jupiter.* Mozart is the sweet composer, there are sweets, sweet liqueurs, sweet wines, at least four sweetshops in North America, desserts in Viennese cookbooks, all named for him. None for Beethoven; all I could find was a meat-and-potatoes restaurant on the coast, and a piano moving company in New York.

The idea of the composer who writes easily, doesn't have to try, for whom problems are solved, as it were, by divine inspiration, in whose music each phrase seems the only logical successor to the one you've just heard, all this correlates with the idea of sweets, which go down easily and represent for us a certain seamlessness. For Mozart, we are sometimes inclined to think, composing was easy as pie, or a piece of cake.

Now, before you say, "Balderdash! What does this tell us about Mozart?," I must remind

you that I'm not talking about Mozart, the historical figure, but about our culture today, in which Mozart and other composers play major roles and become the symbols of important and competing values and of the tensions between them. And so our ideas about music are affected and maybe determined by our desire to juxtapose values, to present life as a set of dichotomies, looking at the universe as the tension between divine and human, divine inspiration and human labor, sweetness and salt. Never mind that the thematic juxtapositions of Mozart's and Beethoven's piano concertos work very much the same way, that Beethoven often picked up where Mozart had left off. The ideas of our culture about music and our perception of the musical thought of composers is very much determined by ways in which we structure our universe. Writers of program notes, music teachers of children, collectors of CDs seem often to be saying, don't confuse me with historical facts, the Mozart and Beethoven myths help me to teach and to clarify for myself the ways in which my society looks at the world.

VI. AUTHORITY AND FREEDOM

We are lucky to live in a society which likes music. What society doesn't? Well, "liking" may often not be the right term, but all societies seem to have and to desire in their lives something that sounds to us like music. But in our society, music is associated with good things; your favorite dog barking is "music to your ears," as is the jingling of money in your pocket; a sound you like is a "musical sound." And if you're singing, you are assumed to be happy.

It's not like that everywhere, of course. The Blackfoot people revere their songs and regard them as essential for human existence; but until recently, I think they did not associate them with the concept of fun. The grand tradition of Carnatic music is much loved by its people in South India, but music is not a metaphor for good and beautiful things; perhaps because it is taken so very seriously. There are parts of the world in which music is viewed with suspicion and ambivalence. It has often been thus in parts of Western culture; maybe it still is. But the example most cited is the Islamic Middle East.

Why devout Muslims avoid music, and how it got that way, is beyond my scope here.[23] I would like to speak a bit to the question of how the fundamental attitude towards music may affect musical thought in the most specific sense. Before beginning, I must tell you that I have hard data for certain of my conclusions, but in other cases I must provide very personal interpretations.

My experience of the Muslim Middle East comes from Iran, of course. And there the situation has always been complex, as we have a society heterogeneous in many ways. But to simplify: Music is something people were careful of, they felt guilty about its enjoyment, they looked down on musicians and visited certain disabilities on them, regarded instruments as particularly dangerous, and kept music away from the mosque. Still, they love and desire music. How do they manage to eat their cake and have it?

There are a number of—shall we call them techniques, or mechanisms, or practices?—which have been established.[24] For one thing, there is the structure of the concept of music. We tend to regard music as a single, comprehensive concept; all kinds of music—Mozart, rock, Carnatic, Machaut, Coltrane—are to the same degree music. They may not be equally good or pleasing, but they are all music. In Iran, different sounds have about them varying degrees of music-ness. People say, in effect, "What we're doing is not really music in the full sense, it is only ... ." The chanting or singing of the Qur'an, which surely sounds to us like music, is not labeled with the Persian word for music. It is, of course, acceptable; and when it comes to real music, the more a sound is like Qur'an singing, the more acceptable it is, and the less music-ness it has. So, music which is vocal, not metric and thus rhythmically unpredictable, improvised on the basis of models, texted, uninfluenced by non-Muslim cultures, and for a sacred, serious, edifying social context, and not for pure entertainment, is acceptable and non-musical. At the other extreme, instrumental music, pre-composed, metric and even with rhythmic ostinato, performed to show off the performer's technique, and possibly even performed in places of entertainment such as night clubs, with women singing and dancing, and maybe with elements of Western

style such as occasional functional harmony, is music in the extreme sense and the most dangerous, eschewed by the devout but also looked down on by secular conservatives. (You can see from this, perhaps, how a classical system of music developed in which non-metric improvisation is central, and in which unpredictability is a major value in the thinking of musicians.)

But this tendency is contradicted by another. If the splitting up of music into varying degrees of music-ness is one technique of dealing with the ambivalence, the splitting up of the concept of musician is an analogue. Few people regard themselves as musicians; especially in villages, one may be a singer of the national epic at teahouses; or an instrumentalist who plays at weddings and similar ceremonies; or a singer of songs to praise the Imam Hossein, martyred son of the prophet's son-in-law; or the reciter of verses and percussionist to accompany gymnastic exercises in the traditional type of gymnasium, the *zurkhaneh*. But not a *musician*. They say, in effect, "We're not musicians, we're only performers of ... ." Well, since each of these genres tends to be dominated by a few tunes or melodic formulae, you can see that these singers may, in their lives as performers, be very predictable indeed. There's a tension between freedom to improvise and having to stick to one's set of basic materials.

But then, also, people will say, in effect, "It's not we who are doing the music," or "What we're doing isn't really making music at all." For the first, it has long been a practice in the Middle East to attract non-Muslim minorities to music, and so a disproportionate number—though by no means a majority—of Persian classical musicians were in my time Jewish; and musicians in the popular music field, Jewish or Armenian Christian; and instrument makers, Armenian; instrument-sellers, Jewish. Having established that music is for minorities, Muslim minorities too were attracted into music; in Northern Iran, Kurds were considered the greatest singers. The structure may have even become reversed in India, where a disproportionate number of musicians in this basically Hindu culture are actually Muslims.

But also, music became a specialty of the various Sufi orders, adherents of the main mystical movement of Islam, who would say, in effect, This isn't music, it's just another way for us to know and come closer to God. And related to this is the conception of the ideal of musicianship being the learned amateur, who knows the system but does not make his living from music. It is possible for such a person to be socially respected, whereas society looked down on professional musicians, associated as they were with a dangerous and undesirable activity, to which was added a reputation for unreliability, sexual promiscuity, homosexuality, habitual tardiness in paying debts, drug addiction, alcoholism, other accusations often visited on minorities, and lots more—the same kinds of things one once heard about jazz musicians. But the upper class amateur almost made a virtue of some of these same things.

My teacher repeatedly made this clear to me. Mood—being in the right mood, and being able to play appropriately corresponding music—is central to Persian musical performance practice. A professional musician must play what his employer asks, when he is commanded, however long is desired; he is told when to begin and when to stop. The amateur has the freedom to make decisions: whether to play at all, which mode, and so on. You can see why this attitude would lead to a system of musical thinking in which improvisation is central and composed music of less esteem; in which the idea of making decisions, from what mode to play all the way to the tiniest ornament, is valued over the pre-planned; in which the unexpected and the exceptional, suggesting freedom to depart even unconventionally from norms, is highly privileged.

I could characterize Persian musical thought as a tension between authority and freedom, between the authority of the radif, which one memorizes, and the freedom to improvise upon it; between knowledge of a canon and ability to depart from it. My work in Persian music has included a great deal of analysis of improvisations based on the same material from the canonic radif; I've tried to see how different musicians differ from each other, how one musician's performances differ over time. The individual differences are extremely interesting: one musician virtually memorizes his improvisations; another plans the temporal relationship sections precisely; a third plays a bit, then rests on long notes while deciding what to do next; a fourth keeps the same tempo for long periods

while a fifth changes constantly; a sixth keeps to the non-metric while a seventh moves in and out of metric structure; one goes through the sections of the radif one by one; another mixes things in an unanalyzable jumble. But how do the musicians evaluate each other, what makes certain performances good and others mediocre? In good measure it is the musician's ability to juxtapose his knowledge of and respect for the tradition with the various musical symbols of freedom.

VII. CONCLUSION

My approach to the concept of musical thought has been to look at the relationship between ideas about music and musical ideas. I have been unable to identify explicitly musical thought as different from other kinds of thinking, and probably I wouldn't be competent to do that. But I do suggest that the way in which musicians think musically, the ways in which they, as it were, "think" their music, depends in large measure on ways in which they think of their world at large. And within that context, the ways in which a society thinks about the concept of music, about music in culture, about musicians, may determine much about the way in which the musicians of that society think their music.

1. This article is based on a lecture given in June, 1992, at Northwestern University. The invitation to deliver this lecture contained the request to speak about the concept of "musical thinking" from an ethnomusicological perspective, but in the hope that this perspective would help to integrate the approaches of scholars and students in musicology, music theory, and music education. I am grateful to Professor Philip Alperson for inviting me to make this lecture into an article, but feel that I must explain the fact that it nevertheless retains a good many aspects of an informal lecture.

2. As in his perhaps best-known sentence: "Der Inhalt der Musik sind tönend bewegte Formen." The view that music is simply music (not representative, to be sure, of Hanslick's total philosophy) is still widespread in the literature of music theory. See, e.g., Robert Cogan and Pozzi Escot, *Sonic Design: The Nature of Sound and Music* (Englewood Cliffs: Prentice-Hall, 1976).

3. The various approaches to musicology, including those

that emphasize cultural and historical context, are discussed critically by Joseph Kerman, *Contemplating Music: Challenges to Musicology* (Harvard University Press, 1985); see also Barry S. Brook and others, eds., *Perspectives in Musicology* (New York: Norton, 1972).

4. Definitions of ethnomusicology abound. See Alan P. Merriam, "Definitions of 'Comparative Musicology' and 'Ethnomusicology': An Historical-Theoretical Perspective," *Ethnomusicology* XXI (1977): 189–204; and Bruno Nettl, *The Study of Ethnomusicology* (University of Illinois Press, 1983), pp. 1–14.

5. University of Washington Press, 1973.

6. During the 1970s, the discussion of cultural universals gained considerable currency in ethnomusicology. See, e.g., Klaus P. Wachsmann, "Universal Perspectives in Music," *Ethnomusicology* XV (1971): 381–84. For a summary, see Nettl, *The Study of Ethnomusicology*, pp. 44–51.

7. See Alan Lomax, *Song Structure and Social Structure* (Washington: American Association for the Advancement of Science, 1968), for general theory; and for an illustration, Nettl, "Musical Values and Social Values: Symbols in Iran," *Asian Music* XII (1980): 129–48.

8. Nettl, *Blackfoot Musical Thought: Comparative Perspectives* (Kent State University Press, 1989), pp. 152–53.

9. Nettl, *The Study of Ethnomusicology*, p. 111.

10. Nettl, *Blackfoot Musical Thought*, pp. 153–54.

11. A number of variants of this myth have been published, some of them by Blackfoot authors. Here I summarize the version in John C. Ewers, *The Blackfeet: Raiders on the Northwestern Plains* (University of Oklahoma Press, 1958), pp. 168–69.

12. The ethnomusicological study of improvisation has been developed only recently. For a publication representing current thought, see *New Perspectives on Improvisation*, with articles by Ali Jihad Racy, Gregory E. Smith, Margaret J. Kartomi, and Leo Treitler, a special issue of the periodical *The World of Music* XXXIII, no. 3 (1991).

13. For detailed description and discussion of the radif, see Nettl, *The Radif of Persian Music: Studies of Structure and Cultural Context* (rev. ed., Champaign: Elephant & Cat, 1992). Although the radif is transmitted aurally, it has been notated in several versions. For examples, see Mehdi Barkechli, *La musique traditionelle de l'Iran* (Teheran: Secreteriat d'état aux beaux-arts, 1963) and Bruno Nettl

with Bela Foltin, Jr., *Daramad of Chahargah, A Study in the Performance Practice of Persian Music* (Detroit: Information Coordinators, 1972).

14. See the extensive bibliography in Nettl, *The Radif of Persian Music*, particularly works by Hormoz Farhat, Mohammad Taghi Massoudieh, Khatschi Khatschi, Jean During, Gen'ichi Tsuge, and Ella Zonis.

15. For detailed explanation of the relationship between social values and musical values in Iran, see Nettl, "Musical Values and Social Values: Symbols in Iran."

16. There have been, of course, attempts to extract "theories" from texts of various sorts. See for example, Hugo Zemp, "'Are'are Classification of Musical Types and Instruments," *Ethnomusicology* XXII (1978): 370–67, and "Aspects of 'Are'are Musical Theory," loc. cit. XXIII (1979): 5–48; Steven Feld, *Sound and Sentiment* (University of Pennsylvania Press, 1982); Paul Berliner, *The Soul of Mbira* (University of California Press, 1978), and for a different perspective, Margaret J. Kartomi, *On Concepts and Classifications of Musical Instruments* (University of Chicago Press, 1990).

17. The following constructed musical theory text is reproduced from Nettl, *Blackfoot Musical Thought*, pp. 171–72.

18. And I did. See Nettl, "Mozart and the Ethnomusicological Study of Western Culture," *Yearbook for Traditional Music* XXI (1989): 1–16.

19. In *Baker's Biographical Dictionary of Musicians*, 6th ed. (New York: Schirmer, 1978), p. 1197.

20. Wolfgang Hildesheimer, *Mozart*, translated from the German by Marion Faber (New York: Vintage Books, 1983), p. 366.

21. Anthony Burgess, *A Clockwork Orange* (New York: Ballantine, 1963 [1981]).

22. Anthony Burgess, *The End of the World News* (New York: McGraw-Hill, 1983).

23. Regarding the complex system of Islamic attitudes towards music, see, for an introductory description, Nettl et al., *Excursions in World Music* (Englewood Cliffs: Prentice-Hall, 1992), pp. 50–55.

24. See Nettl et al., *Excursions in World Music*, for bibliography; also Nettl, *The Radif of Persian Music*, chapters 7 and 10.

Contributors

PHILIP ALPERSON is Professor of Philosophy at the University of Louisville. He has edited two books in aesthetics, *What is Music?: An Introduction to the Philosophy of Music* (1987, 1994), and *The Philosophy of the Visual Arts* (1992), and has written articles on various topics in aesthetics. He is the editor of *The Journal of Aesthetics and Art Criticism*.

NOËL CARROLL is Monroe Beardsley Professor of the Philosophy of Art at the University of Wisconsin at Madison. He has recently completed *A Philosophy of Mass Art* (1997) and *Interpreting the Moving Image* (1998).

STEPHEN DAVIES is Associate Professor of Philosophy at the University of Auckland. He is the author of *Definitions of Art* (1991) and *Musical Meaning and Expression* (1994), and the editor of *Art and Its Messages: Meaning, Morality, and Society* (1997).

CLAIRE DETELS is Associate Professor of Music at the University of Arkansas in Fayetteville where she teaches music history, harpsichord, and gender studies. Her research interests include nineteenth-century opera, feminist musical aesthetics, and the relationship of history and philosophy in the arts.

JOHN ANDREW FISHER is Professor and Chair of the Philosophy Department at the University of Colorado at Boulder. He is the author of *Reflecting on Art* (1993). He is currently writing articles on rock music, recordings, and the sounds of nature.

LYDIA GOEHR is Professor of Philosophy at Columbia University. She is the author of *The Imaginary Museum of Musical Works* (1992). She is currently working on a book on music, censorship, and politics.

PETER KIVY is Professor of Philosophy at Rutgers University, and a past president of the American Society for Aesthetics. He has written numerous essays and books on the philosophy of music including *Authenticities: Philosophical Reflections on Musical Performance* (1995) and *Philosophies of Arts: An Essay in Differences* (1997).

JERROLD LEVINSON is Professor of Philosophy at the University of Maryland. He is the author of *Music, Art, and Metaphysics* (1990), *The Pleasures of Aesthetics* (1996) and *Music in the Moment* (1997), as well as editor of *Aesthetics and Ethics: Essays at the Intersection*, forthcoming (1998) from Cambridge University Press.

JAMES MANNS is Professor of Philosophy at the University of Kentucky. Most of his work centers around aesthetics, and he is the author of a book, *Reid and His French Disciples* (1994).

BRUNO NETTL has taught ethnomusicology at the University of Illinois in Urbana-Champaign since 1964, and has done field research in Iran and South India, with the Blackfoot people of Montana, and in midwestern university schools of music. He is the author of many articles and books on ethnomusicology, including *The Study of Ethnomusicology: Twenty-nine Issues and Concepts* (1983).

JENEFER ROBINSON is Professor of Philosophy at the University of Cincinnati. She has published extensively in aesthetics on such diverse topics as representation in painting and music, style in literature and the visual arts, feminist responses to fiction, fictional discourse and truth, expression, and interpretation.

JOEL RUDINOW teaches philosophy at Sonoma State University and Santa Rosa Junior College in California. His writings on aesthetics have appeared in *The British Journal of Aesthetics, Critical Inquiry, Philosophy and Literature,* and *The Journal of Aesthetics and Art Criticism.* A student of the New Orleans piano tradition, he moonlights currently with several San Francisco Bay Area American roots music bands.

GÖRAN SÖRBOM is Chair of the Department of Aesthetics at Uppsala University, Sweden, and of the Scandinavian Society for Aesthetics. He is the author of *Mimesis and Art: Studies in the Origin and Early Development of an Aesthetic Vocabulary* and two books, in Swedish, on the theory of aesthetic value and on pictorial representation.

FRANCIS SPARSHOTT is University Professor Emeritus of the University of Toronto. His books include *The Structure of Aesthetics* (1963), *The Theory of the Arts* (1982), *Off the Ground* (1988), and *A Measured Pace* (1995).

KENDALL L. WALTON is Professor of Philosophy at the University of Michigan. He has published extensively in aesthetics, and is the author of *Mimesis as Make-Believe: On the Foundations of the Representational Arts* (1990).

Index